This is your hour

MANCHESTER
1824

Manchester University Press

This is your hour

Christian intellectuals in Britain and the crisis of Europe, 1937–49

John Carter Wood

Manchester University Press

Published by Manchester University Press
Altrincham Street, Manchester M1 7JA
www.manchesteruniversitypress.co.uk

British Library Cataloguing- in-Publication Data
A catalogue record for this book is available from the British Library

ISBN 978 1 5261 3253 6 hardback
ISBN 978 1 5261 5256 5 paperback

First published 2019

Typeset by Newgen Publishing UK

For Anja

Contents

Illustrations

Preface

My research on Christian intellectuals in Britain began in 2011, when I became a researcher at the Leibniz Institute of European History (IEG) in Mainz, and it was greatly supported by four years of funding from the German Research Foundation (DFG).

Not least because this book represents a significant change of direction in my historical research (which has previously focused on crime, violence, policing and media), I have accumulated a number of other personal debts while completing it.

My greatest thanks go, collectively, to my colleagues at the IEG, whether on the research or administrative staff. Their helpful pointers and collegial commentaries over the years have been invaluable. In particular, I am grateful to the Institute's co-directors, Johannes Paulmann and Irene Dingel, for their advice, encouragement and support. My work on this book also benefited greatly from a three-month post-doctoral research fellowship at the German Historical Institute (GHI) in London.

I have received countless helpful suggestions – whether in the contexts of invited lectures, research workshops, email exchanges or conference panels – from many colleagues in Europe and the USA. In particular, I thank Pippa Catterall, Keith Clements, Jan De Maeyer, Michael DeJonge, Bernhard Dietz, Andreas Gestrich, Rebekkah Habermas, Andrew Hammel, Rajesh Heynickx, Paul Lawrence, Hugh McLeod, Bob Morris, Patrick Pasture, Axel Schäfer, Katharina Stornig, Till van Rahden, Andreas Rödder and John Wolffe. Frank Cox provided much valued assistance and friendship during my period in London as a GHI fellow. I am grateful to Martin Symons for generously giving me access to items from his father's personal papers, and to Anna Howard for providing a family photo of H. A. Hodges.

As ever, I must separately acknowledge Anja Müller-Wood, without whose steady support and encouragement this book would have never seen the light of day. For that reason – among many others – it is dedicated to her.

The meetings of 'the Moot'

Citations from the minutes of the discussion group referred to as 'the Moot' will include meeting numbers corresponding with those given below. Information on meetings 1–20 is provided in Keith Clements (ed.), *The Moot Papers: Faith, Freedom and Society 1938–1944* (Edinburgh: T. & T. Clark, 2010); other information comes via the Oldham Archive, New College Library, Edinburgh (file reference 12/1/2).

1   1–4 April 1938, High Leigh, Hertfordshire
2   23–26 September 1938, Hampstead, London
3   6–9 January 1939, Haywards Heath, Sussex
4   14–17 April, 1939, Beaconsfield, Buckinghamshire
5   23–24 September 1939, Golders Green, London
6   This meeting, though planned, does not seem to have taken place.
7   9–12 February 1940, Beaconsfield, Buckinghamshire
8   19–22 April 1940, Beaconsfield, Buckinghamshire
9   12–15 July 1940, Beaconsfield, Buckinghamshire
10 10–13 January 1941, Thatcham, Berkshire
11 4–7 April 1941, Thatcham, Berkshire
12 1–3 August 1941, Oxford, Oxfordshire
13 19–22 December 1941, Oxford, Oxfordshire
14 27–30 March 1942, Oxford, Oxfordshire
15 11–14 September 1942, Beaconsfield, Buckinghamshire
16 8–11 January 1943, Beaconsfield, Buckinghamshire
17 18–21 June 1943, Haslemere, Surrey
18 29 October–1 November 1943, Horsham, Sussex
19 14–17 January 1944, Horsham, Sussex
20 23–25 June 1944, Horsham, Sussex
21 15–18 December 1944, Horsham, Sussex
22 6–9 July 1945, Horsham, Sussex
23 4–7 January 1946, Horsham, Sussex
24 10–13 January 1947, Horsham, Sussex

Abbreviations

BBC	British Broadcasting Corporation
BC	John Baillie Collection, University of Edinburgh
BCC	British Council of Churches
CCFCL	Council on the Christian Faith and the Common Life
CCIFSR	Commission of the Churches for International Friendship and Social Responsibility
CERC	Church of England Record Centre
CFC	Christian Frontier Council
CNL	*Christian News-Letter*
COPEC	Conference on Politics, Economics and Citizenship
FU	Federal Union
IMC	International Missionary Council
IOE	Institute of Education (University of London)
LPL	Lambeth Palace Library
MOI	Ministry of Information
MP	Member of Parliament
MSC	W. G. Symons papers provided by Martin Symons
OA	Oldham Archive (New College Library, Edinburgh)
SCM	Student Christian Movement
SVMU	Student Volunteer Missionary Union
UL	Moot Papers, Brotherton Library, University of Leeds
UN	United Nations
UNESCO	United Nations Educational, Scientific and Cultural Organization
USA	United States of America
USSR	Union of Soviet Socialist Republics
UTS	Union Theological Seminary (New York)
WCC	World Council of Churches
WGS	W. G. Symons Papers, University of Birmingham

Introduction: 'This is your hour'

Then Jesus said unto the chief priests, and captains of the temple, and the elders, which were come to him, Be ye come out, as against a thief, with swords and staves? When I was daily with you in the temple, ye stretched forth no hands against me: but this is your hour, and the power of darkness.

Luke 22:52–3

In the foreboding political atmosphere of late 1930s Europe, several Christian activists and thinkers came together in a British-based, internationally connected circle to try to understand – and resist – the apparent cultural disintegration of western society and the rise of totalitarianism. Throughout the Second World War and its aftermath the group's members analysed the world's ills and offered guidelines for post-war 'reconstruction'. Convinced that the crises of the age resulted from Christianity's decline, they sought its 'revolutionary' restoration to dominance in British, European and western culture: in short, a 'Christian society'. While there was no contemporary label for their efforts as a whole, some of which remained out of the public eye, I call them 'the Oldham group', after their organiser, the missionary and ecumenist Joseph H. Oldham.

Active between 1937 and 1949, the Oldham group grew out of the inter-war ecumenical movement and consisted of church-affiliated organisations, an informal discussion group ('the Moot') and publication projects, notably the *Christian News-Letter*. It was substantially Anglican with significant free church (i.e. non-Anglican Protestant) membership; denominational perspectives, however, remained secondary in a search for shared, 'Christian' principles. Participants included prominent figures from the worlds of academic theology and philosophy (such as John Baillie, Alec Vidler and H. A. Hodges), literature and literary criticism (T. S. Eliot and John Middleton Murry) and education (Sir Walter Moberly and Sir Fred Clarke), as well as missionary work and Christian activism (Eric Fenn, Daniel Jenkins, Eleanora Iredale and Kathleen Bliss). Continental refugee scholars Karl Mannheim, Adolf Löwe and Michael Polanyi also took part and played important roles (Löwe Anglicised his name and was often referred to as 'Adolph Lowe'; however, he was almost always referred to within the Oldham group by his original name, and I retain this spelling). Few Roman Catholics were members (only Polanyi and the historian Christopher Dawson), but Catholic ideas influenced the group. Among its contacts and supporters were the leading Christians of the day, whether clergy such as the archbishops Cosmo Lang and William Temple or Bishop George Bell, popular writers such as Dorothy L. Sayers and C. S. Lewis, or theologians and philosophers including Reinhold Niebuhr and Jacques Maritain. In this book, I explore the Oldham group's intellectual influences, show how they mixed, describe the resulting syntheses, trace the group's efforts to impact politics and opinion, evaluate the reception of its ideas, and place its thought in the context of its time. Chapter conclusions contextualise specific topics; the general conclusion, Chapter 8, also draws out the group members' connections to other Christian networks and activities. Explaining my goals for this book means outlining its relationship to intellectual history, defining the Oldham group's main characteristics, summarising the sources used and explaining how the following chapters are structured.

Ideas, agents and contexts

I have written this book primarily as an intellectual rather than, strictly speaking, a religious history, not least to emphasise the mixture of Christian and 'secular' thought within the Oldham group and in British culture at this time more broadly. Intellectual history is marked by 'elusive boundaries' and divergent national historiographical traditions.[1] Nonetheless, recent decades have seen a significant convergence upon a few key points. Ideas – in the sense of 'interpretive systems', 'styles of thought' and 'imagined formations' of the social order[2] – do not *exist* as trans-historical *things* but emerge through interventions in specific arguments at certain times in response to particular events by people with distinct motivations and aims. The claims (and counter-claims) made in such contexts are part of ongoing discussions with particular purposes, institutional frameworks, disciplinary assumptions and, crucially, languages, which both provide *means* of thought and communication and pose *limits* upon legitimate expression.[3] Any use of particular concepts relies upon their accumulated meanings; however, even 'traditional', or purportedly 'eternal', concepts allow for innovation, rethinking and synthesis; at times, new meanings may even depart thoroughly from old ones.[4] But while context matters, no past context was 'a closed province of meaning', separate from other contemporary contexts or the impact of developments over the *longue durée*.[5] Contexts alone, moreover, do not generate meaning: this requires the intentions and efforts of particular actors to create, develop and exchange ideas. Actors are both autonomous agents and constrained by social, institutional and cultural factors, such as, not least, the traditions in which they work. The influence of unconscious (or unintended) influences, self-deception and misunderstandings must also be considered.[6] Finally, intellectual history need not confine itself to the lofty heights of political philosophy but may centre on what Jan-Werner Müller has called the 'in-between figures': 'statesmen-philosophers, public lawyers, constitutional advisors, the curious and at first sight contradictory phenomenon of "bureaucrats with visions", philosophers close to political parties and movements, as well as what Friedrich von Hayek once referred to as "second-hand dealers in ideas".[7]

Such methods have been usefully applied to the history of religion, demonstrating its variable, contested and evolving nature and the ubiquitous tensions between claims of orthodox timelessness and the countless varieties of 'lived belief' or 'discursive Christianity'.[8] Any faith or worldview is defined solely by its adherents' varied and often fragmented beliefs, though more (or less) 'orthodox' forms can be identified in particular times and places. In my analysis, I am always discussing the group's *claims about* Christianity rather than judging the 'accuracy' of such claims. I take into account key tensions and ambiguities: between agency and context, tradition and innovation, and intellectual and popular milieux. The relevant contexts for understanding the Oldham group include its participants' individual experiences and backgrounds, the cultural and religious traditions that inspired them, the organisational structures in which they acted, and the exchanges and discussions in which they engaged. These occurred in still wider contexts: first, the national intellectual public sphere defined mainly by journals, the press, books, pamphlets and radio broadcasts; second, the Christian thought developed in both the emerging, Geneva-based World Council of Churches (WCC, founded in 1948) and in ad hoc exchanges between thinkers in Britain and continental Europe or the United States.

The Oldham group coalesced after a 1937 ecumenical conference in Oxford; by 1949 most of the bodies that defined it had been dissolved (though related activities continued). While strictly theological concerns influenced the group's views, they pursued those issues that seemed most urgent to their society and the world generally. Indeed, the history of the Oldham group illustrates Adrian Hastings's observation that, when it came to religious thought, 'the world set the agenda and could therefore change it'.[9] The period 1937–49 covers three phases of activity – before, during and after the Second World War – and key events in each phase altered the group's evaluation of the need for, and route to, a more Christian social order: the Munich Crisis of 1938, the outbreak of war in 1939, the Dunkirk evacuation and the defeat of France in summer 1940, the entry of the Soviet Union and the United States into the war in 1941, the Allied victory in 1945, the birth of the atomic age, the Labour Party's electoral victory, efforts to rebuild Europe, the formation of the United Nations (UN), and the early stages in the Cold War.

British – Christian – intellectuals

In analysing the Oldham group's responses to totalitarianism, war and post-war reconstruction, I see its members as *British Christian intellectuals*. Each term locates the group in a key sphere: a *national* (British) context featuring specific identities and assumptions (though open to foreign influences); a *religious* (Christian) context shaped by various (not exclusively British) traditions and defined against 'secularism'; and a *public* (intellectual) context marked by certain forms of action and authority.

British

Histories of ecumenical thought have often focused on its *transnational* elements. This approach can be enlightening; however, it is important to attend to the specificities of the *national* contexts in which most Christian groups and individuals lived the far greater parts of their lives and formed their worldviews. Rather than analysing ecumenism as it looked from Geneva (which became the headquarters of the WCC in 1948 and had served more informally as such during the period of its formation), this study takes a primarily national perspective, seeking to draw out a detailed picture of the complexities of Christian social thought in one country: Great Britain. Despite its international scope and transnational connections, the Oldham group's Britishness will become apparent in the chapters that follow. Anglican and free church traditions of socially active Christianity, 'civil society' and 'community' were central to its thinking.[10] Nearly all its participants were British citizens who had – at least mostly – been raised and educated in Britain, inculcating particular outlooks and habits of thought. Participants also included a New Zealander – Scottish-born Presbyterian minister Alexander 'Lex' Miller – and, perhaps more surprisingly, three continental refugee scholars with Jewish backgrounds: Karl Mannheim, Adolf Löwe and Michael Polanyi. However, all three of the latter became naturalised Britons, and they fed the group's conviction that distinct *national* traditions offered valuable resources for cultural renewal. The Oldham group contributed to debates about national social reconstruction, asserted a strong (even patriotic) attachment to the nation and perceived a providential British 'mission' to bring a new order to a disintegrating world.

However, this Britishness was both self-critical and open to influences from abroad and from beyond British Protestantism. As Chapter 2 discusses, these included the 'Christian realism' of American theologian Reinhold Niebuhr, the 'personalist democracy' of French Catholic philosopher Jacques Maritain and the 'I–Thou' approach of Austrian-born Jewish philosopher Martin Buber. References to leading theologians and Christian philosophers – such as Ernst Troeltsch, Karl Barth, Emil Brunner, Eberhard Grisebach, Paul Tillich and Friedrich von Hügel – peppered the group's discussions. Links to the German churches were kept alive during the war, and contacts with American Protestantism were extensive. 'Intercultural transfer' thus played a key role, and members selectively appropriated (and rejected) a range of ideas, adapting them to their own needs, aims and understandings.[11]

Christian

Categorising the Oldham group as religious may seem obvious, but 'religion' has many meanings. This has proved especially true in the scholarly study *of* religion. Indeed, it may be that 'everybody except scholars of religion appears to know what "religion" means.'[12] It can, for example, be used to respond to '*immanent* contexts, events and experiences' and assert group identities that have little to do with, strictly speaking, 'religious' concerns.[13] However, the Oldham group can be seen as 'Christian' in terms of its participants' worldviews, identity, ideas and language. Apart from Mannheim and Löwe – who were agnostic but still saw Christianity as *functionally* useful to social renewal – all its members were personally Christian. Most had been (or remained) active in the missionary, ecumenical or student Christian movements. All the bodies and projects in the group had Christian aims (and often the word 'Christian' in their names), and most were affiliated with the Protestant churches. Concepts such as the Kingdom of Heaven, *agape*, the Incarnation and natural law recurred. But the group's version of Christianity was distinct: it was strongly intellectual, ecumenical and socially oriented. It was connected to official religion (i.e. 'specific ecclesiastical structures') but saw itself as an unofficial, *lay* network and was open to quasi-religious elements.[14] While claiming to speak for a universal Christianity and interested in cross-denominational influences, it was, however, predominantly Protestant.

Intellectuals

While intellectual history is not limited to people defined as 'intellectuals', I aim to place the Oldham group in the intellectual culture of their time.

I am not the first to describe them as intellectuals, but it should be noted that most members would probably not have applied the label to themselves.[15] 'Intellectual' was an ambivalent term in the Britain of the 1930s and 1940s, especially for Christians. In 1938, the *Church Times* saw intellectuals as a clearly secular – and ineffectual – class.[16] The *Christian World* in 1942 depicted the 'left-wing intelligentsia' as leading attacks on Christian views of marriage and family.[17] But in 1938 T. S. Eliot suggested that if an 'intellectual' meant 'a person of philosophical mind philosophically trained, who thinks things out for himself', Christians were as entitled to the label as anyone else.[18]

The group was well educated (most were Oxford or Cambridge graduates) and of a philosophical bent, but rather than taking the term to mean a particular class or profession, I apply Stefan Collini's view of intellectuals as defined by a specific 'structure of relations'. The four relevant 'elements' are, first, 'the attainment of a level of achievement in an activity which is esteemed for the non-instrumental, creative, analytical or scholarly capacities it involves'; second, 'the availability of media or channels of expression which reach publics other than that at which the initial "qualifying" activity itself is aimed'; third, 'the expression of views, themes or topics which successfully articulate or engage with some of the general concerns of those publics'; and fourth, 'the establishment of a reputation for being likely to have important and interesting things of this type to say and for having the willingness and capacities to say them effectively through the appropriate media'.[19] This definition is neither positively nor negatively connoted but describes a *type* of activity; moreover, its applicability to particular individuals varies – being a matter of 'degree not kind' – and the 'public' addressed may be a smaller fraction of the general public.[20] The result is what Collini calls 'cultural authority', which grants its bearers a degree of (at least perceived) social influence.[21] This definition applied more to some group participants than to others; still, it succinctly describes the Oldham group as a whole.

Larger themes

Why, though, should we concern ourselves with the confrontation by a small circle of relatively elite Christians with what may seem historically distant problems: totalitarianism, a crisis of liberal democracy and global war? I suggest that the Oldham group tells us much about a period when Christianity was intricately interwoven in British intellectual and cultural life.[22] Understanding British responses to the inter-war crises, the Second World War and the post-war world thus requires attending to religion. There was a specifically Christian, and widely influential, view

of the meaning of the war. Happily, this study can build upon and con-
tribute to a growing historiography of Christian social thought, the Second
World War, intellectual responses to modernity and the confrontation of
Christians with 'secularisation'.

Relating faith to society

Faith's relevance to society is a matter on which historians have differed.
It is clear, though, that many 'building blocks of Western modernity' –
'states and bureaucracies, revolution and reform, voluntary associations
and social movements, human and civil rights, corporations and welfare
states' – have partly 'religious genealogies'.[23] Far more attention has been
given to Christianity's influence on *nineteenth*-century social thought than
to the century that followed.[24] However, despite secularising trends, religious actors, institutions and ideas were relevant across twentieth-century
Europe. There have been many biographical or institutional studies of
key figures and movements, but broader thematic analyses have sometimes been limited to theological or inner-church contexts.[25] There are
exceptions, and Christianity's role in British national (and imperial) identity through the mid twentieth century has been recognised.[26] There is,
moreover, growing interest in the interactions among European churches,
Christian concepts of order and twentieth-century modernity, with continental Christian Democratic parties and religious influences on European
unification having become active research topics.[27] For Britain, the inter-
war social views of the Church of England, the free churches and Roman
Catholics have been explored, and Christian contributions to pacifism
thoroughly studied.[28] Christian influences on post-1945 domestic policy,
moral debates and international relations have recently been emphasised.[29]
Understanding the Oldham group's perspectives can contribute to existing
interest in inter-war and war-time political culture, and Christianity's
responses to and influence on political decision-making in the twentieth
century remain a vital topic.[30] The Oldham group's efforts to increase the
cultural authority of Christian belief and practice – to gain (or regain) what
has been called 'cultural sovereignty' for the faith in what seemed a deeply
secular age – was part of a larger story of Christianity in the mid twentieth century.[31] The transformative experiences of the 1930s and 1940s are
a context in which these issues can be fruitfully explored.

Christianity, war and social reconstruction

As terrible as the war that began in 1939 was, many Britons thought it
might – should the Allies win – bring a better world, inspiring an explosion

of programmatic visions of new political, economic and social orders. In 1940, prominent British Marxist John Strachey quipped that 'making plans for the world' had become a national 'industry'.[32] 'Almost daily', proclaimed a leader in the *New Statesman and Nation* in March 1941, 'we are told about the Millennium that is to come – after the war'.[33] In 1939, Oldham wrote of 'a babel of voices advocating every variety of blue-print for a new world order'.[34] A writer in the *Catholic Herald* observed: '"Blue-prints," "new orders" and "shapes of things to come" flutter down on us in a veritable leaflet raid'.[35] Indeed, the term 'New Order' became ubiquitous among Christians and non-Christians alike, though its meaning remained unclear. Evoking the need for a Christian-inspired democracy, an essay in the *Spectator* in March 1940 saw the possibility that: 'If bridges are thrown over social gulfs, parade and privilege swept away by voluntary surrender, need met by willing sacrifice as well as by renunciation imposed by drastic but necessary laws, then in this country and in others a new society may yet be built, of architecture both human and divine'.[36] Noting the 'constant phrase' of 'the New Order', a leading Methodist in 1943 commented that 'amidst the confusion and horrors of war', a vision of a better future was emerging: 'Even the smoke over burning cities', he wrote, 'seems to shape itself into a picture of what might and what ought to be'.[37]

The war brought not only social, political and cultural transform-ations but also a language to describe them, from Britain's 'finest hour', the 'Dunkirk spirit' and a nation 'standing alone', to claims that a 'people's war' drove a 'consensus' for 'social reconstruction' and the 'welfare state'.[38] Complacent versions of such myths have been critiqued – and claims of the welfare state as a specifically Christian project refuted[39] – but they continue to shape memories of the war. Revisionism has itself often been narrowly framed: despite attention to the contem-porary rhetoric of a war for 'Christian civilisation', specifically *religious* understandings of the momentous events of the 1930s and 1940s have often been ignored or subsumed within broader, and distinctly secular, narratives (although this has in recent years been changing).[40] Getting behind the accretions of later decades and reconstructing the concepts and languages through which the war and its aftermath were described *at the time* remains an important task.[41]

Committed Christians, of course, shared many of the same responses to the war as their non-Christian (or at least less devout) fellow citizens; however, they also offered distinctive arguments about its causes, con-duct and consequences. There were many opinions (among Christians too) about how – and even whether – the churches should engage in public discussions of social policy. Some Christian contributions proved popular, such as Bishop George Bell's *Christianity and World Order*

(1940) and Archbishop William Temple's *Christianity and Social Order* (1942). Articles about the churches and the emerging 'New Order' were pervasive in the Christian press, and the topic also featured in radio broadcasts. 'Religion and Life Weeks' – organised by the churches and combining worship and lectures on social issues – grew substantially in both frequency and attendance through the war.[42] A letter on peace aims and post-war reconstruction published in *The Times* in December 1940 that had been jointly signed by Anglican, Catholic and free church leaders received much attention.[43] The same was true of Archbishop Temple's conference on Christian (in this case Anglican) social doctrine held at Malvern in 1941. But heated controversy might result if clergy went too far in social advocacy: a substantial part of Christian opinion opposed such interventions.[44] 'There is no room', proclaimed a front-page article in the *Church of England Newspaper*, 'for "Christian" social programmes or a "Christian" sociology'; two years later Labour peer Lord Elton made a similar argument, stressing that Christianity was mainly concerned with personal behaviour rather than any particular '-ism': 'There can be no better Britain', he asserted, 'without better Britons'.[45] However, as it has been recently observed, social policy 'necessarily involves the union of large principles and small facts', and Oldham and his companions aimed to facilitate just such a combination of 'ultimate' values and the minutiae of empirical sociology in guiding post-war social reconstruction, as did other clergy and Christian laypeople.[46] The *Spectator* in 1940 noted a revived interest in the aim of 'Christian politics in a Christian polity', suggesting it was associated with 'Christian laymen of the type of J. H. Oldham, T. S. Eliot, Middleton Murry and Christopher Dawson' (all of whom were Oldham group members).[47] But this was only one episode in a wider discussion of faith and 'modernity'.

The crisis of modernity

Debate rages about how to define 'modernity' as a distinctive stage in history.[48] Clearly, though, many people in early- and mid-twentieth-century Europe *believed* their societies were being revolutionised by secularisation, industrialisation, globalisation, urbanisation, individualisation and rationalisation. The fear that modern society had suffered a catastrophic loss of a stable mental and moral framework for interpreting the world was widespread.[49] What should one believe and how should one act if, as it seemed, traditional certainties had crumbled? Claims of modernity's spiritual emptiness had grown since the turn of the century. The Great War, the wrenching dislocations of the inter-war 'morbid age' and the outbreak

of an even larger global conflict made the sense of modern crisis pervasive, even if it was variously coloured by divergent political allegiances
and worldviews.[50] Religiously inspired writers such as G. K. Chesterton
and Hilaire Belloc made popular arguments against cultural fragmentation, political 'progressivism' and the rising power of the 'servile state'.[51]
'Mass' society inspired widespread unease, particularly among those who
looked down at the masses from a more lofty perspective.[52] Psychologists
diagnosed new feelings of isolation and helplessness and a vulnerability
to increasingly sophisticated forms of political and commercial propaganda.[53] By the 1930s and 1940s, social theorists – such as Karl Polanyi,
Karl Mannheim, Joseph Schumpeter and Peter Drucker – influentially saw
(in Polanyi's terms) a 'great transformation' away from *laissez-faire* liberalism and towards 'integrated' and 'planned' societies.[54] Some welcomed
such trends as a potential boon to 'social justice'; others saw them as threats
to freedom.[55] Christians were among the earliest commentators to develop
a critique of the 'totalitarian state' and to formulate systematic responses
to the new secular 'faiths', both left and right.[56] Even after the Allied victory
in 1945, the outlook remained grim: the birth of the atomic age, revelations
of the Holocaust, a physically and morally devastated European continent,
persistent economic disruption and the emergent superpower rivalry
caused many to think that civilised culture had disintegrated without a
clear sense of the way forward. In 1950, Hannah Arendt expressed the
post-war atmosphere as 'the calm that settles after all hopes have died'.[57]

In the 1930s and 1940s, Christians were on all sides in the debates about
what should be done, their attitudes fed by both distinctly religious traditions
and wider intellectual tendencies. The 'sheer anarchy' of Christian responses
to the events of the period has been noted;[58] nevertheless, there were also clear
patterns rooted in denominational belonging, political allegiance and national
identity. Unsurprisingly, church leaders and Christian thinkers stressed 'spiritual' aspects of world problems and expressed their views via pulpit, newspaper, book and broadcast. For many (whether in the churches or not), faith
provided a familiar and useful language to discuss worldly topics. Across
Europe, it was a resource for the construction of a broad spectrum of politics, from a 'cult of authority' to social protest.[59] Christians often presented
their aims as offering a 'moral regeneration of the community', a 'moral critique of the anomie of secular modernity' and 'an alternative vision of 'modernity' to that of secular liberals, socialists and nationalists'.[60] Here, Christian
thought met a broader trend, as many thinkers, artists and activists – whether
Christian or not – developed a 'romantic' sensibility, insisting on a 'transcendent' level of reality beyond empirical science and philosophical materialism, and aiming to rebuild 'community' against the dominance of large
institutions and a perceived social atomisation.[61] 'Mythic thinking' played a
role in British responses to modernity, 'a new mode of making meaning that

appealed to the imagination by making the claim that myths communicate timeless truths that cannot be apprehended through reason and science'. Rather than *avoiding* modernity, such arguments 'took place within, depended upon, and existed in fruitful tension with fundamental institutions, features and tenets of modernity'.[62] They also provided an opening for Christians. The Oldham group emphasised Christianity's supernatural aspects while stressing its 'realism' and acknowledging the worth of modern, secular knowledge. This, in itself, raises a thorny historiographical debate.

Secularisation

The concept of a 'secularisation process' – a decline in the relevance of religion with modernisation – has, in recent decades, faced vehement attack,[63] attempted revision,[64] and vigorous reassertion.[65] Few would deny that the cultural place of Christianity changed in the twentieth century, but it has been claimed that other concepts better describe what happened, such as diversification, individualisation or deinstitutionalisation. Rather than decline, shifts in the 'religious landscape' or growth in 'believing without belonging' have been stressed.[66] Still, the 1960s have been seen as a turning point in British and European Christianity, marking even the 'death of Christian Britain' or of 'Christendom'.[67] These views see a rapid collapse rather than a gradual subsidence, not only in institutional Christianity but also in the relevance of Christian narratives to individual life. But such arguments stress faith's power *prior* to the 1960s, especially with regard to morality and identity, or what has been called 'discursive' or 'diffusive' Christianity.[68] Inter-war tensions between religion and secularity were 'profound' and 'unresolved'; there was 'a grey area between active worship and active disbelief where the majority were probably to be found'.[69] Faith remained, however, part of most Britons' 'mentality and habits of thought'.[70]

I am less concerned with what *was* happening than with what a group of intellectuals *thought* was happening. Secularisation might be an objectively verifiable phenomenon, but I focus on the motivations, viewpoints and efforts of specific historical actors, seeing secularisation as 'a contingent and active set of strategies' and counter-strategies.[71] Different understandings of religion developed, came into contact (and conflict) and were mutually altered.[72] Signs of what I call 'subjective secularisation' – the *perception* of Christianity's marginalisation by secular movements or by indifference – were legion in intellectual circles. A small but growing and vocal coterie of atheists (or 'rationalists' or 'humanists', as they tended to be known then) welcomed this development; Christians, naturally, did not.

In 1931, T. S. Eliot expressed what would become a common Christian view as the world situation darkened across the next decade: the attempt to build 'a civilised but non-Christian mentality' was doomed, he wrote, and he suggested his fellow believers should prepare for the coming social 'collapse', using their faith 'to renew and rebuild civilisation, and save the World from suicide'.[73] Such sentiments were common. In 1938 popular Roman Catholic historian (and Moot member) Christopher Dawson predicted 'not merely the passing of the Liberal-capitalist order of the nineteenth century' but also 'the End of the Age' and a 'turning point in world history': 'from the emptiness of modern civilization and progress to the vision of spiritual reality which stands all the time looking down on our ephemeral activities like the snow mountains above the jazz and gigolos of a jerry-built hotel'.[74] A review of Arnold J. Toynbee's *Christianity and Civilisation* (1940) found it 'encouraging' that 'if our secular Western civilisation perishes Christianity may be expected not only to endure but to grow in wisdom and stature as the result of a fresh experience of secular catastrophe'. A 'secular calamity', the review concluded, 'may sow the seeds of the spiritual opportunity of a new age'.[75] Even some critics of Christianity could not simply cheer its demise. George Orwell thought the decline in Christian notions of the 'soul' – while 'absolutely necessary' – had driven the rise of totalitarian alternatives. Quasi-sacred (if secular) alternatives were needed: 'We have got to be the children of God', he concluded, 'even though the God of the Prayer Book no longer exists'.[76] Kingsley Martin, editor of the *New Statesman and Nation*, similarly argued that it would be 'useless' to try 'to reimpose a belief in a theology which no longer agrees with knowledge', and he critiqued Christian traditionalists; nonetheless, while he hoped 'the religion of humanism' would someday appeal to 'the mass of mankind', he feared it might not.[77] Martin here was reviewing Harold J. Laski's *Faith, Reason and Civilisation* (1944), which also made the argument that it was necessary to find 'a new system of values' after the decline of religious belief.[78] Such comments suggested that *something* had disappeared from western culture and posed the question of what might replace it. Linking religious decline to the rise of 'political religions' has featured in recent scholarship, but it was a view already then shared by many who saw religion-like qualities in Communism, Fascism and Nazism (and even, some Christians argued, in the 'faith' in scientific progress).[79]

Christian commentators in the 1930s and 1940s despaired of the state of British religion, noting declining church attendance and widespread ignorance about Christian dogma. It is not necessary to argue that they were right to see that their perceptions motivated historically relevant responses. I am thus interested in secularisation as a changing argumentative and motivational context for social, political and cultural claims: secularisation was important because the people in whom I am interested *believed* it was and acted accordingly.[80] Recently, even tendencies towards 'self-secularisation' have been seen in mid-century British Christianity, deriving from new theological currents and some Christian organisations' turn to social activism.[81] The topic of secularisation in these senses – as a subjective viewpoint or conscious strategy – can also be studied through an examination of the Oldham group.

Sources and methods

Many sources give insight into the Oldham group's ideas, efforts, reception and context. As the group was partly formed of bodies affiliated with the Church of England (and free churches), relevant correspondence, memoranda, mission statements, strategy papers and reports are available at the Church of England Record Centre and in the archbishops' papers at Lambeth Palace (both in London). I have also consulted the papers of people active in the group: Oldham himself (New College Library, Edinburgh), John Baillie (University of Edinburgh), Fred Clarke (Institute of Education, London), O. S. Tomkins (University of Leeds) and W. G. Symons (University of Birmingham).[82] Annotated minutes of Moot meetings between 1938 and 1944 have been recently published, and nearly all the papers on which they were based are preserved in the institutional or personal archives noted above.

Public expressions of the group's ideas include individual members' publications – mostly as articles and books – and radio broadcasts published in the BBC's *Listener*. As key group members were editors of journals – such as *Theology* (Alec Vidler) and the *Adelphi* (John Middleton Murry) – they have also been consulted. The public face for the Oldham group, the *Christian News-Letter* (1939–49), has been systematically analysed, and forms – along with Moot discussions and papers – the main source for understanding the shared aspects of the group's ideas. Aiming to gauge public reception of these ideas and contextualise them *vis-à-vis* broader currents in Christian and secular thought, I have examined a range of periodical literature and newspapers. Christian responses and related perspectives have been considered via systematic searches through the Anglo-Catholic periodical *Christendom: A Journal of Christian Sociology*; Anglican newspapers of an Anglo-Catholic orientation (*Church Times* and the *Guardian*) and of a more evangelical bent (the *Church of England Newspaper*); as well as the cross-denominational free church press (*British Weekly* and *Christian World*); and the war-time weekly *Spiritual Issues of the War*, published by the Ministry of Information.[83] I have also consulted the *Catholic Herald* for the years during the war. To get a sense of the group's reception and location in non-explicitly Christian sources, I have read through relevant years of the (left-liberal) *New Statesman and Nation*, conducted digital searches in newspapers and periodicals (*The Times, Times Literary Supplement, Manchester Guardian, Daily Mail, Scotsman, Irish Times, Spectator* and *Picture Post*) and consulted the British Newspaper Archive to cover the provincial press.

These sources have enabled me to analyse the Oldham group's ideas; the sources for them; the internal discussions, debates and disagreements that accompanied their development; the group's efforts to exert influence on politics and public; and the public reception of the thought emerging from the group. They reveal, as subsequent chapters show, an intensive and wide-ranging effort by the group to grapple with numerous topics against the background of a rapidly and dramatically shifting world situation. It would be impossible to present these discussions in their entirety or to account completely for their complexity and diversity. I have thus selected the topics to be considered in accordance with their centrality to the group's concerns and structured my analysis of them via a crucial and recurring intellectual strategy: the search for diverse, but related, 'middle ways'.

Seeking 'middle ways' in an age of extremes

Rather than assembling individual profiles of Oldham group participants, I have sought to stress the collective shape of their ideas: their distinctive style of thought, its changing registers and its place in the war-time public sphere. Reassembling the group's views, however, is a complex issue. Its protagonists shared convictions, worldviews and aims. Yet, they never arrived at a comprehensive, unanimous and detailed vision of a Christian society. No manifesto emerged, and disagreements continued. Still, key texts expressed significant points of agreement, and there was a strong sense of common purpose and identity among participants. Oldham helped build consensus, not only by organising the group's main bodies (and selecting, in some cases, their participants) but also by summarising and synthesising their discussions. The Moot sought to unite diverse opinions (if not *too* diverse); other parts of the group, however, aimed to reach firm – if provisional – conclusions expressed in memoranda or published reports. Producing the *Christian News-Letter* compelled its editors – Oldham and then Kathleen Bliss – to develop a consistent line on many issues, but they also gave space to contrary opinions and frequently acknowledged ambiguities in even the most definitive statements of belief. Group participants, at times, expressed mixed feelings on certain issues. Some changed their minds. To capture this mixture of agreement and dissension, I have pursued three aims in each chapter: first, outlining elements of a significant (if at times unstable) *consensus*; second, accounting for

Figure 1 Joseph H. Oldham, 1937

departures from that consensus; and, third, giving a sense of *change over time* in both consensus and dissent.

Each chapter reveals a recurring dynamic in the group: the search for what I call 'middle ways' through the political and ideological extremes of the age. These might involve taking a *moderate position* between two (or more) perceived extremes; alternatively, the term 'middle way' meant constructing a *synthesis* of two different – possibly contradictory – elements. In some cases, the 'middle way' referred to the intellectual *content* of their ideas, in others to *strategies* for implementing them, both of which are important to understanding Christian efforts to remould European democracy in the mid twentieth century.[84] These middle ways seemed to resolve tensions inherent in the problems the group faced and became typical of the group's approach. Various kinds of 'betweenness' were involved: paths were sought between Protestantism and Catholicism,

between faith and secularity, between *laissez-faire* capitalism and collectivist socialism, between rootless internationalism and aggressive nationalism, between the United States and Russia, between freedom and order,
and between egalitarianism and elitism. While I use the notion primarily
as an analytical term, it also appeared at times in the sources. The vocabulary of the 'middle way' – and the belief that national traditions (such as
the Anglican *via media*) made Britain uniquely qualified to find it – was
common in the 1930s and 1940s.[85] In 1938, for example, Conservative MP
(and future prime minister) Harold Macmillan published a book with that
title, arguing for a centrist economic policy that avoided either *laissez-
faire* or totalitarian collectivism; his book was positively received in the
Christian press.[86] The newsletter *Reality* saw an alternative to either the
'Hitler New Order' or the 'Roosevelt New Order': there was a 'middle way',
a 'straight road to complete individual liberty', neither 'tyranny by force'
nor 'tyranny by money'.[87] However, some, often with Communist sympathies, argued against the possibility of a middle way. Kenneth Ingram,
for instance, gained much attention by claiming that the only choice, particularly for Christians, was between Fascism and Communism, strongly
urging the latter.[88] (There was also a small circle of pro-Fascist clerics
arguing for more radical solutions from a different direction.[89]) Oldham
group member John Middleton Murry admitted that, 'being British, one
dreams of a middle way'; however, he was 'reluctantly' forced to conclude
'that there is no middle way' and advocated a clearly socialist solution.[90]
Murry here departed from the group's consensus, which clung to the possibility of a moderate – yet still somehow 'revolutionary' – way forward.
While the ideal (and language) of the 'middle way' was common to the
period, it meant different things to different people, requiring attention to
the subtleties and ambiguities of its use in the chapters that follow.

Chapter 1 lays out the Oldham group's main participants, structures,
aims and strategies, providing an organisational overview on which later
thematic chapters build. Despite aiming for 'revolutionary' social change,
the group eschewed the options of forming a Christian political party or
seeking to foment popular revolt. Instead, it suggested that a 'revolution
from above' in the main institutions of the political and economic establishment should be brought about by a Christian 'Order' working through
private networks of influence as well as a broader effort to use media and
established Christian networks to create a cultural (Christian) 'leaven'.
Little came of the 'Order', but the group nevertheless sought political
influence through personal relationships while the *Christian News-Letter*
addressed the public and inspired new informal networks.

Chapters 2 and 3 focus on related aspects of one of the key concepts
guiding the group's search for middle ways: what Oldham referred to as the

'frontier' between faith and social life. Chapter 2 examines how the group defined a socially relevant faith amid dramatically different Christian positions on that matter. The group saw an emerging 'convergence' in Christian demands to reshape dominant ideas, cultural norms and social practices in accordance with Christian understandings of human nature and the purposes of social life. It sought 'middle axioms' that could connect eternal, universal Christian principles and the complexities of historically and culturally specific societies. In this effort, certain streams of religious thinking were adopted while others were rejected.

Chapter 3 considers one of the Oldham group's defining aims: bringing Christian principles and secular knowledge into creative relationship. The group's view of secularity combined positive, negative and neutral perspectives. Urging Christians to be more open to scientific knowledge, its members also condemned what they saw as extreme forms of secular 'materialism'. The group idealised a *modus vivendi* that would enable Christianity to influence the 'common life'; however, religion and secularity were conceived as distinct, each with its legitimate role to play. As the group saw Britain as a 'secular' society and likely to remain so, establishing a constructive relationship between Christians and non-Christians was a key goal.

Chapter 4 turns to the role of the State, centring on the ubiquitous 1930s and 1940s discussion about 'planning'. The Oldham group criticised the waste, inequality, greed and chaos of *laissez-faire* capitalism, seen to be at odds with Christian views on human life. Some members valued aspects of Marxist thought, but Marxism was rejected as a utopian ideology and Soviet Communism as a nightmare of totalitarian violence and repression. Karl Mannheim's concept of 'planning for freedom' seemed to offer a middle way (Mannheim called it a 'third way') towards encouraging Christian-inspired norms while leaving room for individual liberty and local initiative. 'Planning for freedom' provoked some dissent in the group and left it with mixed feelings about the emerging post-war welfare state: while welcoming moves towards 'social justice', it was concerned about oppressive statism.

Chapter 5 considers a key tension in the Oldham group's views on national identity. Its participants saw no problem in a close identification with one's national community; indeed, this was thought preferable to an unmoored, rootless 'internationalism'. However, nationalism was viewed negatively as an excessive, even idolatrous extreme. Fascism and National Socialism showed the dangers of nationalism, but similar tendencies threatened the democracies. At the same time, supposedly distinctive British traditions were seen as routes to a better world. What emerged was a 'Christian patriotism' combining a positive image of national characteristics with an emphasis on Christian universalism, national humility, self-criticism and an 'ethic of service' towards other nations. There were also efforts to embed British identity in larger imagined polities, such as 'Christendom', 'Federal Union' and 'the West'.

Chapter 6 considers the group's view of a widely used but variously understood term: 'freedom'. Its members sought to avoid either what they saw as the empty, superficial individualism of liberal capitalism or a violent, totalitarian *Gleichschaltung*. Against both, they sought a 'true' freedom based upon a holistic, organic and community-oriented 'personalism'. While there have been claims that the group's social vision, reflecting a broader Anglo-American Protestant tendency, implied some form of 'Christian totalitarianism', I show how it considered and then rejected this option at an early stage in its consultations. Crucially, already established civil rights and parliamentary government were not questioned. But while their vision of freedom was based upon ideals of political decentralisation and active citizenship, it also assumed democracy would have to take a more constrained form – a view that, however, was not untypical in post-war Europe.

Chapter 7 turns to the issue of social inequality. Here, the group's thinking was shaped by a fundamental tension between two contrasting motives. Participants were nearly unanimous in their opposition to class inequality and their advocacy of a more egalitarian society. Educational reform, in terms of both extending secondary schooling and increasing access to universities, was central to this aim. However, their vision of an ideal education was modelled on the elite variety that most members themselves had experienced. Their aim amounted to a 'democratisation of the aristocracy' rather than its abolition. Also, while committed to democracy and imbued with British libertarian traditions, the Oldham group remained suspicious of the 'masses'. This led them to the conclusion that a Christian (or at least Christian-inspired) elite, possibly in the form of a 'clerisy', was necessary to steer society in the right direction.

Conclusion

The Oldham group sought 'middle ways' through an age of extremes, part of a wider effort by British intellectuals – Christian or not – to reconsider the meaning of democracy and the legitimacy of the liberal, capitalist social order in the years around the Second World War.[91] While parts of the group, particularly the Moot, have received attention, it has been largely ignored in broader studies of British Christian thought or intellectual culture.[92] The group is sometimes mentioned in passing,[93] or it is examined with regard to only individual aspects of its thinking, such as education[94] or the need for a Christian 'elite'.[95] It has been referred to in biographical studies of its key protagonists, particularly those of Oldham himself, T. S. Eliot and Karl Mannheim, but also those of John Baillie and John Middleton Murry.[96] This biographical focus has given a valuable but often partial view determined by the person considered.[97] Figures in the group or related to it have appeared in studies of the ecumenical movement and 'Europe', but little attention has been given to its British context or to themes beyond European integration.[98] Oldham's role in shaping post-war Christian views of the atom bomb has been addressed, but with little attention to his broader vision.[99]

This book offers a more integrated, far-reaching and contextualising perspective on what I call the Oldham group. First, I examine its various component bodies and projects as an interlocking whole. I think it is crucial to take into account the collaborative nature and, in a sense, 'groupness' of the group. Second, more than previous studies, I stress the group's efforts towards influencing public opinion, particularly through the *Christian News-Letter*. While its thinking was often abstract and intellectual, the group – even in its private discussions – aimed at wider relevance and impact. Third, I offer the first broadly thematic study of the interrelated topics with which the group was preoccupied: Christianity's social relevance, the relationship between faith and secularity, the role of the State, the place of national identity, the true meaning of freedom, and ways of balancing egalitarian aims with elitist assumptions. Fourth, this book breaks new ground by considering how the group's ideas were related to and received within British intellectual culture generally.

A close examination of the Oldham group will enable me to contribute to understanding twentieth-century Christian social thought, the Second World War, responses to modernity and perceptions of (and reactions to) 'secularisation'. While it was too small (and elite) to be representative of religious belief and practice in Britain more generally, the Oldham group reveals some dominant trends in Christian thought. Moreover, it was prominent and well connected, and its members' views and publications received substantial attention in both Christian and secular contexts. While they had an ambivalent, often critical, attitude towards ecclesiastical hierarchies, orthodox theology and institutionalised faith, they also benefited from a close relationship to the churches, their most popular leaders (above all Anglican archbishops Lang and Temple) and the foremost theologians and religious philosophers of the age. As an internationally connected group working within the institutions of the ecumenical movement and aiming to synthesise religious thinking beyond denominational boundaries (including even secular thought in the natural and social sciences), the Oldham group is a particularly valuable site for reconstructing the complex and subtle interactions between various intellectual styles of thought in the 1930s and 1940s. As a group self-consciously operating in the misty borderlands between secular and religious worldviews, Oldham and his companions offer insights into both the subjective sense of secularisation and possible tendencies towards 'self-secularisation'.

Seeing the war as a socially and culturally transformative moment, the group sought to ensure that Christian principles could contribute to the 'social reconstruction' to follow. Keeping this hope alive was far from easy but could be expressed in a traditionally Christian language. Commenting on the mounting threat to Britain early in the war, Oldham told *Christian News-Letter* readers that 'Satanic forces' had broken loose in Europe, recalling Jesus' comments to those who arrested him in Gethsemane. 'We are experiencing on a world scale', he wrote, 'what Jesus knew and felt when He said: "This is your hour and the power of darkness."'[100] That moment, leading to the crucifixion, was a pivotal moment in the canonical gospels; however, it was followed, of course, by Jesus' resurrection and thus the inauguration (from a Christian perspective) of a new world. The antidote to destruction, fear and despair, Oldham claimed in drawing upon this text, was 'to fortify our minds with the truth that the Light has shone, and is shining, in the darkness; to remind ourselves every morning that *God is Light*'. The emphasis within Oldham's circle on the war as ushering in a renewal – even 'resurrection' – of Christian cultural, social and political influence (and therefore a reinforcement of liberal democracy) offers a specific example of a wider phenomenon. Metaphorically, Oldham's biblical reference was apt in light of recent research that has highlighted how the engagement with totalitarianism in the mid twentieth century led to a significant reshaping of European democracy, definitions of 'liberalism' and conceptions of 'human rights'.[101] Roger Griffin has stressed the 'palingenetic' promise of social rebirth at the heart of totalitarian movements; however, there were in this era also democratic and pacific visions of constructive social transformation, even if (as in the case of the Oldham group) they believed some lessons might be learned from the successes of their totalitarian opponents.[102] Understanding the Oldham group means accounting for its amphibious nature, both as distinctively British and internationally open; as resolutely Christian but committed to melding faith with useful elements of 'secular' knowledge; and as distinctly intellectual but seeking to address broader publics, whether Christian or not. The Oldham group, as I hope the following chapters show, makes visible many of the key tensions in the contestations around reconceptualising and renewing a democratic social order that took place in the crucible of war and post-war rebuilding.[103]

Notes

1 Riccardo Bavaj, 'Intellectual History', version: 1.0, *Docupedia-Zeitgeschichte* (13 September 2010), http://docupedia.de/zg/Intellectual_History (accessed 3 November 2018).

2 Lutz Raphael, '"Ideen als gesellschaftliche Gestaltungskraft im Europa der Neuzeit": Bemerkungen zur Bilanz eines DFG-Schwerpunktprogramms', and 'Ausschreibungstext', in Lutz Raphael and Heinz-Elmar Tenorth (eds.), *Ideen als gesellschaftliche Gestaltungskraft im Europa der Neuzeit* (Munich: De Gruyter Oldenbourg, 2006), pp. 11–27, 525–31 (pp. 11, 526). Original terms: *Deutungssysteme, Denkstile* and *gedachte Ordnungen*.

3 See Richard Whatmore, 'Intellectual History and the History of Political Thought', in Richard Whatmore and Brian Young (eds.), *Palgrave Advances in Intellectual History* (Basingstoke: Palgrave Macmillan, 2006), pp. 109–29; Richard Whatmore, *What Is Intellectual History?* (Cambridge: Polity, 2016); Q. R. D. Skinner, 'Meaning and Understanding in the History of Ideas', *History and Theory*, 8:1 (1969), 3–53; J. G. A. Pocock, 'The Reconstruction of Discourse: Towards the Historiography of Political Thought', *MLN*, 96:5 (1981), 959–80; J. G. A. Pocock, 'Quentin Skinner: The History of Politics and the Politics of History', *Common Knowledge*, 10 (2004), 532–50; Elías José Palti, 'From Ideas to Concepts to Metaphors: The German Tradition of Intellectual History and the Complex Fabric of Language', *History and Theory*, 49 (2010), 194–211.

4 Reinhart Koselleck, *Futures Past: On the Semantics of Historical Time*, trans. Keith Tribe (New York: Columbia University Press, 2004), pp. 183–9.

5 Peter E. Gordon, 'Contextualism and Criticism in the History of Ideas', in Darrin M. McMahon and Samuel Moyn (eds.), *Rethinking Modern European Intellectual History* (Oxford: Oxford University Press, 2014), pp. 32–55 (p. 48).

6 Mark Bevir, 'Philosophy, Rhetoric, and Power: A Response to Critics', *Rethinking History: The Journal of Theory and Practice*, 4:3 (2000), 341–50 (p. 344).

7 Jan-Werner Müller, 'European Intellectual History as Contemporary History', *Journal of Contemporary History*, 46:3 (2011), 574–90 (p. 588).

8 Thomas Grossbölting, 'Religionsgeschichte als Problemgeschichte der Gegenwart: Ein Vorschlag zu künftigen Perspektiven der Katholizismusforschung', in Wilhelm Damberg and Karl-Joseph Hummel (eds.), *Katholizismus in Deutschland: Zeitgeschichte und Gegenwart* (Paderborn: Ferdinand Schöningh, 2015), pp. 169–85 (pp. 180–1); and Andreas Holzem, 'Die Geschichte des "geglaubten Gottes"', in Andreas Leinhäupl-Wilke (ed.), *Katholische Theologie studieren: Themenfelder und Disziplinen* (Münster: LIT, 2000), pp. 73–103. See also Callum Brown's notion of 'discursive Christianity' in *The Death of Christian Britain: Understanding Secularisation 1800–2000*, 2nd edn (London: Routledge, 2009 [2001]); and Alana Harris, *Faith in the Family: A Lived Religious History of English Catholicism, 1945–82* (Manchester: Manchester University Press, 2013).

9 Adrian Hastings, 'The British Churches in the War and Post-War Reconstruction', in Andrew R. Morton (ed.), *God's Will in a Time of Crisis: A Colloquium Celebrating the 50th Anniversary of the Baillie Commission* (Edinburgh: University of Edinburgh, 1994), pp. 4–13 (p. 4).

10 Matthew Grimley, 'Civil Society and the Clerisy: Christian Elites and National Culture, c. 1930–1950', in Jose Harris (ed.), *Civil Society in British History: Ideas, Identities, Institutions* (Oxford: Oxford University Press, 2003), pp. 231–47.

11 Thomas Adam, *Intercultural Transfers and the Making of the Modern World, 1800–2000* (Basingstoke: Palgrave Macmillan, 2011); Johannes Paulmann, 'Interkultureller Transfer zwischen Deutschland und Großbritannien: Einführung in ein Forschungskonzept', in Rudolf Muhs, Johannes Paulmann and Willibald Steinmetz (eds.), *Aneignung und Abwehr: Interkultureller Transfer zwischen Deutschland und Großbritannien im 19. Jahrhundert* (Bodenheim: Philo, 1998), pp. 21–43.

12 Graham Harvey, 'Defining Religion', in John Wolffe and Gavin Moorhead, 'Religion, Security and Global Uncertainties: Report from a Global Uncertainties Leadership Fellowship' (Milton Keynes: Open University, 2014), pp. 7–8, www. open.ac.uk/arts/research/religion-martyrdom-global-uncertainties/sites/ www.open.ac.uk.arts.research.religion-martyrdom-global-uncertainties/files/ files/ecms/arts-rmgu-pr/web-content/blackburn-programme-may.pdf   [*sic*] (accessed 5 December 2014), pp. 7–8.

13 Samantha May, Erin K. Wilson, Claudia Baumgart-Ochse and Faiz Sheikh, 'The Religious as Political and the Political as Religious: Globalisation, Post-Secularism and the Shifting Boundaries of the Sacred', *Politics, Religion and Ideology*, 15 (2014), 331–46 (p. 339). Emphasis added.

14 John Wolffe, *God and Greater Britain: Religion and National Life in Britain and Ireland 1843–1943* (London: Routledge, 1994), pp. 5–19.

15 Keith Clements (ed.), *The Moot Papers: Faith, Freedom and Society 1938–1944* (Edinburgh: T. & T. Clark, 2010), p. 1 (hereafter *Moot Papers*); William Taylor and Marjorie Reeves, 'Intellectuals in Debate: The Moot', in Marjorie Reeves (ed.), *Christian Thinking and Social Order: Conviction Politics from the 1930s to the Present Day* (London: Cassell, 1999), pp. 24–48.

16 *Church Times*, 2 September 1938, p. 223.

17 *Christian World*, 28 May 1942, p. 5.

18 Shun'ichi Takayanagi, 'T. S. Eliot, the *Action française* and Neo-Scholasticism', in Benjamin G. Lockerd (ed.), *T. S. Eliot and Christian Tradition* (Madison, NJ: Fairleigh Dickinson University Press, 2014), pp. 89–97 (p. 95).

19 Stefan Collini, *Absent Minds: Intellectuals in Britain* (Oxford: Oxford University Press, 2006), p. 52.

20 *Ibid.*, pp. 52–9.

21 *Ibid.*, p. 57.

22 Matthew Grimley, *Citizenship, Community, and the Church of England: Liberal Anglican Theories of the State between the Wars* (Oxford: Oxford University Press, 2004), pp. 10–13; Tom Lawson, *The Church of England and the Holocaust: Christianity, Memory and Nazism* (Woodbridge: Boydell, 2006), pp. 10–14.

23 Philip S. Gorski, David Kyuman Kim, John Torpey and Jonathan VanAntwerpen, 'The Post-Secular in Question', in Philip S. Gorski, David Kyuman Kim, John Torpey and Jonathan VanAntwerpen (eds.), *The Post-Secular in*

Question: Religion in Contemporary Society (New York: New York University Press, 2012), pp. 1–22 (p. 5). See, e.g., Philip S. Gorski, *The Disciplinary Revolution: Calvinism and the Rise of the State in Early Modern Europe* (Chicago: University of Chicago Press, 2003); Sigrun Kahl, 'The Religious Roots of Modern Poverty Policy: Catholic, Lutheran, and Reformed Protestant Traditions Compared', *European Journal of Sociology*, 46 (2005), 91–126; Philip Manow, *Religion und Sozialstaat: Die konfessionellen Grundlagen europäischer Wohlfahrtsregime* (Frankfurt: Campus, 2008); Peter Stamatov, 'Activist Religion, Empire, and the Emergence of Modern Long-Distance Advocacy Networks', *American Sociological Review*, 75 (2010), 607–28.

24 Exceptions include general works such as John Oliver, *The Church and Social Order: Social Thought in the Church of England, 1918–1939* (London: A. R. Mowbray, 1968); Adrian Hastings, *A History of English Christianity 1920–1990* (London: SCM, 1991); G. I. T. Machin, *Churches and Social Issues in Twentieth-Century Britain* (Oxford: Clarendon Press, 1998); and those cited subsequently.

25 E.g. Eleanor M. Jackson, *Red Tape and the Gospel: A Study of the Significance of the Ecumenical Missionary Struggle of William Paton 1886–1943* (Birmingham: Phlogiston, 1980); Christina Scott, *A Historian and His World: A Life of Christopher Dawson, 1889–1970* (London: Sheed & Ward, 1984); John Kent, *William Temple: Church, State and Society in Britain, 1880–1950* (Cambridge: Cambridge University Press, 1992); Andrew Chandler (ed.), *Brethren in Adversity: George Bell, the Church of England and the Crisis of German Protestantism, 1933–1939* (Woodbridge: Boydell, 1997); Diane Kirby, *Church, State and Propaganda. The Archbishop of York and International Relations: A Study of Cyril Foster Garbett 1942–1955* (Hull: University of Hull Press, 1999); Adrian Hastings, *Oliver Tomkins: The Ecumenical Enterprise, 1908–1992* (London: SPCK, 2001); Robert Beaken, *Cosmo Lang: Archbishop in War and Crisis* (London: I.B. Tauris, 2012).

26 Wolffe, *God and Greater Britain*; Grimley, *Citizenship*; Keith Robbins, *Great Britain: Identities, Institutions, and the Idea of Britishness* (London: Longman, 1998); S. C. Williams, *Religious Belief and Popular Culture in Southwark c. 1880–1939* (Oxford: Oxford University Press, 1999); Hastings, *A History*; Stephen Parker, *Faith on the Home Front: Aspects of Church Life and Popular Religion in Birmingham, 1939–1945* (Bern: Peter Lang, 2005).

27 Emiel Lamberts (ed.), *Christian Democracy in the European Union (1945–1995)* (Leuven: Leuven University Press, 1997); Patrick Pasture, 'Religion in Contemporary Europe: Contrasting Perceptions and Dynamics', *Archiv für Sozialgeschichte*, 49 (2009), 319–50; Wolfram Kaiser, *Christian Democracy and the Origins of European Union* (Cambridge: Cambridge University Press 2007); Heinz Duchhardt and Małgorzata Morawiec (eds.), *Die europäische Integration und die Kirchen: Akteure und Rezipienten* (Göttingen: Vandenhoeck & Ruprecht, 2010); Patrick Pasture, *Imagining European Unity since 1000 AD* (Basingstoke: Palgrave Macmillan, 2015); Patrick Pasture, 'Between a Christian Fatherland and Euro-Christendom', in John Carter Wood (ed.), *Christianity*

and National Identity in Twentieth-Century Europe: Conflict, Community, and the Social Order (Göttingen: Vandenhoeck & Ruprecht, 2016), pp. 169–87.

28 Oliver, *Church and Social Order*; Grimley, *Citizenship*; Bruce Wollenberg, *Christian Social Thought in Great Britain between the Wars* (Lanham, MD: University Press of America, 1997); Peter Catterall, 'Morality and Politics: The Free Churches and the Labour Party between the Wars', *Historical Journal*, 36:3 (1993), 667–85; Peter Catterall, *Labour and the Free Churches, 1918–1939: Radicalism, Righteousness, and Religion* (London: Bloomsbury, 2016); Tom Villis, *British Catholics and Fascism: Religious Identity and Political Extremism between the Wars* (Basingstoke: Palgrave Macmillan, 2013); Alan Wilkinson, *Dissent or Conform? War, Peace and the English Churches 1900–1945* (London: SCM, 1986); Martin Ceadel, *Semi-Detached Idealists: The British Peace Movement and International Relations, 1845–1945* (Oxford: Oxford University Press, 2000); Richard Overy, 'Pacifism and the Blitz, 1940–1941', *Past and Present*, 219 (2013), 201–36.

29 Diane Kirby (ed.), *Religion and the Cold War* (Basingstoke: Palgrave, 2003); Philip M. Coupland, *Britannia, Europa and Christendom: British Christians and European Integration* (Basingstoke: Palgrave Macmillan, 2006); Peter Itzen, *Streitbare Kirche: Die Church of England vor den Herausforderungen des Wandels 1945–1990* (Baden-Baden: Nomos, 2012); Paul T. Phillips, *Contesting the Moral High Ground: Popular Moralists in Twentieth-Century Britain* (Montreal: McGill-Queen's University Press, 2013); Jonathan Gorry, *Cold War Christians and the Spectre of Nuclear Deterrence, 1945–1959* (Basingstoke: Palgrave Macmillan, 2013); Sam Brewitt-Taylor, 'The Invention of a "Secular Society"? Christianity and the Sudden Appearance of Secularisation Discourses in the British National Media, 1961–64', *Twentieth Century British History*, 24:3 (2013), 327–50; Sam Brewitt-Taylor, 'From Religion to Revolution: Theologies of Secularisation in the British Student Christian Movement, 1963–73', *Journal of Ecclesiastical History*, 66:4 (2015), 792–811; Mark T. Edwards, '"God's Totalitarianism": Ecumenical Protestant Discourse during the Good War, 1941–45', *Totalitarian Movements and Political Religions*, 10 (2009), 285–302; Mark T. Edwards, *The Right of the Protestant Left: God's Totalitarianism* (New York: Palgrave Macmillan, 2012); Michael G. Thompson, *For God and Globe: Christian Internationalism in the United States between the Great War and the Cold War* (Ithaca, NY: Cornell University Press, 2015).

30 Helen McCarthy, 'Whose Democracy? Histories of British Political Culture between the Wars', *Historical Journal*, 55:1 (2012), 221–38.

31 Gregor Feindt, Bernhard Gißibl, and Johannes Paulmann (eds.), *Kulturelle Souveränität: Politische Deutungs- und Handlungsmacht jenseits des Staates im 20. Jahrhundert* (Göttingen: Vandenhoeck & Ruprecht, 2016).

32 Quoted in Coupland, *Britannia, Europa and Christendom*, p. 18.

33 *New Statesman and Nation*, 8 March 1941, p. 230.

34 *Christian News-Letter* (*CNL*) 5S, 29 November 1939, J. H. Oldham, 'Preliminaries to the Consideration of Peace Aims', p. 3. (References from *CNL* include issue number, date and a notation (L or S) indicating the 'letter'

(written by the editor or guest editor) or 'supplement' (by the editor or an invited author). Author names (when known) and titles of supplements are given. Pagination varied and was often absent entirely. I provide page numbers, when present, as they originally appeared; otherwise, they are counted separately for letters and supplements.)

35 *Catholic Herald*, 1 August 1941, p. 6.

36 *Spectator*, 22 March 1940, pp. 400–1.

37 Speech by Dr Leslie F. Church, President of the Methodist Conference, in *Christian World*, 15 July 1943, p. 4.

38 David Edgerton, 'Becoming a Nation: Nationalism, "Alone", and "People's War" in British History and Historiography since 1940', unpublished essay, 2016.

39 Correlli Barnett, *The Audit of War: The Illusion and Reality of Britain as a Great Nation* (London: Macmillan, 1986). See a critique in Jose Harris, 'Enterprise and Welfare States: A Comparative Perspective', *Transactions of the Royal Historical Society*, 40 (1990), 175–95.

40 Keith Robbins, 'Britain, 1940 and "Christian Civilisation"', in Keith Robbins (ed.), *History, Religion and Identity in Modern Britain* (London: Hambledon, 1993), pp. 195–214; Philip Williamson, 'Christian Conservatives and the Totalitarian Challenge, 1933–1940', *English Historical Review*, 115:462 (2000), 607–42. Sonya Rose's *Which People's War* largely ignores religion, except with regard to pacifism: Sonya O. Rose, *Which People's War? National Identity and Citizenship in Britain, 1939–1945* (Oxford: Oxford University Press, 2003). Exceptions include Lawson, *Church of England and the Holocaust*; Parker, *Faith on the Home Front*; Michael Hughes, *Conscience and Conflict: Methodism, Peace and War in the Twentieth Century* (Peterborough: Epworth, 2008); Stephen G. Parker and Tom Lawson (eds.) *God and War: The Church of England and Armed Conflict in the Twentieth Century* (Aldershot: Ashgate, 2012); and Alan Jacobs, *The Year of Our Lord 1943: Christian Humanism in an Age of Crisis* (Oxford: Oxford University Press, 2018).

41 Edgerton, 'Becoming a Nation'.

42 'Religion and Life Weeks' were sponsored by the Commission of the Churches for International Friendship and Social Responsibility (about which more is said in Chapter 1). See *Spiritual Issues of the War*, no. 225, 24 February 1944, pp. 1–2 for a description of a typical 'Religion and Life Week'; and *ibid.*, no. 235, 4 May 1944, p. 1 for the growing frequency of the events (1940: 1; 1941: 5; 1942: 21; 1943: 60; 1944: 51). Oldham group members took part in such events.

43 *The Times*, 21 December 1940, p. 5. See commentary in *Spectator*, 27 December 1940, pp. 690–1, and 10 January 1941, p. 37; *British Weekly*, 6 February 1941, p. 191; *Spiritual Issues of the War*, no. 80, 15 May 1941.

44 *Church Times*, 31 January 1941, p. 27; *Church Times*, 16 January 1942, p. 35; *Church of England Newspaper*, 17 January 1941, pp. 4–5; *Christian World*, 8 October 1942, p. 6; *Christian World*, 12 November 1942, p. 1.

45 *Church of England Newspaper*, 22 August 1941, p. 1.

46 Stefan Collini, 'Saint or Snake', *London Review of Books*, 8 October 2015, pp. 29–33 (p. 29).

47 *Spectator*, 23 February 1940, pp. 241–2.

48 A useful summary is offered by Joris van Eijnatten, Ed Jonker, Willemijn Ruberg and Joes Segal, 'Shaping the Discourse on Modernity', *International Journal for History, Culture and Modernity*, 1 (2013), 3–20.

49 See, e.g., Itzen on *Sinnstiftung* (meaning-making) and religion: *Streitbare Kirche*, pp. 11–18.

50 Richard Overy, *The Morbid Age: Britain and the Crisis of Civilisation, 1919–1939* (London: Penguin, 2010); Wilkinson, *Dissent or Conform?*, pp. 193–231.

51 Villis, *British Catholics and Fascism*, pp. 76–83.

52 D. L. LeMahieu, *A Culture for Democracy: Mass Communication and the Cultivated Mind in Britain between the Wars* (Oxford: Clarendon Press, 1988).

53 See a review of Erich Fromm's *The Fear of Freedom* in *British Weekly*, 7 January 1943, p. 183.

54 Gareth Dale, *Karl Polanyi: The Limits of the Market* (Cambridge: Polity, 2010), pp. 45–6.

55 See, generally, Julia Stapleton, 'Resisting the Centre at the Extremes: "English" Liberalism in the Political Thought of Interwar Britain', *British Journal of Politics and International Relations*, 1:3 (1999), 270–92.

56 Markus Huttner, *Totalitarismus and säkulare Religionen* (Bonn: Bouvier, 1999), esp. pp. 265–322.

57 Hannah Arendt, *The Origins of Totalitarianism*, 3rd edn (London: George Allen & Unwin, 1967 [1950]), p. xxix (preface to the 1st edn).

58 Samuel Moyn, *Christian Human Rights* (Philadelphia: University of Pennsylvania Press, 2015), p. 21.

59 Friedrich Wilhelm Graf, 'Euro-Gott im starken Plural? Einige Fragestellungen für eine europäische Religionsgeschichte des 20. Jahrhunderts', *Journal of Modern European History*, 3 (2005), 231–56 (pp. 241–2).

60 John Hutchinson, *Modern Nationalism* (London: Fontana, 1994), pp. 41, 65, 66.

61 Meredith Veldman, *Fantasy, the Bomb, and the Greening of Britain: Romantic Protest, 1945–1980* (Cambridge: Cambridge University Press, 1994), pp. 1–3.

62 Matthew Sterenberg, *Mythic Thinking in Twentieth-Century Britain: Meaning for Modernity* (Basingstoke: Palgrave Macmillan, 2013), pp. 1, 3–4.

63 Rodney Stark, 'Secularisation R. I. P.', *Sociology of Religion*, 60:3 (1999), 249–73; David Nash, 'Reconnecting Religion with Social and Cultural History: Secularization's Failure as a Master Narrative', *Cultural and Social History*, 1 (2004), 302–25; David Nash, *Christian Ideals in British Culture: Stories of Belief in the Twentieth Century* (Basingstoke: Palgrave Macmillan, 2013).

64 See José Casanova, *Public Religions in the Modern World* (Chicago: University of Chicago Press, 1994).

65 Roy Wallis and Steve Bruce, 'Secularization: The Orthodox Model', in Steve Bruce (ed.), *Religion and Modernization: Sociologists and Historians Debate the Secularization Thesis* (Oxford: Clarendon Press, 1992), pp. 8–30; Steve Bruce, 'Secularisation in the UK and the USA', in Callum G. Brown and Michael Snape (eds.), *Secularisation in the Christian World* (Farnham: Ashgate, 2010), pp. 205–18; Steve Bruce, *Secularization: In Defence of an Unfashionable*

Theory (Oxford: Oxford University Press, 2011); Detlef Pollack and Gergely Rosta, *Religion in der Moderne: Ein internationaler Vergleich* (Frankfurt: Campus, 2015).

66 Gladys Ganiel, 'Secularization, Ecumenism and Identity on the Island of Ireland', in Wood, *Christianity and National Identity*, pp. 73–89; Patrick Pasture, 'Dechristianization and the Changing Religious Landscape in Europe and North America since 1950: Comparative, Transatlantic, and Global Perspectives', in Nancy Christie and Michael Gauvreau (eds.), *The Sixties and Beyond: Dechristianization in North America and Western Europe, 1945–2000* (Toronto: University of Toronto Press, 2013), pp. 367–402. On individualisation, see also Grossbölting, 'Religionsgeschichte als Problemgeschichte der Gegenwart', pp. 180–4; and Grace Davie, *Religion in Britain since 1945: Believing without Belonging* (Oxford: Blackwell, 1994).

67 Brown, *Death of Christian Britain*; Hugh McLeod, 'Introduction', in Hugh McLeod and Werner Ustorf (eds.), *The Decline of Christendom in Western Europe, 1750–2000* (Cambridge: Cambridge University Press, 2003), pp. 1–26; Pollack and Rosta, *Religion in der Moderne*, p. 464.

68 Brown, *Death of Christian Britain*, pp. 12–13; Parker, *Faith on the Home Front*, pp. 15–17.

69 Ross McKibbin, *Classes and Cultures: England, 1918–1951* (Oxford: Oxford University Press, 1998), pp. 272, 289.

70 *Ibid.*, pp. 276, 294.

71 Jonathan Sheehan, 'Enlightenment, Religion, and the Enigma of Secularization: A Review Essay', *American Historical Review*, 108:4 (2003), 1061–80 (pp. 1079–80).

72 Russell T. McCutcheon, '"They licked the platter clean": On the Co-Dependency of the Religious and the Secular', *Method and Theory in the Study of Religion*, 19 (2007), 173–99; Timothy Fitzgerald, *Discourse on Civility and Barbarity: A Critical History of Religion and Related Categories* (Oxford: Oxford University Press, 2007), p. 24; Markus Dressler and Arvind-Pal S. Mandair, *Secularism and Religion-Making* (Oxford: Oxford University Press, 2011), p. 21; Marion Eggert and Lucian Hölscher (eds.), *Religion and Secularity: Transformations and Transfers of Religious Discourses in Europe and Asia* (Leiden: Brill, 2013). See also James Chappel, 'Beyond Tocqueville: A Plea to Stop "Taking Religion Seriously"', *Modern Intellectual History*, 10:3 (2013), 697–708.

73 T. S. Eliot, 'Thoughts after Lambeth' (1931), in *Selected Essays, 1917–1932* (New York: Harcourt, Brace, 1932), pp. 310–32 (p. 332). Eliot expressed similar sentiments in verse in 1934: 'Choruses from "The Rock"', in T. S. Eliot, *The Poems of T. S. Eliot*, Vol. I: *Collected and Uncollected Poems*, ed. Christopher Ricks and Jim McCue (London: Faber and Faber, 2015), pp. 169–70.

74 Christopher Dawson, *Religion and the Modern State* (London: Sheed & Ward, 1938 [1935]), p. 153.

75 *British Weekly*, 19 September 1940, p. 279.

76 George Orwell, 'Notes on the Way', in George Orwell, *The Collected Essays, Journalism and Letters of George Orwell*, Vol. II: *My Country Right or Left*

1940–1943, ed. Sonia Orwell and Ian Angus (London: Penguin, 1970 [1958]), pp. 30–3.

77 See Kingsley Martin's review of Harold J. Laski's *Faith, Reason and Civilisation* in *New Statesman and Nation*, 18 March 1944, p. 192.

78 Harold J. Laski, *Faith, Reason, and Civilisation: An Essay in Historical Analysis* (London: Victor Gollancz, 1944), pp. 54–5.

79 See, e.g., Emilio Gentile, 'Fascism, Totalitarianism and Political Religion: Definitions and Critical Reflections on Criticism of an Interpretation', *Totalitarian Movements and Political Religions*, 5:3 (2004), 326–75.

80 'Säkularisierung war existent, weil sie von den Akteuren erfahren und reflektiert wurde und sie ihr Handeln danach ausrichteten'; Itzen, *Streitbare Kirche*, p. 13.

81 Brewitt-Taylor, 'Invention of a "Secular Society"?'; and 'From Religion to Revolution'.

82 The following archives have been consulted: the J. H. Oldham Papers, New College Library, Edinburgh (the 'Oldham Archive' (OA)); Fred Clarke Papers, Institute of Education, University of London (IOE); Church of England Record Office (CERC); Lambeth Palace Library (LPL); John Baillie Collection, University of Edinburgh (BC); Moot Papers, Brotherton Library, University of Leeds (UL); W. G. Symons Papers, University of Birmingham (WGS). Papers belonging to W. G. Symons – who was on the *Christian News-Letter*'s editorial board – were also generously given to me by his son, Martin (references to sources from that collection will be prefaced 'MSC').

83 On the *British Weekly* and *Christian World* see Catterall, *Labour and the Free Churches*, p. 9.

84 Jan-Werner Müller, 'Towards a New History of Christian Democracy', *Journal of Political Ideologies*, 18:2 (2013), 243–55, esp. pp. 246–51.

85 Joanne Pemberton, 'The Middle Way: The Discourse of Planning in Britain, Australia, and at the League in the Interwar Years', *Australian Journal of Politics and History*, 52:1 (2006), 48–63. *British Weekly*, 17 October 1940, pp. 23, 26; 2 October 1947, p. 349; 13 May 1948, p. 4; and 15 July 1948, p. 6. *Guardian*, 17 March 1939, p. 166. *Catholic Herald*, 8 September 1944, p. 4. CNL 274S, 27 November 1946, J. Middleton Murry, 'Can Democracy Survive?', p. 15.

86 *Church Times*, 1 July 1938, p. 19; *Guardian*, 24 June 1938, p. 406.

87 B. R., 'The Middle Way', *Reality*, no. 185, Vol. 4, no. 35, 13 November 1942, pp. 3–4.

88 Review of *The Christian Challenge to Communists*, *Church Times*, 12 August 1938, p. 157. See also Kenneth Ingram, *Christianity: Right or Left?* (London: George Allen & Unwin, 1937).

89 Thomas Linehan, '"On the Side of Christ": Fascist Clerics in 1930s Britain', *Totalitarian Movements and Political Religions*, 8:2 (2007), 287–301.

90 OA 14/5/48 [J. M. Murry], 'The Way to Beat Hitler' [n.d.], p. 2.

91 This was part of a broader European pattern: Jan-Werner Müller, *Contesting Democracy: Political Ideas in Twentieth-Century Europe* (New Haven: Yale University Press, 2011).

92 Oliver, *Church and Social Order*; David Lyon, 'The Idea of a Christian Sociology: Some Historical Precedents and Current Concerns', *Sociological Analysis*, 44 (1983), 227–42. Maurice Cowling discusses Temple but not the Oldham group: *Religion and Public Doctrine in Modern England*, Vol. III: *Accommodations* (Cambridge: Cambridge University Press, 2001). Jonas Kurlberg, 'Resisting Totalitarianism: The Moot and a New Christendom', *Religion Compass*, 7 (2013), 517–31 provides a thorough overview of existing research on 'the Moot'. See also Jonas Kurlberg, 'The Moot, the End of Civilisation and the Re-Birth of Christendom', in Erik Tonning, Matthew Feldman and David Addyman (eds.), *Modernism, Christianity and Apocalypse* (Leiden: Brill, 2015), pp. 222–35.

93 Robbins, 'Christian Civilisation', esp. pp. 206–9; Stephen G. Parker, 'Reinvigorating Christian Britain: The Spiritual Issues of the War, National Identity, and the Hope of Religious Education', in Parker and Lawson, *God and War*, pp. 61–79 (p. 67).

94 Tom Steele and Richard Kenneth Taylor, 'Oldham's Moot (1938–1947), the Universities and the Adult Citizen', *History of Education*, 39 (2010), 183–97.

95 Grimley, 'Civil Society and the Clerisy'; Phil Mullins and Struan Jacobs, 'T. S. Eliot's Idea of the Clerisy, and Its Discussion by Karl Mannheim and Michael Polanyi in the Context of J. H. Oldham's Moot', *Journal of Classical Sociology*, 6 (2006), 147–76.

96 On Oldham: Keith Clements, *Faith on the Frontier: A Life of J. H. Oldham* (Edinburgh: T. & T. Clark, 1999). On Eliot, e.g.: Roger Kojecky, *T. S. Eliot's Social Criticism* (London: Faber and Faber, 1971); Collini, *Absent Minds*, pp. 316–22; Barry Spurr, *'Anglo-Catholic in Religion': T. S. Eliot and Christianity* (Cambridge: Lutterworth Press, 2010), esp. pp. 190–1; Christopher McVey, 'Backgrounds to *The Idea of a Christian Society*: Charles Maurras, Christopher Dawson and Jacques Maritain', in Benjamin G. Lockerd (ed.), *T. S. Eliot and Christian Tradition* (Madison, NJ: Fairleigh Dickinson University Press, 2014), pp. 179–93. On Baillie: Keith Clements, 'John Baillie and "the Moot"', in David Fergusson (ed.), *Christ, Church and Society: Essays on John Baillie and Donald Baillie* (London: T. & T. Clark, 1993), pp. 199–219; Andrew R. Morton, ed., *God's Will in a Time of Crisis: A Colloquium Celebrating the 50th Anniversary of the Baillie Commission* (Edinburgh: University of Edinburgh, 1994). On Mannheim: Wolf Lepenies, *Between Literature and Science: The Rise of Sociology* (Cambridge: Cambridge University Press, 1988), pp. 329–33; David Kettler and Volker Meja, *Karl Mannheim and the Crisis of Liberalism* (New Brunswick, NJ: Transaction, 1995). On Murry: Frank Alfred Lea, *The Life of John Middleton Murry* (London: Methuen, 1959).

97 Collini, for example, gives the impression that Eliot's views were representative of the Moot. The elitist notion of 'cultural leadership' did shape the group's thought; however, it also stressed local activity and public dialogue. Collini, *Absent Minds*, pp. 316–22. Spurr doubts that Eliot valued his participation with the group at all; Spurr, *'Anglo Catholic in Religion'*, pp. 188–93. I address this issue in Chapter 4.

98 Jurjen A. Zeilstra, *European Unity in Ecumenical Thinking 1937–1948* (Zoetermeer: Boekencentrum, 1995); Coupland, *Britannia, Europa and Christendom*.

99 Gorry, *Cold War Christians*.

100 *CNL* 30L, 22 May 1940, p. 3, citing Luke 22:53. See also John Painter, *1, 2 and 3 John* (Collegeville, MN: Liturgical Press, 2002), pp. 382–3.

101 Martin Conway, 'The Rise and Fall of Western Europe's Democratic Age, 1945–1973', *Contemporary European History*, 13:1 (2004), 67–88; Müller, *Contesting Democracy*; Duncan Bell, 'What Is Liberalism?', *Political Theory*, 42:6 (2014), 682–715; Moyn, *Christian Human Rights*.

102 Roger Griffin, *Modernism and Fascism: The Sense of a Beginning under Mussolini and Hitler* (Basingstoke: Palgrave Macmillan, 2007). Roger Griffin, 'The Legitimizing Role of Palingenetic Myth in Ideocracies', in Uwe Backes and Steffen Kailitz (eds.), *Ideokratien im Vergleich: Legitimation – Kooptation – Repression* (Göttingen: Vandenhoeck & Ruprecht, 2014), pp. 279–95.

103 Müller, *Contesting Democracy*.

1

The 'Oldham group', 1937–49: people, organisations and aims

What I call the Oldham group grew out of J. H. Oldham's efforts to advance the conclusions of the 1937 Oxford ecumenical conference on 'Church, Community and State', itself a summary of decades of Christian thought about the social order. Oldham set up the group's official and unofficial bodies, selecting their members, guiding their discussions, synthesising their views and publicising their conclusions. But his efforts were assisted by others and enabled by the wider institutional infrastructure of British Christianity. He gained the backing of the Protestant churches, bringing resources, contacts and prestige; nevertheless, group members saw institutional religion as not only an ally but also an obstacle to their goals. While the group shared an intellectual consensus, it also experienced interpersonal tensions, political clashes, theological disputes and a chronic failure of resources to match ambitions. Introducing the group thus means describing Oldham himself, the people who joined him, the organisations they formed and the strategies they pursued.

Creating the Oldham group

Joseph Houldsworth Oldham (1874–1969), 'Joe' to his friends and colleagues, was born in India, where his father was an engineer for the East India Company.[1] When he was seven, the family returned to Scotland. Oldham attended Edinburgh Academy and then Trinity College, Oxford, where he not only read Greats between 1892 and 1896 but was also convinced by visiting American evangelists Dwight L. Moody and John Mott to become a missionary. He was the first full-time General Secretary of the Student Volunteer Missionary Union (SVMU), spending three years in India (where he wed) until a case of typhoid forced his return in 1901. He attended New College, Edinburgh, and studied with Gustav Warneck, professor of the theology of missions, in Halle, Germany in 1904 and 1905. (He received honorary doctorates in divinity from Edinburgh University in

1929 and Oxford in 1937.) Though never ordained, Oldham became a leader in the missionary and ecumenical movements, the latter emerging from the former after the 1910 Edinburgh World Missionary Conference, which he co-organised. He was then secretary of the conference's Continuation Committee. In 1912, he founded the *International Review of Missions*.

The 'ecumenical movement' referred to individuals in various countries, denominations and organisations working for Christian unity in theology and social action. Dominated by Europeans and North Americans, its reach extended to Africa, Asia and South America. Protestants led it, but Orthodox churches were represented; the Roman Catholic Church refused participation until the 1960s. Within the movement, there were various views on the meaning of 'unity' and the relationship between faith and society. A key fault line ran between Anglo-American social activism and the continental European Protestant – especially German – insistence on separating divine and secular categories.[2] The movement arose piecemeal through the coordination of conferences. Key organisations were the World Alliance for Promoting International Friendship through the Churches (founded in 1914), Faith and Order (1920) and the Universal Christian Council on Life and Work (1925).

Oldham became a key figure in inter-war ecumenism, particularly in Life and Work. Though raised a Presbyterian, he became an Anglican upon moving to London after the Great War.[3] In 1921 he was appointed secretary of the International Missionary Council (IMC), where he remained until 1938. It allowed him to develop contacts with colonial administrators, contributing to his popular book *Christianity and the Race Problem* (1924). Without denying 'racial' differences (a question, as he saw it, for science), Oldham here set them in 'a fundamental human unity' and argued against racism and exploitation.[4] One chapter, 'The Christian View and Its Relation to Facts', made assertions central to his later work: Christianity was less an ethical code than a claim about reality; Christians should engage with social issues; faith provided key beliefs about life's meaning and purpose rather than 'explicit direction' for policy; and 'secular' knowledge could further Christian aims.[5] He organised important ecumenical meetings and published his successful *Devotional Diary* (1923). He also became the first administrative director of the International Institute of African Languages and Cultures.

Oldham's focus shifted decisively to Europe in the 1930s. Russian Communism and Italian Fascism had long caused concern; however, the Great Depression, development of Stalinism, rise of the Nazis and apparent weakness of the democracies brought the issues of freedom, secularity and the social order to the top of his agenda. In 1934, he became chair of Life and Work's 'Research Committee'. Increasingly convinced of the need for

Christian responses to what seemed a terminal western crisis, Oldham and William Temple (then Archbishop of York) organised the 1937 Life and Work Conference on 'Church, Community and State' in Oxford.[6] Oldham was then in his early sixties (and nearly deaf), but the next decade saw him embark on a period of furious organisational activity.

The 1937 Oxford conference was the most significant inter-war meeting on Protestant and Orthodox social thought. It built upon and expanded existing strands of ecumenical thinking, such as those expressed at 'COPEC' (as the 'Conference on Politics, Economics and Citizenship' held in Birmingham in 1924 was widely known), and also reflected the specific political and theological atmosphere of the late 1930s. Over twelve days in July 1937, 425 delegates (and a similar number of visitors) from 120 churches in over 40 countries met in thematic committees to discuss pre-circulated draft resolutions.[7] Oldham had issued a pre-conference pamphlet, and he co-wrote a summary of the conference's main issues with Willem A. Visser 't Hooft, *The Church and Its Function in Society* (1937).[8] A series of reports were published on society, economics and international relations, the fruits of decades of Christian thought. Archbishop Temple saw inter-war ecumenism as defined by its critique of 'acquisitive society', assertion that social life must reflect true human 'ends', emphasis on 'personal freedom' and commitment to a fair deal for workers.[9] However, the conference also exemplified Christians' political divisions, particularly those related to the German 'church struggle' between the pro-Nazi *Deutsche Christen* ('German Christians') and the oppositional *Bekennende Kirche* ('Confessing Church'). Agreement had been reached on joint participation by both sides, but at the last minute Hitler personally ordered that no German delegation attend.[10] Nonetheless, the conference approved the creation of the WCC, a step matched by Faith and Order that year in Edinburgh: delayed by war, the WCC was inaugurated in 1948. After 'Oxford 1937', Oldham was at the centre of efforts by the British churches to continue the conference's momentum, enabling what I call 'the Oldham group' to come together.

Oldham set up two church-funded organisations – the Council on the Christian Faith and the Common Life (CCFCL, 1938–42) and, later, the Christian Frontier Council (CFC, 1942–75) – as well as a discussion group called 'the Moot' (1938–47). With the outbreak of war, he founded a weekly (later biweekly) periodical, the *Christian News-Letter* (*CNL*, 1939–49), and a related book series. These projects formed an interlocking whole. The Moot was a private arena for discussing ideas. The two 'Councils' gave links to official Christianity, bringing prestige and material resources. The *News-Letter* was published under their auspices, with some of its content developed in the Moot and CFC. The Moot was the group's main intellectual laboratory and the *News-Letter* its public face: it had a recognisable style and editorial line and proved to be popular. It was seen within the group as its most important joint production.

People

The members of the Moot

The crucial sites for developing the group's thinking were the Moot, CFC and the editorial office of the *CNL*. The detailed minutes and voluminous papers from the Moot offer a systematic insight into its meetings. Across its existence, the Moot had twenty-three 'members', aptly described as a 'cross-section of the liberal, intellectual British establishment' based in the churches, lay organisations, media and universities.[11] They included clergy and theologians, such as the Anglicans Gilbert Shaw, Oliver Tomkins and Alec Vidler (editor of the journal *Theology*) as well as the Presbyterians John Baillie, H. H. Farmer and Alexander ('Lex') Miller. Eric Fenn and Daniel Jenkins (like Tomkins) had backgrounds in the Student Christian Movement (SCM) and later became ministers (Presbyterian and Congregationalist, respectively); Fenn had also helped Oldham organise Oxford 1937 and was assistant director of religious broadcasts at the BBC from 1939 to 1945. H. A. Hodges was a professor of philosophy at Reading University. The poet and critic T. S. Eliot was a member, as was John Middleton Murry: author, editor, pacifist and Christian Communist. Senior educationalists were involved, such as Sir Walter Moberly (chair of the University Grants Committee between 1935 and 1948 and former vice-chancellor of Manchester University), Sir Fred Clarke (director of the Institute of Education at the University of London, 1936–45), Walter Oakeshott (assistant master of Winchester College and later High Master of St Paul's School) and Sir Hector Hetherington (principal and vice-chancellor of Glasgow University). The group's Christians were almost entirely Protestant (with Anglicans as the largest group, followed by Presbyterians), save for the Roman Catholics Christopher Dawson (a historian) and, from 1944, Michael Polanyi (a chemist and philosopher).[12] Polanyi was one of three academics with Jewish origins in the group, alongside sociologists Karl Mannheim and Adolf Löwe. The latter two were agnostic and took British citizenship in 1939; Polanyi did so in 1940. Three women were centrally involved: Oldham's wife Mary, the missionary and Anglican lay theologian Kathleen Bliss and the ecumenical activist Eleanora Iredale. There were also several 'visitors' to the Moot, and people outside the group (such as C. S. Lewis) were sometimes invited to comment on discussion papers.[13]

Participants' involvement varied: some Moot members, such as Tomkins, attended only a few times; others, such as Dawson, were at odds with its views.[14] A kind of 'inner circle' of the group, based in the Moot, can be defined both by quantitative factors (e.g. frequency of attendance or number of papers contributed) and by an evaluation of their influence. This group included Oldham, Mannheim, Hodges, Baillie, Eliot, Murry, Vidler and Bliss. The nature of their influence also varied. Murry's and Eliot's departures from the group's consensus were as important as their agreements with it. Others outside this circle contributed enormously to specific topics, as later chapters show: e.g. Polanyi's critique of planning or Clarke's thoughts on education. Iredale raised vital funds for Oldham's projects and was CCFCL treasurer. (Oldham was seen as 'helpless' without her when it came to finances.[15]) Fenn undertook key secretarial tasks and co-organised the CCFCL. Moberly helped run the CCFCL and CFC (of which he was chair) and regularly attended the Moot, but he was mainly a discussant and commentator. Such contributions cannot be ignored; however, I turn now to a closer look at those eight participants who will play a central role in what follows.

The inner circle

Oldham's life has already been described, but his leadership role should be stressed. The CCFCL was informally known as 'Joe's Council': he was clearly the CFC's guiding spirit, and the Moot was 'firmly Oldham's project' with regard to its membership and agenda.[16] He was the moving force behind the *CNL*, writing up (after discussions with its board), most of the editorial content and contributing a large number of essays. He was the figure most publicly associated with it, and his *Resurrection of Christendom* (1940) inaugurated the '*CNL* Books' series. But Oldham did not always get his way, and his efforts were, as we shall see, sometimes marked by conflict, frustration and occasional failure. The group was, clearly, collaborative, and Oldham's talent lay mainly in bringing people together and synthesising what resulted. Still, in all these activities his distinctive 'voice' is recognisable.

Next to Oldham, the Hungarian sociologist Karl Mannheim (1893–1947) dominated the Moot. From Budapest circles around Marxist critic Georg Lukács and liberal sociologist Oscar Jászi, Mannheim moved to Heidelberg after the 1919 Hungarian revolutions. He helped found the sociology of knowledge with *Ideologie und Utopie* (*Ideology and Utopia* (1929 [1936])), extending Marxist claims about the social determination of bourgeois knowledge to *all* knowledge, radical 'utopias' no less than reactionary 'ideologies'. Intellectuals, he argued, should synthesise these partial truths, reflecting his own approach to melding romanticism and idealism, Marxism and liberalism, and religion and sociology.[17] Mannheim having been awarded a professorship in Frankfurt in 1930, his Jewish origins soon brought his dismissal in 1933. British political scientist Harold Laski invited him to teach at the London School of Economics, after which he met Oldham. Often at odds with British sociologists, Mannheim became a well-known public intellectual via *Man and Society in an Age of Reconstruction* (1940: a translation of *Mensch und Gesellschaft im Zeitalter des Umbaus* [1935]) and *Diagnosis of Our Time: Wartime Essays of a Sociologist* (1943). Fred Clarke invited him to lecture at the University of London, where Mannheim taught until his sudden death in January 1947.

When he joined the Moot in 1938, Thomas Stearns Eliot (1888–1965) was an eminent poet, playwright and literary critic. Born and raised in St Louis, Missouri as a Unitarian, he became a British citizen and an (Anglo-Catholic) Anglican in 1927. He had developed his status as a Christian social thinker as editor of the literary journal the *Criterion*. Once drawn to the right-wing monarchism of the *Action française*, after the mid 1920s Eliot turned to the more democratic Catholic thought of Christopher Dawson and Jacques Maritain.[18] He was active in several Christian circles, such as the Anglo-Catholic 'Christendom Group'. Oldham was brought to his attention by Bishop George Bell during a shared train journey in 1930.[19] Eliot spoke at Oxford 1937 and was on its economics committee with fellow Moot members Baillie and Iredale and alongside V. A. Demant, Sir Josiah Stamp and R. H. Tawney.[20] Eliot helped set up the CCFCL, attended the Moot and was on the *CNL*'s editorial board. His books *The Idea of a Christian Society* (1939) and *Notes towards the Definition of Culture* (1948, the year he received the Nobel Prize for Literature) were influenced by Oldham's circle, but, as noted in Chapter 4, he became increasingly critical of its aims.[21]

The role of John Middleton Murry (1889–1957) in the group also combined devotion and discord. Of humble origins, he won scholarships to attend Christ's Hospital School and to study classics at Brasenose College, Oxford.[22] Through marriage to Katherine Mansfield and editorship of the *Athenaeum* (1919–21) and the *Adelphi* (1923–48), he became a prominent literary critic and a leading figure in the foundation of English literary modernism in the 1910s and 1920s, a movement he publicly rejected by the late 1920s, notably engaging in a literary debate with Eliot.[23] Exemplifying the 'indeterminate, fluid character' of inter-war intellectual life, Murry promoted a shifting and unorthodox (even eccentric) amalgam of social and religious thought.[24] In *The Necessity of Communism* (1932) he argued for an 'English' Communism suffused with liberty. Turning to Christianity, Murry then proclaimed *The Necessity of Pacifism* (1937). He formed a pacifist community in rural Essex – the 'Adelphi Centre' (1935–37) – and edited *Peace News* (1940–46), also advocating faith, pacifism and socialism in *The Price of Leadership* (1939) and *The Betrayal of Christ by the Churches* (1940).[25] He ceased attending the Moot in 1942 but remained in contact with it. His *Europe in Travail* (1940) was the second in the *CNL*'s book series. During the war, he argued for religious social renewal in books such as *Christocracy* (1943) and *Adam and Eve* (1944) and led an experimental communal farm in Norfolk.[26] It failed as a commune (though succeeded financially), and the war's end saw yet another turn, expressed in *The Free Society* (1948): away from pacifism and towards a fervent anti-Communism.[27]

Alec R. Vidler (1899–1991) was a well-known Anglican clergyman.[28] From a Sussex family that ran a shipping firm, he read theology at Selwyn College, Cambridge, was ordained in 1922 and joined a celibate Anglo-Catholic society, the Oratory of the Good Shepherd. Vidler publicly supported the Labour Party, and – like many Anglo-Catholics – he served in a 'slum ministry' (in Newcastle). He was active in efforts to connect Christianity and social policy, and published *Magic and Religion* (1930), *Sex, Marriage and Religion* (1932) – which supported women's economic equality and the use of contraception within marriage – and *A Plain Man's Guide to Christianity* (1936). The 1930s and 1940s saw him drift towards 'cultural pessimism and criticism of political and theological liberalism', views he elucidated in *God's Judgement on Europe* (1940), *Secular Despair and Christian Faith* (1941) and *Christ's Strange Work* (1944).[29] While in the Moot, Vidler was Warden of St Deiniol's Library, Hawarden (1939–48) and edited the monthly Anglican journal *Theology* (1939–64). He was on the *CNL*'s editorial board and editor of its associated book series. From 1948, Vidler's new offices at the canonry of St George's Chapel, Windsor became CFC headquarters. He was 'at the forefront of trends in Anglican theology for three decades', later contributing to the controversial collection *Soundings: Essays in Christian Understanding* (1962).[30]

John Baillie (1886–1960) was a Church of Scotland minister and theology professor at Edinburgh University and, with his brother Donald, among the most significant twentieth-century Scottish theologians.[31] Baillie met Oldham as a student assistant at the 1910 Edinburgh conference. He studied philosophy and theology in Edinburgh, Jena and Marburg; after the war, he attended the Auburn Theological Seminary in New York, being ordained in 1920. After a brief spell in Toronto, he went to Union Theological Seminary (UTS) in New York in 1930, returning to Edinburgh in 1934 to take up the divinity professorship he held until 1956. He stayed part of a group of prominent UTS scholars: Reinhold Niebuhr, Henry Sloane Coffin and Pitney Van Dusen.[32] The Church of Scotland appointed him to head its 'Commission on God's Will in the Present Crisis' in 1940.[33] The Oldham group's influence is apparent in its report, *God's Will for Church and Nation* (1946), and in Baillie's Riddell Lectures, *What Is Christian Civilization?* (1945). In 1952, he became a president of the WCC.

When he joined the Moot, Herbert Arthur Hodges (1905–76) was the chair in philosophy at the University of Reading (where he had lectured since 1928), a post he held until retirement in 1969.[34] Hodges was from Sheffield, the son of a commercial traveller and an elementary school teacher; he won a scholarship to the King Edward VII School and later graduated from Balliol, Oxford, obtaining firsts in Classical Moderations and *Literae Humaniores*, and his doctorate in 1932. His research focused on the philosopher Wilhelm Dilthey, and he was fascinated by Kierkegaard. Although raised a Methodist, Hodges was received into the Church of England in 1928.[35] He advocated socialism and a dialogue between Christianity and Marxism. He missed only one Moot meeting for which records exist and shared the distinction with Mannheim of having written the most Moot papers. In the war, Hodges served in the Home Guard and lectured for the Services College and the Workers' Educational Association. He was later an Anglican delegate to the WCC's 1948 Amsterdam assembly and published works such as *The Pattern of Atonement* (1955), *Anglicanism and Orthodoxy* (1955) and *Death and Life Have Contended* (1964).

Like Hodges, Kathleen Bliss (née Moore, 1908–89) was one of the younger members of Oldham's circle.[36] A graduate of Girton College, Cambridge (history and theology), she had joined SCM and been a missionary in India (1932–39). After returning to Britain, she worked with Oldham, becoming the *CNL*'s assistant editor.[37] She joined the Moot in June 1943 and took over the editorship of the *CNL* in May 1945, where she remained until publication ceased in July 1949. She was granted the title of Doctor of Divinity by the University of Aberdeen in 1949.[38] Raised a Congregationalist, she became an Anglican and was a Church of England delegate to the WCC's 1948 assembly. She has been called one of the most 'dynamic and creative figures' in the post-war British ecumenical movement.[39]

Organisations and strategies

Group members thought institutional Christianity was ill-prepared for what Oldham called the 'new world' or 'new mode of human existence' brought by science, technology, industry, and 'mass' culture and politics.[40] Memoranda of the CCFCL emphasised the epoch's uniqueness and the inadequacy of existing Christianity to face it. Compared to the 'great *novum*' of modern propaganda, traditional methods of shaping values in family, church and school seemed 'of a home-spun order'.[41] Christians needed 'fresh ways' to respond to 'new needs'.[42] Statements by the CCFCL in 1938 stressed the depth of the modern crisis, pointing to war, unemployment, totalitarianism, feelings of 'insecurity and futility', the arbitrary use of power, diminishing respect for 'life and personality', and declining mercy and compassion.[43] Oldham decried the 'repudiation' of Christian truths in what had once been 'Christendom'.[44] Without 'a heroic effort' to align social life with Christianity, the faith could only offer 'consolations of a life to come' in a society 'alien to the Christian spirit'.[45] The modern crises were seen as 'spiritual' and 'cultural', involving profound shifts in norms, beliefs and behaviours. The Christian task seemed clear: developing a new social vision and promoting it in the public sphere. Group members were painfully aware of their meagre resources and that a far larger effort was needed; still, they sought to set an example that others – in larger numbers – could follow.

The Council on the Christian Faith and the Common Life (CCFCL): enabling an 'Order'

Already before Oxford 1937, Oldham had wanted to bring together 'the best minds' to increase Christian influence upon public policy; encouraged by Moberly, Iredale and Eliot and supported by Temple, he convinced Cosmo Lang, the Archbishop of Canterbury, of his plan.[46] Between January and March 1938, meetings were held at Lambeth Palace, chaired by Lang, with representatives from the largest Protestant churches.[47] Their proposal for a new 'Council on the Christian Faith and the Common Life' was approved by the Anglican, Presbyterian, Methodist, Congregationalist and Baptist churches in spring and summer, and it began meeting in November.[48] The Council was to coordinate the existing 'spontaneous' actions of small groups, sometimes called 'cells'.[49] They were seen as crucial; however, Oldham described Christians then as 'an army in which every platoon defined its own strategy'.[50] He aimed to unite this potential, believing that an 'Order' of lay Christians – a few hundred people in key institutions – could transform society.[51] Enabling such an order required, in turn, 'some small body at the centre giving a coherent lead': *this* was to be the role of the CCFCL.[52] Oldham and his collaborators believed the churches' intellectual inertia had added to the crisis. Still, the churches' cultural authority made their cooperation essential. The CCFCL was thus a hybrid body: it was officially supported (and funded) by the churches but stressed lay leadership; its official proposal even insisted it 'must not be predominantly ecclesiastical in character'.[53]

The aim of being both *a part of* and *apart from* the churches shaped its structure. It had twenty-four members: fourteen of them were chosen by the churches and they then selected ten laypeople with experience in public life.[54] The members oversaw a small staff working to join up the 'spontaneous, creative forces' scattered in church and community, enabling 'hundreds, or thousands, of other persons to do what they could not otherwise do and to be what they could not otherwise become'.[55] An experimental effort to introduce a 'leaven' into the churches, this 'open conspiracy' aspired to a new dynamism.[56] It sought connections with government, social services, youth organisations, universities, schools, industry, labour and the media, aiming to assemble the 'best', 'ablest' and most 'creative' thinkers.[57] Christian newspapers labelled it a 'Religious Brain Trust' or 'Christian intelligence service'; Oldham compared it to Chatham House, an early think tank.[58] It was, however, also criticised in the Christian press, with the *Church of England Newspaper* calling it 'yet another project' to 'increase the machinery without switching on the Power'.[59]

The Council, indeed, was a troubled venture from the start, preoccupied with personnel issues, lobbying for funds and defining its mission.[60] Then the war intervened. On 31 August 1939, Oldham told Lang that a possible conflict would only increase the need for 'a reborn Christendom'; two days later he informed Temple that the Moot had agreed war would make such work more vital.[61] At an 'emergency meeting' on 27 September Oldham urged the need to 'pool our spiritual resources', interpret the war's 'religious meaning' and 'establish a means of communication with as wide a constituency as possible'.[62] Thus was born the *Christian News-Letter*, which is discussed in more detail below. The Council also produced reports on religious conditions in the armed services and factories, and on youth education.[63] However, the CCFCL was hobbled by limited resources: 'six to eight' staff members had been envisioned, but in the end there were only two (at first Fenn and Iredale, then Fenn was replaced by A. C. Craig). Its trouble was only magnified by its co-existence with another body, the Commission of the Churches for International Friendship and Social Responsibility (CCIFSR), which had been formed under the CCFCL's own auspices in late 1938. They were to work together: the CCFCL's aims required 'a programme of education of the Church constituencies' to be undertaken by the CCIFSR.[64] Despite efforts to maintain this division, the CCIFSR – chaired by Temple – did as much 'intelligence work' as the CCFCL, published a bulletin (*The Church in the World*) and organised public events ('Religion and Life Weeks') throughout Britain. It was larger, better resourced and had a clearer role. Meanwhile, the short-staffed CCFCL became almost entirely focused on producing the *CNL*.

The CCFCL was also undermined by ecumenical politics. A rivalry between Oldham and a leading CCIFSR figure, William Paton, proved decisive. Oldham was at loggerheads with Paton – secretary of the IMC and joint-secretary (with Visser 't Hooft in Geneva) of the WCC-information. Paton wanted a single British ecumenical body under ecclesiastical control; Oldham did not.[65] Oldham sought a 'small prophetic band of scholars' studying and working behind the scenes; Paton aimed for a council officially representing the churches and coordinating large-scale public activities.[66] (A. C. Craig saw the two models as 'a small family business' and 'a public corporation accountable to its shareholders'.[67]) Oldham obstructed Paton, straining relations with Geneva. Paton manoeuvred Iredale and Oldham into resigning in summer 1941, and he took Oldham's place.[68] However, this worked to Oldham's benefit. A sub-committee recommended, first, combining the CCFCL and the CCIFSR into a new body and, second, forming a 'semi-independent Committee' for 'pioneer work'.[69] In 1942, the CCFCL and CCIFSR were duly merged into the British Council of Churches (BCC), and – with support from outgoing Archbishop Lang (who was being succeeded at Canterbury by Temple) – a new body, the 'Christian Frontier Council' (CFC), was born, with Moberly as its chair, and Oldham and his young assistant F. C. Maxwell named its officers.[70]

The Christian Frontier Council (CFC): 'tunnelling from the opposite end'

The CFC proved a more coherent and successful undertaking. Oldham told Temple that he had been inspired by a conversation in the late 1920s with A. D. Lindsay – master of Balliol College and later vice-chancellor of the University of Oxford – about how an unofficial body of Christians might influence State policy. The idea had been partly realised in the CCFCL, but Oldham concluded it had been wrong to mix social thought and an 'ecclesiastical organisation': 'The new set-up', he found, 'offers much better prospects'.[71] The CCFCL (and then the BCC) would coordinate *church* efforts and provide a British link to the WCC in Geneva, leaving the CFC free, as Oldham put it, for the 'pioneer work' of intellectually 'tunnelling from the opposite end': i.e. not deriving social policy from religion but rather examining modern society and working *back* to the relevance of faith.[72] (Paton and Eliot critiqued this approach, but Oldham also tried to infuse it into the WCC.[73]) The CFC was under the 'aegis' of the CCFCL (and later BCC), but despite some oversight it was 'free to experiment' with ways of increasing Christian influence: it would be, Oldham wrote, 'a body of guerrilla troops' and a 'powerful new reinforcement' for the churches.[74]

The 'frontier' in the CFC's name expressed a key idea of Oldham's: it meant, first, the divide between those in the churches and the 'interested and sympathetic' people outside them; second, the difference between 'the Kingdom of God and the new life in Christ' and 'the community as a whole'.[75] It could be described as 'the borderland between the normal work of the Churches and the general life of society'.[76] These perceived frontiers influenced the group's thinking about faith and secularity and defined the CFC's role: it would seek contact with non-Christians, analyse society and link groups working for Christian ends. It sought to attract Christians 'engaged in practical affairs' and holding 'responsible positions' in politics, business and the labour movement.[77] These connections were vital given the changes brought by the war and the need to reshape the post-war world. Responsibility for the *CNL* passed to the CFC, which came to be seen as the group's 'spear-head' and means of communication with those seeking 'a new order of society'.[78] Its main aim, Oldham wrote in 1946, was 'to help people in fulfilling their public responsibilities' in more Christian ways.[79]

Amid the surfeit of Christian responses to the crisis, Oldham saw the CFC as having to 'venture out into the unknown' to develop a 'unifying idea' to guide the renewal of industry, education and politics.[80] He here stressed the reassertion of the transcendental Christian views of the 'realities of human existence' against a pervasive materialism.[81] Such work was crucial: if 'men's thinking is fundamentally wrong [and] based on a false understanding of what is real', he argued, then 'the most *practical* thing we can do is to change their thinking'.[82] The time seemed ripe: from the apparent 'chaos of ideas and babel of voices' he saw an emerging 'clarification of thought', a Christian–secular consensus that questioned radical individualism and stressed healthy relations with nature, community and God.[83] This clarification was exemplified by a 1943 *CNL* essay by Temple (which was based on a draft by Oldham) on 'What Christians Stand for in the Secular World'. It articulated a vision of renewal based upon five 'decisions': for 'God', for 'neighbour', for 'man as rooted in nature', for 'history' and for 'the gospel and the Church'.[84] Oldham told Temple the essay successfully encapsulated the CFC's programme.[85] Books such as C. S. Lewis's *The Abolition of Man* (1943) and Leslie Paul's *The Annihilation of Man* (1944) were also seen as evidence of an intellectual convergence.[86] A 1947 CFC pamphlet suggested that the two main Christian insights into social life were, first, 'that man is truly man only by virtue of his responsibility to an authority superior to himself' and, second, 'that the essential meaning of human life is found in the relations of persons with one another'.[87]

Such ideas are discussed in later chapters, but a few words should be said about the CFC's activities. It gathered some two dozen members, mainly prominent lay Christian establishment figures from the realms of politics (including both Conservative and Labour MPs), industry, press, the civil service (such as the Ministries of Labour and of Information), the voluntary sector, and literary and cultural criticism.[88] It organised discussions (held monthly by the early post-war period), often with invited experts, and had subgroups on industrial relations, new management theories, planning, youth problems, community, education, medicine and post-war demobilisation.[89] Its reports appeared in the *CNL*, such as a series on 'Responsibility in the Economic System', and fed into publications such as Moberly's *The Crisis in the University* (1949).[90] CFC member George Goyder – who was general manager of the war-time Newsprint Supply Company – wrote in the *CNL* about the British press.[91] Dr Desmond Pond, a young psychiatrist who was part of the CFC's 'Medical Group', contributed an essay on mental illness.[92] Needing to concentrate on other matters (such as the WCC), Oldham resigned from the CFC at the end of 1947, but he continued to serve it in an 'honorary capacity'.[93] The CFC seems to have continued to exist into the 1970s.

The Moot: 'companions in affliction'

The CCFCL and CFC provided contexts for exploring Christian social ideas, but between April 1938 and January 1947 the informal circle known as 'the Moot' – Old English for an assembly or discussion – was the Oldham group's intellectual heart. It was a 'free, autonomous and anonymous' body at first intended to advise the CCFCL.[94] It quickly, however, took on a life of its own, meeting over weekends at conference centres, hostels and schools near London to discuss pre-circulated papers, two to four times a year between 1938 and 1944, and annually between 1945 and 1947. Debate continued between meetings via correspondence, and a sense of corporate identity as 'members of the Moot' emerged. At meetings, participants shared prayers and – pooling their rations during the war – meals. Apart from some changes in membership, the Moot's structure did not alter until Oldham disbanded it after Mannheim's sudden death in January 1947.

The Moot analysed the modern crisis, outlined what a more Christian society would look like and considered ways of reaching it. Unlike the other bodies in the Oldham group, it remained a private gathering, and its name was not publicised. It could thus ignore the sensitivities of the churches, the ecumenical movement or public, lending its discussions a greater freedom than those in the CCFCL, CFC and *CNL*. Its members agreed that Christian principles, if effectively implemented, could change society. Murry summarised its aim as defining a 'Christian Doctrine of Man' for the modern age, a goal that brought together 'Christian sociology,

Christian psychology and Christian theology.[95] Later chapters explore the Moot's ideas, but some tensions that shaped them should be noted here.

Disagreements recurred about the Moot's relation to 'thought' and 'action': were its members exploring *ideas* or seeking *influence*? In 1937, Oldham urged ecumenical efforts towards 'common study and thought' but – citing Mannheim's *Ideology and Utopia* – warned against 'scholastic, academic and lifeless' ideas detached from life's 'concrete problems'.[96] He described the Moot ambivalently as an agent of thought – even 'pure thought' – but with 'a lively interest also in action'.[97] Mannheim often urged action (or at least 'talking with a view to action') but gradually came to see the Moot as 'a formulating group' that could act only in spheres such as religion and education.[98] Murry complained in 1942 that the Moot had given up on 'taking action', critiquing its 'lack of reality' and 'dilettantism': it was a 'philosophical club'.[99] Vidler, too, doubted the value of expending 'hot air' about 'new world orders'.[100] Eliot, however, was perfectly happy with the stress on thought: for him, the Moot's value lay not in the enforced unity of political action but rather in creative *dis*agreement.[101] It was in any case, he claimed, 'too gentlemanly' for active politics.[102] In 1943, he stated he was interested in thinkers 'who are not concerned with any immediate solution of anything' and argued the Moot could not take 'collective action' or develop a comprehensive 'programme'.[103] (Mannheim found himself 'in final agreement' with Eliot on this point.[104]) The Moot thus remained a discussion circle, but its members came to see innovative thinking itself as a form of political activity. They would seek, Hodges said, 'new possibilities of Christian action', thereby encouraging others' efforts.[105] In 1944, he saw the Moot's aim as 'awakening' people in groups such as the 'intelligentsia, students, teachers, scholars, professional men, public servants and the like'; it might influence movements with similar aims.[106]

But even within the realm of thought, tensions remained. Was the group to articulate specific policies or proclaim broad 'principles'? Mannheim frequently critiqued papers (often Oldham's) as vague and, joined by Löwe, called for 'concrete' proposals.[107] Citing Christ's example, Mannheim thought it necessary 'to begin living in another way' before discovering a philosophy: 'practical tasks', he argued, preceded principles, a position on which Hodges and Shaw agreed.[108] Oldham sought neither an abstract philosophy nor a 'programme': he agreed that change must come in *practice* but insisted there had to be 'some form of words' describing the new life.[109] Wanting to avoid detailed 'blueprints' – a bugbear for the group (and many other Christians) – Oldham nevertheless saw 'some formulation of criteria in the light of which practical steps are to be judged' as a priority.[110]

Arguments over the balance between thought and action or about the need for concrete ideas led to frustrations. At the eighth and ninth meetings (April and July 1940), Mannheim, Hodges, Moberly, Shaw, Murry, Löwe and Vidler complained about a lack of progress.[111] The Moot, Hodges said, had become 'a group of intellectuals in the bad sense'.[112] The minutes recorded difficulty in agreeing on a programme that was neither 'too general to be useful' nor 'too detailed to be readable'.[113] Oldham admitted glumly that he could not tell a government minister that any two Moot members agreed on what 'Christian values' even were.[114] In 1943 he could still not identify faith's specific contribution 'to social and political wisdom', and he doubted the group agreed on 'fundamentals', even after having 'analysed and unrolled problem after problem'.[115] But members remained committed to the group, sometimes saw progress and agreed on key points. A late 1943 draft essay that served as the basis of Archbishop Temple's *CNL* essay on Christians and secularity marked a milestone, being praised by Moot members (including Eliot, Murry and Mannheim) and external readers.[116] Eliot encapsulated the Moot's mix of amity and discord by calling its members 'companions in affliction'; but even here Hodges thought that, given the circumstances, they were having 'only a small fraction of the difficulty the world is finding'.[117]

The Christian News-Letter (CNL): *'Britain's ecumenical voice'*

The *CNL* appeared within weeks of the war's outbreak and was the Oldham group's most successful venture. The original idea may have been Iredale's (who also wisely bought thirty tonnes of paper before it was rationed), but Oldham set it up, edited it and wrote much of its content.[118] In April 1939, the Moot had foreseen a need for 'articles and pamphlets' should war come, and it made plans in late September.[119] In terms of its format and approach it was clearly modelled on the popular *King-Hall News-Letter* issued by naval officer, politician and author Stephen King-Hall from 1936. While King-Hall's publication was not specifically Christian (and he does not appear to have had contact with the *CNL*), it offered commentary supportive of 'the democratic faith'.[120] A promotional issue of the *CNL* was sent to 32,000 potential subscribers, about half of them laypeople, in mid October 1939. Publication began in November and ended, after 341 issues, on 6 July 1949.[121] It consisted of a 'letter' and 'supplement', its total length varying between six and sixteen pages throughout its existence. The letter was signed by the editor – a 'personal touch' on which the Moot had insisted – and contained news, announcements, reader comments and discussions of other publications.[122] The 'supplement' was an essay usually by a named (but sometimes anonymous, pseudonymous or group) author. Vidler was co-editor, and guest editors included T. S. Eliot, Bishop George Bell, Mary Stocks, George MacLeod, Barbara Ward and Daniel

Jenkins. In mid 1945 Oldham passed the editorship to Bliss. At first it appeared weekly, then rising postal rates led to fortnightly supplements from May 1940; paper restrictions then brought the entire *CNL* to a fortnightly schedule from April 1943.[123] Among its 'collaborators' were well-known Christian clergy, thinkers and activists, including William Temple, C. H. Dodd, Stafford Cripps, Reinhold Niebuhr, Charles Raven, Dorothy L. Sayers, Arnold Toynbee, R. H. Tawney, Nathaniel Micklem, Kurt Hahn, Alfred Zimmern, Viscount Hambleden (chair of W. H. Smith), A. D. Lindsay, and the bishops of Sheffield and Winchester. Its editorial board included Oldham, Eliot, Vidler, Iredale, Bliss, Lord Hambleden, Philip Mairet, Mary Stocks, F. C. Maxwell, Daniel Jenkins and W. G. Symons. Vidler edited a related series of 1s. books: the first five '*Christian News-Letter* Books' appeared in January 1940, selling 30,000 copies by July.[124] They were given a front-page review in the *Church of England Newspaper*. The *Catholic Herald* labelled it as a series of 'Anglican "Penguins"' (referring to that publisher's short, inexpensive and highly popular 'Specials' on contemporary issues) and particularly praised Oldham's *The Resurrection of Christendom* (1940).[125] By 1942, fourteen volumes had appeared. In all, eighteen books were published.[126]

The *CNL* set up its office in Balcombe Street, near Regent's Park, announcing that duplicate member lists were kept in case 'our office is destroyed by a bomb'.[127] Indeed, bomb damage in September 1940 forced a move to the SCM headquarters in Golders Green. When they too were damaged, the *CNL* went to Manchester College, Oxford. By July 1942 it was back in London (in Westminster), finally returning to Balcombe Street in December 1944.[128] There were eighteen staff, many of whom were volunteers. Packing and mailing was done by twelve German 'Christian non-Aryan refugees'.[129] It was funded by subscriptions (10s. annually, rising to 12s. 6d. in 1940 and £1 in 1948), donations, and the budgets of the CCFCL and CFC. Money was tight: Oldham described it as 'not in any way a paying proposition', with its staff stretched thin.[130] When Bliss resigned in 1949 shortly before giving birth to her third child, it folded.

The *CNL* became the centrepiece of the Oldham group's strategy to 'bridge the gulf' between Christianity and social life. It was seen as a way to help Christians achieve a 'common mind, outlook and purpose' and a vehicle for 'the ideas current in the Moot'.[131] It addressed many topics, such as military operations, peace aims, social reconstruction, family life, sexual morality, totalitarianism, educational reform, state planning and the atomic age. While focused on social questions, it also discussed theology and spirituality. Contributors included prominent Christian thinkers and commentators such as William Temple, George Bell, Reinhold Niebuhr, Dorothy L. Sayers, Barbara Ward, V. A. Demant, C. H. Dodd, John Marsh,

Figure 2 Kathleen Bliss, undated photo

Gerhard Leibholz, F. B. Welbourn, A. D. Lindsay, Kenneth Grubb, John Foster Dulles and Karl Jaspers.

Subscriber numbers grew rapidly: there were 9,081 'members' in February 1940, over 10,000 in July and by February 1941 a peak of about 11,500.[132] Between 1943 and 1946 they drifted down from about 10,000 to slightly over 9,000.[133] Post-war circulation dropped to 5,000, and then rose again by late 1948 to 7,221.[134] Dozens of discussion groups quickly formed, some based in church congregations, others originating in direct outreach efforts.[135] Parish priests and ministers referenced the *CNL* in their sermons.[136] Overseas subscriptions were between 9 and 15 per cent of the total in the early 1940s, roughly half of which were in North America.[137] There were also subscribers in Europe (Switzerland, unoccupied France, Iceland, Gibraltar and Malta), Africa (over 250 in 20 territories), Asia (mostly India, but also Free China, Syria, Palestine, Iran and Iraq), Oceania (130 members in New Zealand and Australia), the West Indies (Jamaica, Grenada, Barbados and Trinidad) and South America (British Guiana, Brazil, Peru, Paraguay, Uruguay, Argentina and Chile).[138] Copies were sent to the WCC in Geneva, some being smuggled to the German resistance.[139] Post-war currency restrictions hindered continental distribution, but outstanding subscriptions interrupted by occupation were filled, and British readers were asked to sponsor gift memberships.[140]

Oldham aimed the *CNL* 'at all who helped to mould public opinion': it should, he thought, have a depth that would appeal to senior academics but also be readable by teachers and adult-education students.[141] He reported to the CCFCL that it was read by 'privates in the army, Anglican and Roman Catholic Archbishops, school teachers in elementary and secondary schools, lawyers, doctors, miners, business men, civil servants, nurses, [and] housewives'; indeed: 'every variety of person seems to be represented'.[142] In fact, its readership was largely limited to the middle class. A survey showed that despite some support in the Labour Party for Christian efforts towards social renewal, the *CNL* was seen as too complicated, irrelevant to working people's concerns and not clearly on their side.[143] Even those who contributed to the *CNL* complained at times about its 'academic character'.[144] The *Liverpool Daily Post* admitted it was 'high-brow', hoping that, while its essays 'quite rightly' could continue demanding some 'intellectual effort', the letters might nonetheless 'concede something to the requirements of a popular man-in-the-street or man-in-the-pew circulation'.[145] Oldham admitted privately that 'the circumstances of my life have never brought me into contact with the working classes in this country'; however, he insisted: 'I see with entire clarity their significance'.[146]

Nonetheless, the *CNL* was seen to have 'a wide influence on thoughtful people'.[147] Visser 't Hooft called it 'Britain's ecumenical voice'.[148] Despite his concern that its intellectual tone made it unappealing to working-class readers, W. G. Symons assured Oldham that the *CNL* 'has an unparalleled sphere of influence in these days of crisis'.[149] Issues were exchanged with *Picture Post, New English Weekly*, the *Listener, Time and Tide* and others.[150] Even local newspapers cited *CNL* essays or books.[151] Up to 200 reader letters arrived daily.[152] One supplement titled 'Pater Noster' – a version of the Lord's Prayer tailored to the war – had over 35,000 requests.[153] Temple's essay 'What Christians Stand for in the Secular World' was widely read.[154] Bliss thought the *CNL* was 'the focus of a vast amount of thinking', though some readers, she noted, 'wished we talked about God more'.[155] A reader letter listed complaints that the *CNL* repeated itself, had a sometimes 'condescending' attitude towards the free churches, and too often avoided 'controversial' issues.[156] Eliot thought the *CNL* 'often tends to be too polite, and to accept the official pronouncements of ecclesiastics somewhat uncritically'. However, he admitted that the *CNL*'s delicacy on controversial topics was probably essential to maintaining its subscription numbers.[157] Nonetheless, reader reactions, at times, sharply diverged. In 1948, some readers found a previous issue 'a new high water mark', others 'quite nauseous'.[158] It was often accused, said Bliss, 'of giving balanced statements with which nobody can disagree'.[159] Still, many readers valued 'a sense of belonging to something' and felt 'an acute sense of loss' when publication ceased.[160]

Conclusion

Broadly speaking, the Oldham group developed in five stages between 1937 and 1949. A first period stretches from Oxford 1937 to the CCFCL's formation in autumn 1938. During this time the Moot also began meeting. A second stage extended from the CCFCL's first meeting in November 1938 to the outbreak of war in September 1939. Here, discussions continued about the CCFCL's aims, and early Moot meetings established key elements of the group's agenda for the following decade. The war opened a third phase marked by the publication of the *CNL*, beginning in November 1939, and lasting until the CCFCL was dissolved in early 1942. A fourth phase stretches between the foundation of the CFC in 1942 (which took over the *CNL*) and the war's end in September 1945. In it, the improving fortunes of the Allies focused attention on post-war reconstruction. The war's end brought a fifth phase defined by Bliss's shift to editor of the *CNL* and by new conditions and challenges: peace, European reconstruction, a growing welfare state, the atomic age and the emerging Cold War. This phase saw the Moot disbanded in January 1947 after Mannheim's death, Oldham's retirement from the CFC late in the same year and the *CNL*'s closure in 1949.

The group's contexts extended both before and after the period of its actual existence. Its members had been involved in various ways in the vibrant worlds of Christian social thought and activism that flowered across the inter-war decades. And long after it ceased to exist in the constellation I have sketched out, its influences continued. Commenting on the *CNL*'s demise, Bliss observed, 'as for persons, so for institutions, obedience to the universal rule of death is the only condition of new life'.[161] Indeed, it seemed that a new set of ideas and strategies was needed at the close of the 1940s. A follow-on publication – a quarterly titled *Frontier* that was edited by Vidler and Mairet – began in 1950. In spirit, the *CNL* lived on: early issues of *Frontier* labelled it a 'continuation of the work of *The Christian*

News-Letter. Even in the early 1960s, by which time *Frontier* was a monthly, its title page still harked back to the *CNL*. Throughout the Oldham group's existence, there were continuous overlapping memberships and activities within its component parts. Some of the leading members of the Moot, for example, were also active in the CFC and helped produce and edit the *CNL* (particularly Oldham, Eliot, Vidler, Iredale and Bliss, and also the Moot visitors Philip Mairet and W. G. Symons). There was also overlap between *CNL* 'collaborators' and participants in the CFC, such as – apart from Moot members – Lord Hambleden (chair of W. H. Smith), A. D. Lindsay (master of Balliol), Dorothy L. Sayers (popular author) and Henry Brooke (Conservative MP).

In its composition, the Oldham group was exclusively white, mostly middle-class, largely Oxbridge-educated and mainly male. While worth mentioning in a descriptive sense, these categories ultimately tell us little about what group members thought. Other intellectual circles with similar (or even identical) ethnic, class and gender profiles were coming to very different conclusions about the world. More important to its ideas was the fact that it was overwhelmingly Protestant, dominated by Anglicans and Presbyterians. Although clergy participated (especially in the CCFCL), the group saw itself as a lay circle, convinced that only the laity could drive real social change. With the exception of Löwe, Mannheim and Polanyi, the group's personnel was very British (predominantly English but with a prominent Scottish element). It spanned the political right (Eliot and Dawson) and left (Murry, Hodges, Vidler, Miller, Löwe). It also crossed generations: many of its leading figures (e.g. Baillie, Oldham, Moberly, Clarke, Murry and Eliot) were in their fifties or sixties by the end of the 1930s, but others (e.g. Hodges, Bliss, Fenn, Jenkins, Oakeshott, Miller and Vidler) were in their thirties (or, in Jenkins's case, twenties), with some of the others in between (Löwe and Mannheim were both in their mid forties when they joined the Moot). While participants were relatively well heeled, well educated and well connected, they were also at odds with their respective institutional and intellectual contexts, whether theology, the churches, ecumenism or the universities. Indeed, while the group bene-fited from its close connection to the churches, this relationship was often seen as a potential liability. The first page of the *CNL*'s promotional issue expressed awareness that 'for some at least whose interest we want to enlist any mention of the Churches is an unpromising beginning'.[162] This combin-ation of authority and alienation suggests the Oldham group represented a *critical* establishment: it possessed significant social capital and was ensconced in key institutions, but it questioned the leading orthodoxies of its main intellectual contexts.

There were various routes for disseminating the group's ideas. Alongside the *CNL* and a few jointly produced documents, group members used their own publications to promote ideas influenced by their participation in it. Their articles and books were also recommended reading for the outreach-oriented 'Religion and Life Weeks' organised by the CCIFSR. Eric Fenn became associate editor of SCM Press, which published books by some group members, and members participated as well in SCM conferences as speakers. Via Fenn, the group also gained access to the BBC, enabling the occasional radio broadcast. Vidler's editorship of *Theology* and Murry's of the *Adelphi* provided other vectors for group-related ideas. Oldham and Bliss, as well as W. G. Symons and Kenneth Matthews, were on the BCC's Committee on Evangelism (which considered how the Christian message could be most effectively disseminated post-war), bringing group impulses directly into British ecumenism more broadly.[163]

All of the group's main activities were seen as small or preliminary steps within the context of a larger strategy. Its members saw 'culture' as a key battleground in renewing western society, and they aimed to return Christian norms, attitudes and ideas to dominance. Despite agreement that 'revolutionary' social change was necessary, the group sought neither to create a Christian 'party' nor to foment popular revolt; however, they also found existing efforts by the churches to influence democratic politics to be insufficient. As a result, they envisioned a two-pronged effort. First, they aimed towards what was sometimes referred to as a 'revolution from above' guided by an 'Order' of committed Christians working behind the scenes. (The efforts to define an 'Order' proved, however, particularly frustrating.) The group also sought broader means of 'permeating' society with new values through the action of Christian ideas as a kind of cultural 'leaven'.[164] The image of the Kingdom of Heaven as 'leaven' – starting in imperceptible ways but then bursting forth with revolutionary impact – is derived from New Testament parables and epistles.[165] An article on the CCFCL, for example, envisioned 'hundreds and thousands' of 'cells', describing them as 'a true lay ministry and a means by which the national life might gradually be permeated by Christian influence'.[166] The *CNL* was part of this strategy of 'permeation': assisting the dissemination of new thinking, bringing together separate streams of Christian action and influencing public opinion. (Essay drafts were also distributed to as many as a couple of dozen readers.[167]) The aim was to develop an idea of what a Christian society would be and the means of achieving it.

The grandiose ambition of a small circle of Christian thinkers to reorient western society might seem, in retrospect, absurd and even, it has been suggested, 'delusory'.[168] Indeed, Oldham himself and others were plagued by self-doubt. 'I do not think that anyone is more sensible than I am of the difficulties of what is proposed', Oldham admitted in March 1938: 'I am sometimes tempted to think that it is impossible.'[169] In a letter to W. G. Symons in May 1941, he wrote: 'The sense that we were failing to do more than a fraction of the things that needed to be done has gnawed at me the whole time.'[170] But that a small group might have revolutionary impact seemed confirmed by recent history. As Moberly asked in May 1938: 'Who could have seemed less practical in 1850 than Marx, sitting down in the Reading Room of the British Museum to work year after year at very abstract studies? Or, sixteen years ago, than Hitler, with a few unpromising associates, redrawing the map of Europe and making a programme for his coming into power?'[171] H. H. Farmer thought Christians might 'learn something by looking at the Nazi party and the methods whereby it moved from the position of a minority to dominance'.[172] Fenn compared the Moot to the efforts of the pre-1917 Bolsheviks ('formulating a theory of revolutionary action, elaborating a view of society and building a party'): action, however, had to await 'our kind of revolutionary situation'.[173] They could begin with 'small things': 'a gradual building of a group or two, seeking very patiently for those who have the possibilities of revolution in them'.[174] Vidler saw the group seeking a peaceful 'revolution'.[175]

As Chapter 6 discusses, this fascination with totalitarian models should not be overstated. Other comparisons were also drawn. Moberly suggested that 'convinced Christians are not so small a minority as the Fabians had been when they began'.[176] Oldham pointed to the nineteenth-century Utilitarians as 'the outstanding example of what can be accomplished by a comparatively small band of men who have *read the signs of the times, who are united in their principles and in their aims* and have thought out and can preach a systematic but fundamentally simple doctrine'.[177] Hodges compared the Moot to the Puritans.[178] Mannheim thought that enabling Britain to play a role in a world dominated by the Soviet Union and United States depended upon 'the vitality of small groups such as the Moot'.[179] Creating a 'new order' would be 'beyond us', Shaw admitted in 1941, but he thought the group might influence 'at least the atmosphere and the attitude of mind and character of those who must form it'.[180] The CCFCL, as Oldham put it, would not be the 'engine' of a Christian social revolution but rather 'the oil which assists the smooth working of the engine'.[181] While it may be that Oldham and at least some other members of the group were influenced by the vision of a revolutionary 'vanguard' party (like that advocated by Lenin), the traditional Christian emphasis on small, 'leavening' groups was undoubtedly far more decisive in his decision to set up his projects – especially the Moot and the CFC – in the way that he did.

As discussed in Chapter 3, the group was also convinced Christians could rely upon supernatural power to achieve their specific aims, to which the following chapters now turn, considering how the group applied Christian principles to social reality, seeking, in each case, middle ways through the age's political extremes. Given the centrality of faith to the group's worldview and efforts, our journey through its thinking begins there.

Notes

1 On Oldham, Clements, *Faith on the Frontier*; Keith W. Clements, 'Oldham and Baillie: A Creative Relationship', in Morton, *God's Will in a Time of Crisis*, pp. 45–59; and Kathleen Bliss, rev. Andrew Porter, 'Oldham, Joseph Houldsworth (1874–1969)', in *Oxford Dictionary of National Biography* (Oxford: Oxford University Press, 2004); online edn, May 2007, www.oxforddnb.com/view/article/35301 (accessed 18 October 2011).

2 Alan Wilkinson, *The Church of England and the First World War* (Cambridge: Lutterworth Press, 2014 [1996]), p. 285. Kenneth C. Barnes, *Nazism, Liberalism, and Christianity: Protestant Social Thought in Germany and Great Britain, 1925–1937* (Lexington: University Press of Kentucky, 1991), pp. 58–9. Thompson, *For God and Globe*, pp. 117–18.

3 Clements, *Faith on the Frontier*, pp. 2, 161; Kathleen Bliss, 'The Legacy of J. H. Oldham', *International Bulletin of Missionary Research*, 8:1 (1984), 18–23 (p. 19).

4 See Keith Clements, '"Friend of Africa": J. H. Oldham (1874–1969), Missions and British Colonial Policy in the 1920s', in Frieder Ludwig and Afe Adogame (eds.), *European Traditions in the Study of Religion in Africa* (Wiesbaden: Otto Harrasowitz, 2004), pp. 175–86; George Bennett, 'Paramountcy to Partnership: J. H. Oldham and Africa', *Africa: Journal of the International African Institute*, 30:4 (1960), 356–61; Clements, *Faith on the Frontier*, p. 207; Wollenberg, *Christian Social Thought*, p. 46.

5 J. H. Oldham, *Christianity and the Race Problem* (London: SCM, 1924), pp. 17, 21, 23.

6 Barnes, *Nazism, Liberalism, and Christianity*, pp. 102–3; John C. Bennett, 'Breakthrough in Ecumenical Social Ethics: The Legacy of the Oxford Conference on Church, Community and State (1937)', *Ecumenical Review*, 40:2 (1988), 132–46 (pp. 132–3).

7 Clements, *Faith on the Frontier*, p. 354. Asia, Africa and Latin America had thirty representatives, often western missionaries. There were nineteen female delegates; Bennett, 'Breakthrough', p. 133. See also *The Churches Survey Their Task* (London: George Allen & Unwin, 1937), pp. 10–12; Graeme Smith, *Oxford 1937: The Universal Christian Council for Life and Work Conference* (Frankfurt: Peter Lang, 2004); and Thompson, *For God and Globe*, pp. 120–44.

8 J. H. Oldham, *Church, Community and State: A World Issue* (London: SCM, 1935); W. A. Visser 't Hooft and J. H. Oldham, *The Church and Its Function in Society* (London: Allen & Unwin, 1937).

9 *Guardian*, 11 July 1941, p. 330.
10 Barnes, *Nazism, Liberalism, and Christianity*, pp. 98–101.
11 Steele and Taylor, 'Oldham's Moot', p. 188. See *Moot Papers*, pp. 24–34.
12 There was one Orthodox Moot visitor: Evgeny (Eugene) Lampert, a Russian-born theologian.
13 Visitors: Melville Chaning-Pearce, O. S. Franks, A. C. Goyder, W. D. L. Greer, Eugene Lampert, Philip Mairet, Lesslie Newbigin, Reinhold Niebuhr, Frank Pakenham, William Paton, Gilbert Russell, W. G. Symons, R. H. Tawney and Geoffrey Vickers. OA 12/1/2: C. S. Lewis commented on Mannheim's 'Planning for Freedom' paper.
14 Hastings, *Oliver Tomkins*, p. 35. Scott, *Historian and His World*, p. 133.
15 LPL Lang 25, fo. 35, Lidgett to Lang, 25 November 1937, pp. 1–2.
16 Jackson, *Red Tape and the Gospel*, p. 271; Clements, *Faith on the Frontier*, p. 373.
17 David Kettler, Volker Meja and Nico Stehr, *Karl Mannheim* (London: Tavistock, 1984), p. 34.
18 Benjamin G. Lockerd, 'Beyond Politics: T. S. Eliot and Christopher Dawson on Religion and Culture', in Lockerd, *T. S. Eliot and Christian Tradition*, pp. 217–36. Eliot, somewhat equivocally, distanced himself from Maurras in *CNL* 44L, 28 August 1940, p. 2.
19 T. S. Eliot, *The Letters of T. S. Eliot*, Vol. VII: *1934–1935*, ed. Valerie Eliot and John Haffenden (London: Faber and Faber, 2017), pp. 226–7.
20 *The Times*, 17 July 1937, p. 18; Kojecky, *T. S. Eliot's Social Criticism*, p. 156.
21 In *Notes towards the Definition of Culture* (London: Faber and Faber, 1962 [1948]), p. 9, Eliot thanked V. A. Demant, Christopher Dawson and Karl Mannheim. See also Collini, *Absent Minds*, pp. 314–22.
22 Kate Fullbrook, 'Murry, John Middleton (1889–1957)', in *Oxford Dictionary of National Biography* (Oxford: Oxford University Press, 2004); online edn, September 2012, www.oxforddnb.com/view/article/35171 (accessed 24 November 2014).
23 Sydney Janet Kaplan, *Circulating Genius: John Middleton Murry, Katherine Mansfield and D. H. Lawrence* (Edinburgh: Edinburgh University Press, 2010), pp. 1–12.
24 Wollenberg, *Christian Social Thought*, p. 103.
25 The Adelphi Centre (1935–37) was in Langham, Essex.
26 Dennis Hardy, *Utopian England: Community Experiments 1900–1945* (London: E. & F. N. Spon, 2000), pp. 44–5. John Middleton Murry, *Community Farm* (London: Country Book Club, 1953).
27 Lea, *John Middleton Murry*, pp. 312–15.
28 This summary of Vidler's life is based upon his autobiography: A. R. Vidler, *Scenes from a Clerical Life* (London: Collins, 1977); and on Matthew Grimley and Sam Brewitt-Taylor, 'Vidler, Alexander Roper [Alec] (1899–1991)', in *Oxford Dictionary of National Biography* (Oxford: Oxford University Press, 2004); online edn, September 2012, www.oxforddnb.com/view/article/50491 (accessed 23 June 2014).

29 Grimley and Brewitt-Taylor, 'Vidler'; Vidler, *Scenes*, p. 119.

30 Grimley and Brewitt-Taylor, 'Vidler'.

31 George Newlands, 'Baillie, John (1886–1960)', in *Oxford Dictionary of National Biography* (Oxford: Oxford University Press, 2004); online edn, September 2012, www.oxforddnb.com/view/article/40282 (accessed 23 June 2014).

32 Alec C. Cheyne, 'The Baillie Brothers', in David Fergusson (ed.), *Christ, Church and Society: Essays on John Baillie and Donald Baillie* (Edinburgh: T. & T. Clark, 1993), pp. 34–7.

33 David A. S. Fergusson, 'Theology in a Time of War: John Baillie's Political Writing', in Morton, *God's Will in a Time of Crisis*, pp. 32–44 (p. 32).

34 See Hodges's obituary in *The Times*, 8 July 1976, p. 18; and Alan P. F. Sell, *Four Philosophical Anglicans: W. G. de Burgh, W. R. Matthews, O. C. Quick, H. A. Hodges* (Farnham: Ashgate, 2010): pp. 203–6.

35 Dewi Morgan (ed.), *They Became Anglicans: Personal Statements of Sixteen Converts to the Anglican Communion* (London: A. R. Mowbray, 1960), p. 64.

36 David L. Edwards, 'Bliss, Kathleen Mary Amelia (1908–1989)', rev., in *Oxford Dictionary of National Biography* (Oxford: Oxford University Press, 2004); online edn, May 2007, www.oxforddnb.com/view/article/39995 (accessed 23 June 2014).

37 Clements, *Faith on the Frontier*, p. 402. She attended Moot-related meetings from February 1942: OA 13/4/212 (21–2 February 1942), 13/4/219 (16–17 May 1942), 13/4/228 (16 July 1945).

38 *CNL* 336L, 27 April 1949, p. 135.

39 Clements, *Faith on the Frontier*, p. 402.

40 LPL Lang 25, fo. 2, Oldham to Lang, 15 October 1937. *CNL* 312S, 26 May 1948, J. H. Oldham, 'Mr. Murry on the Free Society – II', p. 14.

41 LPL Lang 25, fos. 104–12, 'A Proposed Council of the Churches in Great Britain on the Relation of the Christian Faith to the National Life', n.d. [January 1938], pp. 1–2.

42 LPL Lang 25, fos. 130–5, 'A Council of the Churches in Great Britain on the Christian Faith and the Common Life', 23 February 1938, pp. 1–2.

43 LPL Lang 25, fos. 242–5, 'The Christian Faith and the Common Life: A Proposal Submitted to the Churches in Great Britain. Summary Statement', p. 4 (hereafter 'CCFCL final summary') and fos. 246–57, 'The Christian Faith and the Common Life: A Proposal Submitted to the Churches in Great Britain', p. 5 (hereafter 'CCFCL final proposal'); *Scotsman*, 2 May 1938 (in Lang 25, fos. 258–9).

44 LPL Lang 25, fos. 246–57, CCFCL final proposal, p. 5.

45 LPL Lang 26, fos. 10–13, 'Memorandum B: The Programme of the Council', n.d. [November 1938], p. 1.

46 Clements, *Faith on the Frontier*, p. 354; LPL Lang 25, fo. 1, Temple to Lang, 30 September 1937.

47 The CCFCL proposal was issued on 17 March 1938 by the Church of England, Church of Scotland, English Presbyterian Church, Methodist Church, Congregationalist Union and Baptist Union: LPL Lang 25, fos. 230–1.

48 LPL Lang 26, fos. 5–9.

49 Visser 't Hooft and Oldham, *Church and Its Function in Society*, p. 198.

50 *Moot Papers*, M19, p. 680.

51 LPL Lang 25, fos. 130–5, 'A Council of the Churches in Great Britain on the Christian Faith and the Common Life', 23 February 1938, p. 5. *Moot Papers*, M3, p. 154.

52 *Moot Papers*, M19, 680; LPL Lang 25, fos. 3–4, 'Suggested Action by Churches in Great Britain', sent to Lang on 15 October 1937; LPL Lang 25, fo. 5, meeting between Lang and Oldham on 19 October 1937; LPL Lang 25, fos. 19–28, 'The Situation Disclosed by the Oxford Conference and Its Demands on the Churches', sent to Lang on 4 November 1937; LPL Lang 25, fos. 29–32, 'An Order of Christian Explorers', sent to Lang on 4 November 1937.

53 LPL Lang 25, fos. 246–57, CCFCL final proposal, p. 18.

54 There were five Church of England members; two from the Church of Scotland; and one each from the Methodist Church, Congregational Union, Baptist Union, Presbyterian Church of England, Free Churches of Wales, Church of Ireland and Presbyterian Church of Ireland. LPL Lang 25, fos. 242–5, CCFCL final summary, p. 7; Lang 26, fo. 17, 10 November 1938.

55 LPL Lang 25, fos. 246–57, CCFCL final proposal, p. 9.

56 *Ibid.*, pp. 8, 16–18; LPL Lang 25, fos. 242–5, CCFCL final summary, p. 5. H. G. Wells had popularised the term 'open conspiracy'.

57 LPL Lang 25 fos. 3–4, 'Suggested Action by Churches in Great Britain'; LPL Lang 25, fos. 242–5, CCFCL final summary, pp. 5, 6. *Moot Papers*, M3, p. 172. *CNL* 245S, 17 October 1945, 'The Conversion of England', p. 6.

58 *Church Times*, 6 May 1938, pp. 508–9; *Guardian*, 6 May 1938, p. 293. *Moot Papers*, M3, p. 162. The CCFCL was welcomed by Dr A. E. Garvie (who had participated in its founding) in *British Weekly*, 12 May 1938, p. 111.

59 *Church of England Newspaper*, 6 May 1938, quoted in OA 13/8/1, n.d., p. 4.

60 In February 1939, Oldham, Fenn and Iredale were officers: LPL Lang 26, fo. 282. In May 1940, the following were members: Cosmo Lang (President), Revd M. E. Aubrey, A. D. Lindsay, Dr S. M. Berry, the Bishop of Bristol, J. C. S. Brough, Dr J. Hutchinson Cockburn, John Craig, Professor J. E. Davey, the Bishop of Down, Revd E. J. Hagan, Viscount Hambleden, Harold G. Judd, Dr J. Scott Lidgett, Sir Walter Moberly, the Bishop of Monmouth, W. F. Oakeshott, Miss M. E. Popham, H. G. Tanner, Professor R. H. Tawney, the Bishop of Winchester, the Archbishop of York. Officers: Oldham, Iredale and A. C. Craig; LPL Lang 26, fo. 176. By May 1941, the Bishop of Monmouth had been replaced by the Bishop of Winchester; LPL Lang 26, fo. 244, Oldham to Lang, 2 May 1941.

61 LPL Lang 26, fos. 151–3, Oldham to Lang, 31 August 1939, p. 2; LPL W. Temple 6, fos. 58–9, Oldham to Temple, 2 September 1939.

62 LPL Lang 26, fo. 156; LPL Lang 26, fos. 160–1, 'The Task of the Council in War Time', 19 September 1939, p. 1.

63 LPL Lang 26, fos. 213–22, 'Minutes of the Fifth Meeting of the CCFCL', 9 July 1940; LPL Lang 26, fo. 265.

64 CERC CCIFSR 2/1/1, 'Minutes of Sub-Committee Meeting on Proposed Commission', 6 December 1938, p. 1.

65 Jackson, *Red Tape and the Gospel*, pp. 271–3; E. Templeton, *God's February: A Life of Archie Craig* (London: CCBI, 1991), pp. 60–2; Clements, *Faith on the Frontier*, pp. 408–14.

66 Jackson, *Red Tape and the Gospel*, p. 272.

67 *Ibid.*, p. 273.

68 See LPL W. Temple 6, fos. 93–7, 'Minutes of Seventh Meeting of the CCFCL', 29 July 1941, esp. p. 5.

69 LPL Lang 26, fos. 264–5, 'Report of the Sub-Committee on Staffing', 11 July 1941.

70 Clements, *Faith on the Frontier*, p. 412. LPL Lang 26, fos. 277–8, 'The Christian Frontier', pp. 2–3.

71 LPL W. Temple 11, Oldham to Temple, 12 January 1942, fo. 190, pp. 1–2.

72 LPL Lang 26, fos. 273–6, 'Minutes of the Eighth Meeting of the CCFCL', 3 February 1942, p. 1; OA 9/4/3, Oldham to Visser 't Hooft, 19 March 1942, p. 2.

73 LPL Lang 26, fos. 273–6, 'Minutes of the Eighth Meeting of the CCFCL', 3 February 1942, p. 2. OA 9/6/58, Eliot to Oldham, 28 April 1944. On the WCC: OA 9/8/26, Oldham to Van Dusen, 28 May 1948, pp. 3–4.

74 LPL Lang 26, fos. 273–6, 'Minutes of the Eighth Meeting of the CCFCL', 3 February 1942; LPL W. Temple 11, fos. 269–70, Oldham to Temple, 28 September 1944.

75 LPL W. Temple 11, fos. 191–3, Oldham, 'The Christian Frontier', n.d. [sent 12 January 1942], p. 1.

76 *CNL* 154S, 7 October 1942, Walter Moberly, 'The Christian Frontier', p. 2.

77 *Ibid.*, p. 1.

78 LPL W. Temple 11, fos. 191–3, Oldham, 'The Christian Frontier', n.d. [sent 12 January 1942], p. 2. LPL Lang 26, fos. 264–5, 'Report of the Sub-Committee on Staffing', 11 July 1941.

79 MSC, Oldham to Symons, 18 December 1946, p. 5.

80 IOE MOO/83, Oldham, 'The Religious Foundations of the Frontier', July 1942, pp. 1, 2.

81 *Ibid.*, pp. 5–6.

82 *Ibid.*, p. 7. Emphasis in original.

83 *Ibid.*, pp. 3, 5.

84 *CNL* 198S, 29 December 1943, William Temple, 'What Christians Stand for in the Secular World'.

85 LPL W. Temple 11, fos. 269–70, Oldham to Temple, 28 September 1944.

86 *CNL* 218L, 4 October 1944, pp. 1–3. See also *Moot Papers*, M19, pp. 659–60; and *CNL* 232S, 18 April 1945, Daniel Jenkins, 'A Map of Theology To-day', p. 8.

87 OA 20, 'The Christian Frontier', n.d. [1947], p. 3.

88 In February 1942, CFC members included, alongside the Moot members Moberly, Eliot and Oakeshott: A. D. Lindsay (Balliol), Edwin Barker (Young Men's Christian Association), Henry Brooke (MP, Con., and later Home Secretary), Melville Chaning-Pearce (author and Christian philosopher),

Lord Hambleden (chair of W. H. Smith), H. G. Judd (accountant and Director of Salvage and Recovery at the Ministry of Supply), Mary Stocks (Westfield College), J. F. Wolfenden (headmaster, Uppingham School), Lady Cripps (international aid organiser and wife of Sir Stafford Cripps), H. C. Dent (*The Times*), Sir Wilfred Garrett (Ministry of Labour), F. H. Ogilvie, Reginald Pugh, Clifton Robbins (Ministry of Information (MOI)), Dorothy Sayers, Ivor Thomas (MP, Lab.), Barbara Ward (economist and Roman Catholic activist), H. W. Willink (MP, Con.) and George Woodcock (anarchist and writer); Clements, *Faith on the Frontier*, p. 412. Kenneth Grubb of the MOI later joined (*CNL* 219L, 18 October 1944, p. 4), as did the industrialist Samuel Courtauld (LPL W. Temple 34, fo. 162) and the businessman George Goyder. *CNL* 285L, 14 May 1947, pp. 1–7. OA 20, 'The Christian Frontier', n.d. [1947], p. 4.

89 *CNL* 154S, 7 October 1942, Walter Moberly, 'The Christian Frontier', p. 3; Clements, *Faith on the Frontier*, p. 413; *CNL* 208L, 17 May 1944, p. 3; OA 20, 'The Christian Frontier', n.d. [1947], p. 5.

90 *CNL* 190S, 8 September 1943, 'Responsibility in the Economic System'; *CNL* 204S, 22 March 1944, 'Responsibility in the Economic System: Government Regulation'.

91 *CNL* 279L, 5 February 1947, p. 9.

92 *CNL* 317L, 4 August 1948, p. 10; *CNL* 317S, 4 August 1948, Desmond Pond, 'On Trying to Be a Psychiatrist'.

93 OA 9/7/52, Oldham to members of the Moot, November 1947; OA 9/7/56, Oldham to Van Dusen, 4 November 1947.

94 *Moot Papers*, M3, p. 182; M4, p. 188; M5, p. 244.

95 LPL W. Temple 6, fos. 28–31, 'Notes by J. Middleton Murry' [*c.* May 1938], pp. 1–2.

96 *Churches Survey Their Task*, pp. 252–3.

97 *Moot Papers*, M4, pp. 188–9.

98 *Ibid.*, M8, pp. 292–5; M13, p. 476.

99 IOE MOO/93, letter from J. M. Murry, 14 September 1942, p. 1; IOE MOO/ 129, n.d., p. 1; *Moot Papers*, M11, p. 385; M13, p. 476; M16, pp. 538–9. Clements, *Faith on the Frontier*, pp. 384–5.

100 IOE MOO/44, Alec Vidler, 'Notes on Some Cultural Issues', *c.* March 1941, pp. 2–4.

101 IOE MOO/35, 'Notes on Mannheim's Paper by T. S. Eliot', 10 January 1941, pp. 2–3. Emphasis in original.

102 IOE MOO/50, 'Letter from T. S. Eliot', n.d. [*c.* March 1941], p. 2.

103 Kojecky, *T. S. Eliot's Social Criticism*, p. 184; OA 9/5/17, 'Extracts from Letters from T. S. Eliot', 6 September 1943, p. 1.

104 *Moot Papers*, M10, p. 347.

105 OA 9/2/39, Hodges to Oldham, 17 September 1939, pp. 4–5.

106 OA 14/1/71, H. A. Hodges, 'The Collective Commonwealth and the Christian', 22 January 1944, p. 9; OA 14/1/43, H. A. Hodges, 'Politics and the Moot', 9 June 1943, p. 10.

107 *Moot Papers*, M2, p. 117; M3, p. 149; M13, p. 446; M18, p. 622. IOE MOO/47, Letter from Karl Mannheim, n.d. [*c.* March 1941], p. 1.

108 *Moot Papers*, M18, pp. 622, 623, 626, 627.
109 IOE MOO/52, J. H. Oldham, letter to members of the Moot, 2 April 1941, p. 1.
110 *Ibid*. Karl Mannheim, *Diagnosis of Our Time: Wartime Essays of a Sociologist*, 2nd edn (London: Kegan Paul, Trench, Trübner, 1943), pp. 144, 149. *Moot Papers*, M11, pp. 382, 384 (Mannheim). *CNL* 212S, 12 July 1944, J. H. Oldham, 'Christianity and Power', p. 8.
111 *Moot Papers*, M8, pp. 293–5, 298–9, 316, 319.
112 *Ibid*., M8, p. 298.
113 *Ibid*., M9, p. 338.
114 *Ibid*., M13, pp. 477–8.
115 *Ibid*., M17, p. 595; M18, pp. 622, 641.
116 OA 9/5/19, 'The Christian Witness in the Present Crisis', 6 October 1943, pp. 11–13. *Moot Papers*, p. 15.
117 OA 9/4/42, 'Extract from a Letter from T. S. Eliot', 20 December 1942, p. 1; IOE MOO/94, letter from H. A. Hodges, 6 November 1942, p. 1.
118 Oldham credited Iredale: *CNL* 136S, 3 June 1942, J. H. Oldham, 'The Growth of Co-operation between the Churches', p. 4. See Vidler, *Scenes*, pp. 119–20; and Kojecky, *T. S. Eliot's Social Criticism*, pp. 161, 172. Bliss credited Oldham, Temple and Lang: *CNL* 338L, 25 May 1949, pp. 161–2.
119 *Moot Papers*, M4, p. 220; M5, pp. 234–8.
120 First annual report, 1936–37, *King-Hall News-Letter Service*, 2 (December 1936–June 1937), p. 1. See Arthur N. Prior, 'Christian News', *Theology*, 41:243 (September 1940), 165–9.
121 CERC CCFCL 2/2/1, 'Minutes of the Second Meeting of the Business Committee', 16 October 1939, p. 1.
122 *Moot Papers*, M5, p. 237. *CNL* 338L, 25 May 1949, p. 162.
123 *CNL* 29L, 15 May 1940, pp. 3–4; *CNL* 179L, 7 April 1943, p. 1.
124 CERC CCFCL 2/1/2, 'Report to Council on *CNL*' [9 July 1940], p. 2.
125 *Church of England Newspaper*, 29 March 1940, p. 1; *Catholic Herald*, 21 March 1940, p. 4. Vidler clarified that the series was not purely Anglican and that a Catholic book was forthcoming; *Catholic Herald*, 5 April 1940, p. 4.
126 I thank Keith Robbins for helpful information on *CNL* Books.
127 *CNL* 0L, 18 October 1939, p. 3.
128 *CNL* 48L, 25 September 1940, p. 4; *CNL* 51L, 16 October 1940, p. 2. *CNL* 144L, 29 July 1942, p. 2; *CNL* 223L, 13 December 1944, p. 6.
129 CERC CCFCL 2/1/2, 'Report to Council on *CNL*' [9 July 1940], p. 3.
130 *CNL* 29, 15 May 1940, p. 3. See also *CNL* 52L, 23 October 1940, p. 4; and OA 9/7/56, Oldham to Van Dusen, 4 November 1947, pp. 1–2.
131 *CNL* 0S, 18 October 1939, J. H. Oldham, 'What Is a "Christian" News-Letter?', pp. 1, 4. Oldham used similar language in CCFCL 2/1/1, 'The Task of the Council in War Time', 19 September 1939, p. 1.
132 CERC CCFCL 2/1/2, 'Minutes of the Fourth Meeting of the Council', 6 February 1940. CCFCL 2/1/2, 'Report to Council on *CNL*' [9 July 1940], p. 1; CCFCL 2/1/3, 'Minutes of the Sixth Meeting of the Council', 3 February 1941, p. 1.

133 MSC, 'Subscription Department Report', n.d., p. 1.

134 *CNL* 338L, 25 May 1949, p. 165.

135 In July 1940 there were 43 reading groups with 476 members: CERC CCFCL 2/1/2, 'Report to Council on *CNL*' [9 July 1940], p. 1. By 1942, there were 52 groups: Clements, *Faith on the Frontier*, p. 394.

136 *CNL* 341L, 6 July 1949, p. 211.

137 CERC CCFCL 2/1/3, 'Minutes of the Sixth Meeting of the Council', 3 February 1941, p. 1: 11,500 members, 1,800 overseas, 'the larger part' in the USA. *CNL* 132L, 6 May 1942, p. 2: 1,500 overseas (600 in USA, 200 in Canada).

138 *CNL* 132L, 6 May 1942, p. 2.

139 Clements, *Faith on the Frontier*, pp. 397–8; and Jackson, *Red Tape and the Gospel*, pp. 242–58.

140 *CNL* 247L, 14 November 1945, p. 4. *CNL* 307L, 17 March 1948, pp. 6–7. MSC, 'Subscription Department Report', n.d., pp. 1–2.

141 *Moot Papers*, M5, p. 237.

142 CERC CCFCL 2/1/2, 'Report to Council on *CNL*' [9 July 1940], p. 2; *CNL* 152L, 23 September 1942, p. 2.

143 WGS DA 43, Box 4, File: Christian working-class tradition, 'A Christian World Order and the Working Class: An Enquiry'. The report is probably that by Gwendoline Hill (secretary to Stafford Cripps) referenced in CCFCL 2/1/2, 'Minutes of the Fifth Meeting of the Council, Held at Lambeth Palace on 9 July 1940', p. 1.

144 MSC, Symons to Greer (General Secretary of SCM), 17 October 1941, p. 1.

145 *Liverpool Daily Post*, 6 April 1940, p. 5.

146 MSC, Oldham to Symons, 12 May 1941, pp. 1, 2.

147 Alan Richardson, 'The Religious Situation of Wartime Britain', *Christianity and Society* (Autumn 1941), 8–17 (p. 16).

148 *CNL* 338L, 25 May 1949, p. 163.

149 MSC, Symons to Oldham, 22 October 1941, p. 1.

150 CERC CCFCL 2/1/2, 'Report to Council on *CNL*' [9 July 1940], p. 2.

151 See *Tamworth Herald*, 11 April 1942, p. 4, and 9 May 1942, p. 5; *Aberdeen Journal*, 18 March 1940, p. 2.

152 CERC CCFCL 2/1/2, 'Report to Council on *CNL*' [9 July 1940], p. 2.

153 *CNL* 62S, 1 January 1941, 'Pater Noster'; 101L, 1 October 1941, p. 4.

154 Oldham: it had had 'exceptionally good press'; OA 9/5/41, Oldham to Visser 't Hooft, 30 December 1943, p. 1.

155 *CNL* 235L, 30 May 1945, p. 1; *CNL* 288L, 25 June 1947, p. 5.

156 MSC, Barnati to Oldham, 6 November 1941.

157 MSC, Eliot to Symons, 17 June 1944. Symons agreed: MSC, Symons to Eliot, 21 June 1944.

158 *CNL* 307L, 17 March 1948, pp. 6–7.

159 *CNL* 309L, 14 April 1948, p. 5.

160 *CNL* 341L, 6 July 1949, p. 209.

161 *CNL* 338L, 25 May 1949, p. 165.

162 *CNL* 0L, 18 October 1939, p. 1.

163 See WGS, DA 43, Box 2, File CC 30, BCC '46, 'Mission and Evangelism', especially BCC report on the inter-church conference on evangelism held at Emmanuel College, Cambridge, 2–5 July 1946.

164 *Moot Papers*, M2, pp. 81, 90; M3, 182. J. H. Oldham, *The Resurrection of Christendom* (London: Sheldon Press, 1940), pp. 52, 66, 67; *CNL* 10L, 3 January 1940, p. 2; *CNL* 93L, 6 August 1941, p. 2; *CNL* 94L, 13 August 1941, p. 1.

165 Matthew 13:33, Luke 13:20–1 and 1 Corinthians 5:6.

166 Walter Moberly, 'The Christian Faith and the Common Life', *Contemporary Review*, 153 (May 1938), 555–62 (p. 561).

167 MSC, Oldham to Symons, 29 May 1941, p. 2.

168 Hastings, *Oliver Tomkins*, p. 34.

169 LPL Lang 25, fos. 164–6, Oldham to Lang, 15 March 1938, p. 3.

170 MSC, Oldham to Symons, 12 May 1941, p. 1.

171 Moberly, 'Christian Faith and the Common Life', p. 562.

172 *Moot Papers*, M1, p. 44.

173 IOE MOO/48, Fenn to Oldham, 31 March 1941, p. 1.

174 *Ibid.*, p. 2.

175 IOE MOO/44, Vidler, 'Notes on Some Cultural Issues', n.d. [*c.* March 1941], p. 1.

176 *Moot Papers*, M4, pp. 199–200.

177 LPL W. Temple 11, fos. 210–20, 'A Common Christian Strategy', p. 1. Emphasis in original.

178 *Moot Papers*, M19, p. 662.

179 *Ibid.*, M18, pp. 628–9.

180 IOE MOO/51, letter from Gilbert Shaw, n.d. [*c.* March 1941], p. 1.

181 LPL Lang 26, fos. 38–49, 'The Council on the Christian Faith and the Common Life, Statement of Policy', 25 November 1938, p. 9.

2

Explorations on the frontier:
I Faith and the social order

As Christians seeking to change what seemed a deeply secularised society, members of the Oldham group navigated tensions between 'religious' and 'secular' principles, worldviews and practices. Their views on how these categories were related to each other shaped their engagement with a range of other issues. We thus begin with their understanding of faith. Important points of consensus within the group developed with regard (and in opposition) to competing perspectives. Rather than expressing a timeless, self-evident 'Christianity', their outlook emerged through a process of faith-building *vis-à-vis* broader trends in theological and secular knowledge. The group's 'middle way' here was via Oldham's notion of a 'frontier' at which sacred and secular met and interacted (while remaining distinct). Understanding this frontier requires mapping the territories on either side of it. This chapter focuses on religion, examining the group's views on how faith related to society, its theological influences and its vision of a more 'Christian' society. The next chapter thus turns to its views on secularity, efforts to bring religious and secular viewpoints into a creative relationship, and assertions of faith's distinctive resources for cultural renewal.

Seeking a useful faith

The members of the Oldham group largely shared the view that Christianity had to be rethought for a modern age and that this effort had to be undertaken in interaction with emerging forms of 'secular' knowledge. God was the 'Lord of History', shaping distinct social contexts for human action across different historical eras.[1] Faith's social meaning had to be actively *discovered*. Murry saw the Moot as agreeing that 'the Christian mind' was 'something which is created (or more truly *re-created*) in us by our knowledge of reality'.[2] Gilbert Shaw urged a 'rebirth' of social Christianity rather than a recovery of earlier models (such as 'medievalism').[3] Europe awaited, a *CNL* essay insisted, 'a new Reformation'.[4] Oldham saw the

CNL's mission as 'to define a faith and purpose', combining 'new' aspects with rediscovered 'lost' ones.[5] Mannheim also saw a need to 're-state' the faith – 'a dynamic entity in process of regeneration' – to account for a changing social structure and human psychology: a large-scale society had to 'retranslate' biblical values.[6] In 1944, Oldham expressed the goal as 'a re-discovered and revivified Christianity, apprehended afresh in living relation to the conditions of our time'.[7] Faith's link to the 'true ends' of life, he insisted, had to be 'continually renewed by the creative initiative and courage of pioneers and prophets'.[8] 'The fight' must be 'waged in the field of *public decision and action*': religion could not 'remain aloof from the world of the machine'.[9]

However, as Oxford 1937 had shown, Christian opinions on the social order varied widely. Conference reports sought a compromise: the Church should not engage directly in politics but could still 'judge' society, economics and politics in the light of the gospel.[10] But it was also emphatically stressed that Christians had a 'duty' to scrutinise 'the institutional framework of organized society' according to the 'canons of their faith'.[11] Oldham and his companions accepted this view, critiquing Christians' 'relative feebleness and ineffectiveness' against 'the modern Leviathan', and the churches' distance from real life: for most people faith seemed 'irrelevant to life as it has actually to be lived'.[12] There was a 'gulf' between 'Christianity as it is ordinarily presented' and 'the minds of ordinary men'.[13] A 'bridge', Oldham argued, had to be built 'from both ends': faith and social life.[14] Christianity centred on individual salvation, but Oldham insisted that in an epoch of mass politics 'personal religion' was insufficient to combat malignant ideologies.[15] The Church might well exist 'to make Christians', but there were also 'Christian criteria or standards' for society.[16] Each person had a personal 'predicament', but some predicaments were typical of a specific age.[17] The gospel offered contrasting impulses: it was both 'a call away from the world' and 'a call back into the world'.[18] Murry believed the Christian's 'prime duty' was to propagate 'a truly Christian conception of modern society'.[19] Hodges insisted that the Christian life was not merely 'cult and private devotion' but had to be worked out in secular activities.[20]

Looking back from the 1960s, Oldham saw Christians in the 1930s as divided into rival camps arguing either for or against faith's social relevance. He understood the reluctance to bring religion into social matters or vice-versa, but he also thought it 'intolerable' to 'leave things exactly as they were'.[21] Indeed, in April 1940, he asserted that the ability to lead a Christian life depended on defeating totalitarianism.[22] Christianity, he later argued, had to be *lived* in a secular society: it was a 'deception' to believe that totalitarianism would make no difference to 'a Christian existence'.[23] In *Theology* in 1944, Oldham denied either that faith was irrelevant to society or that these two 'spheres' could simply be joined. A 'middle term' was needed, 'a *social and political philosophy*' that was 'avowedly secular' but also compatible with Christianity and open to its influences, insights and values.[24]

That faith was socially relevant was a core conviction of the group, one that appealed to many Christians. In the *Spectator*, Canon F. R. Barry urged the recently founded CCFCL to consider topics such as law, economics, marriage, education, unemployment and leisure. What significance did allegiance to Christ have in understanding the role of the State, the 'limits of political obedience' and 'the duty of Christian citizens in a world of armaments and power politics'?[25] Moberly, in the *Contemporary Review*, saw 'limitless' areas for research: education, industry, class society, secular culture and international relations.[26] Four years later, the aim of the CFC was described not as interpreting the Bible but as understanding society.[27] In the Moot, Baillie described Christians as 'an influential minority in a world with a Christian past', even if they were not making much of their potential.[28] The social imperative was clear: God, Oldham wrote, 'has to be served not only in the Church, but in the State'.[29] Lex Miller called for a better 'doctrine of the purpose of God for the secular order itself'.[30] In 1947, Bliss highlighted the centrality of social action for the Christian:

> It is clear from the Scriptures that when a man comes to judgment he will be asked what he *did* with cups of cold water, and bread and clothing, that is to say, in his work and business, in his relations with creditors and debtors and his everyday living with neighbours, and he will not be able to evade the issue by inviting attention to his activities as a churchwarden, or his participation in a discussion group on a Christian Social Order, important as these are.[31]

Christians, Moira Symons wrote in the *CNL*, were 'the leaven in the lump' but must still 'live in the lump' and involve themselves with 'practical secular affairs'.[32] For Oldham, faith was not a separate 'sphere of life' but 'a force entering into the whole human struggle and progressively changing it'.[33] But how did the sacred and social connect?

The group's answer was based on 'middle axioms', a concept pioneered by Oldham that linked Christian ideals to social action, defining 'a way of being the Church in the world'.[34] In *Christianity and the Race Problem* (1924), Oldham had outlined the essential idea: the Bible contained no specific social programme for a world of capitalism, industry and bureaucracy; however, the vision of the Kingdom of Heaven gave 'an outlook, a temper, a spirit' and guidance about 'the meaning and purpose of life'.[35] In 1930, he defined a middle axiom as a formulation 'in the light of the Christian view of life' of the 'governing principle of action in regard to a given situation'.[36] The Church could not give detailed policy advice, about which Christians might in any case legitimately differ; moreover, policy-making belonged to 'the practical statesman' with experience 'lacking to the clergy or to the ordinary Christian citizen'. Nonetheless, middle axioms, while abstract, enabled evaluating politics according to how they related to Christian purposes. Oldham defined middle axioms as lying between 'purely general statements of the ethical demands of the Gospel' and 'decisions that have to be made in concrete situations': they showed the 'directions' in which faith should be expressed 'at a given period and in given circumstances'.[37]

Middle axioms thus emphasised *historicity, moral ambiguity* and *expert knowledge.* The group repeatedly stressed that Christians – *as* Christians – had no special insights into secular problems. The churches were also proclaiming much that was irrelevant: 'What help does it bring to the banker as banker, the industrialist as industrialist or the trades-unionist as trades-unionist or the statesman as statesman', Oldham asked, 'to tell him that he must act in accordance with the law of love?'.[38] What did loving one's neighbour as oneself even mean in industrial society? Christians must show mercy, but did it follow, for example, that they had to accept a 'lenient peace' with Germany?[39] Without a direct way from the faith's 'deepest insights' to the political decisions of the day, a 'third term' was needed 'between Christian teaching and the problems of society'.[40] Middle axioms occupied this in-between level. While not always concretely referred to in group discussions, they defined what W. G. Symons called 'the intervening country between ordinary "morals" and "politics"' on which those exchanges focused.[41] Hodges saw the Moot as seeking 'valid middle axioms' and 'a moral and social philosophy adequate to our times'.[42] Middle axioms have been criticised as imprecise or even useless; nonetheless, they were employed by Oldham, Temple and Baillie and were important to twentieth-century British (and especially Anglican) Christianity.[43] Temple, for example, took a middle-axiom approach at his influential 'Malvern' conference in 1941, and they underlay his popular *Christianity and Social Order* (1942).[44] But alongside the general method of middle axioms, the group also shared specific theological influences.

Theological influences

The Oldham group reworked diverse religious and secular influences into a selective synthesis. Oldham aimed to generate a 'school of thought' that was not 'exclusive' but included 'the elements of truth in the different schools already in existence'.[45] Individual members' views certainly reflected their denominational backgrounds, generational trends and personal experiences, but they were also broadly ecumenical. While recognisably 'evangelical' in outlook, for example, Oldham was inspired by diverse theologians and philosophers such as Paul Tillich, Emil Brunner, Ernst Troeltsch, Eberhard Grisebach, Nikolai Berdyaev, Martin Buber, Jacques Maritain and Reinhold Niebuhr.

The Oldham group's participants often spoke as if a socially relevant, non-denominational Christianity could be distilled from these influences. The aim was a 'common profession of Christian dogma' for social purposes (which family and Church might then supplement with specific denominational teachings).[46] Some members doubted the approach (Eliot in particular), and confessional perspectives periodically fuelled disagreements.[47] But the synthesising emphasis remained. 'Differing theologies must realise', Oldham told the Moot, 'that they were agreed on certain things which were vastly more important than the points of difference.'[48] Indeed, the group saw a broad theological 'convergence' already emerging from efforts to apply faith to society. In a *Theology* editorial in 1945, Vidler argued that, 'beneath the surface', Protestant writers such as Brunner and Niebuhr, and Catholics such as Maritain and Dawson, were 'saying much the same thing.'[49]

Still, various faith traditions saw the sacred and secular as connected in different ways, defined by varying degrees of *continuity* or *discontinuity*. Seeking a 'Copernican revolution' in theology, the group stressed continuity, aiming to put social teachings at Christianity's centre.[50] They were thus attracted to theological arguments that supported this aim, and correspondingly sceptical of those that did not. Mannheim urged Christians to take responsibility for the social order and 'Christian thinkers' to 'blend theological thought with sociological knowledge.'[51] Oldham agreed but complained to Temple that, unfortunately, 'some of the theologians' were the 'most stupid' about faith and society: their rarefied 'theological atmosphere' was remote from 'the actual world.'[52] Nonetheless, five theological influences on the group stand out: (1) domestic traditions of 'liberalism'; (2) the 'Christian realism' of Reinhold Niebuhr; (3) the neo-Thomist philosophy of Jacques Maritain; (4) 'continental' Protestant theology, particularly that of Karl Barth; and (5) personalism.

A self-critical 'liberalism'

'Liberal' Protestantism had many facets, and it must be kept in mind that 'liberalism' was often a term of abuse used by opponents of particular theological positions. It was also the case that theological liberalism (sometimes called 'modernism') was a less coherent position in Britain than in Germany. Nonetheless, in the early twentieth century, Protestant liberalism can be seen to have involved certain perspectives: (1) a scientific approach to knowledge (including scriptural claims); (2) a downplaying of supernatural faith; (3) a stress on human goodness and moral improvement through social action; and (4) optimism about building (at least partially) the Kingdom of Heaven on earth.[53] There was also a distinct and specific-ally Anglican religio-political 'liberalism' that idealised 'organic national community', opposed 'economic competition and class conflict', foresaw a 'comprehensive church' and 'active state', and emphasised education's culturally integrative power.[54] This liberalism also influenced the Oldham group, but here I focus on *theological* liberalism.

Theological liberalism was often critiqued in the 1930s and 1940s as sentimental, optimistic, naïve, utopian and secularised. The world, indeed, seemed not to be playing by the liberal script, though this realisation was in some cases slow in coming. The Great War had shaken belief in progress, but British Christians had quickly channelled a renewed post-war hope into support for the League of Nations.[55] In inter-war ecumenical debates, German theological pessimism often confronted Anglo-American liberal optimism.[56] Times were changing, however. While the 1925 Life and Work conference in Stockholm saw Anglo-American calls for Christianity 'to be a new world order', the mood in 1937 at Oxford – both theologically and politically – was gloomier.[57] Indeed, Oxford 1937 has been seen as marking the peak of 'post-liberal' theology in the ecumenical movement, with influences flowing together from continental Europe and the United States.[58] Modernistic liberalism seemed 'tired and conservative' while 'theological conservatism' appeared an 'exciting, radical option', and a gen-eration gap divided younger theologians drawn to the continental 'the-ology of crisis' (described below) from older, more 'liberal' colleagues.[59] But for all such opposition, liberalism was not swept aside: leading British clergy – such as Temple and Bell – maintained their liberal convictions, if more measuredly.[60]

The Oldham group distanced itself from liberal failings but was less *anti*-liberal (or 'post-liberal') than *self-critically* liberal. Its members claimed to reject theological liberalism while still adhering – if only tacitly or partially – to recognisably liberal positions. True, they emphasised the ontological transformation of Christ's incarnation and atonement, seeing Christianity, in contrast to liberalism, not as an *ideal* but as a *reality*: not as an ethic but as a 'faith'.[61] However, Oldham and his companions still derived 'values' from that faith. While rejecting liberalism's 'materialism', they praised secular knowledge. They condemned liberal utopianism but continued to see Christianity as a world-renewing force, even if they added emphases on human sin-fulness. Liberalism's resilience derived partly from its influence on ecclesiastical leaders and academics, and it was arguably strengthened through its critics' insights. At war's end, Daniel Jenkins perceived a 'revaluation of Liberalism' and even the dawning of a 'post-anti-Liberal period'.[62] The Oldham group's stance resembled that of the era's leading 'anti-liberal liberal', Reinhold Niebuhr, who was similarly 'theologically to the right and politically to the left' of liberal Protestantism.[63]

'Christian realism'

The disagreements of the American Protestant theologian Reinhold Niebuhr (1892–1971) with liberalism were not unique, but he formulated them particularly effectively in books such as *Moral Man and Immoral Society* (1932), *The Nature and Destiny of Man* (1943) and *The Children of Light and the Children of Darkness* (1944). Niebuhr, 'the single greatest theological influence' in 1930s Britain, became a leading representative of Anglo-American 'neo-orthodoxy' (a theological tendency discussed below), and he formulated what was widely called 'Christian realism'.[64] He knew members of the Oldham group personally (being especially close to Baillie). He attended the Moot in 1939 and 1943 and was on the *CNL*'s advisory committee.[65] He also founded the American periodicals *Christianity and Society* and *Christianity and Crisis*, which cooperated with the *CNL*.

Niebuhr critiqued liberalism from a position *within* liberalism, even if some liberals – or even Niebuhr himself – would have struggled to think so at the time.[66] He had been influenced by the 'social gospel', a liberal Protestant view that downplayed individualist faith, sought to reform earthly life and critiqued capitalism.[67] But in the 1930s Niebuhr rejected naïve optimism about human progress. Still critical of capitalism, he attacked liberal Christian pretensions of building an earthly Kingdom and highlighted humanity's innate sinfulness. Opposing liberal philosophers, such as John Dewey, and totalitarian efforts to remake human nature, Niebuhr claimed groups, communities, institutions and nations *amplified* rather than limited human faults.[68] Individuals might overcome self-interest, but groups were always riven by struggles for power. Still, he urged Christians to *engage with* rather than *withdraw from* an inherently immoral public life: Christian love – *agape* – should motivate *action*. Niebuhr saw continuities between the divine and temporal realms but insisted that political action was inevitably morally ambiguous: Christians had to be willing to 'get their hands dirty'.[69] In 1944, Oldham approvingly quoted Niebuhr's evocation of his 'tragic' vision: with victory imminent, Niebuhr had written 'let there be contrite thoughts over the evil we must do in order to conquer evil'.[70] Dangerous power could only be met by a more moral power; but power *always* posed a moral threat to those who wielded it. This was Christian realism.

Niebuhr's thought was useful to the Oldham group. He urged Christians to think sociologically about modern life, telling the Moot in June 1943 that 'a combination of social science and theology' was necessary.[71] His political conclusions were democratic and anti-totalitarian.[72] He believed all societies experienced struggles for political domination but insisted that democracy maintained tolerable conditions for 'fallen' humankind: 'Man's capacity for justice makes democracy possible', he famously asserted, 'but man's inclination to injustice makes democracy necessary'.[73] He justified combating totalitarianism militarily, arguing against Christian pacifism. His critique of capitalism and calls for State action during the 1930s – tempered by a growing emphasis on liberty in the 1940s – dovetailed with the Moot's consensus on 'planning for freedom' (discussed in Chapter 4).[74]

Neo-Thomism

The Oldham group – and leading Anglicans such as Temple – also found useful qualities in the thought of French Roman Catholic philosopher Jacques Maritain (1882–1973).[75] Maritain's worldview developed in the early-twentieth-century revival of medieval Scholasticism, particularly the philosophy of Thomas Aquinas. The Vatican encouraged this movement to resist cultural liberalism, secularism and relativism as well as inner-church tendencies towards 'modernism' (e.g. via biblical criticism or arguments that dogma evolved historically).[76] In 1879, Aquinas's writings were officially endorsed by Pope Leo XIII as an antidote to modern philosophy, enabling the rise of 'neo-Thomism' to intellectual predominance in the Roman Catholic Church.[77] The furiously partisan (and partly anti-clerical) politics in early-twentieth-century France made the Catholic confrontation with secularity especially intense there.[78]

Throughout his works, Maritain diagnosed modernity's disintegrative tendencies and argued for cultural renewal through Christianity. But his political views evolved. A passionate anti-modernist by the outbreak of the Great War, he published *Antimoderne* (1922) and became editor of *Revue universelle*, linked to Charles Maurras's reactionary, monarchist, nationalist and anti-Semitic *Action française*.[79] But Maritain came to think Catholicism was capable of a profound synthesis with modernity. Two 'about-turns' resulted: he rejected *Action française* (after the papal condemnation of Maurras in 1926) and supported Republican Spain after 1936.[80] This was the Maritain who influenced the Oldham group, mainly through his book *Humanisme intégral* (1936), published in English as *True Humanism* in 1938. His British reception was smoothed by the 1930s 'high summer of Anglo-Catholic theology', but he also had personal connections to the Oldham group.[81] He had known Eliot since the 1920s, and had written for his journal, *Criterion*; Maritain's *Religion and Culture* (1931) had been published in a series edited by Dawson; and he had met with Moot members at one of Eliot's gentlemen's clubs.[82] Oldham introduced *True Humanism* to many others, including Archbishops Lang and Temple.

The group welcomed Maritain's ideas – which were cited in CCFCL mission statements – not least since they had reached similar conclusions independently.[83] *True Humanism* was discussed at the Moot's third meeting in January 1939.[84] Importantly, Baillie – a Presbyterian – was chosen to introduce Maritain's Catholic ideas. Even more significantly, he agreed

Figure 3 John Baillie, 1942, by Elliott & Fry

with them. Maritain had, Baillie pronounced, largely avoided 'aspects of Romanism', and his argument concerned less the saving of souls than 'the salvation of civilization'.[85] Maritain argued that medieval 'Christian absolutism' had given way to 'anthropocentric humanism' in the Renaissance; in the 1930s this was, in turn, succumbing to 'totalitarian absolutism'. He proposed, in response, an 'integral' or 'theocentric' humanism that stressed human dependence on God and sought a 'looser and more elastic' unity of the sacred and the secular than that of the Middle Ages.[86] The 'secular Christian order' he described would have 'relative autonomy' from faith, with politics seen 'as an end in itself, but not as an absolute end in itself': the aim was the social order reimagined as 'a temporal city vivified and impregnated with Christianity'.[87]

The Moot immediately accepted Maritain as one of its intellectual guiding lights. His theological value lay less in his absolute originality than his clarity of expression and reinforcement of key ideas already held by the group. First, he shared the group's diagnosis of the modern crisis as resulting from the divide between the sacred and the secular. Christians, he argued, should encourage 'a truly and fully human life' in a society shaped by principles of 'justice', 'the dignity of human personality' and 'brotherly love'.[88] Maritain, Baillie saw, had the same opponents: Catholic medievalism, secular liberalism, atheist Communism, neo-pagan Fascism and the radical 'dualism' of continental Protestantism.[89] Second, Maritain asserted the *relative* autonomy of religious and secular spheres: churches would not interfere in 'politics, economics, education, legislature, science and art', providing instead only 'general ethical principles' (except in issues such as divorce); a 'lesser-evil' principle would enable political compromise.[90] Third, Maritain's ideal of the 'pluralist commonwealth' lay, Baillie wrote, 'perhaps half way' between liberalism and totalitarianism, bringing it close to Mannheim's vision of 'planning for freedom'.[91] Maritain's goals – a 'Christian secular order' or a 'Christianised earthly city' – resembled the group's own aims.[92] Fourth, he condemned both Communism and capitalism, seeking 'a half-way-house' to transcend their contradictions: his 'new Christendom' would have Christian leadership and inspiration but be pluralist, allowing 'a very large diversity of men and of views'.[93] Baillie thought Maritain had a useful 'appreciation' for Communism's 'truth and goodness' as well as its 'evil and error'.[94] Fifth, Maritain suggested Christian unity would be won not by a political party but rather by 'a sort of Christian diaspora', echoing Moot discussions about 'cells' and the permeation of culture.[95]

There were aspects of the specifically Roman Catholic position from which Maritain argued that appealed to members of the Oldham group;

however, far more decisive were Maritain's distinctive theological openness and commitment to political democracy as well as the intellectual 'convergence' his book seemed to embody. The Oldham group was clearly not 'neo-Thomist' in the sense of consistently or coherently arguing from that theological-philosophical standpoint, not least since other (non-Thomist) ideas and perspectives were equally important to shaping its consensus.[96] Despite enthusiasm for Maritain, much of the Oldham group – apart from Dawson and Eliot – expressed doubts about Catholic political thinking. The *CNL* praised some Vatican statements and supported the Catholic-led 'Sword of the Spirit' movement during the war.[97] But, privately, the group critiqued a political Catholicism that even some of its adherents (such as Dawson) admitted was 'authoritarian and hierarchical'.[98] The group, ultimately, shared a broader Protestant antipathy towards Catholic politics, and Maritain's commitment to democracy and position somewhat *outside* the Catholic mainstream made his ideas easier to approach and appropriate.

'*Continental Protestantism*'

Even within Protestantism, however, there were disagreements. As we have seen, a self-critical liberalism and the ideas of Niebuhr offered resources for rethinking Christianity and society. This was in contrast to what the group – like many British Christians – referred to as 'continental Protestantism'. Various theological positions were lumped together under this term, above all Lutheranism and the theology of Swiss Reform theologian Karl Barth. Barth's approach (referred to variously as 'dialectical theology', the 'theology of crisis' or 'neo-orthodoxy') had been welcomed in the inter-war period by group members, including Oldham.[99] Oldham had, for example, helped organise Barth's first visit to England in 1930.[100] He also sought commentary on Moot papers and *CNL* texts from advocates of continental theology, which he thought was 'more original and creative' than traditional British liberalism.[101] The *CNL* published several supplements by or about Barth, including a positive summary and review of his *Kirchliche Dogmatik*.[102] Moreover, the group sometimes doubted whether what seemed 'the extreme Barthian position' could fairly be taken as representative of continental thought. Still, despite such open-minded views, for the Oldham group, 'continental' Protestantism (and Barth in particular) served as an important counter-example *against which* its own thought was developed.[103]

Barth saw a deep discontinuity between sacred and secular, adapting Kierkegaard's 'infinite qualitative distinction' between God and humanity.

God was 'the Wholly Other', utterly unlike anything human and reachable only through revelation.[104] As Baillie wrote, this made for 'a complete dualism between the heavenly and the earthly cities': 'It teaches that the revealed economy of the City of God gives us no guidance for the economy of actual society on earth ... It makes the political problem a purely "human" problem, setting it in contrast with the divine; a purely "secular" problem, setting it in contrast with the sacred.'[105] Lutheranism was seen to draw a similar division between sacred and secular, one that denied the Oldham group's aim of bringing these categories into mutually enriching dialogue.[106] Some members of the Moot (H. H. Farmer, John Baillie, Lex Miller and Daniel Jenkins) and guests (such as Lesslie Newbigin) were influenced by Barth, but they remained a small minority.[107] (Farmer attended only twice; Newbigin once.[108]) Jenkins disagreed that Barth denied faith's social relevance; right or wrong, however, the group largely held the view that his theology did precisely that.[109] Murry condemned the 'neo-Protestant' (or 'neo-Lutheran') claim of 'absolute heterogeneity' between God and the world: its continental popularity was, Murry claimed, 'psychological compensation' for a faith that had caused social 'indifferentism' and brought 'disastrous consequences'.[110] (In *The Price of Leadership*, he called this Protestantism 'retrograde', 'pernicious' and 'alien to the temper of English Christianity'.[111]) Niebuhr told the Moot that the radical continental divide between sacred and secular 'destroyed the relative distinctions of good and evil' essential for engagement with politics.[112] Barth's ideas fared poorly in the group against Maritain's.[113] The Moot respected Barth's socialism and leadership of the Confessing Church, but his politics, in their view, contradicted his theology. Vidler concluded that 'continental criticism could be left out' of group deliberations.[114] Löwe saw dialectical theology 'in retreat' and as 'a typical professorial position' appropriate to peace-time: 'no one in the Moot took that point of view'.[115] Oldham said Barth asked only 'the Church question' and ignored politics; while understandable on a totalitarian-dominated continent, it did not fit the British situation.[116]

Overall, then, the group ignored Barthian positions, but there were a few direct engagements. Hodges presented a Moot paper titled 'Christian Thinking To-day'. With Barth clearly in mind, he critiqued 'an intransigent neo-Protestantism' that denied 'any way from the world to a genuine knowledge of God'.[117] A response to this paper by Thomas F. Torrance, a British Barthian, attacked the attempt by Hodges – and the Moot – to make divine will 'intelligible'.[118] Shaw and Hodges responded vigorously. Shaw saw 'a fundamental cleavage' between Barth's views 'and all that the Moot stands for': there was 'no possibility of any fruitful common action'.[119] Barthian 'axioms' opposed the Moot's, and Shaw urged the group not to engage in what he saw as a futile battle.[120] Hodges also saw Torrance's Barthian viewpoint as posing a 'challenge to the whole Moot', saying the group had ultimately to decide whether their aim of a socially relevant faith was legitimate or not.[121] Clearly, the group's long-term members thought it was.

Thus, while there was much sympathy in the group for theological positions that questioned liberal assertions of human perfectibility, Barth was seen as turning a worthy cautionary insight into an extreme rejection of human politics. Typical for the public expressions of this view was a *CNL* essay from 1948 in which Niebuhr critiqued 'continental theology', focusing on Barth's denial at the Amsterdam WCC conference that Christians were responsible for the world.[122] Niebuhr thought Barth had usefully corrected overly enthusiastic visions of 'Christian economics' or 'Christian sociology'; however, he claimed that Barth took this insight too far.[123] Barth's theology had powerfully responded to crisis, he argued, but offered nothing to Christians in their day-to-day political responsibilities. Niebuhr allowed that the 'Anglo-Saxon' view was corrupted by Pelagianism (a heretical view that stressed innate human goodness and the possibility of moral action even in the absence of God's grace); however, continental views ignored 'the foothills where human life must be lived'.[124] Barth's reply – also published in the *CNL* – claimed 'Anglo-Saxons' paid little attention to the Bible.[125] Niebuhr agreed that 'Anglo-Saxon thought' saw more mixture between culture and 'Biblical faith' than did its continental counterparts; but while American 'liberalism' or Anglican tendencies towards 'bourgeois individualism' went wrong, Niebuhr defended such intellectual exchange against insistence on biblical 'purity'.[126] A *Theology* editorial both accepted Niebuhr's critique and defended Barth, arguing that while Barth himself could not be reproached for advocating social quietism, Niebuhr had nonetheless 'spoken a word in season': there was an emerging theological tendency to withdraw from social concerns into 'the inner life of the Church'.[127] The editorial urged Christians to resist such trends.

Lutheranism was similarly critiqued. Hodges accused it of a 'guilt-obsession', excessive focus on the 'isolated individual' and reluctance to address social issues.[128] Murry thought Lutheran claims of an 'essential heterogeneity' between a possible 'earthly commonwealth' and God's Kingdom were as 'un-Christian' as liberal optimism.[129] Niebuhr claimed Lutheranism had always been too focused on 'ultimate answers to the ultimate issues of life' to consider 'questions of civic virtue and political justice'.[130] Barth – though neither German nor Lutheran – was reproached for strengthening German Lutheranism's worst qualities. In 1940, Niebuhr suggested Barth had revived an excessive Lutheran focus on sinfulness, thereby reducing relative political evaluations to 'insignificance'. Indeed, he claimed Lutheranism had caused Germany's 'present plight' by assuming that 'men are evil' and that a 'strong state' must control them.[131] Mannheim argued similarly.[132] Bliss likewise reproached German Protestantism for lacking 'a strong sense of responsibility for the ordering of the life of society'.[133] Anglicans broadly shared this criticism of Lutheranism, seen as 'super-Erastian', excessively obedient to the State and unwilling to apply faith to social action.[134]

The influential Swiss Reformed theologian Emil Brunner was less often counted by the group as representing the 'continental' positions they so roundly critiqued. Brunner had influenced Oldham and knew him personally.[135] Indeed, his book *Das Gebot und die Ordnungen* (1933) shared the group's preoccupations, emphasising the social relevance of Christian ethics, the *relative* autonomy of society from Christian ideals, the centrality of 'Christian anthropology', the place of human 'dependence', the grounding of responsible freedom in the relationship to God, the relational nature of individual development, the importance of secular knowledge, the justification for Christian opposition to capitalism and Marxism, and an ambivalence towards the State.[136] Brunner also, similarly, aimed to 'discover the significance of Christian faith' for 'conduct in the complex modern world of economics, politics and culture'.[137] The *CNL* reprinted an address of his on 'Man and Technics' in January 1948.[138] He was rarely mentioned in the Moot but was, like Barth, critiqued for 'overstating the corruption of man'.[139] Indeed, many British and American Christians saw Brunner – despite his many conflicts with Barth – as a 'Barthian'.[140]

Personalism

The group's thinking was also shaped by 'personalism', an emphasis on the unique value of persons and their holistic development in relationships (as opposed to allegedly more 'atomistic' ideals of 'individualism').[141] Some of those in or close to the Oldham group had long promoted personalist thinking, such as Farmer, Temple and Niebuhr.[142] A key personalist influence on Oldham was German Protestant philosopher Eberhard Grisebach, particularly his book *Gegenwart* (1928).[143] Grisebach saw reality becoming '*present to* us in the encounter with others' and examined human nature via 'the interhuman realm of concrete encounters, demands and opportunities'.[144] Oldham was also drawn to Jewish philosopher Martin Buber's 'I–Thou' philosophy: his *Ich und Du* (1923) had deeply influenced Oldham, who could read German. (An English translation appeared only in 1937,

delaying his British reception.) Nikolai Berdyaev's Orthodox personalism was a recurring reference point, and Maritain's *True Humanism*
brought personalist influences from Catholicism. British philosopher John
Macmurray also emphasised holistic, relational individual development
in *Freedom in the Modern World* (1932) and *Interpreting the Universe*
(1933).[145]

Personalist emphases were scattered throughout group discussions,
documents and publications.[146] Oldham explained its essence in a
December 1941 *CNL* supplement, 'All Real Life Is Meeting', a phrase
that had long been his motto and one that has remained associated with
him.[147] Oldham argued that the key social issue was whether people
were only judged according to their usefulness or whether life's true
significance was found 'in the mutual relations of persons'.[148] The latter
was essential to building a decent society and resisting totalitarianism,
and he insisted that encouraging such relationships depended on faith.
With Buber (and Macmurray) Oldham distinguished human relations
to *things* ('the world of "It"') from those to *each other* ('the world of
"Thou"'). The former could be understood through science, but the
latter saw two equals meeting: 'We are persons', Oldham insisted, 'only
in our relation with other persons'.[149] The problem was not science
itself but the growing 'extent and domination of the world of things'
and decline in 'man's power to enter in to relation'.[150] Oldham asserted
that even the most 'spiritual' view of the 'will to power' – the attitude
of modern 'impersonal' society – led to the 'annihilation of man'.[151] In
1947, Oldham (citing Buber) argued that a relational principle was a
'saving corrective' to the dominance of scientific thought.[152] Even when
not referring to 'personalism' as such, the group emphasised the need
for individual development 'in relation' and in 'community'.

As the foregoing shows, rather than representing a single denominational viewpoint, the Oldham group's thought was shaped by a
selective combination of Protestant, Catholic, Orthodox and Jewish
influences. Although untangling the various motivations involved
is challenging, this selection was clearly biased towards those theological principles that would support the group's social and political
aims. Allowing for continuities between divine and human categories
was essential: bridging the sacred and secular, after all, required that
the chasm between them be not impossibly broad. At the same time,
they thought it important to avoid theological liberalism's easy mixture
of broadly Christian ethics and progressive politics. For the Oldham
group, the balance was found in a *self-critical* liberalism, Niebuhr's
'Christian realism', Maritain's 'new Christendom' and varieties of 'personalism'. These stood in contrast (as most in the group saw it) to both

political Catholicism and 'continental Protestantism', whether Lutheran or Barthian. It was suggested that Britain – and British Christianity – might be suited to what Niebuhr, writing in the *CNL* just after the war, called a 'new synthesis'. British socialism, for example, unlike its continental variety, had not denied the West's 'Christian foundations', and Anglicanism combined Protestant and Catholic strengths.[153] But in what direction might these hopes of a Christian middle way lead?

A 'fundamental re-orientation of outlook'

The Oldham group saw that cultural 'disintegration' resulting from secularisation required a new cultural 'unity' supported by faith and renewed forms of 'community'. In a much-noted letter to *The Times* in October 1938 (in the wake of the 'Munich crisis'), Oldham argued that modern society's 'structure, institutions and activities' often violated 'the Christian understanding of the meaning and end of man's existence'. It was necessary, in response, to 'work out a Christian doctrine of modern society and to order our national life in accordance with it'.[154] The goal, as a CCFCL document put it, was *not* a return to an earlier society but – here echoing Maritain's language – a 'new Christendom'.[155] But what did *that* mean?

The group was ambivalent about calling for an explicitly *Christian* social order. Early Moot discussions of a 'Christian society' sparked concerns about excessively blurring the boundaries between sacred and secular, worries about 'utopian' thinking, and doubts about whether an entire society of professed Christians was even remotely feasible in such a deeply secular age. The aim came to centre on a '*more* Christian' society that would at least enable Christian influence to survive and, possibly, flourish.[156] Oldham suggested they might 'refrain from the outright use of the word Christian' and instead work towards a 'social and political faith and philosophy which is compatible with the Christian understanding of the end of man, is leavened with Christian values and owes some of its major insights to Christian minds which have cooperated in its formulation'.[157] In March 1942 he even mused that the aim was not 'a Christian order of society' but rather 'an alternative to totalitarianism'.[158] Such comments, however, were exceptions: a more Christian 'order of society' was a clear goal, driving efforts to define a 'social philosophy', a 'Doctrine of Man and Society', an 'alternative political society' or a new 'combination of social science and theology'.[159] Tentative language was common in the group's vision of a society that was 'compatible with' faith or 'in some sense Christian': the aim was a social order that 'conforms in some measure' to Christianity or could be 'leavened', 'enriched' or 'impregnated' by Christian values.

Still, specifically Christian aims were needed, even if participants usually denied faith offered 'blue-prints' or 'a specific programme'. (Though they sometimes said it might.[160]) They wanted to define the 'minimum content' of Christian social thought with regard to 'certain major questions'; as Oldham put it, they sought 'a common basis among Christian minds discoverable (say) by an inhabitant of Mars if he investigated the earth'.[161] (Shaw saw the Moot looking to define 'the central mean' of Christian teachings.[162]) Discussion therefore often tended to remain on the level of generalities. Aware that political reforms would inevitably be pursued by flawed individuals in a context of political conflict and compromise, they sought to avoid 'abstract systems' and warned against 'utopias'.

Instead, the aim came to focus strongly on understanding the 'nature and the end of man'.[163] All societies, Oldham observed in a broadcast in 1941, were built 'consciously or unconsciously, on a certain conception of man'.[164] A true *anthropology* seemed more vital than a list of ideals or policies. The main 'disorder' of the West was, after all, that people had 'in their minds a false picture of what they really are'.[165] Society must be 'consciously directed' towards the true ends of man's existence understood in the light of the Christian revelation'.[166] Like the Oxford conference reports, the group stressed Christianity's view of an essentially stable, divinely created human nature in opposition to regimes that sought to remake people ideologically.[167] Mannheim saw some 'plasticity' in 'human nature', but he also opposed a 'misdirected utopianism' that thought individuals could be 'moulded at will', stressing instead long-term and global regularities in human societies.[168] There was a consensus that, as Oldham put it, a *false* view of 'the nature and the end of man' had become deeply entrenched in the modern West's consciousness, determining even 'the climate which we breathe'.[169]

In the view of the Oldham group, all contemporary social orders – whether capitalism, Communism, Nazism or Fascism – violated humanity's 'true nature'.[170] A distinct Christian answer was needed, and recovering 'a vital Christianity' meant identifying 'the true predicament of men in modern society' and working for what Oldham called 'a fundamental reorientation of outlook'.[171] If people came to see themselves differently, it was hoped, they would *live* differently. In the Moot he stressed articulating Christian social aims and creating 'a body pledged to get these accepted by public policy'; five years later, he similarly argued that 'effective action' required a 'group united by a conscious common purpose'.[172] The crisis was 'religious', involving 'the whole Christian understanding of life'.[173] Christians thus needed guiding *principles* (on the level of middle axioms) and a realistic understanding of political *power* to bring society in harmony with them. This emphasis on changing 'beliefs', 'values', 'aims', 'understandings', 'habits' and 'outlooks' highlights the group's focus on *culture*.

Within the group, culture was often understood in the 'anthropological' sense already common in the 1940s, i.e. a non-normative term for the ideas, norms, values and practices common to a specific group.[174] But unlike most anthropologists, they distinguished religion *from* culture. With the exceptions of Mannheim and Löwe – who had functional, sociological views on faith – members saw God as an eternal supernatural *reality*, and Christ's incarnation, crucifixion and resurrection as events that changed the *nature* of human life. But Christianity, if not reducible *to* culture, had to be brought into a healthy relationship *with* culture. Two broad elements are important to understanding this relationship.

First, both the group's diagnosis of and its solution for the modern crisis were cultural in that they focused on ideas, attitudes and practices. In *The Times* in October 1938 Oldham intertwined both meanings: the undermining of the 'spiritual foundations of Western civilization' had been demonstrated by the 'extent to which Christian ideals have lost their hold over, or faded from the consciousness of, large sections of the population'.[175] Expressing a group consensus in 1941, he insisted that 'history is shaped by what men fundamentally believe about themselves and the world in which they live'.[176] 'Conduct', he wrote two years later, was determined by 'ultimate beliefs'.[177] In 1946, Mairet argued that the world's crisis only seemed economic or political: it was, in fact, 'cultural'.[178] The West's 'worship of false gods', Oldham wrote, meant it could only return to 'health' through 'a true scale of values'.[179] The pursuit of 'false ends' meant 'the ends must be changed' through a 'conversion of the mind'.[180] Christians had to change 'the thought, practice and institutional forms of society'.[181] Introducing the CFC to *CNL* readers, Moberly emphasised the need to change 'fundamental attitudes of mind and modes of behaviour', both 'the ideas in people's minds and also their practice'.[182] In the Moot, Oldham quoted a refugee German educator in calling the war ' "A Hell-sent opportunity" to change values'.[183] Murry insisted that 'a new and different system of values' had to become 'dominant and decisive of actual behaviour'.[184] In May 1944, Oldham asserted that the 'real crisis' was 'cultural', curable only through re-establishing 'a unity between men's ultimate beliefs and habits and their conscious aims'.[185] In 1945, Bliss claimed all reforms were 'doomed to failure without a radical revolution in men's minds'.[186] In the *CNL*, Owen Barfield insisted that 'a new society' required 'a change in people's ways of thought and feeling'.[187] As Chapter 4 explains, Mannheim put cultural 'valuations' at the heart of 'planning for freedom'; in a different

way, Eliot and Dawson also stressed the relation between a healthy culture
and religion.[188]

Second, the Oldham group stressed a *non-relativist understanding of
culture*. The group insisted that Christianity could not be understood as
the sum of its cultural manifestations, insisting it offered a relationship
with a level of *reality* independent of human beliefs, desires or standards.
This relationship between God and culture was often defined, Oldham
complained, 'the wrong way round': 'We take the world for granted and
ask where God comes in.'[189] But God's will applied not only to individuals
but also to societies: there was an inherent, divine order in the natural and
social worlds. It was argued that Christianity offered a standpoint *above*
cultural relativism and political instrumentality: divine 'laws' defined a
'true' relationship to reality, enabling distinctions between 'genuine' and
'false' culture. However, as the next chapter emphasises, the group sought
to translate this Christian understanding into terms that non-believers
could also accept.

There were variations in the specific formulations of the group's
understanding of an objectively *right* culture in line with human needs,
but Oldham's *The Resurrection of Christendom* (1940) was typical,
asserting that social life should 'contribute to the growth of free and
responsible persons, realizing their vocation as sons of God and living in
relations of mutual trust, obligation and service'.[190] God, Oldham wrote
in the *CNL* that year, had meant people to live 'as responsible persons
serving one another in a genuine community'.[191] The stress on *responsible* freedom was seen as distinctly Christian. It was not a *laissez-faire*
argument for leaving people to fend for themselves: *genuine* freedom
and responsibility, given focused attention in Chapter 6, required an
ethic of service to others, a healthy *community* and acceptance of human
dependence. In his introduction to the Oxford conference report,
Oldham described 'the fundamental demonic element common to all
forms of social life' as the aim to be 'absolutely sovereign, free from all
constraint, wholly self-sufficient'.[192] This argument was made by other
Christians, and recurred often in the group.[193] The modern 'boundless
ego of the isolated self' encouraged an individualist denial of 'man's true
nature' as 'dependent' on God and his 'fellow-men'.[194] The 'humanist cult
of personality', Oldham claimed, was based upon 'a false view of human
nature' that ignored the need for bonds of 'obligation and responsibility'
to God and to other people.[195] Oldham saw the Christian mission as
elucidating a 'massive social philosophy', making mutual interdependence 'part of the furniture of the mind of the common man', advocating
social reforms and creating forms of Christian 'community'.[196]

Enabling responsible freedom, awareness of dependence, an ethic of service and community meant bringing people into 'right relations' with God, other people and nature.[197] In an early CCFCL document, Oldham approved Maritain's description of a 'rational' society compatible with Christianity as 'communal', 'personalist' and 'peregrinal'.[198] He later enumerated seven principles for judging 'social and political systems and policies': after responsible freedom came tolerance, social justice, pluralism, the family, reverence for nature and the universality of the Church.[199] Temple's *CNL* supplement, 'What Christians Stand for in the Secular World' (which had been originally drafted by Oldham in consultation with the Moot), named five core Christian 'decisions': 'for God who has spoken'; 'for neighbour'; 'for man as rooted in nature', 'for history' and 'for the gospel and the Church'.[200] These relationships had to be not only accepted but also lived out in 'community': 'mass society', however, had extinguished the communities in which they could be experienced. In a world of false ideas and decayed social bonds, living a Christian life was nearly (or utterly) impossible: 'the free, responsible person, living in community with other persons, whom the New Testament has in view', Oldham argued, 'has in modern society to an alarming degree ceased to exist'.[201] There was only one way out: 'We have to live our way back to social health'.[202]

Conclusion

In the *CNL* in January 1946, Kathleen Bliss claimed that Christianity (unlike some eastern religions and 'certain modern movements') did not encourage 'a mystical withdrawal from the world': 'for Christians the world is God's creation and the sphere in which His will has to be fulfilled'.[203] The 'modern' world, however, posed fundamental obstacles in achieving Christian aims. In 1948, Emil Brunner (in an essay in the *CNL*) identified three false 'watchwords of modern man' that violated Christianity's view 'of the essence of man as person': 'freedom as independence, creativity without responsibility and power without reverence'.[204] The Oldham group saw Christianity as a guide for steering society away from such a false culture. The group held that human and divine realms were distinct but could be brought into mutually constructive relation. Bridging the divide depended on 'middle axioms' and a true anthropological understanding of what humans *are* and the lives they needed to flourish. A new society would come not simply from new ideas but only through constructing a new social reality in line with human nature. Utopianism was rejected, and the relative aim of a '*more* Christian society' was a key middle way.

Individualist interpretations of the faith and those that sharply divided sacred and secular realms were rejected, as was an optimistic anthropocentrism seen to be common to secularism and liberal Protestantism. A return to 'social health' was not simply a religious issue but involved renewal of society as a whole.

Several theological streams came together in the Oldham group's religious synthesis: a self-critical Protestant liberalism, Niebuhr's 'Christian realism', Maritain's democratic 'New Christendom' and varieties of 'personalism'. There were periodic concerns that, in the process of combining different influences, the group's would become insufficiently specific and Christian.[205] However, for some, Anglicanism's own ambivalent position was one of its strengths, making it uniquely capable as a basis for ecumenical leadership: 'No single view of the Church', Oldham wrote, 'can be regarded as expressing the mind of the whole of the Church of England': 'It has "a character and a story which are hard to fit into the conventional categories of continental Christianity. The Anglican was and is a bad Lutheran, a bad Calvinist, and certainly no Papist."'[206] These influences were 'theological' but also had a secular utility. Oldham demanded that Christians devote themselves to understanding 'the relevance of Christian teaching to life as it has to be lived in the dust and heat of the conflicts of modern society'.[207]

Niebuhr and Maritain seemed to offer guideposts for a Christianity that would correct 'liberal' errors while remaining socially engaged, generating a political alternative to totalitarianism. However, 'continental' Protestantism – referring mainly to Lutheranism and to Barth's 'theology of crisis' – served, in contrast, primarily as something *against which* the group positioned themselves: for all their interest in (and agreement with) aspects of Barth's stress on God's ultimate unfathomability as a corrective to liberalism, his insistence on a radical discontinuity between God and man was of no use in building a 'more Christian society'. Baillie noted that many continental Protestants argued, as he put it in their language, for an *'absolute Trennung zwischen Religion und Politik'*, i.e. 'an absolute separation between religion and politics'. Whether this view of continental Protestantism in the 1930s and 1940s is *correct* is beyond my scope, but some will no doubt see the group's rejection of Barth as based upon (possibly wilful) misunderstandings of his theology. However, the point is that for all of its eclecticism and belief in a theological 'convergence', the Oldham group's endeavour was laden with intellectual conflict. Then, too, international ecumenism – the Oldham group's main context – was itself not always welcomed by Christians: Roman Catholics and conservative evangelicals in Britain and America, for example, were particularly critical of its positions.[208] Despite its claims of discerning a generally 'Christian' viewpoint, then, the group's perspectives remained highly selective and distinct from the views of many Christians. But alongside such religious debates, the Oldham group's pursuit of a more Christian society also required it to enter into a profound engagement with the 'secular', to which the next chapter turns.

Notes

1 *CNL* 1S, 1 November 1939, J. H. Oldham, 'What Is God Doing?', p. 1.
2 LPL W. Temple 6, fos. 28–31, 'Notes by J. Middleton Murry' [*c.* May 1938], p. 4. Emphasis in original.
3 *Moot Papers*, M2, p. 114.
4 *CNL* 51S, 16 October 1940, Richard Russell, 'The Rebuilding of Europe', p. 2.
5 *CNL* 88S, 1 July 1941, J. H. Oldham, 'The Predicament of Society and the Way Out. II', p. 1; *CNL* 228L, 21 February 1945, p. 7.
6 *Moot Papers*, M2, p. 119; M14, p. 506.
7 *CNL* 209L, 31 May 1944, pp. 3–4.
8 *CNL* 223L, 13 December 1944, p. 5.
9 *CNL* 241L, 22 August 1945, p. 8. Emphasis in original.
10 *Churches Survey Their Task*, p. 41.
11 *Ibid.*, p. 110.
12 *CNL* 88S, 1 July 1941, J. H. Oldham, 'The Predicament of Society and the Way Out. II', p. 6; *CNL* 59S, 11 December 1940, J. H. Oldham, 'Predicament and Salvation', p. 2.
13 *CNL* 70S, 26 February 1941, J. H. Oldham, 'Predicament', p. 1.
14 *CNL* 59S, 11 December 1940, J. H. Oldham, 'Predicament and Salvation', p. 2; *CNL* 71L, 5 March 1941, p. 3.
15 Oldham, *Resurrection of Christendom*, p. 13; *CNL* 45S, 4 September 1940, J. H. Oldham, 'The Way Out', p. 4.
16 *CNL* 57S, 27 November 1940, J. H. Oldham, 'The Demand for a Christian Lead', pp. 2–3.
17 *CNL* 59S, 11 December 1940, J. H. Oldham, 'Predicament and Salvation', p. 3.
18 J. H. Oldham, *Work in Modern Society* (London: SCM, 1950), p. 44.
19 LPL Lang 25, fos. 315–25, J. M. Murry, 'Towards a Christian Theory of Society', n.d. [discussed September 1938], p. 11.
20 OA 14/2/12, H. A. Hodges, 'Comments on Middleton Murry's Paper', n.d. [discussed September 1938], p. 3.
21 OA 13/4/87, 'Appendix B'.
22 *CNL* 24L, 10 April 1940, p. 2.
23 *CNL* 312S, 26 May 1948, J. H. Oldham, 'Mr. Murry on the Free Society – II', p. 14.
24 *Theology*, 47:291 (September 1944), 207–9 (p. 208). Emphasis in original.
25 F. R. Barry, 'The Churches and the Common Life', *Spectator*, 13 May 1938, in LPL Lang 25, fos. 272–3.

26 Moberly, 'Christian Faith and the Common Life', pp. 560–1.
27 IOE MOO/83, 'The Religious Foundations of the Frontier', July 1942, p. 5.
28 *Moot Papers*, M15, p. 537.
29 *CNL* 205L, 5 April 1944.
30 *CNL* 206S, 19 April 1944, Alexander Miller, 'Theological and Lay Responsibility', p. 11.
31 *CNL* 278L, 22 January 1947, p. 2. Emphasis in original.
32 *CNL* 303S, 21 January 1948, Moira Symons, 'Home and Community', p. 10.
33 *CNL* 318L, 18 August 1948, p. 3.
34 Duncan B. Forrester, 'God's Will in a Time of Crisis: John Baillie as a Social Theologian', in David Fergusson (ed.), *Christ, Church and Society: Essays on John Baillie and Donald Baillie* (Edinburgh: T. & T. Clark, 1993), pp. 221–33 (p. 229).
35 Oldham, *Christianity and the Race Problem*, pp. 21–2.
36 LPL LC 168, no. 9 (1930), Oldham, 'The Christian Attitude to Racial Relations', pp. 1–2.
37 Visser 't Hooft and Oldham, *Church and Its Function in Society*, pp. 209–10. See also Clements, 'Oldham and Baillie', pp. 47–9.
38 OA 13/5/1, J. H. Oldham, 'The Christian Ethos: Its Source, Nature and Authority', July 1939, p. 3.
39 *CNL* 216L, 6 September 1944, p. 6; *CNL* 220L, 1 November 1944, p. 1.
40 *CNL* 125L, 18 March 1942, p. 3; *Moot Papers*, M12, p. 429 (Moberly).
41 *CNL* 124S, 11 March 1942, W. G. Symons, 'Changing Industry and Moral Decision', p. 3.
42 *Moot Papers*, M19, p. 662.
43 *Ibid.*, M2, p. 103; Clements, *Faith on the Frontier*, pp. 326–7; Smith, *Oxford 1937*, pp. 29–38. For criticism, see Duncan B. Forrester, *Beliefs, Values and Policies: Conviction Politics in a Secular Age* (Oxford: Clarendon Press, 1989), pp. 16–35. On Baillie, see Clements, 'Oldham and Baillie', p. 48; Forrester, 'God's Will in a Time of Crisis', p. 229; and Baillie's report, *God's Will for Church and Nation* (London: SCM, 1946), pp. 45–6.
44 *Malvern, 1941: The Life of the Church and the Order of Society* (London: Longmans, 1941), p. vii; *Christian World*, 10 September 1942, p. 5.
45 *Moot Papers*, M14, pp. 487–8.
46 IOE MOO/5, 'Notes on the "Order" by A. R. Vidler', n.d., p. 1.
47 T. S. Eliot, *The Idea of a Christian Society* (London: Faber and Faber, 1939), p. 47; *Moot Papers*, M2, p. 92; *CNL* 97L, 3 September 1941, pp. 2–3.
48 *Moot Papers*, M19, p. 683.
49 *Theology*, 48:302 (August 1945), p. 169.
50 *Moot Papers*, M18, pp. 638–9; M1, p. 51.
51 Mannheim, *Diagnosis*, p. 115.
52 LPL W. Temple 11, fo. 274, Oldham to Temple, 4 October 1944, p. 2.
53 Bernard G. Reardon (ed.), *Liberal Protestantism* (London: Adam & Charles Black, 1968), pp. 51–65; Eric Lord and Marjorie Reeves, 'Themes of the 1930s', in Marjorie Reeves (ed.), *Christian Thinking and Social Order: Conviction*

Politics from the 1930s to the Present Day (London: Cassell, 1999), pp. 3–18 (p. 4); Barnes, *Nazism, Liberalism, and Christianity*, pp. 47–9.

54 Grimley, *Citizenship*, pp. 6–7.

55 Barnes, *Nazism, Liberalism, and Christianity*, p. 58.

56 *Ibid.*, p. 59; Markku Ruotsila, *The Origins of Christian Anti-Imperialism: Conservative Evangelicals and the League of Nations* (Washington, DC: Georgetown University Press, 2008), pp. 25–6; Edwards, 'God's Totalitarianism', p. 286; Lyon, 'Idea of a Christian Sociology', p. 236.

57 Zeilstra, *European Unity in Ecumenical Thinking*, pp. 9–10; Richard Wightman Fox, *Reinhold Niebuhr: A Biography* (New York: Pantheon, 1985), pp. 180–1.

58 Thompson, *For God and Globe*, pp. 22, 122–7.

59 Hastings, *A History*, p. 294; Lawson, *Church of England and the Holocaust*, pp. 8–9; John Nurser, 'The "Ecumenical Movement" Churches, "Global Order", and Human Rights: 1938–1949', *Human Rights Quarterly*, 25:4 (2003), 841–81 (p. 847); *Moot Papers*, M10, p. 350; M19, p. 656.

60 Lord and Reeves, 'Themes of the 1930s', p. 4. Wilkinson, *Dissent or Conform?*, p. 88; Lawson, *Church of England and the Holocaust*, p. 9. Thompson, *God and Globe*, p. 122.

61 LPL Lang 25, fos. 305–14, 'The Problems and Tasks of the Council on the Christian Faith and the Common Life', n.d. [discussed September 1938], p. 1.

62 *CNL* 232S, 18 April 1945, Daniel Jenkins, 'A Map of Theology To-day', pp. 11–12. See similar suggestions of a continuing vitality of liberalism in *Christian World*, 12 September 1946, p. 1.

63 Gary J. Dorrien, *The Making of American Liberal Theology: Idealism, Realism and Modernity, 1900–1950* (Louisville, KY: Westminster John Knox Press, 2003), esp. pp. 534–44; Gary J. Dorrien, *Social Ethics in the Making: Interpreting an American Tradition* (Chichester: John Wiley, 2011 [2008]), p. 239.

64 Hastings, *A History*, p. 293. See also Paul T. Phillips, *A Kingdom on Earth: Anglo-American Social Christianity, 1880–1940* (University Park: Pennsylvania State University Press, 1996), p. 46; Fox, *Reinhold Niebuhr*, p. 181; Heather A. Warren, *Theologians of a New World Order: Reinhold Niebuhr and the Christian Realists, 1920–1948* (Oxford: Oxford University Press, 1997). R. John Elford and Ian S. Markham, eds., *The Middle Way: Theology, Politics and Economics in the Later Thought of R. H. Preston* (London: SCM, 2000), pp. 46–51.

65 Niebuhr attended the fifth (September 1939) and seventeenth (June 1943) meetings.

66 Phillips, *Kingdom on Earth*, pp. 33–4; Fox, *Reinhold Niebuhr*, 180–1.

67 Wilfred M. McClay, *The Masterless: Self and Society in America* (Chapel Hill: University of North Carolina Press, 1994), p. 100.

68 *Ibid.*, p. 178.

69 Wilfred M. McClay, in 'Obama's Favorite Theologian? A Short Course in Reinhold Niebuhr', 4 May 2009, www.pewforum.org/2009/05/04/obamas-favorite-theologian-a-short-course-on-reinhold-niebuhr/(accessed4November 2018).

70 *CNL* 223L, 13 December 1944, p. 2.

71 *Moot Papers*, M17, p. 610.

72 Patrick Deneen, *Democratic Faith* (Princeton: Princeton University Press, 2005), pp. 246–60; Stanley Hauerwas, *Dispatches from the Front: Theological Engagements with the Secular* (Durham, NC: Duke University Press, 1994), pp. 98–104.

73 Reinhold Niebuhr, *The Children of Light and the Children of Darkness: A Vindication of Democracy and a Critique of Its Traditional Defense* (Chicago: University of Chicago Press, 2011 [1944]), p. xxxii.

74 Gary Dorrien, foreword to Niebuhr, *The Children of Light and the Children of Darkness*, p. xii.

75 Hastings, *A History*, pp. 256, 293.

76 Stephen Schloesser, 'The Rise of a Mystic Modernism: Maritain and the Sacrificed Generation of the Twenties', in Rajesh Heynickx and Jan De Maeyer (eds.), *The Maritain Factor: Taking Religion into Interwar Modernism* (Leuven: Leuven University Press, 2010), pp. 28–39 (p. 30). Moyn, *Christian Human Rights*, pp. 65–100.

77 Bernard McGinn, *Thomas Aquinas's 'Summa theologiae': A Biography* (Princeton: Princeton University Press, 2014), pp. 117–209, esp. p. 163. Thomas F. O'Meara, *Thomas Aquinas: Theologian* (Notre Dame: University of Notre Dame Press, 1997), pp. 152–200.

78 Schloesser, 'Mystic Modernism', pp. 30–1.

79 *Ibid.*, 30.

80 Michael Einfalt, 'Debating Literary Autonomy: Jacques Maritain versus André Gide', in Heynickx and De Maeyer, *Maritain Factor*, pp. 152–63 (p. 154).

81 Hastings, *A History*, p. 298.

82 Grimley, 'Civil Society and the Clerisy', pp. 239–41. Jason Harding, ' "The Just Impartiality of a Christian Philosopher": Jacques Maritain and T. S. Eliot', in Heynickx and De Maeyer, *Maritain Factor*, pp. 181–91.

83 Maritain's ideas were similar to Oldham's 'before and during and since the Oxford Conference', and fitted 'Murry's conception of a clerisy': LPL Lang 26, fos. 52–64, John Baillie, 'Paper on Maritain's *True Humanism*', n.d. [discussed January 1939], p. 9. A draft CCFCL memo 'owed much to *True Humanism*', but 'its main positions had been arrived at independently': Lang 26, fos. 38–49, 'Statement of Policy', 25 November 1938, p. 5.

84 *Moot Papers*, M3, pp. 126–83.

85 LPL Lang 26, fos. 52–64, John Baillie, 'Paper on Maritain's *True Humanism*', pp. 1–2.

86 *Ibid.*, p. 2.

87 *Ibid.*, p. 7. Emphasis in original.

88 *Ibid.*, p. 7.

89 *Ibid.*, pp. 5, 8.

90 *Ibid.*, pp. 9, 12. See also LPL Lang 26, fos. 98–124, Oldham's 'Handbook' sent to Lang on 4 January 1939, p. 9.

91 LPL Lang 26, fos. 52–64, John Baillie, 'Paper on Maritain's *True Humanism*', p. 10.

92 *Ibid.*, pp. 7–8.

93 *Ibid.*, p. 10.

94 *Ibid.*, pp. 4–5.

95 *Ibid.*, pp. 9–10.

96 Kurlberg has suggested the Moot could be classified as neo-Thomist in 'Resisting Totalitarianism', p. 517; and 'The Moot', p. 228.

97 E.g. *CNL* 9S, 27 December 1939, Ernest Barker, 'The Papal Encyclical'; 11L, 10 January 1940, p. 4; 38L, 17 July 1940, pp. 3–4; 78L, 23 April 1941, p. 1; 64L, 15 January 1941, pp. 1–2; 83L, 28 May 1941, p. 4; 127L, 1 April 1942, p. 4.

98 Dawson, *Religion and the Modern State*, pp. 135–6. Critiques of political Catholicism: *Moot Papers*, M10, p. 360 (Hodges); M18, p. 628 (Mannheim), pp. 648–9 (Hodges and Miller); *CNL* 246S, 31 October 1945, Reinhold Niebuhr, 'The Religious Level of the World Crisis', p. 10.

99 Clements, *Faith on the Frontier*, pp. 270–2. J. H. Oldham, *Life Is Commitment* (London: SCM, 1953), pp. 41–2.

100 Clements, *Faith on the Frontier*, p. 272; D. Densil Morgan, *Barth Reception in Britain* (Edinburgh: T. & T. Clark, 2010), p. 35.

101 OA 16/2/115, J. H. Oldham, 'Can Christianity Become an Effective Historical Force?', *Christianity and Crisis*, 6 March 1944, pp. 2–5 (p. 3).

102 See also his *CNL* book: Karl Barth, *A Letter to Great Britain from Switzerland* (London: Sheldon Press, 1941).

103 *Moot Papers*, M3, p. 139.

104 Karl Barth, *The Epistle to the Romans* (1933), quoted in Lord and Reeves, 'Themes of the 1930s', pp. 4–5. Nurser, 'Ecumenical Movement', p. 847.

105 OA 14/7/10, John Baillie, 'Comments on Middleton Murry's Paper', n.d. [discussed September 1938], p. 2.

106 *Moot Papers*, M3, p. 171; and M4, p. 205.

107 See Morgan, *Barth Reception*, pp. 164, 177–9, 183, 185–6, 189–90. *Moot Papers*, M18, p. 627.

108 Clements, *Faith on the Frontier*, p. 373.

109 *CNL* 232S, 18 April 1945, Daniel Jenkins, 'A Map of Theology To-day'.

110 OA 14/5/1, 'Paper Read at the Moot, Sept. 23–26, 1938', p. 3. See also *Moot Papers*, M2, pp. 72–4.

111 John Middleton Murry, *The Price of Leadership* (London: SCM, 1939), pp. 108–9.

112 *Moot Papers*, M17, p. 602.

113 *Ibid.*, M3, pp. 138–43.

114 *Ibid.*, M3, p. 141.

115 *Ibid.*, M3, pp. 141, 171.

116 *Ibid.*, M3, p. 156.

117 IOE MOO/63a, H. A. Hodges, 'Christian Thinking To-day', p. 11. These critiques were left out of the published version of the paper: *CNL* 305S, 18 February 1948, H. A. Hodges, 'Christianity and the Modern World View – I'.

118 BC BAI-05-06, Revd Thomas F. Torrance, 'Christian Thinking Today'. See also *Moot Papers*, pp. 441–3; and Clements, *Faith on the Frontier*, p. 383. On Torrance, see Morgan, *Barth Reception*, pp. 224–8, 248–51.

119 IOE MOO/70, Shaw, 'Criticism of T. F. Torrance's Paper', pp. 1, 2.

120 *Moot Papers*, M13, p. 468.

121 IOE MOO/71, H. A. Hodges, 'Barthianism and Christian Thinking', p. 1. Also *Moot Papers*, p. 443.

122 *CNL* 323S, 27 October 1948, Reinhold Niebuhr, 'We Are Men and Not God', p. 11.

123 *Ibid.*, p. 13.

124 *Ibid.*, pp. 14, 10.

125 *CNL* 326S, 8 December 1948, Karl Barth, 'A Preliminary Reply to Dr. Reinhold Niebuhr'.

126 *CNL* 332S, 2 March 1949, Reinhold Niebuhr, 'An Answer to Karl Barth', pp. 75, 76–7.

127 *Theology*, 52:344 (February 1949), 41–3.

128 LPL Lang 26, fos. 65–74, H. A. Hodges, 'Towards a Plan for a New *Summa*', n.d. [discussed January 1939], p. 7.

129 Murry, *Price of Leadership*, pp. 108–9.

130 *CNL* 246S, 31 October 1945, Reinhold Niebuhr, 'The Religious Level of the World Crisis', p. 10.

131 *CNL* 11S, 10 January 1940, Reinhold Niebuhr, 'Christianity and Political Justice', p. 3. *CNL* 299S, 26 November 1947, Michael Foster, 'Some Remarks on the Relations of Science and Religion', p. 15.

132 Mannheim, *Diagnosis*, p. 113.

133 *CNL* 324L, 10 November 1948, p. 1.

134 *Church Times*, 23 July 1937, p. 79. Cf. Michael P. DeJonge, 'Martin Luther, Dietrich Bonhoeffer, and Political Theologies', in *Oxford Research Encyclopedia (Religion)*, August 2016, DOI: 10.1093/acrefore/9780199340378.013.307 (accessed 14 September 2016).

135 Brunner had participated in Oldham's 'Christianity and Reality' group in the 1930s; Thompson, *God and Globe*, p. 125. See also Smith, *Oxford 1937*, p. 194; and Clements, *Faith on the Frontier*, pp. 263, 272, 317–18.

136 Clements, *Faith on the Frontier*, p. 272. Terence Renaud, 'Human Rights as Radical Anthropology: Protestant Theology and Ecumenism in the Transwar Era', *Historical Journal*, 60:2 (2017), 493–518.

137 OA 12/5/1, Brunner, 'On Christian Ethics, I', n.d., p. 4.

138 *CNL* 302S, 7 January 1948, Emil Brunner, 'Man and Technics – Whither?'

139 *Moot Papers*, M7, p. 282.

140 Thompson, *God and Globe*, p. 125.

141 Clements, *Faith on the Frontier*, pp. 270–3; Oldham, *Life Is Commitment*, pp. 23, 31, 40–1.

142 Paul Helm, *Faith with Reason* (Oxford: Clarendon Press, 2000), p. 120; *Moot Papers*, M1, pp. 44–5.

143 Oldham, *Life Is Commitment*, pp. 29–32.

144 Clements, *Faith on the Frontier*, p. 273. Emphasis in original.

145 *Ibid.*, pp. 28–9. See also *CNL* 281S, 19 March 1947, J. H. Oldham, 'Life as Dialogue'.

146 *Moot Papers*, M1, pp. 44–5, 47, 50; M14, p. 491; M16, pp. 547–8; M17, p. 578; M19, pp. 681, 684. See also J. H. Oldham (ed.), *Real Life Is Meeting* (London: Sheldon Press, 1942), no. 14 in the *CNL* Books series.
147 *CNL* 112S, 17 December 1941, Oldham, 'All Real Life Is Meeting'.
148 *Ibid.*, p. 1.
149 *Ibid.*, pp. 2–3.
150 *Ibid.*, p. 3.
151 *CNL* 114S, 31 December 1941, Oldham, 'Superman or Son of God?', p. 1; *CNL* 104L, 22 October 1941, p. 1.
152 *CNL* 281S, 19 March 1947, J. H. Oldham, 'Life as Dialogue', p. 7.
153 *CNL* 246S, 31 October 1945, Reinhold Niebuhr, 'The Religious Level of the World Crisis', p. 11.
154 *The Times*, 5 October 1938, p. 15.
155 LPL Lang 26, fos. 38–49, CCFCL Statement of Policy, 25 November 1938, p. 5.
156 LPL Lang 26, fos. 147–9, Oldham to Lang, 25 April 1939; IOE MOO/14, 'Resolution Passed at Meeting of the Council on February 6th, 1940'; *CNL* 86S, 18 June 1941, J. H. Oldham, 'The Predicament of Society and the Way Out', p. 3.
157 Oldham, *Resurrection of Christendom*, p. 25.
158 *Moot Papers*, M14, p. 518.
159 *Ibid.*, M8, p. 308 (Oakeshott); M17, p. 610 (Oldham); M13, p. 448 (Oldham); M17, p. 610 (Niebuhr).
160 'It won't do to be too much afraid of the "blue-print"': LPL Lang 26, fos. 205–8, Hetherington to Oldham, 1 July 1940, p. 2.
161 *Moot Papers*, M2, p. 102; M18, p. 622. The image of a 'visitor from Mars' also appeared in OA 9/5/19, 'The Christian Witness in the Present Crisis', 6 October 1943, p. 1.
162 OA 9/3/65, Gilbert Shaw to Oldham, n.d. [1941], p. 1.
163 *CNL*, 45S, 4 September 1940, J. H. Oldham, 'The Way Out', p. 1.
164 J. H. Oldham, *The Root of Our Troubles: Two Broadcast Talks* (London: SCM, 1941), p. 4.
165 *CNL* 218L, 4 October 1944, p. 2.
166 Oldham, *Resurrection of Christendom*, p. 52.
167 *CNL* 241L, 22 August 1945, p. 1.
168 Karl Mannheim, *Man and Society in an Age of Reconstruction: Studies in Modern Social Structure* (London: Kegan Paul, Trench, Trübner, 1942 [1940]), pp. 121–5, 200; Karl Mannheim, *Freedom, Power and Democratic Planning* (New York: Oxford University Press, 1950), pp. 179–81.
169 *CNL* 45S, 4 September 1940, J. H. Oldham, 'The Way Out', p. 1. Also, *CNL* 237S, 27 June 1945, J. H. Oldham, 'Prospect for Christendom', p. 8.
170 *CNL* 45S, 4 September 1940, J. H. Oldham, 'The Way Out', p. 4.
171 *CNL* 59S, 11 December 1940, J. H. Oldham, 'Predicament and Salvation', p. 3.
172 *Moot Papers*, M2, p. 92; M18, p. 620.
173 *CNL* 88S, 1 July 1941, J. H. Oldham, 'The Predicament of Society and the Way Out. II', p. 5.

174 IOE MOO/44, A. R. Vidler, 'Notes on Some Cultural Issues' [Spring 1941]. See also OA 14/6/4, T. S. Eliot, 'Cultural Forces in the Human Order', 1 November 1944; and *CNL* 257S, 3 April 1946, V. A. Demant, 'The Incompetence of Unaided Virtue or the Mischief of Ideals', p. 5.

175 *The Times*, 5 October 1938, p. 15.

176 *CNL* 88S, 1 July 1941, J. H. Oldham, 'The Predicament of Society and the Way Out. II', p. 7.

177 *CNL* 175L, 3 March 1943, p. 2.

178 OA 13/6/43, typed extract from the *New English Weekly*, 28 November 1946, p. 3.

179 *CNL* 6L, 6 December 1939, p. 3.

180 *CNL* 57S, 27 November 1940, J. H. Oldham, 'The Demand for a Christian Lead', pp. 1–2.

181 IOE MOO/83, 'The Religious Foundations of the Frontier', 19 July 1942, p. 11.

182 *CNL* 154S, 7 October 1942, Walter Moberly, 'The Christian Frontier', p. 2.

183 Oldham was quoting Kurt Hahn: see *Moot Papers*, M9, p. 325.

184 OA 14/5/13, J. M. Murry, 'The Agricultural Community and the Future of Society', 17 June 1943, p. 3.

185 *CNL* 209L, 31 May 1944, pp. 3–4.

186 *CNL* 244L, 3 October 1945, p. 2.

187 *CNL* 39S, 24 July 1940, Owen Barfield, 'Effective Approach to Social Change', p. 2.

188 McVey, 'Backgrounds', pp. 187–8.

189 *CNL* 69L, 19 February 1941, p. 1.

190 Oldham, *Resurrection of Christendom*, p. 29; see also *ibid.*, pp. 13, 27.

191 *CNL* 57S, 27 November 1940, J. H. Oldham, 'The Demand for a Christian Lead', p. 4.

192 *Churches Survey Their Task*, p. 41.

193 See, e.g., *Guardian*, 24 February 1939, p. 120; and *Church Times*, 2 April 1948, p. 183.

194 *CNL* 45S, 4 September 1940, Oldham, 'The Way Out', p. 1. *CNL* 88S, 1 July 1941, Oldham, 'The Predicament of Society and the Way Out. II', p. 4. *CNL* 154S, 7 October 1942, Walter Moberly, 'The Christian Frontier', p. 3.

195 *CNL* 14L, 31 January 1940, p. 2. Oldham, *Root of Our Troubles*, pp. 4–5.

196 *CNL* 57S, 27 November 1940, J. H. Oldham, 'The Demand for a Christian Lead', pp. 3–4.

197 LPL Lang 26, fos. 223–5, 'An Initiative of the Churches towards a More Christian Society', July 1940, p. 1.

198 'Communal' meant subordinating personal and sectional interests to those of the community. 'Personalist' meant enabling the growth of the 'human person, who has ends that reach beyond society'. 'Peregrinal' meant recognizing 'that man is created for a spiritual and eternal destiny and has on earth no continuing city. It would thus be free from illusory hopes of an earthly utopia.' LPL Lang 26, fos. 38–49, 'Statement of Policy', 25 November 1938, p. 6.

199 Oldham, *Resurrection of Christendom*, pp. 27–33.

200 *CNL* 198S, 29 December 1943, Temple, 'What Christians Stand for in the Secular World'. OA 9/5/12, Oldham to Murry, 24 August 1943, p. 1. See also Clements, *Faith on the Frontier*, pp. 401–2.

201 *CNL* 57S, 27 November 1940, J. H. Oldham, 'The Demand for a Christian Lead', p. 4.

202 *CNL* 45S, 4 September 1940, Oldham, 'The Way Out', p. 4.

203 *CNL* 251L, 9 January 1946, p. 5.

204 *CNL* 302S, 7 January 1948, Emil Brunner, 'Man and Technics – Whither?', p. 14.

205 *Moot Papers*, M2, p. 100 (Vidler and Paton); M12, p. 414 (Oakeshott); M9, p. 332 (Murry); M14, p. 521 (Chaning-Pearce).

206 OA 15/2/64, 'The Church in the Context of the Oxford Conference' (April 1936), p. 7.

207 *CNL* 206L, 19 April 1944, p. 4.

208 *CNL* 319L, 1 September 1948, p. 7.

3

Explorations on the frontier:
II Engaging with 'the secular'

The Oldham group shared religious motivations, theological influences and the aim of a more Christian society, but it also called on Christians to be open to 'secular' knowledge and to work with non-Christians. The term 'secularisation' first appeared widely in the British media from the 1960s, but it was already common in Christian circles – including the Oldham group – from the 1930s. It has been suggested that finer distinctions among 'secularism', 'secularity' and 'secularisation' – a movement, condition and process, respectively – were drawn only in the 1960s; however, these and related words were also being used in similar senses thirty years previously.[1] 'Secular' had neutral, negative and positive connotations in the Oldham group, evoking, respectively, a shared 'common life', a dangerous 'materialism' and an appreciation of science. Group members even saw a role for secular actors and ideas in pursuing a more Christian culture. However, finding a middle way along Oldham's 'frontier' also meant emphasising faith's distinctiveness and its absolute necessity in building a better society. In this chapter, I will consider the group's varied understandings of secularity, lay out the opportunities it saw for working with non-Christians and consider what resources only Christians had that others lacked.

Variations of the secular: neutral, negative and positive

There were neutral, negative and positive views of the 'secular' in the Oldham group, which sometimes even co-existed within a single text.[2] Group members respected the secularity of 'the common life', a label Christians used for everyday relations in a society shared with non-Christians. Putting that term in the CCFCL's name signalled its aim of addressing Christians 'in the hurly-burly of secular activity'.[3] Every Christian, Bliss wrote, lived 'on the frontier', expressing their faith in work, politics and leisure; it was in the common life, Oldham wrote, that 'God's will must be done'.[4] The health of the common life depended on spiritual influences, a degree of cultural homogeneity and a strong sense of community. Society, however, had become materialistic, mixed and mass. Faith was no longer 'the hub of things', in Hodges's words: it persisted via 'the sheer inertia of tradition'.[5] In *The Times* and *CNL*, Oldham condemned the mixed society's aim of 'a post-Christian world'.[6] After the war, the *CNL* and others even labelled Britain a 'post-Christian society', a term that had already been used during the conflict.[7] However, while critical of this trend, the group largely accepted 'the claims of the secular in the secular sphere'. Oldham saw various 'provinces of life' as having 'distinctive ends', some of which could not be subordinated to religion.[8] He insisted on the 'autonomy of the secular', even in areas previously under Church authority; Eliot, similarly, urged the group to resist both radical forms of secularism and what he called a religious 'imperialism of thought' over 'the secular disciplines'.[9] Oldham labelled the *CNL* as 'secular' in the sense of being focused on 'the actual, present world of men's strivings and conflicts': Christians belonged to both 'earthly' and 'heavenly' cities, and they fulfilled their duties to God in the former.[10] Daniel Jenkins saw the *CNL*'s goal as finding a 'Christian duty' in a secular society.[11] Christianity, Hodges said, had both to be 'a formative force' and to receive influences 'from without'.[12] Christianity and secularity thus needed each other.

A potentially healthy balance, however, had been seriously eroded. The Oxford conference report decried the 'secularisation of modern life' and 'secularists', terms also used in the Moot.[13] The Christian press often referred to 'secularism' as a consciously anti-religious (or at least areligious) worldview. As early as the end of the 1920s, Oldham believed that 'secularism' – which he described as 'the demonic attempt to put the world or the self in the place of God' – had already 'stricken the heart of Europe'.[14] Dawson thought secularising tendencies of various kinds had pushed religion out of society and restricted it to 'the inner life', and a 1944 *CNL* essay condemned 'epidemic secularisation'.[15] Oldham argued that the 'mechanisation of life' and collapse of community had destroyed faith.[16] There had been a centuries-long uprooting of Christianity, particularly, it was thought, in the Renaissance, Enlightenment and Victorian eras. Hodges saw a 'steady departure' from Christianity since the Middle Ages, with diverse cultural developments acting as 'a solvent upon the inherited Christianity of Europe'.[17]

Such fears seemed confirmed in army reports, sociological studies, and letters from military chaplains and urban (and suburban) priests. Taken together, they suggested that 90 per cent of youth had no connection to Christianity, that there was widespread ignorance of Christian teachings and that active Christians were a tiny minority, even if most people clung to some vague faith.[18] (In 1947, the *CNL* reported on Mass Observation's survey *A Puzzled People*, which reached similar conclusions.[19]) Oldham argued in 1941 that Britain was 'much more pagan' than people generally supposed.[20] In 1945, Bliss thought the figure of 90 per cent indifference to religion had become widely accepted, even a 'commonplace'.[21]

Many Christians were convinced that religious decline had enabled the rise of a *negative* variety of secularity, namely a 'materialist' worldview. In the 1920s, Oldham had called materialism Christianity's greatest challenge, and he had put addressing secularism at the heart of the Oxford conference's agenda.[22] In the Moot, Walter Oakeshott complained that 'a material view of life was dinned into us by poster, newspaper, magazines, etc', a trend that showed what was 'fundamentally wrong with the present age'.[23] Oldham decried a 'new materialistic religion' in both capitalist and Communist varieties and condemned a secularist ideology promoted by left-wing scientists – such as Julian Huxley, J. D. Bernal and C. H. Waddington – who were now seen by the public as 'the saviours of society'.[24] Hodges complained that only knowledge created by materialist science was taken seriously.[25] Modern atheism, Bliss wrote, defined dependence on God – which was at the heart of the Christian social message – as incompatible with dignity, freedom and responsibility.[26] The 1948 Kinsey Report on male sexuality, for example, was seen as 'powerful propaganda' for a dangerously animalistic view of humanity.[27]

That secularisation had led to totalitarianism became a standard Christian trope across the 1930s.[28] At Oxford 1937, the 'secularist revolt' and subsequent birth of materialist 'cults' were seen as decisive cultural forces.[29] A CCFCL document argued that 'spiritual realities' had been replaced by 'the supremacy of nation, race or class'.[30] At an SCM conference in 1938, Moberly warned that a British totalitarianism might result from 'secularisation' or a 'Godless self-containedness'.[31] A religious vacuum had been filled by the worship of dictators and the deification of nation, party, class or *Volk*. The totalitarianisms – and even science – were depicted in the Moot and *CNL* as political 'religions' or 'faiths'. Dawson thought secularisation had culminated in Communism; Murry called totalitarianism 'a secularised Church'.[32] Michael Polanyi saw totalitarianism resulting from materialism and the divorce of power from morality: Nazism showed 'the plain logic of all purely secular power'.[33] Hodges thought power worship was common to democracy, Communism and Fascism.[34] Oldham argued that ideals of secular self-sufficiency had culminated in totalitarianism; Bliss, similarly, viewed 'German technocrats' as western materialism's 'logical conclusion'.[35] Without transcendental values, only power and self-interest remained: a 'spiritual vacuum', Vidler thought, had made 'fertile seed plots' for authoritarianism.[36] A post-war 'spiritual void' was likewise feared.[37] (For their part, secularists made the counter-argument that totalitarianism had fed on the 'absolute and prescriptive standards' of religion itself.[38])

Even many kinds of explicitly democratic political visions were separated from Christianity by an 'unbridgeable gulf', guided as they were by 'purely secular', materialist assumptions.[39] There seemed little difference between the Communist 'faith' in harnessing material forces to political ends and the liberal belief in progress: both saw humanity as the architect of its destiny.[40] A post-war *CNL* essay praised Karl Popper's *The Open Society and Its Enemies* (1945) for its commitment to freedom but critiqued the author's view of human 'self-sufficiency'.[41] Christians, Vidler wrote, knew that humanity was 'fundamentally incapable' of solving its own destiny.[42] The decay of community – i.e. 'organic social life' – was clearest in totalitarianism (which artificially rebuilt it), but such advanced trends also cast a 'searchlight' on the western situation as a whole.[43] Oldham saw 'corroding' influences everywhere: defeating Nazism would be only the 'first round' in a long spiritual conflict.[44] In the *CNL* in 1940, Niebuhr influentially called Communism and Fascism 'wrong answers to unanswered problems', i.e. perverse responses to what was nonetheless a genuine and disastrous loss of cultural coherence.[45] In 1945 he identified three 'political and social religions': liberal democracy (which envisioned a 'universal community' and 'frictionless harmony' of social development), Marxism (a 'catastrophic' rather than 'evolutionary' version of the same goal) and Fascism ('distinguished by its nationalism, particularism and cynicism').[46] Violet Markham saw a post-war disillusionment that resulted from a materialist view of humanity as 'an accident in a planless universe'.[47]

Nonetheless, the Oldham group also saw secular knowledge as having a positive sense – particularly the natural and social sciences – and critiqued Christians' scepticism about science. Documents of the CCFCL urged that science must have a 'full and rightful place' in any new social order.[48] A social ethic that ignored medical psychology and psychotherapy, for example, would be incomplete.[49] Christians, Oldham proclaimed in 1942, must cast fears of scientific knowledge (by which he meant new medical, psychological, economic and sociological findings) 'to the winds' and instead welcome it 'with both arms as an indispensable ally'.[50] Even atheism, Bliss wrote, offered a 'searching challenge' to the faithful to reconsider the meaning of God.[51] Christian failures were admitted. Oldham deplored the Church's 'defensive attitude' to the 'gift' of science, the authority of which – in its own 'province' – had to be 'unreservedly acknowledged'.[52] He insisted there were benefits that only science could offer and regretted that scientists seemed to have a greater 'zeal and missionary fervour' for social improvement than did Christians.[53] In the *CNL* in 1943, Temple critiqued the 'timidity' that had led Christians to oppose science.[54] Niebuhr thought Christians had wrongly insisted on the literal truth of their 'pre-scientific symbols and myths': their 'cultural obscurantism' had limited the appeal of their faith to 'the cultured classes of western Christendom'.[55] Violet Markham admitted that the Church had 'nailed very unfortunate flags to its mast', including hostility to science.[56]

A distinction had to be made, the argument went, between science *as knowledge* and science *as a value system*, a task the war made even more urgent. Control over nature had grown so far, Fenn argued, that the problem was 'its rightful use'.[57] Oldham thought the Church must recognise science's claim to 'cure moral evil' while also pointing to its limits.[58] For Murry, only science, not morality, had advanced, and humanity was thus 'morally quite unprepared' for its new powers.[59] Oldham even called for 'more science, more knowledge, more intelligent planning, more bold and venturesome experiment': such efforts had, however, to be undertaken in the right 'temper'.[60] Hodges, similarly, called science a great achievement but saw Christianity in conflict with 'the spirit and temper of the scientific age'.[61] Clarke thought science could avoid being an 'instrument of Satan' only if seen as 'a gift of the Spirit'.[62] It was not, however, being used in this way: science, originally marked by 'humility and reverence', had become instead, Oldham wrote, a tool of 'pride and ambition'.[63] In 1942 he warned of the dangers of science's 'dazzling possibilities'.[64]

Such 'possibilities' expanded vastly with the birth of the atomic age. Humanity now had an 'unlimited' energy source without knowing what to do with it.[65] The atomic bomb, Bliss wrote, symbolised science's amplification of human power, showing that its place in society had to be rethought in cooperation with scientists and in the light of a clear Church stance towards 'the creative possibilities of man's nature'.[66] Science for the sake of truth – or scientific knowledge that could minister to 'human needs', ameliorate 'the human lot' or enlarge 'human possibilities' – should be welcomed; yoked to the pursuit of power, however, it was a 'disaster'.[67]

The group's consensus thus combined welcoming the natural and social sciences with asserting their limits in understanding reality, humanity's true nature and the purposes of social life. Science was, Oldham wrote, 'not everything': it failed to comprehend the 'living' world of personal relations.[68] Without questioning the 'indispensable' value of 'the scientists as scientists', he insisted that 'science as the instrument of mistaken purposes can land us in hell'.[69] Temple similarly found science to be not necessarily 'the most fundamental and important' perspective on the world.[70] The Moot member Michael Polanyi – a renowned scientist and committed Christian – contributed important arguments about the compatibility of science and Christianity: his *Science, Faith and Society*

(1946) became a late touchstone in this regard.[71] When, in 1948, the *CNL* described 'belief in salvation by knowledge' as Christianity's main cultural rival, it still insisted the Church nevertheless had to 'incorporate' that knowledge in furthering its own aims.[72]

The argument that science and faith might fruitfully work together emerged again in October 1948, when the *CNL* reported on meetings of the Lambeth Conference – the decennial Anglican ecclesiastical assembly – and of the British Association for the Advancement of Science. Bliss saw the gatherings as not opposed to one another: the bishops at Lambeth had welcomed scientific findings and hoped for a 'marriage of true science and true religion'; at the same time, some scientists at the British Association were, she suggested, likely to be practising Christians.[73] Still, they seemed different worlds: one saw science driving progress, the other sought a Christian 'doctrine of man'.[74] But Bliss quoted the claim expressed in the journal *Nature* that science and religion stood together 'in the defence of freedom and the moral, spiritual and cultural values of civilization'.[75] Science and religion were thus inextricably linked, she argued. Christianity should welcome scientific findings, but the Church seemed trapped in traditional forms of thought and evangelism, failing to comprehend 'modern knowledge'.[76] Letters followed from the Bishop of Sheffield and from physicist Sir Lawrence Bragg lamenting the Church's obstinate hostility towards science.[77] Soon thereafter, a *CNL* supplement by Alex Comfort (later known for *The Joy of Sex* but then a doctor and declared 'non-theist') criticised religion's reliance on 'assertions' and resistance to 'evidence'.[78] In replying, Bliss was adamant, however, that Christianity offered equally valid, if different, knowledge.[79]

Going 'part of the way together': religious–secular engagements

The Oldham group's aims, openness to scientific knowledge and assessment of Christianity's weak position in society led it to consider closely secular ideas, movements and institutions. In April 1941, Oldham urged Christians to work on 'the borderland between religion and politics', as politics alone would be powerless against the 'forces which threaten to engulf the life of men'.[80] Modern ethics could no longer be defined solely by religion, however, but required 'pooling many types of experience'.[81] Christian aims had to be translated into secular terms, since professing Christians were a minority (and 'active' Christians a *tiny* minority); policy-making must express a 'common mind' and, ideally, reflect a secular morality 'vitalised and regenerated' by faith.[82] The aim was not an anodyne minimum agreement but a distinctly *Christian* politics that could – somehow – also be expressed in a non-religious language. In the Moot in 1941, Eliot, Hodges, Vidler and Murry agreed that a mixed society limited the potential for an expressly Christian politics.[83] Vidler publicly observed that the 'small minority' of believing Christians would have to cooperate with non-Christians in pursuing secular political objectives.[84] The *CNL* stressed that Christians had to accept that they lived in a society 'ruled by other presuppositions'.[85] A mixed society could not have a directly Christian philosophy; it might, however, have one 'imbued' with a Christian understanding of the 'true ends of life'.[86] The Oldham group thus sought a secular definition of the good society as one that was 'at least *compatible* with the pursuit of Christian ends' and where 'the Christian leaven is free to do its work'.[87]

The idea that cooperation with non-Christians would be possible was eased by the group's belief in a spiritual significance in *some* secular concepts, and its suggestion that there were non-Christians 'equally bewildered' by modernity's 'moral anarchy' who might agree with certain religious principles.[88] In a CFC document, Oldham argued that 'purely secular' movements could contribute to a Christian society, such as those aiming at reorienting education and industry better to serve 'human' needs for 'social relationship'. 'The people whose thought I have been trying to absorb', he explained here, 'are not for the most part preachers; some of them would not call themselves Christians'.[89] Even atheists might express 'Christian' ideas: 'Christ', Oldham stated in a radio talk, 'plainly taught that there would be people in heaven who would be utterly surprised to find themselves there'.[90] He told *CNL* readers that many agnostics and 'rationalists' were as fervent in seeking justice as were Christians.[91] An atheist's life, he claimed, might in fact be even more 'committed to the service of the God whose existence he denies than that of many a professing Christian'.[92] Moberly, too, saw secular social movements potentially contributing to a 'common Christian society'.[93] He voiced a Moot consensus that modern nations could base their politics only on values that were 'common to Christians and humanists'.[94] Ultimately, detaching spiritual *values* from specifically Christian *identity* enabled an openness to diverse initiatives. Temple wrote in the *CNL* that, while the gospel demanded resisting the age's 'dominant tendencies', Marxists and humanists might at times express 'elements of truth' better than Christians.[95] Niebuhr found important insights in modern secularism despite what he called its 'libertarian or equalitarian illusions'.[96]

There were varying opinions in the Moot about just how essential a specifically religious leadership would be and the extent to which its aims were shared with secularists; but a Christian lead was clearly seen as a uniquely motivating force. Hodges addressed religious–secular cooperation in a 1940 *CNL* supplement titled 'Social Standards in a Mixed

Figure 4 Herbert A. Hodges, *c.* 1934

Society', which was based on an earlier Moot paper.[97] He saw roles both for 'natural reason' in defining social ideals and for 'revelation' in discerning a 'common good'.[98] In a mixed society, Christians had to seek non-Christian support by appealing to 'less than the full Christian principle': not only Christians, for example, saw humans as responsible persons, even if only Christianity allowed this ideal to 'yield its full consequences'.[99] Introducing Hodges's essay, Eliot pondered whether 'common principles of behaviour' might enable cooperation with those of other faiths (or of none) in making a 'tolerable' society.[100] Hodges argued that a society where 'everyone is a Christian and behaves accordingly' was unrealisable.[101] Concepts such as 'common sense', 'social health' and 'natural law' (or 'natural reason') were believed capable of supporting a dialogue: Christian positions could be defended on other grounds (such as Kant's prohibition on treating others as means to an end).[102] Still, deeper truths – such as altruism – required Christianity's specific 'moral wisdom'.[103] In January 1944, Hodges argued that the group sought 'a pattern of social health' that would appeal to 'men of intelligence and good will, Christian or not'.[104] Marjorie Reeves used a *CNL* supplement to argue for educating youth in principles shared between Christians and 'humanists' while also 'preparing the ground' for Christianity itself.[105] Murry thought Christianity added little to the principles of a good society derived from natural reason, which were valid 'if all, or some, or no members of the society were Christians'.[106] Oldham likewise separated the 'specific task' of the churches from more general social convictions on which Christians and non-Christians might agree.[107]

In early 1940, the group discussed articles by the enormously popular author H. G. Wells – a leading secularist voice in this period – based on the 'charter of the Rights of Man' in his book *The New World Order* (1940). Oldham had earlier classified Wells's vision of a 'World-State' as a 'democratic' form of totalitarian thinking; here, he lamented that the churches left Wells 'to proclaim on the housetops truths that are inherent in the Christian faith', such as social justice and peace.[108] But he thought Wells understood neither true human 'ends' nor the need for a 'change of heart', leaving his analysis in the end unconvincing.[109] The Moot broadly agreed with V. A. Demant's critique that Wells ignored the necessity of rejuvenating 'community'.[110] Fred Clarke even saw Wells's materialist aims as 'a triple dose of the very thing which had failed', and it was held that his focus on states (especially the *world*-state) and individuals ignored the 'smaller organisations' that existed in between.[111] But Löwe thought it would be wrong to hinder Wells by publicly labelling him a totalitarian, ultimately siding with him over Demant because of the latter's medievalism: such 'allegiance to past forms' was, he said, 'reactionary'.[112] Murry, too, wanted to avoid ' "crabbing" Wells' effort', since Christians lacked a detailed alternative.[113] Moberly praised Wells for at least 'raising a banner against Totalitarianism'.[114]

Education exemplified the need for religious–secular cooperation but also its complexities. Oldham, for example, avoided framing the *CNL* supplement 'Educating for a Free Society' as a 'professedly Christian viewpoint'.[115] Discussing government plans for Christian education in state schools, he cited Catholic modernist philosopher Friedrich von Hügel to argue that, for Christians, religion was both 'everything' and '*not* everything': God's creation had 'spheres and levels' that were 'separate and distinct from the specifically religious sphere', each with its own 'distinctive aims, laws, principles and methods'.[116] Christians must distinguish the generally *human* from the specifically *religious*: the 'full Christian interpretation of life' could hardly predominate in education in a society that was divided about its beliefs.[117] Oldham saw 'no choice' except 'to work with the other nine-tenths of the world on a basis of joint decisions'.[118] A Christian society could nevertheless be seen as a genuinely *human* society, and Christians valued both 'a good human education' and 'a specifically Christian education'.[119] Here, there was room for negotiation. Eliot agreed that even if 'full Christian virtue' required 'full Christian belief', Christians and non-Christians could agree on a 'natural virtue'; still, he warned that Christians often compromised with the world on the shallow and false principle that 'a little Christianity all round' was more vital than 'the full Christian life on the part of the few'.[120] Group members also supported the youth-oriented 'County Badge movement', which – if not explicitly religious – encouraged standards of achievement shared by members of all cultures and faiths within the 'natural or human sphere'.[121] A 'true natural order' that enabled 'a genuinely human life' would help resist the totalitarian denial of human dignity and freedom, offering 'common ground': 'Christians and non-Christians', Oldham urged, 'can travel at least part of the way together'.[122]

The *CNL*'s emphasis in late 1941 on the categories of 'natural' or 'human' as possible bridges to secular thought grew out of Moot discussions about the mainly Lutheran concept of the 'orders of creation' and the Catholic notion of 'natural law'. The orders of creation suggested there was divine legitimation of certain social institutions and conventions, but the concept's misuse by the pro-Nazi *Deutsche Christen* and scepticism about 'continental Protestantism' limited its appeal within the group.[123] Oldham saw pre-war German debates over them as a 'mistake'.[124] However, 'natural law' kept reappearing in Moot discussions (in Vidler's words) 'like a recurring decimal'.[125] It was a focus at Moot meetings in July 1940 and August 1941. The latter discussed a paper by Anglican Christian socialist Ruth Kenyon, who saw natural law as useful in defining the political order, demarcating natural from supernatural and legitimating critical reason: it seemed an objective social standard that was applicable to (and discernible by) all people, not just Christians. It specified a 'hierarchy of ends' that, first, corresponded to the medieval social order 'as a community of communities, not as a congeries of individual atoms' and, second, gave standards for evaluating social life: the economy, for example, should be judged by its satisfaction of human needs rather than by the profits it generated.[126] But natural law had its limits. Hodges thought it medieval, Moberly called it 'static' and Oldham saw it as a distraction.[127] But Vidler explored natural law in the pages of *Theology*, seeing it as a basis for a new social order, and he later co-edited a book on the concept.[128] (Reviewing that book, Hodges doubted that non-Christians would agree with a view of a natural order that, however open-minded, was obviously and deeply Christian.[129]) The group broadly concluded that natural law was too freighted by past interpretations and present disputes in a similar way to that in which the 'orders of creation' were theologically flawed and politically tainted: one was too

Catholic, the other too Lutheran. (Niebuhr argued that there was a need for a 'Protestant natural law'.[130]) Still, this discussion moved the group forward in its search for evaluative principles for the social order that did not depend on specifically *Christian* ideas (or at least on Christian *revelation*). The Church could contribute to defining 'a healthy *natural* order' and circumvent 'hindrances to the good life'.[131]

Ultimately, the group developed a style of thinking that, if theologically vague, was at least reminiscent of natural law: by mixing anthropology and history, Oldham thought, Christianity's truth could win over even those who denied its 'creedal basis'.[132] There were various ways of describing what resulted. Baillie compared natural law to what 'the ordinary Englishman' would call 'certain eternal moral laws'; Dawson saw it as essentially saying 'everybody knew the difference between right and wrong'.[133] Fenn compared it to a social ideal that 'most decent, unprejudiced men can see and desire'.[134] Mannheim envisioned 'basic functional rules for society' – such as honesty, mutual helpfulness and social justice – that were shared by the major religions and derived from 'family and the basic social group'.[135] (Dawson saw similarities between natural law and Mannheim's 'demand for a basic minimum ethic'.[136]) The goal of seeking what was genuinely 'human' was one way of expressing this type of thinking in the group, not least as a means to bring Christians and non-Christians together.[137] In early 1945, Oldham suggested that renewing Christianity required fighting for 'the *human* as part of God's created order'.[138] In the *CNL*, Barbara Ward insisted that Europeans need not choose between American or Soviet versions of 'centralization, mass organization, mass diffusion of ideas, uncritical scientificism [*sic*] and naïve materialism' but should instead work for 'the more human and therefore more Christian order'.[139] Oldham praised Murry's *The Free Society* (1948) for its defence of 'a genuinely human life'.[140]

Defending the truly 'human' was not satisfactory for everyone, and arguments continued to be made for a more specific equivalent to natural law.[141] However, the group remained committed to translating Christian precepts into non-religious idioms after the war. In 1946, Bliss reported comments by George MacLeod arguing that, for non-Christians, the usual presentation of the gospel seemed like 'some mediaeval treatise in demonology', internally logical but meaningless in the present 'frame of discourse'. While Christians assumed that 'Christendom' (in which religious standards were widely accepted) still existed, McLeod argued, it had already disappeared: no longer 'like an army billeted in every house in the land', faith had 'withdrawn into hedge-hog positions in a vast waste of incomprehension and of alien thought forms'.[142] And in a context in which God had ceased to be intelligible, Bliss wrote, Christian affirmations were useless: a vast effort was needed 'to give a fresh and living content to the conception of God in the light of modern knowledge'.[143] In January 1948, she announced that the *CNL* would seek to define a modern Christian social attitude. A six-part series by Hodges on 'Christianity and the Modern World View' – which was based on some of his Moot papers – followed. He urged, for example, enquiry into specifically Christian 'forms or attitudes of imagination' or even a distinctive 'logic'.[144] Christians were both modern and part of an institution that was like a 'foreign body' in society, speaking an 'un-intelligible' language: Christians, in response, had to make their faith 'visible', 'intelligible' and 'desirable'.[145]

The notion of 'travelling part of the way together' on the basis of common values is also exemplified by the group's appropriation of ideas from non-Christian sources. Mannheim and Löwe were especially important in this regard, but there were other examples. One of the first *CNL* supplements was by Geoffrey Vickers, a solicitor and social theorist who did not see himself as a Christian. Introducing Vickers's essay, Oldham stressed that the CCFCL and the *CNL* aimed to link Christian institutions with the wider community and that those in the churches had to listen to those 'who stand outside'.[146] The left-wing economist and political scientist G. D. H. Cole likewise 'stood outside' the churches but contributed an influential *CNL* essay in 1941.[147] Personally atheist, Cole had long cooperated with Christian socialists, with whom he shared concerns about social disintegration and an emphasis on democratic fellowship in small groups. Oldham also praised Kenneth Barlow's *The Discipline of Peace* (1942): without mentioning religion, the book expressed a 'profound religious understanding' and illustrated, Oldham suggested, how secular thought could reinforce 'the Christian understanding of reality'.[148] In May 1942 he described two books on business management – Mary Parker Follett's *Dynamic Administration* (1941) and T. N. Whitehead's *Leadership in a Free Society* (1936) – as guideposts for creating a better society, particularly Follett's focus on social integration and Whitehead's stress on interpersonal communication. Although the ideal of integration was not specifically Christian, both authors addressed what Oldham called a 'true *natural* order' where 'men can live as *men*', i.e. 'as persons in genuine communication and co-operation with other persons'.[149] Oldham also argued that the psychological sciences seemed to confirm the Christian critique of the view of 'man as a self-contained personality, master of his fate and captain of his soul'.[150] Walter Lippmann – who had long advocated humanism to replace a vanished religion – was recommended to *CNL* readers, especially his essays on atomic weapons and the future of democracy.[151] Hans J. Morgenthau's *Scientific Man versus Power Politics* (1946) was praised for debunking the idea of humanity as 'rational and good': his secular view,

Bliss suggested, would be familiar to readers of Niebuhr. It was part of a tradition of European thought reaching back to Augustine and a resource 'against the neo-pelagianism [sic] of modern rationalism'.[152] While a secular morality would be incomplete, Bliss argued, efforts to create one might still 'broaden and re-enforce Christian ethical teaching'.[153] She thought, for example, that Alex Comfort's 1949 CNL supplement was 'exceptionally sensitive to what is going on in the world'.[154]

'Spiritual resources which others have not': asserting Christian distinctiveness

Group members were clearly willing to cross the religious–secular frontier, but they also reinforced it by identifying what they saw as Christianity's distinctive political and social contributions. In the CNL's first issue, Oldham listed four 'Christian' ideas: belief in 'an objective rightness in things', 'extreme realism', a 'creative spirit', and the aim of a just peace reached by negotiation and agreement.[155] The Christian claim that the Kingdom of God was a present reality, he later argued, was Christianity's 'distinctive and fundamental contribution' to social regeneration.[156] An emphasis on transcendence set the faith apart, but its precise limits remained unclear. Eliot warned against adopting a vague 'spirituality': the group's views must remain 'definitely religious' and 'dogmatically Christian', and he thought it was too reserved on this point.[157] The CNL, however, directly opposed watering down faith by denying its supernatural aspects or turning it into a merely ethical 'philosophy'. It defended the reality of the resurrection and asserted 'the historic Christian creeds': 'That is where we stand, and we do not propose to change our position.'[158]

Cooperation was thus to be refused with versions of secularism that were clearly anti-Christian or even in themselves totalitarian, a label Oldham applied, for example, to John Dewey's philosophy.[159] He warned against supporting movements that expressed only a vague affinity to Christian values, even if this was often, in practice, a difficult distinction. Indeed, his own summary in the Moot of Christian aims – i.e. a society where people lived in responsibility to God and each other, experienced 'a growing realisation of our membership one of another' and received respect as children of God – was itself critiqued as insufficiently Christian.[160] The problem, he insisted, was finding common ground with secularity while ensuring 'that the issue is decided in the sense that their faith demands'.[161] As noted, the category of (truly) 'human' was seen as a possible point of agreement; however, 'merely human' values were also, Oldham warned, 'irremediably tainted with arbitrariness'.[162] Vidler favoured cooperation between secular and religious spheres as long as differences were openly stated: from political necessity, Christians had to collaborate with the forces of 'decency without vitality' (i.e. established political parties) and of 'vitality without decency' (i.e. Marxism).[163] But using Christian language for purely secular ends was condemned. God, Oldham insisted, could not be thought of 'as a glorified Henry Ford or Lord Beaverbrook, re-enforcing the cause of right in much the same way as a man of superlative energy might speed up the production of munitions'.[164] Bliss argued that allegiance to Christianity must not be confused with support for a particular policy.[165] There were fears of Christian *self*-secularisation, reflecting Temple's view that Christians were 'already too like the world'.[166] The era's entire intellectual climate, Oldham claimed, took for granted 'the view of the universe built up by the secular mind'.[167]

Among its benefits, faith offered the kind of armaments necessary for waging 'spiritual warfare'; indeed, evocations of a 'spiritual front' became common.[168] Christians, Moberly insisted, had spiritual resources others lacked.[169] Three features were particularly stressed: spiritual 'energy', a distinct 'realism' and a non-relativist morality. Faith's explicitly *supernatural* power or energy gave strength to resist enemies, wisdom to fight morally and creativity to regenerate society.[170] A 1938 CCFCL memorandum insisted that a 'radical' social transformation required 'the release of new spiritual energies on a vast scale'.[171] Oldham wrote that only the 'audacity' of asserting that the war was God's will could sustain the nation.[172] Trusting in humanity alone would deny 'spiritual energies' needed to defeat 'demonic forces of evil'.[173] Victory required acknowledging the 'infinite obligation' owed to others based on the 'infinite obligation' owed to God: faith could overcome 'despondency and faint-heartedness' through 'unseen powers' that could bring a new vitality via 'visitations from the unseen world'.[174] An 'anchor' was needed 'that will hold, even if the floods sweep everything else away'.[175] The notion of anchoring or grounding *earthly* activity in *transcendental* contexts was common in the group, as it was among Christians generally.[176] One could face reality, Oldham wrote, only with the supernatural faith that God was 'greater than the world'.[177] Christianity gave access to 'vast untapped reservoirs of power' containing, Oldham claimed (using an image of Dawson's), 'a vitalism more dynamic than the vitalism of blood and soil'.[178]

It was hoped that this spiritual power would lead to Britain fighting a moral war and achieving a just peace. Despite the presence of a few pacifists in the Moot (such as Murry, who changed his views after 1945) and occasional presentation of pacifist arguments in the *CNL*, the Oldham group's consensus consistently supported Britain's war effort. But it also probed its morality, seeing the war as a divine judgement on universal sins and insisting on humane methods in prosecuting the war when possible.[179]

The first *CNL* claimed that through the war God was 'unmasking' evil forces, ending a 'false peace', judging 'idolatries', disclosing 'false values' and enabling a more profound understanding of 'charity, penitence and forgiveness'.[180] Faith provided a moral guide for walking what Oldham called the 'knife's edge' between the irresponsibility of strict pacifism and the destructiveness of unlimited war.[181] H. H. Farmer argued Christians had to bring everything 'back to the Cross' to ensure emotions were not 'hardened' and to encourage 'the *distinctively* Christian mind' to emerge.[182] Christian influence would allow Britain not to lose its soul in saving itself, responding to fears that fighting totalitarianism abroad could encourage it at home. A 'black-out of mind' could only be avoided via an internal 'second front' that defended sacred principles.[183] The *CNL* repeatedly warned against succumbing to vindictiveness, and it frequently questioned Allied bombing strategy.[184]

Spiritual energies would also fuel the necessary, but immense, task of social renewal. Like other Christians, the group argued that there should be clear peace aims and urged social reconstruction. Oldham insisted faith could bring about no mere 'reorganisation of existing forces' but a 'revolution' greater than Communism and Nazism.[185] Mannheim agreed, believing Christianity could inspire commitment to a new social order. But the group also thought an impetus towards revolution had to be matched by a Christian realism distinct from revolutionary Marxism, racialist Fascism, materialist scientism or progressivist liberalism.[186] Making 'utopian plans' for a new world, Oldham claimed, was 'quite alien' to Christianity, even if some Christians' views had been tainted by modern assumptions.[187] Vidler asserted Christians should 'deflate all Utopian illusions'; Hodges thought they could better confront life's contradictions.[188] Moberly saw the CFC as guided by realism.[189] This realism derived from Christian understanding of sin's ubiquity and inescapability.[190] In the *CNL*, Niebuhr attacked modern optimism as a caricature of Christianity's 'profounder hope': utopianism strove towards sinlessness but brought only 'new forms of anarchy or tyranny'.[191] Vidler mocked a 'facile and optimistic' progressivism: liberalism had 'begotten a fierce progeny' (i.e. totalitarianism) that it could neither control nor understand.[192] Moberly emphasised the Christian need for an 'unsentimental understanding of the modern world'.[193] Mannheim, though he doubted liberal optimism, held to the belief in progress in science and social techniques (as distinct from progress in 'moral consciousness').[194] He also denied that secularism was inherently naïve. Freud, after all, believed in 'deep evil': the 'radical optimist', in Mannheim's view, was the behaviourist.[195] But post-war secularity seemed to have learned little, and, referring to the creation of the UN, Bliss argued that a Christian understanding of humanity's tainted mind and soul remained essential.[196]

But true Christian realism also resisted pessimism. In *The Price of Leadership* (1939), Murry called Christianity 'the only realism that does not lead to despair'.[197] Christianity, Oldham wrote, opposed *both* a 'facile optimism' and 'despairing pessimism'.[198] Readers accused the *CNL*, variously, of excessive optimism or pessimism. The group, however, located Christianity beyond this dichotomy: Oldham saw its realism mixed with 'hope', 'confidence' and 'joy'.[199] In the Moot, Vidler called the gospel both a rebuke to 'Utopianism' and an assertion of the power of love.[200] In print, he praised the Christian 'paradox' that found hope *in* despair via a life centred on God.[201] In this view, *secular* realism meant power-politics and cynicism; *Christian* realism, in contrast, had transcendent optimism about the meaning of life and history, a firm sense of morality and access to supernatural power.[202] Thus, there were true and false varieties of realism. In January 1948, Bliss praised Christians' willingness to face the world situation without either fear or naïveté, and she highlighted Christians' acceptance of 'suffering and death' and their hope of eternal life.[203] Shortly thereafter, Moira Symons argued in the *CNL* that Christian politics must derive from 'a *realistic* view of responsibility in the ordering of community life'.[204] But realism did not contradict the goal of revolution. Human realities did not alter, but Oldham denied it was utopian to think faith might 'change the course of history'.[205] Christian hope offered more than idle dreaming. The war might be God's judgement on a sinful humanity, but His grace also offered forgiveness and renewal. Seeing the world in the midst of a historic transformation, Oldham thought uniting the scattered forces of renewal involved not only human assertion but also discovering 'something that carries us' (i.e. the Holy Spirit).[206] Shaw admitted that the group had to think in reformist terms, but he saw them as 'revolutionaries' cooperating with 'the Spirit of God'.[207]

Christianity was also claimed to offer a timeless, universal standpoint from which to define a 'true' relationship to reality. Group members faulted secular liberalism for its moral 'neutrality' and lack of unifying principles, which had led to a drastic form of cultural relativism.[208] Christianity, in contrast, envisioned a natural moral order that could be disregarded 'only at the cost of unending frustration and suffering'.[209] Properly understood, it was argued, Christianity encouraged tolerance. Belief in a transcendent, meaning-giving reality would, Oldham claimed, hinder giving 'absolute value' to any merely human cause or aim; those who were aware of their 'finitude' would tend not to adopt extreme views while also resisting the predominant 'anaemic indifferentism' in which 'every opinion is as good as another'.[210] Reality, Vidler argued, had a divinely willed 'normative character'. Christianity defined 'permanently right ways of dealing with things and people', providing a basis for morally grounding a mixed society.[211] Hodges argued in a Moot paper that while Christianity – with a 'peculiar way of looking at the world' – could only be defended 'within its own universe of discourse', it was not more peculiar in this regard than science. Science required 'the presupposition of uniformity'; religion needed, in contrast, the 'metaphysical presupposition', i.e., the prior belief that there was a transcendental level of existence.[212]

Christianity thus knew not what *should be*, in the sense of an abstract ethical ideal, but what *was*: a true understanding of reality. Citing an article by Murry, Oldham saw a 'vertical relation to the eternal' as the only way to give life meaning: the human soul could not endure 'the nullity and vacuity of a personal life severed from all vertical sources'.[213] Violating the divine order, Oldham wrote in 1944, could lead only 'to self-destruction and disaster'.[214] Christianity named 'unalterable realities' by which people must abide 'if society is not to suffer shipwreck'.[215] In this view, a democracy built on an atheism that saw values as solely determined by human aims and power would inevitably fail; belief in an 'infinitely greater' wisdom could, in contrast, encourage peaceful co-existence.[216] Emphasis continued after the war on grounding human dignity in something other than social conventions.[217] A *CNL* essay lamented a decline in belief in legal principles beyond purely human interests.[218] Murry complained that the Soviet Union had destroyed belief in an objective moral law.[219] In 1947, the *CNL* cited a list compiled by Emil Brunner of modern axioms that included moral relativism, a denial of transcendental reality and the equation of truth with majority opinion.[220] In early 1948, Bliss found the world's most worrying aspect not in 'famine, or ruined cities or deserted conference tables' but rather in a widespread 'practical atheism' that had lost belief in 'a world in which truth and goodness exist and are discoverable and realizable'.[221]

However, not just any version of Christianity would do in confronting secular materialism, utopianism and relativism. In a mid-1940 *CNL* essay, 'What Difference Does Christianity Make?', Hodges criticised the clergy for either tending to 'boil down' Christianity's message to mere brotherly love or clinging to the utopian vision of mass conversion.[222] The war's moral complexities denied clear divisions between right and wrong: not only did actions undertaken for good reasons (such as appeasement) have evil results, but morally questionable acts (such as the aerial bombardment of cities) were necessary to fight evil.[223] The only solution seemed to come not from Christianity's *maxims* (even Socrates and Buddha had, after all, taught goodwill) but from the *powers* it released from 'another order or dimension of existence', and its wisdom, 'which stands outside and above the stream of history'.[224]

Here, Hodges combined the energy, realism and non-relativism he saw in Christianity into a message that could be asserted to non-believers and Christians alike. In 1947, another, jointly written, *CNL* supplement was also titled 'What Difference Does Christianity Make?'. In it, three Christian perspectives on politics were argued to be relevant: an awareness of 'the corrupting power of unconscious bias', admission by each individual of 'the fallibility of his own judgment as a sinful man' and 'finite being', and a willingness to make 'difficult and costly decisions'.[225]

Conclusion

The last two chapters have drawn a complex map of the geography straddling Oldham's religious–secular 'frontier'. It was both a border between and meeting point for the Christian churches and the 'common life'. There was an 'unceasing tension', Oldham wrote in 1939, between the earthly and heavenly cities: Christians must both 'cooperate in the work of the world' and 'contend against the world'.[226] In the Moot, Baillie admitted that the issue of relating faith to society had 'never been solved', and in a post-war report for the Church of Scotland he urged accepting that there would always be 'some unresolved tension' between sacred and secular.[227] Without aiming to *overcome* such tensions, Christians had to seek a more nuanced, constructive way of dealing with them. The lack of a Christian 'doctrine of the secular', Oldham wrote in 1944, only strengthened secular worldviews, including 'pseudo-religions or disguised Churches' that threatened the 'collapse of civilisation' and the 'abolition of man'.[228] Only real religion (i.e. Christianity) could recreate a 'genuine' culture to resist the false unities of totalitarianism or the naïve optimism of secular relativism.

The Oldham group's engagement with 'the secular', secularisation and secularism – a cultural and social realm, sociological process, and worldview, respectively – was thus motivated by a concern that the common life had become divorced from vital religious influences, leaving only thoroughly materialist ideals based upon an assumption of human self-sufficiency. Group members believed religion's decline had opened the door to a sacralisation of the secular categories of nation, class, *Volk*, party and even science itself. But secular knowledge was also seen to offer something crucial to Christians. There was much, Oldham observed, that belonged to the 'natural' rather than the specifically Christian sphere of human activity. Ignoring ('as Christians have often done') realities such as 'sex, the nation or economic activities' would divorce faith from life, with 'devastating consequences'.[229] The journal *Nature* similarly suggested that science and technology had outstripped moral progress, seeing a post-war 'new world order' as an opportunity for a 'partnership' between science and faith.[230] Such comments emerged against a cultural background in early-twentieth-century Britain in which many philosophers, and even some scientists, were sceptical (or at least ambivalent) about fully materialist worldviews.[231] The Oldham group's engagement with secular knowledge came from a religious conviction about what Christianity *was* (or *should be*) and the belief that totalitarianism would have to be defeated – in alliance with non-Christians – if any truly Christian life were to remain possible.

A middle way was envisaged, with secular knowledge sovereign in its own sphere but faith orienting its *purposes*. Christians and non-Christians could cooperate via a true understanding of what was 'human' or 'natural', according to rules that any 'honest', 'decent' or 'intelligent' person could recognise, a common ground that would enable Christian principles to be translated into secular contexts. The 'social and political philosophy' that Oldham saw his group seeking would be both 'avowedly secular' and open to Christian influence, and he insisted that the churches should accept the 'autonomy of the secular sphere'.[232] The clergy had to learn to discuss political questions 'in political terms' without claiming that any specific policy was the only 'Christian' option.[233]

In reshaping society, then, group members hoped to go part of the way with secularists (and even atheists): a new social philosophy was needed that would not be 'specifically Christian' (so as not to 'antagonise indispensable allies') but rather 'compatible with' Christianity and capable of being 'leavened' by it.[234] In matters of faith, however, the group criticised the liberal Protestant demotion of Christianity's supernatural elements. Christianity, they agreed, was not 'an optimistic humanitarian idealism'.[235] Prayer, in their view, enabled communication with 'a new order or dimension of reality', and God's actions were not to be counted 'among the natural causes of events'.[236] No matter how open to secular ideas, they insisted on Christianity's distinctiveness. 'We must learn to understand the two sides of ourselves', wrote Hodges, 'so that the Christian in us may explain himself to the modern man in us in language which the modern man can recognise, without the Christian becoming absorbed into the modern man'.[237] Christianity provided power to withstand totalitarianism, realism about human nature and a non-relativist understanding of existence. These were vital both to winning the war and to rebuilding post-war society. The group both tried to *connect with* and *distinguish itself from* the secular, generating tensions that, while never resolved, provided a vital dynamic in its thinking.

The idea that the present crisis was the result of a long-term replacement of faith in God by a limitless belief in human capacities was a widespread notion in the Christian press. 'By weakening religion', a leading article in the Anglican *Guardian* argued, 'the agnostics and positivists have a definite responsibility for the growth of pagan cults, and it is, in effect, such cults that have created the war'.[238] The *Church of England Newspaper* in 1940 editorialised about a 'moral disintegration' – apparent, among other things, in the popular craze for media celebrities – that had set in from the eighteenth century onwards: driven by the increasing dominance of science, 'scepticism' and 'materialism', this tendency had caused a breakdown in 'the system of restraints, inhibitions and decencies so painfully built up by centuries of belief in Christian doctrine and morality'.[239] The 'root sin', argued D. R. Davies, was 'affirming man as the centrality of things': 'Our generation is draining the bitter lees of the cup which the men of the Renaissance ecstatically sipped'.[240] In *Christendom*, Maurice Reckitt insisted that the war was 'the natural climax' of a secularised view of life.[241] Even non-Christians made similar arguments. Harold J. Laski, in *Faith, Reason, and Civilisation* (1944) saw the nineteenth century as a turning point at which 'religious creeds' were superseded by 'political creeds'.[242] There were various calls for reinstating Christianity to its former cultural dominance. Oldham, for example, devoted a *CNL* supplement to Lionel Curtis's plan for a religious world federation, as described in his book *Civitas Dei: The Commonwealth of God* (1938).[243] In contrast, the 'Christendom Group' – a loosely affiliated circle of Anglo-Catholic writers and thinkers with which Eliot was also involved – tended to reject secular knowledge.[244] While Oldham and his companions sought *an engagement with* secular knowledge on its own terms, the Christendom Group aimed to *replace* a secular sociology with a religious one and downplayed 'technical' knowledge. It was, it has been observed, 'reluctant to recognise the autonomy of the social sciences', a position in marked contrast to Oldham and most of his collaborators.[245]

The Oldham group argued that a process of social, political and cultural transformation driven by secularisation had long been underway and that a new Christianity was needed to meet this historically unique challenge. Such ideas would re-emerge in the 1960s in what has been called a broader 'elite re-imagination of British religiosity'.[246] The group's perceptions of a radical cultural secularisation were probably overstated, part of a much longer history of Christian jeremiads about their fellow citizens' irreligiosity. After all, substantial majorities of Britons identified as Christian, even if their understandings of what that meant were often theologically shallow or unorthodox. Nevertheless, in the 1930s and 1940s, the group's *perception* of secularisation was driven by the political, economic, social and military crises of the age: given what seemed the chronic weakness of capitalism, the dynamic rise of totalitarianism and the apparent collapse of liberal-democratic polities, the notion of a momentous, epochal cultural change was newly tangible. For the Oldham group, a socially and politically attuned Christianity that was open to secular knowledge was the only alternative to a quietist retreat of faith into the private sphere or to a quixotic attempt to reinstate religious sovereignty over all aspects of life. Meeting the radically new problem of modernity meant, in their view, rethinking Christianity. As the next chapters show, this basic dynamic shaped their views on the State, economics, national identity, freedom and social equality.

Notes

1 Clements, 'Oldham and Baillie', p. 47.
2 Eliot noted Oldham's use in one document of 'secular' both as something 'good and proper' and as a 'term of abuse': OA 9/6/58, Eliot to Oldham, 28 April 1944, pp. 1–2.
3 *CNL* 59S, 11 December 1940, J. H. Oldham, 'Predicament and Salvation', p. 4.
4 *CNL* 278L, 22 January 1947, p. 2; *CNL* 88S, 1 July 1941, J. H. Oldham, 'The Predicament of Society and the Way Out. II', p. 4.
5 IOE MOO/63a, H. A. Hodges, 'Christian Thinking Today' [July 1941], p. 2.
6 *The Times*, 5 October 1938, p. 15; *CNL* 0L, 18 October 1939, p. 1.
7 *CNL* 278L, 22 January 1947, p. 7. *Christian World*, 15 August 1946, p. 11. Maurice Reckitt, 'Editorial: The "Failure" of the Church', *Christendom*, 13:54 (June 1944), 163–6 (p. 165).
8 LPL Lang 26, fos. 98–124, Oldham's 'Handbook', sent to Lang on 4 January 1939, p. 8.
9 OA 13/6/35, 'Christianity and the Secular', 19 April 1944, p. 4. OA 9/6/58, Eliot to Oldham, 28 April 1944, enclosure, 'Note on Memorandum "Christianity and the Secular"', p. 2.
10 *CNL* 9L, 27 December 1939, pp. 2, 3.
11 *CNL* 293L, 3 September 1947, p. 1.
12 *CNL* 183S, 2 June 1943, H. A. Hodges, 'The Problem of Archetypes', p. 4.
13 *Churches Survey Their Task*, pp. 139–42, 196; *Moot Papers*, M1, p. 51 (Dawson); M2, pp. 72–3 (Murry); M2, p. 83 (Oldham); M17, p. 596 (Niebuhr); M19, p. 661 (Moberly), p. 680 (Oldham).
14 Oldham quoted in Udi Greenberg, 'Protestants, Decolonization, and European Integration, 1885–1961', *Journal of Modern History*, 89 (2017), 314–54 (p. 329).

15 IOE MOO/65, letter from Christopher Dawson, n.d. [late 1941], p. 2; *CNL* 219S, 18 October 1944, Kenneth Grubb, 'Europe – the Christian Outlook', p. 6.

16 *CNL* 86S, 18 June 1941, J. H. Oldham, 'The Predicament of Society and the Way Out', p. 3.

17 OA 14/2/12, H. A. Hodges, 'Comments on Middleton Murry's Paper', n.d. [discussed September 1938], pp. 3–4.

18 *CNL* 25L, 17 April 1940, p. 1; *CNL* 28S, 8 May 1940, R. Roseveare, 'The Story of a New Community', p. 1; *CNL* 32L, 5 June 1940, p. 3; *CNL* 43L, 21 August 1940, p. 3; *CNL* 59S, 11 December 1940, J. H. Oldham, 'Predicament and Salvation', p. 1; *CNL* 164L, 16 December 1942, pp. 1–2; *CNL* 172L, 10 February 1943, p. 1; *CNL* 172S, 10 February 1943, Mass Observation, 'Religion and the People', p. 1.

19 *CNL* 295L, 1 October 1947, pp. 4–7.

20 *CNL* 108S, 19 November 1941, J. H. Oldham, 'The Need for a Fresh Approach to Christian Education', p. 2.

21 *CNL* 227L, 7 February 1945, p. 1.

22 Clements, 'Oldham and Baillie', p. 46; Smith, *Oxford 1937*, pp. 25, 74–95.

23 *Moot Papers*, M2, p. 106; M8, p. 308.

24 IOE MOO/83, 19 July 1942, H. H. Oldham, 'The Religious Foundations of the Frontier', p. 6; *CNL* 118L, 28 January 1942, pp. 1–2; *CNL* 120L, 11 February 1942, pp. 1–2.

25 *CNL* 120S, 11 February 1942, H. A. Hodges, 'Christianity in an Age of Science', p. 2.

26 *CNL* 323L, 27 October 1948, p. 9.

27 *CNL* 317L, 4 August 1948, p. 6.

28 Huttner, *Totalitarismus und säkulare Religionen*, pp. 265–322.

29 *Churches Survey Their Task*, p. 196.

30 CERC CCFCL 2/1/1, 'The Churches and the International Crisis', n.d., p. 3.

31 *Church Times*, 14 January 1938, p. 46.

32 Dawson, *Religion and the Modern State*, pp. 148, 152–3. *Moot Papers*, M13, p. 454 (Murry). See also Murry, *Price of Leadership*, p. 62.

33 BC, BAI 1/7/2, Michael Polanyi, 'Science and the Modern Crisis', 14 November 1944, p. 4.

34 *CNL* 272L, 30 October 1946, p. 5.

35 *CNL* 9L, 27 December 1939, p. 4; *CNL* 241L, 22 August 1945, p. 6; *CNL* 242L, 5 September 1945, p. 3.

36 A. R. Vidler, *Christianity's Need for a Free University* (London: SCM, 1946), p. 14.

37 *CNL* 235L, 30 May 1945, p. 2. Also: *CNL* 240S, August 1945, Barbara Ward, 'The Fate of Europe', p. 8.

38 McClay, *Masterless*, pp. 192–3.

39 *CNL* 46L, 11 September 1940, p. 4.

40 IOE MOO/83, J. H. Oldham, 'Religious Foundations of the Frontier', 19 July 1942, p. 6.

41 *CNL* 299S, 26 November 1947, Michael Foster, 'Some Remarks on the Relations of Science and Religion', p. 14.

42 A. R. Vidler, *Secular Despair and Christian Faith* (London: SCM, 1941), p. 16.

43 *CNL* 86S, 18 June 1941, J. H. Oldham, 'The Predicament of Society and the Way Out', p. 2; LPL Lang 25, fos. 104–12, 'A Proposed Council of the Churches in Great Britain on the Relation of the Christian Faith to the National Life', p. 1. Oldham, *Church, Community and State*, pp. 8–9.

44 *CNL* 218L, 4 October 1944, p. 2.

45 *CNL* 16S, 14 February 1940, Reinhold Niebuhr, 'Wrong Answers to Unanswered Problems'.

46 *CNL* 246S, 31 October 1945, Reinhold Niebuhr, 'The Religious Level of the World Crisis', p. 1.

47 *CNL* 267S, 21 August 1946, Violet Markham, 'The Man and the Machine', p. 6.

48 LPL Lang 26, fos. 38–49, 'Statement of Policy', 25 November 1938, p. 5. LPL Lang 26, fos. 98–124, Oldham's 'Handbook', sent to Lang on 4 January 1939, p. 8.

49 OA 13/5/1, 'The Christian Ethos: Its Source, Nature and Authority', July 1939, p. 1.

50 *CNL* 120L, 11 February 1942, p. 2.

51 *CNL* 280L, 5 March 1947, p. 8.

52 *CNL* 163L, 9 December 1942, pp. 1–3.

53 *CNL* 183L, 2 June 1943, p. 4.

54 *CNL* 198S, 29 December 1943, William Temple, 'What Christians Stand for in the Secular World', p. 7.

55 *CNL* 246S, 31 October 1945, Reinhold Niebuhr, 'The Religious Level of the World Crisis', pp. 9–10.

56 *CNL* 267S, 21 August 1946, Violet Markham, 'The Man and the Machine', p. 10.

57 Eric Fenn, *The Crisis and Democracy* (London: SCM, 1938), p. 31.

58 OA 13/5/1, 'The Christian Ethos: Its Source, Nature and Authority', July 1939, p. 1. *CNL* 14L, 31 January 1940, p. 1.

59 Murry, *Price of Leadership*, pp. 101–3; John Middleton Murry 'Ends and Means', *Listener*, 23 May 1940, 1014–15.

60 *CNL* 6L, 6 December 1939, p. 2.

61 *CNL* 120S, 11 February 1942, H. A. Hodges, 'Christianity in an Age of Science', p. 3.

62 IOE MOO/7, 'Notes on English Educational Institutions in the Light of the Necessities of Planning for Freedom in the Coming Collectivised Regime by F. Clarke', 21 August 1939, p. 25.

63 *CNL* 88S, 1 July 1941, J. H. Oldham, 'The Predicament of Society and the Way Out', pp. 2–3.

64 *CNL* 163L, 9 December 1942, p. 1.

65 *CNL* 244L, 3 October 1945, p. 2.

66 *CNL* 251L, 9 January 1946, 1, p. 6.

67 *Ibid.*, p. 7.

68 *CNL* 163L, 9 December 1942, p. 3. See also *CNL* 164S, 16 December 1942, Oldham, 'Christmas 1942', p. 3.

69 IOE MOO/83, 19 July 1942, Oldham, 'The Religious Foundations of the Frontier', p. 6.

70 *CNL* 198S, 29 December 1943, William Temple, 'What Christians Stand for in the Secular World', p. 7.

71 *CNL* 292S, 20 August 1947, A. D. Ritchie, 'Science and the Free Society', pp. 10, 14; *CNL* 302L, 7 January 1948, p. 5.

72 *CNL* 313L, 9 June 1948, p. 7.

73 *CNL* 323L, 27 October 1948, pp. 1–2.

74 *Ibid.*, pp. 2–4.

75 *Ibid.*, p. 4, quoting *Nature*, 11 September 1948, p. 385. See also *Nature*, 16 October 1948, pp. 589–91.

76 *CNL* 323L, 27 October 1948, pp. 5–7.

77 *CNL* 324L, 10 November 1948, pp. 7–10.

78 *CNL* 329L, 19 January 1949, p. 27; *CNL* 329S, 19 January 1949, Alex Comfort, 'Scientific Evidence and Religious Assertion'.

79 *CNL* 330L, 2 February 1949, p. 36.

80 LPL Lang 26, fos. 227–30, memo submitted to the CCFCL by Oldham, 23 April 1941, p. 2.

81 *CNL* 59S, 11 December 1940, J. H. Oldham, 'Predicament and Salvation', pp. 3, 4.

82 LPL Lang 26, fos. 98–124, Oldham's 'Handbook', sent to Lang on 4 January 1939, p. 9. LPL Lang 25, fos. 305–14, 'The Problems and Tasks of the Council on the Christian Faith and the Common Life', p. 5.

83 See papers for M13, 19–22 December 1941: IOE MOO/123 (Eliot); 125 (Hodges); 126 (Vidler); 127 (Murry).

84 Vidler, *Secular Despair*, p. 74.

85 *CNL* 0S, 18 October 1939, J. H. Oldham, 'What Is a Christian News-Letter?', p. 1.

86 *CNL* 88S, 1 July 1941, J. H. Oldham, 'The Predicament of Society and the Way Out. II', p. 7.

87 *CNL* 125L, 18 March 1942, p. 3. Emphasis in original.

88 CERC CCFCL 2/1/1, 'The Churches and the International Crisis' [1939], p. 2.

89 IOE MOO/83, 'The Religious Foundations of the Frontier', July 1942, pp. 5, 8, 11.

90 Oldham, *Root of Our Troubles*, p. 22. *CNL* 114L, 31 December 1941, p. 3.

91 *CNL* 197L, 15 December 1943, p. 1.

92 *CNL* 223L, 13 December 1944, p. 4.

93 *CNL* 154S, 7 October 1942, Walter Moberly, 'The Christian Frontier', p. 2.

94 *Moot Papers*, M20, p. 713.

95 *CNL* 198S, 29 December 1943, Temple, 'What Christians Stand for in the Secular World', pp. 2, 4, 11. See also *Moot Papers*, M18, pp. 615–16.

96 *CNL* 332L, 2 March 1949, p. 79.

97 *CNL* 43S, 21 August 1940, H. A. Hodges, 'Social Standards in a Mixed Society'.

98 IOE MOO/125, Hodges, 'Notes on Social Philosophy', n.d. [discussed July 1940], p. 1.

99 *Ibid.*, p. 2.

100 *CNL* 43L, 21 August 1940, p. 4.

101 *CNL* 43S, 21 August 1940, H. A. Hodges, 'Social Standards in a Mixed Society', p. 1.

102 *Ibid.*, p. 3.

103 Hodges, 'Notes on Social Philosophy', p. 1.

104 OA 14/1/71, H. A. Hodges, 'The Collective Commonwealth and the Christian', 22 January 1944, p. 1.

105 *CNL* 200S, 26 January 1944, Marjorie Reeves, 'Religious Education', pp. 4–5.

106 IOE MOO/127, Murry, 'Notes on Social Philosophy', n.d. [discussed July 1940], p. 2.

107 *CNL* 88S, 1 July 1941, J. H. Oldham, 'The Predicament of Society and the Way Out. II', p. 7. *Moot Papers*, M11, p. 381. *CNL* 237S, 27 June 1945, J. H. Oldham, '*Prospect for Christendom*', p. 11.

108 Oldham, *Church, Community and State*, pp. 12–13. *CNL* 14L, 31 January 1940, p. 2; *CNL* 15L, 7 February 1940, p. 2.

109 *CNL* 28L, 8 May 1940, p. 3.

110 *Moot Papers*, M7, p. 275.

111 *Ibid.*, M7, pp. 258, 276.

112 *Ibid.*, M7, pp. 281, 275.

113 *Ibid.*, M7, p. 286. Murry and Eliot sparred directly with Wells on the letters page of the *Guardian*; see, e.g., *Guardian*, 19 January 1940, p. 19; 26 January 1940, p. 43; 2 February 1940, p. 55; 16 February 1940, p. 79.

114 *Moot Papers*, M7, pp. 272–3.

115 *CNL* 14L, 31 January 1940, p. 1.

116 *CNL* 72S, 12 March 1941, Oldham, 'Christianity and Manhood', p. 1. Emphasis in original.

117 *CNL* 76L, 9 April 1941, p. 2.

118 *Moot Papers*, M14, p. 505.

119 *CNL* 94L, 13 August 1941, p. 1.

120 *CNL* 97L, 3 September 1941, p. 3.

121 *CNL* 102L, 8 October 1941, p. 2. Clarke, Oakeshott, Moberly and Oldham were involved. Nick Veevers and Pete Allison, *Kurt Hahn: Inspirational Visionary, Outdoor and Experiential Educator* (Rotterdam: Sense, 2011), pp. 40–2. A. D. Lindsay, 'A Plan for Education', *Picture Post*, 4 January 1941, 27–31.

122 *CNL* 108S, 19 November 1941, Oldham, 'The Need for a Fresh Approach to Christian Education', pp. 2–3.

123 See, e.g., *Moot Papers*, M2, p. 101; M9, pp. 335–7; M12, p. 426; M14, p. 502.

124 *Ibid.*, M9, p. 335.

125 IOE MOO/78, Vidler, 'Two Approaches to "Natural Law"', March 1942, p. 1.

126 IOE MOO/64, Ruth Kenyon, 'The Idea of the Natural Law', 28 July 1941, pp. 3–4. *Moot Papers*, M12, p. 411.

127 *Moot Papers*, M9, pp. 326–7, 335; M12, p. 429.

128 A. R. Vidler, 'Inquiries Concerning Natural Law', *Theology* 44:260 (1942), 65–73; A. R. Vidler and W. A. Whitehouse, *Natural Law: A Christian Reconsideration* (London: SCM, 1946).

129 H. A. Hodges, review of *Natural Law*, *Theology*, 49:310 (April 1946), 122–4.

130 OA 9/3/42, n.d.

131 *CNL* 59S, 11 December 1940, Oldham, 'Predicament and Salvation', p. 4. Emphasis in original.

132 *Moot Papers*, M9, pp. 335–6.

133 *Ibid.*, M12, pp. 426–7.

134 IOE MOO/48, Fenn to Oldham, 31 March 1941, p. 2.

135 *Moot Papers*, M9, p. 328; M12, p. 409. Mannheim, *Diagnosis*, pp. 7, 29, 110, 114.

136 IOE MOO/65, letter from Christopher Dawson, n.d. [probably late summer or early autumn 1941], p. 2.

137 *CNL* 32L, 5 June 1940, pp. 1–2; *Moot Papers*, M12, pp. 429–30.

138 OA 21/1/12, 'Weekend Meeting, January 26–29, 1945: Notes on the Church and Society', 10 January 1945, p. 3. Emphasis in original.

139 *CNL* 289L, 9 July 1947, 11.

140 *CNL* 312S, 26 May 1948, J. H. Oldham, 'Mr. Murry on the Free Society – II', p. 16.

141 Moberly: *Moot Papers*, M16, p. 566; Oldham: LPL, W. Temple 11, fos. 272–3, Oldham to Archie Craig, 3 October 1944.

142 MacLeod was a Church of Scotland minister and founder of the Iona Community. *CNL* 255L, 6 March 1946, p. 2.

143 *CNL* 291L, 6 August 1947, p. 8.

144 *CNL* 302L, 7 January 1948, p. 2. *CNL* 305S, 18 February 1948, H. A. Hodges, 'Christianity and the Modern World View – I', p. 14. It was revised from OA 14/2/5, H. A. Hodges, 'Christian Thinking Today'. Emphasis in original.

145 *CNL* 305S, 18 February 1948, H. A. Hodges, 'Christianity and the Modern World View – I', p. 15.

146 *CNL* 2L, 8 November 1939, p. 3.

147 *CNL* 90S, 16 July 1941, G. D. H. Cole, 'Democracy Face to Face with Hugeness'.

148 IOE MOO/83, 19 July 1942, J. H. Oldham, 'The Religious Foundations of the Frontier', p. 9.

149 *CNL* 132S, 5 May 1942, J. H. Oldham, 'Of These Stones', pp. 2–3, 4. Emphasis in original.

150 *CNL* 164S, 16 December 1942, J. H. Oldham, 'Christmas 1942', pp. 3–4.

151 *CNL* 269S, 18 September 1946, J. H. Oldham, 'The Control of Atomic Energy', pp. 8–9. *CNL* 274L, 27 November 1946, p. 3.

152 *CNL* 313L, 9 June 1948, pp. 3–4.

153 *CNL* 334L, 30 March 1949, pp. 101–5.

154 *CNL* 329S, 19 January 1949, Alex Comfort, 'Scientific Evidence and Religious Assertion'.

155 *CNL* 1L, 1 November 1939, p. 2.

156 *CNL* 57S, 27 November 1940, J. H. Oldham, 'The Demand for a Christian Lead', p. 1.

157 IOE MOO/50, letter from T. S. Eliot, n.d. [*c.* March 1941], p. 1.

158 *CNL* 187L, 28 July 1943, p. 1.

159 *CNL* 171L, 3 February 1943, pp. 2–3.

160 *Moot Papers*, M2, pp. 91–106.

161 *CNL* 88S, 1 July 1941, Oldham, 'The Predicament of Society and the Way Out', p. 6.

162 *CNL* 164S, 16 December 1942, J. H. Oldham, 'Christmas 1942', p. 2.

163 *Moot Papers*, M14, pp. 502, 505.

164 *CNL* 69L, 19 February 1941, p. 1.

165 *CNL* 231L, 4 April 1945, p. 2.

166 *Churches Survey Their Task*, p. 57; *CNL* 6S, 6 December 1939, p. 3; *CNL* 69L, 19 February 1941, p. 1.

167 *CNL* 192S, 6 October 1943, J. H. Oldham, 'Belief in the Resurrection', p. 3.

168 *CNL* 48L, 25 September 1940, p. 1. *CNL* 30L, 22 May 1940, p. 1; *CNL* 82L, 21 May 1941, p. 1. LPL Lang 26, fos. 194–203, 'The Spiritual Front', n.d. (*c.* June 1940).

169 *CNL* 98L, 10 September 1941, p. 1.

170 *CNL* 18L, 28 February 1940, p. 3; *CNL* 35L, 26 June 1940, p. 2; *CNL* 82L, 21 May 1941, p. 2; *CNL* 59S, 11 December 1940, J. H. Oldham, 'Predicament and Salvation', p. 1; *CNL* 276L, 25 December 1946, pp. 1–2.

171 LPL Lang 26, fos. 38–49, CCFCL, 'Statement of Policy', 25 November 1938, p. 6.

172 *CNL* 1S, 1 November 1939, J. H. Oldham, 'What Is God Doing?', p. 1.

173 *CNL* 6L, 6 December 1939, p. 3.

174 *CNL* 187L, 28 July 1943, p. 2.

175 *CNL* 17L, 21 February 1940, p. 2.

176 See, e.g., *Church of England Newspaper*, 21 June 1940, p. 9, and 25 February 1944, p. 8; *Guardian*, 29 September 1939, p. 607.

177 *CNL* 59S, 11 December 1940, J. H. Oldham, 'Predicament and Salvation', p. 1.

178 *CNL* 82L, 21 May 1941, p. 2; *CNL* 88S, 1 July 1941, J. H. Oldham, 'The Predicament of Society and the Way Out', pp. 2, 3, 7. OA 14/4/1, Christopher Dawson, 'The Sword of the Spirit', December 1940, p. 4. *CNL* 313L, 9 June 1948, p. 8.

179 Alec Vidler, *God's Judgment on Europe* (London: Longmans, Green, 1940); Christopher Dawson, *The Judgement of the Nations* (London: Sheed & Ward, 1943).

180 *CNL* 1S, 1 November 1939, Oldham, 'What Is God Doing?', pp. 1–3.

181 *CNL* 79L, 30 April, 1941, pp. 3–4.

182 *CNL* 7S, 13 December 1939, H. H. Farmer, 'Can the Feelings be Changed?', p. 3. Emphasis in original.

183 *CNL* 0S, 18 October 1939, J. H. Oldham, 'What Is a Christian News-Letter?', p. 3; *CNL* 6L, 6 December 1939, p. 1.

184 *CNL* 7L, 13 December 1939, p. 1; *CNL* 22L, 27 March 1940, p. 1; *CNL* 34L, 19 June 1940, p. 4; *CNL* 48L, 25 September 1940, p. 2; *CNL* 56L, 20 November 1940, pp. 3–4; *CNL* 57L, 27 November 1940, pp. 1–2; *CNL* 58L, 4 December

1940, p. 3; *CNL* 75L, 2 April 1941, p. 3; *CNL* 79L, 30 April 1941, pp. 3–4; *CNL* 81L, 14 May 1941, pp. 1–3; *CNL* 84L, 4 June 1941, pp. 1–2; *CNL* 101L, 1 October 1941, pp. 2–3; *CNL* 133L, 13 May 1942, pp. 2–4; *CNL* 147L, 19 August 1942, pp. 2–4; *CNL* 181L, 5 May 1943, pp. 2–4; *CNL* 185L, 30 June 1943, pp. 1–3; *CNL* 223L, 13 December 1944, pp. 1–3; *CNL* 224L, 27 December 1944, pp. 3–4; *CNL* 225L, 10 January 1945, pp. 5–8.

185 *CNL* 6L, 6 December 1939, p. 3; *CNL* 9L, 27 December 1939, p. 4. Oldham, *Resurrection of Christendom*, pp. 7, 11, 12.

186 *CNL* 1L, 1 November 1939, p. 2.

187 *CNL* 6L, 6 December 1939, p. 2; *CNL* 13S, 24 January 1940, 'Our Members Contribute', p. 2; *CNL* 14L, 31 January 40, p. 2.

188 Vidler, *Secular Despair*, p. 77; *CNL* 27S, 1 May 1940, H. A. Hodges, 'What Difference Does Christianity Make?'.

189 *CNL* 154S, 7 October 1942, Walter Moberly, 'The Christian Frontier', p. 4.

190 *CNL* 1L, 1 November 1939, pp. 1–2; *CNL* 14L, 31 January 1940, p. 2; *CNL* 212S, 12 July 1944, J. H. Oldham, 'Christianity and Power', p. 8; *CNL* 126S, 25 March 1942, Philip Mairet, 'The Gospel Drama and Society', p. 2.

191 *CNL* 16S, 14 February 1940, Reinhold Niebuhr, 'Wrong Answers to Unanswered Problems', pp. 3–4.

192 Vidler, *God's Judgment on Europe*, p. 19.

193 *CNL* 154S, 7 October 1942, Walter Moberly, 'The Christian Frontier', p. 4.

194 Mannheim, *Diagnosis*, p. 122.

195 *Moot Papers*, M7, p. 283.

196 *CNL* 242L, 5 September 1945, p. 2. *CNL* 296L, 15 October 1947, p. 1.

197 Murry, *Price of Leadership*, pp. 7–8.

198 *CNL* 5S, 29 November 1939, J. H. Oldham, 'Preliminaries to the Consideration of Peace Aims', p. 1.

199 CERC CCFCL 2/1/1, 'The Churches and the International Crisis', n.d. [probably 1939], p. 1; *CNL* 17L, 21 February 1940, p. 1; *CNL* 37L, 10 July 1940, p. 3; *CNL* 237S, 27 June 1945, J. H. Oldham, 'Prospect for Christendom', p. 9.

200 *Moot Papers*, M7, p. 271.

201 Vidler, *Secular Despair*, pp. 7, 31.

202 IOE MOO/57, Eliot to Clarke, Good Friday [11 April] 1941, pp. 1–2.

203 *CNL* 302L, 7 January 1948, p. 1; *CNL* 307L, 17 March 1948, pp. 3–4.

204 *CNL* 303S, 21 January 1948, Moira Symons, 'Home and Community', p. 16. Emphasis in original.

205 *CNL* 88S, 1 July 1941, J. H. Oldham, 'The Predicament of Society and the Way Out', p. 7. *CNL* 223L, 13 December 1944, p. 4.

206 IOE MOO/83, 'The Religious Foundations of the Frontier', July 1942, p. 4.

207 IOE MOO/51, letter from Gilbert Shaw, n.d. [*c*. March 1941], p. 1.

208 *CNL* 50L, 9 October 1940, p. 3; John Baillie, *The Mind of the Modern University* (London: SCM, 1946), p. 27.

209 *CNL* 9L, 27 December 1939, p. 4.

210 IOE MOO/2, J. H. Oldham, 'A Reborn Christendom', p. 13.

211 IOE MOO/126, A. R. Vidler, 'Notes on Social Philosophy', n.d. [discussed 19–22 December 1941], p. 2. IOE MOO/67, copy of letter from the Revd A. R. Vidler, n.d., p. 1.

212 OA 14/1/9, H. A. Hodges, 'Towards a Logic of Christian Thinking', 27–30 March 1942, p. 1. Moberly called Hodges's paper 'of first importance': *Moot Papers*, M14, p. 490.

213 *CNL* 104L, 22 October 1941, p. 1.

214 *CNL* 212S, 12 July 1944, Oldham, 'Christianity and Power', p. 9.

215 *CNL* 223L, 13 December 1944, p. 4.

216 *CNL* 175L, 3 March 1943, p. 2.

217 *CNL* 237S, 27 June 1945, J. H. Oldham, '*Prospect for Christendom*', p. 9.

218 *CNL* 285S, 16 April 1947, Arthur fforde, 'What Then Is That Law?'.

219 *CNL* 284S, 30 April 1947, J. Middleton Murry, 'The Free Society', p. 15. John Middleton Murry, *The Free Society* (London: Andrew Dakers, 1948), pp. 99–112.

220 *CNL* 278L, 22 January 1947, pp. 7–8.

221 *CNL* 302L, 7 January 1948, pp. 3–4.

222 *CNL* 27S, 1 May 1940, H. A. Hodges, 'What Difference Does Christianity Make?', p. 1.

223 *Ibid.*, p. 2.

224 *Ibid.*, pp. 3–4.

225 *CNL* 277S, 8 January 1947, anon., 'Christians in Politics: III. The Temptations of a Politician', p. 16.

226 LPL Lang 26, fos. 98–124, Oldham's 'Handbook', sent to Lang on 4 January 1939, p. 9.

227 *Moot Papers*, M16, p. 559; Clements, 'Oldham and Baillie', p. 53.

228 OA 13/6/35, 'Christianity and the Secular', 19 April 1944, p. 3.

229 *CNL* 157L, 28 October 1942, p. 1.

230 'The Church as a Social Force', *Nature*, 150:3808 (24 October 1942), 469–72.

231 Peter J. Bowler, *Reconciling Science and Religion: The Debate in Early-Twentieth-Century Britain* (Chicago: University of Chicago Press, 2001).

232 J. H. Oldham, letter to the editor, *Theology*, 47:291 (September 1944), 207–9.

233 *Ibid.*, p. 207.

234 IOE MOO/121, Walter Moberly, 'Religious Education in Our National Schools', n.d., pp. 1–2.

235 *CNL* 1L, 1 November 1939, pp. 1–2.

236 *CNL* 34L, 19 June 1940, p. 2; *CNL* 69L, 19 February 1941, p. 1.

237 *CNL* 120S, 11 February 1942, H. A. Hodges, 'Christianity in an Age of Science', p. 4.

238 *Guardian*, 12 April 1940, p. 175. See also *Guardian*, 19 April 1940, p. 191.

239 *Church of England Newspaper*, 23 February 1945, p. 12.

240 *Church of England Newspaper*, 26 March 1943, p. 1.

241 *Christendom*, 13:51 (September 1943), 67–9 (p. 69).

242 Laski, *Faith, Reason, and Civilisation*, p. 52.

243 *CNL* 185S, J. H. Oldham, 'A Prophet on the Prevention of War', 30 June 1943, pp. 3–4.

244 The Christendom Group included V. A. Demant, Maurice Reckitt, W. G. Peck, P. E. T. Widdrington, Ruth Kenyon, Dorothy Sayers, William Temple and T. S. Eliot. See Oliver, *Church and Social Order*, pp. 118–39; and Wollenberg, *Christian Social Thought*, pp. 31–2. Its 'dogmatic' and 'traditional' theology was critiqued by John Macmurray: *New Statesman and Society*, 20 October 1945, p. 269.

245 Oliver, *Church and Social Order*, p. 136. John D. Brewer, 'Sociology and Theology Reconsidered: Religious Sociology and the Sociology of Religion in Britain', *History of the Human Sciences*, 20:2 (2007), 7–28 (pp. 19–20). Elford and Markham, *Middle Way*, pp. 2–3, 96–7. Eric W. Brewin criticised the Christendom Group's 'grossly unfair accusations against modern scientists' and unwillingness 'to seek a sympathetic understanding of modern economics': *Theology*, 48:303 (September 1945), 206–9 (p. 209).

246 Brewitt-Taylor, 'Invention of a "Secular Society"', p. 349.

4

Between mammon and Marx: capitalism, Communism and 'planning for freedom'

The Oldham group saw a 'spiritual' malaise permeating modern economic, political and social life: liberal capitalism had, in its view, failed, but the authoritarian regimes that had arisen to oppose it were even more inhuman and un-Christian. The group sought an alternative to an allegedly chaotic liberalism that would nonetheless maintain liberty, a middle way that coalesced around Karl Mannheim's idea of 'planning for freedom'. The group's discussions in this area took place within (and drew and commented upon) a wider intellectual fascination in the late 1930s and throughout the 1940s with planning and even with aspects of Communism. The group's commitment to planning, even in the carefully hedged form that it took, is striking in light of British Christians' general scepticism about the State. Indeed, the expansion of State power throughout the West had become central to ecumenical analyses of 'totalitarianism' in the 1930s. Planning, it was feared, too easily became idolatry. The totalitarian State, Oldham wrote in 1935, 'lays claim to man in the totality of his being', thus denying the independence of religion, culture, education and family.[1] Such tendencies were perceived not only in Soviet Russia, Fascist Italy or Nazi Germany but were also visible, if in a milder form, in Britain. It was not doubted that State action had improved education; economic regulation; and the provision of pension, welfare and health benefits, but Christians, it was insisted, could never accept the dictates of what Oldham called an 'omnicompetent state', a view also taken at Oxford 1937.[2] The Oldham group was, on the one hand, part of a resurgence of Christian 'civil society' ideals, such as Maritain's personalist democracy; but it also, on the other hand, resisted *anti*-planning arguments, Christian or not.[3] It distinctively combined religious principles *and* secular sociology as well as personalism *and* planning: it represented, in a sense, a meeting of Maritain *and* Mannheim. In this chapter, I outline Mannheim's ideas about planning, explore their role in the group's critiques of capitalism and Communism and, finally, consider important departures from the planning consensus.

'Planning for freedom': Mannheim's 'third way'

Mannheim's essay 'Planning for Freedom' was discussed at Moot meetings in January and April 1939. It derived from his *Mensch und Gesellschaft in einem Zeitalter des Umbaus* (1935), which was translated as *Man and Society in an Age of Reconstruction* (1940).[4] Mannheim expressed his views in the Moot (and its subgroup on education), in comments on others' papers, and in essays on a 'new social philosophy' and on 'values' in 1941 and 1942. Some of these essays were published in *Diagnosis of Our Time: Wartime Essays of a Sociologist* (1943), and his later thinking appeared posthumously in *Freedom, Power and Democratic Planning* (1950).

'Planning' was a popular if variously understood term.[5] Mannheim used it broadly, referring to the coordination of cultural, social and economic life through 'social techniques', particularly by the State. Social techniques included forms of communication, strategies of business organisation, weapon systems and methods of education.[6] Planning could take dictatorial or democratic forms but always fostered 'minority rule' by those in 'key positions'. All countries were 'in the same boat', with *laissez-faire* society – one of Mannheim's key terms – inexorably giving way to planning.[7] The era of *laissez-faire* had featured competing interests (preventing authoritarianism), rule by elites (making mass politics unnecessary) and a residual cultural tradition (providing an unconscious unity). By the 1920s, it had seemed that 'man could live on Hollywood and ice-cream soda alone'.[8]

However, a 'crisis in valuation' had enveloped the West: the cultural consensus had evaporated just when it was most needed. Mannheim saw 'values' (morals or norms) and 'valuation' (the means of making them) not in Marxist terms as a superstructure of economics but as independent influences. Modernity's interconnected transformations – a move from 'primary groups' such as family, neighbourhood and guild to 'great society'; a shift from handicraft to industry; a growth in contact among groups via trade and migration; and a proliferation in authorities – had destroyed 'commonly accepted values' and 'spiritual consistency'.[9] Society no longer knew its own mind, as was shown by incessant disputes over education, punishment, work, leisure, sexual morality, gender roles and religion. The results were 'confusion', social and psychological disintegration, rule by the 'mob', and a 'herd spirit'.[10] Western mores had been replaced by 'fads and fashions' driven by propaganda and advertising (people, for example, 'changed their sex habits as they changed their clothes'). The media taught people 'what to strive for, whom to obey, how to be free, how to love'.[11] Amid such cultural chaos, fragmented cultures could be more easily

Figure 5 Karl Mannheim, 1943, by Elliott & Fry

captured by small groups skilled in social techniques (as demonstrated by the Bolsheviks, Fascists and Nazis).

Convinced that all societies needed 'a certain basic conformity', Mannheim saw the need for a unifying social purpose like that of the war.[12] This unity might seem 'semi-totalitarian', but, while totalitarian efficiency offered lessons, it 'was the efficiency of the devil'.[13] He envisioned something else. The planned society would only enforce a consensus on 'basic' values, such as 'brotherly love, mutual help, decency, social justice, freedom, respect for the person, etc.' 'Complicated' values would be left to individuals. For Mannheim, moreover, democracy was not 'everybody deciding about everything' but rather constitutional planning overseen by Parliament; he warned against either oligarchy or 'private armies, sabotage and mob rule'.[14] This was his 'third way': neither 'goose-step coordination' nor 'helpless confusion' but rather a tolerant but 'militant' democracy.[15] On basic values, he argued, 'we could be as militant as the totalitarian states': democracy did not mean 'one must tolerate the intolerant'.[16] (Fascism should, if necessary, be prevented by violence.) Since society was built of many 'little publics', intermediate groups between individual and State were crucial. A type of planning compatible with freedom meant coordination 'in the spirit of polyphony' rather than 'monotony' to encourage growth, experimentation, 'spontaneity' and 'a many sided individuality'.[17] Planning would be self-limiting (smart planners knew when *not* to plan) and would encourage self-government and decentralisation.[18] It might, he thought, require 'a body somehow similar to the priests' to enforce core standards, but there would be 'regions' of experimentation by 'pioneer groups' and 'citadels of self-determination'.[19] A psychology melding conformity with individuality was needed, and a value consensus would encourage security and counteract the appeal of totalitarianism.[20]

Mannheim thought revolutions were 'apt to go wrong' and lead to tyranny, whether successful (as in the Soviet Union) or not (as in Germany); he deprecated class struggle in favour of a 'united front' – 'the Churches, the Civil Service, the middle classes and the proletariat' – to pursue a 'revolution from above' and gradual change.[21] Elites, too, had to be transformed, and institutions reshaped, by a 'revolution from within' undertaken by small, committed groups (the 'Church within the Church' or 'university within the university').[22] A democratic social transformation was thus feasible, he argued, insisting that religious faith should be identified not with one party but rather with all of them through a society-wide consensus on values.[23]

Values would guide social techniques to defend and even rejuvenate liberty. Fascism had clarified the choice facing the democracies, uniting them in 'a kind of holy war' and preparing them for a great transformation.[24] Britain's traditions of freedom and 'spontaneous reform' – and its unique blend of conformity, individualism and privacy – gave it a special role. Indeed, Britain's 'destiny' was to create 'a vision of a better future', inspiring all those 'rising against universal aggression'.[25] It was, Mannheim argued, the only nation where industrialisation had not abolished religion; moreover, its religious forces had been *both* 'progressive' and 'conservative', unlike on the Continent, where (largely) secular progressivism had confronted (mostly) religious conservatism.[26]

Mannheim saw Christianity's decline as a cause of the crisis in valuation: it had led other institutions – 'family, community, business, trade unions, parties, army, public opinion and its exponents, press, wireless, cinema, associations, age groups, groups of intelligentsia, clubs, etc.' – to compete for influence in mutually neutralising ways.[27] The resulting cultural disintegration was accompanied by 'despiritualisation'. Mannheim often used the term 'spiritual', contrasting it to pure rationality or 'mere analysis and sophistication'.[28] This stress on non-rational thought departed from his earlier work, and he concluded that the need for a 'transcendental religious foundation' of social life was embedded in human nature.[29]

Mannheim saw the cure for *de*spiritualisation in *re*spiritualisation, explaining his interest in the Moot. The Church, he thought, knew how to propagate moral codes and how to be the community's 'visible con-science': it could 'crystallise' morality and create 'dynamic impulses to action'. Prayer encouraged integration, church rituals spiritualised 'mass emotion' and Christianity's global nature aided international understanding.[30] Mannheim also speculated that the Moot might be the basis of an 'Order' to 'revitalize the social body', citing as examples – in terms of their effect-iveness rather than their specific beliefs – the Communist and Nazi parties as well as the Jesuits.[31]

Here 'archetypes' and 'paradigmatic experiences' were key. Archetypes were 'basic valuations underlying civilisation', such as justice or mutual love or other 'basic images' with a 'deep, irrational appeal': they were ancient, powerful ideals or basic mental figures.[32] Paradigmatic experiences preserved 'primordial' impulses deep in the mind.[33] Hodges wrote a series of papers in this vein from 1942. He departed from Mannheim's definitions – and his own varied – but saw archetypes as psychologically meaningful symbols, concepts and experiences that might support cultural reinte-gration.[34] While the language and idea of archetypes recalled Carl Jung's theories, he was rarely mentioned. Hodges even distanced the group's con-cept of 'archetypes' from Jung's, which were seen as too 'uncanny' (even 'demonic') and hereditary.[35] Christianity possessed many archetypes – figures of the hero, the sage, the virgin, the saint, the good shepherd, or concepts of baptism, absolution and the Eucharist – and shared its values through paradigmatic experiences of sin, redemption, love and suffering.[36] Mannheim and Hodges agreed that these precepts had to be rethought for mass society without being diluted or warped. There were doubts whether such a 'translation process', in Clarke's words, was feasible, given that, as Moberly argued, 'small-scale values' lost elements of 'personal encounter' in larger contexts; still, educating people to apply Christian principles in modern life was the goal.[37] Protestant and Catholic influences were seen as complementary. Catholicism had a sociological tradition but was prone to 'mediaevalism' and authoritarian corporatism. Protestantism tended towards individualism and neglected the social order, but its emphases on individual freedom, voluntarism, self-help and mutual aid could resist cen-tralism.[38] Mannheim sought something like a Catholic moral system that was allied to Protestant elements to prevent it becoming oppressive. He agreed with Oldham that only the churches – rather than, say, the universities, in which he saw 'no hope' – could stop planning from becoming 'blind and disastrous'.[39]

Planned societies also needed unity and enthusiasm for carrying out arduous social transitions. The group saw totalitarianism as relying on pseudo-religious integration, but Mannheim hoped for a 'genuine' democratic reunification through a 'rebirth' of religion.[40] Planning *for freedom* thus also meant planning *for religion*. Mannheim saw religion as manifested in various ways: personal experience, fellowship, social organisation and rituals. Planning could support all of these, encouraging experiences of God (e.g. in new forms of monastic life), restoring community and developing a ceremonial 'religious behaviourism'.[41] Imbuing social work with a new spirit and a 'devotion to human interests' would tame bureaucracy ('the dry spirit of the desk'); 'inwardness and transcendence' were needed for life to be 'more than the satisfaction of biological needs or a jig-saw puzzle of objective social institutions'.[42] 'Planning for freedom' thus offered a framework for thinking about how religion might play a central role in reshaping State and society.

Mannheim's persuasiveness within the Oldham group rested on his authority as a sociologist, the utility of his ideas, the importance he ascribed to Christianity and his direct experience of totalitarianism in Germany. He convinced the group that some form of planning was inevitable. Moberly quickly agreed there was no alternative: Mannheim's programme had to be pursued 'with all our might'.[43] By early 1941 the Moot generally seemed to agree on it.[44] Clarke labelled it a 'plan of action for the democracies'; Vickers saw a need for 'revolutionary ferment among the middle aged and the well-to-do' and a new institutional 'custodian of our scale of values'.[45] Some members, such as Vidler, were only gradually persuaded. In 1939, he thought a planned democracy unlikely and modern society 'irredeemable'; even so, he saw no alternative to Mannheim's approach, 'even though it might fail', suggesting that Mannheim had convinced him that, in Britain at least, democratic planning was possible.[46] He continued to argue that mass society was more likely to disintegrate than become 'Mannheim's Brave New World', and he suggested that Christians might instead go underground to outlast 'the coming tyranny' and defend 'personal freedom'.[47] But by 1944 Vidler had come round to the idea of planning guided by 'a doctrine of the true ends of human existence'. Christians rightly feared State planning, but their 'sneers about bureaucracy' were, he thought, mistaken: pluralism needed a strong State with a sense of moral responsibility.[48] In *Theology* he argued that a 'planned society' (but not totalitarianism as such) was inevitable.[49] He remained, however, ambivalent: in 1946 he reproached an advocate of 'Beveridgism' for too easily dismissing fears that 'the social service State may become the servile State'.[50] Vidler here referenced Hilaire Belloc's formulation of the oppressive 'servile state': though originally coined shortly before the First World War, it enjoyed a new popularity in the 1940s as a shorthand term expressing concerns about Government power. But despite lingering doubts of this kind, Mannheim's ideas came to permeate CCFCL memoranda, which called for 'deliberate planning and ordered integration' and for 'powerful new social techniques' to 'serve the cause of freedom'.[51] Oldham's *Resurrection of Christendom* (1940) – the first in the *CNL* Books series – was imbued with a similar spirit and language.[52] In 1943 the Moot agreed to seek non-revolutionary social change in order to ensure political power was used 'responsibly'.[53]

Although Oldham initially shared Vidler's scepticism, he was soon packaging Mannheim's ideas for readers of the *CNL*. He called *Man and Society* 'one of those rare books which open the mind to a new dimension of reality': he also argued a planned society was 'inescapable' and required 'radical' change and efforts at 'Christianising the new state'.[54] In June 1941 he asserted it was necessary *'consciously to plan for freedom'* while encouraging 'spontaneous activity and responsible actions'.[55] In a *CNL* essay titled 'Planning for Freedom' he stated that modern society had to be planned: without a 'good' plan a 'bad one' would result. Reassuring readers that Mannheim did not seek 'a band of intellectuals running society from above' but rather a new 'consciousness', he stressed the roles of 'smaller groups', an agreement on values and the importance of Christian 'archetypes'.[56] There were exceptions to the group's consensus, but before discussing them I will first locate the group's thinking about planning with regard to what it saw as the age's key extremes in the economic sphere: *laissez-faire* capitalism and totalitarian Communism. (Fascism was addressed more as a form of extreme nationalism than as an economic theory, as the next chapter discusses.)

Between mammon and Marx: the contexts of 'planning for freedom'

Worshipping false gods: critiques of capitalism

Critiques of 'capitalism', '*laissez-faire*', 'the present economic structure', the 'world-economic system', 'financial values', the 'profit motive', 'mammon-worship' and 'cut-throat competition' recurred in the Oldham group. The pseudo-religious veneration of economic rationality was seen to encourage greed and exploitation. From its origins the *CNL* attacked the 'idolatry of commercial and financial values' as the 'worship of false gods'.[57] Oldham denounced generations of British sacrifices to the 'Moloch' of economic efficiency, citing enclosure acts, labour exploitation, imperial land seizures and the ill-treatment of colonial populations.[58] The 'tyranny' of false values, dominance of the profit-motive and loss of meaning in work were symptoms of capitalism's violation of human needs.[59] In the *CNL*, Temple argued economics must be subordinated to the 'truly human' (and the human, in turn, to the 'divine').[60] In 1946, Oldham claimed that 'unregulated capitalism' shared a 'demonic element' with totalitarianism: 'The soulless pursuit of power', he stated, 'is matched by the soulless pursuit of profit'.[61]

True community, it was alleged, had dissolved in the 'machine age', what Demant called 'two centuries of life dominated by mechanical, industrialised and financial values'.[62] The group stressed the violation of natural rhythms, limits and resources. Artist Eric Gill's *CNL* Book, *Christianity and the Machine Age* (1940), depicted faith and industrialism as incompatible. (The connection between Gill – who was a prominent figure in pacifist and 'anti-mechanisation' circles – and the *CNL* may have come about via Philip Mairet, who was friends with Gill and involved with both the Moot and CFC.[63]) The Bishop of Sheffield deplored a 'machine age' in which spirituality was thought to be 'strange'.[64] In the *CNL* in 1946, Violet Markham saw 'a mechanical civilization out of hand' at the heart of the world crisis.[65] Oldham lamented the 'perverted' urban economy and the 'ruthless exploitation' of resources.[66] Temple decried 'the sacrilegious sacrifice of rural England to urban interests'.[67] Murry relentlessly idealised village life.[68] An 'inescapable dependence on nature' topped a list of 'elements of a political and social faith' agreed upon in the Moot in 1942.[69] Such idealised rural imagery was of a piece with a broader trend from the 1920s onwards, visible in contexts as varied as prime minister Stanley Baldwin's speeches, the foundation of the Council for the Protection of Rural England (1926) and J. B. Priestley's *English Journey* (1934).

But the group also distinguished itself from other Christians' allegedly naïve ruralism.[70] Planning for freedom was understood as moving *with* technological development, and Oldham – reviewing Peter Drucker's *The Future of Industrial Man* (1942) – insisted that 'the Christian mind' must be 'industrially conscious'.[71] Even Murry, who founded a rural commune, saw not machines themselves but rather the lack of Christian control over them as the 'lethal' element of modern life.[72] In 1945, Bliss reproached the Christian 'Council for the Church and Countryside' for idealising nature, later complaining that many Christians sought simply to 'escape from our machines' rather than face the difficult work of redefining neighbourly love in industrial contexts.[73] The *CNL* also distinguished a properly Christian reverence for nature from its 'pagan' worship.

Capitalism was reproached for causing poverty, misery, waste and inequality. Mannheim saw the destructive effects of the trade cycle – primarily unemployment – as one of *laissez-faire*'s key failures.[74] In *The Idea of a Christian Society* (1939), Eliot suggested that Britain was a 'financial oligarchy', and condemned 'moral deterioration', 'malnutrition' and 'unregulated industrialism'. He doubted whether liberal society was anything more than 'a congeries of banks, insurance companies and industries'.[75] Hodges identified the 'evil' of capitalism through four linked historical processes: the capture of politics by wealth, the separation of economic power from the people, the divorce of personal ambition from public interest and the alienation of 'the product of labour' from workers.[76] The *CNL* and Moot deplored a 'plutocratic', un-Christian Britain. Reducing inequality and eliminating 'the domination of financial interests' were essential, Oldham argued, to 'social justice and harmony', and he highlighted the crippling effects of the class system on youth.[77] The phrase 'social justice' – meaning specifically a reduction in poverty and the provision of equal opportunities – was often invoked, and Mannheim named it as a key aim of planning.

Similar to attitudes towards science, practices of production, trade and banking were condemned *not* as such but rather for having become amoral ends in themselves. In the *CNL*, Temple argued that the economic 'natural order' – in which 'consumption should control production' and 'production should control finance' – had become 'inverted'.[78] (The consumer was, after all, 'the only truly human interest in the whole process', a view shared by a 1943 CFC report.[79]) 'Planning for freedom' suggested that by reorienting economic activity on *values* – which the vast war-time mobilisation of resources for non-commercial purposes demonstrated was possible – capitalism's destructive effects could be avoided, mitigated or repaired. It also, importantly, offered a competing vision of social justice to that offered by Communism. And this, too, was vitally important to the group.

'Elements of truth': addressing Marxism and Communism

Linking planning with 'freedom' distanced the group's anti-capitalism from Marxism and Communism, terms frequently used as synonyms, though the latter often referred specifically to the Soviet Union. In Britain, Marxism was politically marginal but intellectually influential. The *CNL* lamented that atheist Communism had become 'the rallying point of social reconstruction', blaming Christians' lack of a social message and their support for the status quo, a point that had also been made at the Oxford ecumenical conference in 1937.[80] Communism's universalism and stress on social justice made it, unlike Fascism or National Socialism, appealing to some in the Oldham group. Indeed, Murry, Hodges and Miller openly advocated some version of Marxism. In *The Necessity of Communism* (1932) Murry had called for a distinctively 'English', democratic and tolerant Communism; later, he praised Marxist views on the social determination of thought, which Christians, he complained, had ignored.[81] Hodges thought Communism appealed to Christians seeking 'drastic social changes', and his own Moot papers had clear Marxist influences.[82] In *Biblical Politics* (1943) and *The Christian Significance of Karl Marx* (1946) – which Oldham and Bliss praised – Miller mixed Barthian theology and Marxist sociology.[83] The *CNL* reproached the churches for ignoring economic exploitation and, except for some of the free churches, for alienating the working class.[84] In 1946, Bliss thought Christians underestimated Communism's 'powerful attraction', singling it out three years later as Christianity's main opponent.[85]

In general, the group claimed 'elements' or 'aspects' in Communism had a spiritual relevance.[86] Mannheim saw a personalist idea of 'meeting' in Marxist critiques of capitalist 'reification'.[87] Oldham thought Marx was right that 'life is essentially conflict' and harmonious progress an 'illusion'.[88] Soviet entry into the war seemed to promise that the post-war world would not be 'an Anglo-Saxon settlement' based solely on *laissez-faire*, opening the possibility for social reconstruction.[89] Hodges urged Christians to learn from Marx's analysis of morality, politics, law and religion: he called for a *Christian* dialectic and theory of class struggle.[90] *CNL* guest editor Mary Stocks – a leading figure in movements for women's suffrage, family allowances and birth control – called Communism 'a good seed-bed' for religion: it had, she thought, an 'essentially religious' view of history and valued cooperation over competition.[91] Temple saw 'elements of truth' that Marxists had expressed better than Christians, and, at times, theologians and philosophers such as Maritain, Niebuhr and Berdyaev agreed.[92] Niebuhr used Temple's distinction between Communism's 'Christian heresy' and Nazism's 'anti-Christian paganism'. The former was a materialist 'illusion', but it nonetheless promoted universal values, instilled a 'passion for social justice', rejected belief in a master race and denied 'self-justifying' power.[93] Berdyaev saw, Oldham said, 'important and necessary truths' in Communism (despite its 'fundamental untruth'): its 'spirit of community' and rejection of exploitation.[94] Oldham stated that Communism was 'this-worldly' but insisted it nonetheless had 'religious elements', whether via Hebrew influences on Marx or through the Russian 'soul'.[95] In 1945, he divided Communism's laudable, if secularised, effort to realise the Kingdom of God from its contemptible view that ends justify means.[96] Marxism expressed 'truths about human relationships', the Oxford philosopher Ian Crombie wrote in the *CNL*, and 'liberalism expresses others', a passage Oldham quoted in a draft report for Amsterdam 1948.[97]

However, the group also vehemently critiqued Communism, especially after the Nazi–Soviet pact and the Russian invasion of Finland in November 1939. As had been the case at Oxford 1937, the critique of Communism focused on its utopianism, materialism and disregard for human dignity.[98] Dawson told Oldham the sole consolation of that 'dark time' was that the cooperation of the two totalitarianisms broke the 'false issue of Left and Right'; the first *CNL* supplement likewise suggested that such an 'unmasking of forces' and 'destruction of false peace' were among God's purposes in the war.[99] Stalinism's atheism, religious repression and perversion of socialist ideals were denounced. Marxism's own materialism was stressed: like capitalism, it valued the economic over the spiritual, and, like Fascism, its violation of human nature could only bring 'evil and misery'.[100] Russia showed the 'folly' of believing any class possessed superior virtue.[101] The German invasion of the Soviet Union in June 1941 brought, Oldham wrote, a welcome ally but also 'a new confusion', since aspects of the Russian regime were 'hardly distinguishable' from Nazism.[102] Letters to the *CNL* were ambivalent. While detesting 'dictatorship, the secret police, the periodical mass-trials, the absence of civil liberty and the use – or alleged use – of torture', one praised Russian society as more Christian than Britain's 'frank mammon-worship'.[103] Another decried Communism's 'hate, murder and untruth' but saw it as an alternative to 'bourgeois' forms of 'godlessness'.[104] That correspondent, Russian-born Orthodox theologian Evgeny Lampert, also wrote a 1941 *CNL* essay doubting that 'bourgeois' Christianity was better than Marxist atheism, citing the West's aimless freedom and lack of 'a unity and a centre in life'.[105] However, an anonymous *CNL* essay in 1944 argued that the imposition of the Soviet model would mean 'suicide' for Europe, whose tradition was Christian, 'personalistic' and 'anti-totalitarian'.[106]

As the war ended, the Oldham group became increasingly anti-Communist. For one, the Moot gained a fervent anti-Marxist with Michael Polanyi becoming a member from 1944; for another, Murry turned decisively against Communism. The *CNL* continued to give voice both to those well disposed towards Communism (such as the Czech Lutheran theologian Josef Hromádka) and to those opposed to it.[107] In 1948, for example, the *CNL* summarised a Swiss church newspaper exchange sparked when Emil Brunner had reproached Karl Barth for not taking a stand against Communism.[108] Barth responded that the Church need not 'systematize her actions in political situations'; in any case, Communism, with few western adherents, was 'not worth it'.[109] That year, George Every wrote to Oldham to insist Christianity's 'libertarian elements' could inspire resistance to the Soviets; R. H. Crossman – editor of the influential collection

The God that Failed (1949) – urged 'fighting for the soul of Europe against the Communists'.[110] The WCC's Amsterdam conference indeed stressed freedom, but the organisers (Oldham included) downplayed elements of anti-Communism in order to enable Eastern Orthodox churches to participate.[111] There continued to be differing ecumenical viewpoints on how to deal with Soviet Communism and the Cold War, and the movement has been reproached both for insufficiently condemning Soviet human-rights violations and for allegedly becoming an instrument of western interests.[112] Throughout its existence, the Oldham group sought to avoid either pitfall, a stance that also reflected its internal political tensions.

'Active and discriminating support': the welfare state

The 'planning for freedom' consensus also shaped the group's reactions to war-time and post-war steps towards State action on employment, social security, housing, health and education, later known collectively as 'the welfare state'. In the general election of July 1945, the *CNL* maintained its studied party-political neutrality but urged Christians to help build a new post-war society.[113] It neither praised nor condemned Labour's resounding victory, but it did assert – against some Conservative accusations to the contrary – that the party was well within 'the British liberal democratic tradition'.[114] A 1946 *CNL* essay gave Christian arguments for either 'radical' or 'conservative' positions.[115] Here was another middle way: the aim of building a welfare state was conditionally defended, but the need for strong communities beyond it was also stressed.

In January 1943, the Moot was visited by Frank Pakenham, assistant to Sir William Beveridge. Pakenham presented a paper on political morality and discussed the 'Beveridge Report' on post-war social security, the release of which the previous month had sparked intense debate and fundamentally shaped the emerging welfare state. Beveridge's plan featured an insurance system, family allowances and a national health service. Pakenham, a socialist and Roman Catholic (Beveridge was a Liberal of vaguely Protestant beliefs), saw a specifically Christian justification for the plan. Christians, he said, had to decide whether to 'shrink back in alarm every time the State did anything' – which too many, he thought, were doing – or to 'face the implications and seek appropriate safeguards'.[116] No basic opposition to the plan emerged in the Moot, where Mannheim had earlier foreseen a right to work, a 'living wage', free health care and 'economic security in old age' as components of 'planning for freedom'.[117] In the Moot, Bliss critiqued Austrian economist F. A. Hayek's *The Road to Serfdom* (1944), a paean to free-market competition and critique of planning, for its exaggerated 'fear of state control'.[118] Likewise, Oldham, though warning about excessive State power, cheered Beveridge's aim of eliminating 'want', urging Christians to cultivate an attitude of 'active and discriminating support' for the plan.[119] The goal of social justice was stressed, and the war-time government's tepid support for the plan critiqued.[120]

The *CNL*'s support for the welfare state was in fact both 'active' and 'discriminating'. An essay on pensions stressed there was no one-size-fits-all solution, but it nonetheless welcomed Beveridge's plan.[121] A CFC research group accepted that the State could encourage equality but warned against giving it too much power.[122] A 1945 essay pressed Christians to support full employment from a duty to their neighbours.[123] (Eliot, as noted below, disagreed and wrote a rejoinder.) In June 1945 Bliss distinguished between the post-war housing crisis, when State planning was essential, and a longer-term return to a greater reliance on the free market.[124] Churches were urged to help plan 'new towns'.[125] (There had been smaller efforts by the churches to contribute to town planning and local civic life after the 1924 COPEC conference.) Some Christians opposed the Education Bill introduced in December 1943 – passed in 1944 and widely known as the 'Butler Act' – for expanding State influence in that area. However, Oldham argued that its provisions for free schooling, raising the school-leaving age and religious education in state schools led the *CNL* to be 'wholly' in favour.[126] He pointed out, though, that Douglas Woodruff, editor of the Catholic weekly *The Tablet*, had been editorialising against both Beveridge and Butler for taking 'dangerous strides towards totalitarianism'.[127] Given a *CNL* supplement, Woodruff – who had taken a friendly line towards Mussolini and Franco (though a critical one towards the Nazis) – reproached those Christians who supported State welfare for betraying liberty.[128] Oldham, in public, respected Woodruff's view (which he linked to Hayek's), but he also stressed the dangers of *private* power and the State's duty to restrain it.[129] Private letters show that, behind the scenes, the decision to publish Woodruff's supplement had led to controversy within the editorial board. Symons was especially concerned that the essay was part of a worrying trend in which the *CNL* only referred to 'government action' in ways that had been 'cautious and negative': this was justifiable but only, he argued, 'if we not merely refer to but also *put forward* a *positive* picture of state action as, within its limits, a beneficial thing'.[130] Not long afterwards, A. D. Lindsay rebutted both Woodruff and Hayek in the *CNL*, arguing that the State could address the 'frightful but remediable evils' of capitalism while also promoting liberty.[131] (In other venues around this time, Woodruff and Pakenham publicly debated the Beveridge plan.[132]) In the 1950s, Vidler had come to argue that the welfare state could encourage Christian values.[133]

However, this advocacy, while active, was also discriminating, stressing the need to limit State power and develop a strong community life separate

from it. Oldham viewed working-class institutions, such as the adult education movement, cooperatives, friendly societies and other clubs, as the core
of a potentially 'self-governing social sphere'.[134] In early 1945, he contrasted
the Nazis' 'ruthless, scientific power state' with the Allies' 'scientific welfare state': society must move towards the latter but the two threatened
to 'coalesce'.[135] Bliss stressed the danger of too much State planning and
pointed instead to the 'Peckham experiment' – a privately run, progressive London health centre – which, while secular, exemplified local community organisation.[136] The CFC stressed the *limits* of State control of
industry, preferring changes to be made within industrial organisation
itself.[137] Reducing economic antagonisms and increasing cooperation were
advocated in the *CNL*.[138] The need for small-scale voluntarism was consistently emphasised. Even well-intentioned welfare, Bliss argued, caused
more of life to be 'dealt with on forms, in card indexes, over post office
grills by bureaucrats who regard you as a name on a card, and technical
experts who see you as a medical or social "case"'.[139] Murry complained
that 'bureaucracy is choking creativity', suggesting Britain had to seek a
synthesis of Communism and 'capitalist democracy'.[140] Hodges similarly
bemoaned Labour's bureaucratic collectivism and the 'dehumanising' tendencies of the State.[141] The group's stress on the local, voluntary and small-
scale echoes various strains within British political thought, from guild
socialism to Burkean conservatism (the latter to this day still evoked in
references to 'little platoons'). However, group members saw such ideals
less as tied to a specific *political* tradition – there were few references, for
example, to Burke – and more as distinctively *Christian* insights that had
found various expressions throughout history.

A contested consensus: debates, dissensions and departures

In March 1949, Bliss pointed to what she saw as a praiseworthy British consensus: in the USA, a WCC report seeking alternatives to what it defined
as the 'extremes' of *laissez-faire* and Communism had been attacked by
business interests, conservatives and evangelical Christians for promoting the 'leftist beliefs of the Churchmen of Europe'.[142] In Britain, she
wrote, such Christian social questioning was not denounced, and Britain's
main political parties were 'committed to discovering a middle way'. She
admitted, though, that the approaching 1950 election made clear 'that
even middle ways have two sides to them, and that the two sides may be
very far apart'.[143] Such divisions are also apparent within the Oldham group
itself: 'planning for freedom' certainly moulded its aims, strategies and language, but it remained a contested consensus. In the latter stages of the
war and into the post-war period, group dynamics and broader political

developments changed how the concept was seen. Four persistent critics of planning for freedom – Murry, Hodges, Eliot and Polanyi – drew variously on left-wing, conservative and liberal perspectives to question it from different directions.

Murry and Hodges offered perspectives from the left. Murry had long advocated an 'English', democratic and socialist revolution, seeing the modern crisis as caused not by 'values' but by inherent capitalist dynamics.[144] In early Moot meetings, he called for State and Church to bring 'machine society' under 'Christian control'.[145] What he described as a 'national Christian society' seemed, in his eyes, amenable to Mannheim's vision. (Indeed, in July 1940, Oldham associated 'planning for freedom' with Murry's name.) Still, Murry noted a 'sense of futility' at the lack of concrete planning policies, feeling 'forced' to agree with the idea only by the lack of an alternative.[146] Reviewing Mannheim's *Man and Society* in 1940, he agreed that planning was inevitable.[147] But, privately, he needled the Moot for being too afraid of 'popular movements' and overly 'diplomatic'.[148] He doubted democracy could be maintained in an industrial society at war, reinforcing his aim to create a *local* community to survive the social collapse.[149] But some saw Murry's and Mannheim's views as complementary: local experiments were vital to Mannheim, and Murry admitted planning might stave off a 'lapse into anarchy'. Löwe and Eliot even suggested that Murry's plan depended on the success of Mannheim's.[150] What Murry called his own 'obstinate condition of pessimism', however, made him doubtful.[151] Mannheim, in turn, found Murry's commune appealing but ultimately 'romantic'.[152] Oldham thought Murry usefully corrected the planners' hubris but stressed that 'living an autonomous life on the fringes of society in close relation to nature' – here referring to Murry's experimental rural commune – was an option only for 'a tiny minority'.[153] In the same vein, Niebuhr saw Murry as offering 'monasticism' rather than a 'real-world' ethic.[154]

Concerned that planning for freedom had become an unquestioned 'socio-political orthodoxy', however, Murry quit attending the Moot from September 1942.[155] He thought Mannheim's plan ignored the need for broad social transformation and depended on dangerous large-scale institutions. Still, he stayed in contact with Oldham and the Moot.[156] His writings, in turn, were sympathetically reviewed in the *CNL*.[157] Labour's victory in 1945 lessened his despair about British democracy. More dramatically, he abruptly rejected pacifism and Communism, admitting he had underestimated totalitarianism's ruthlessness. Indeed, earlier in the war, he had both publicly and privately downplayed the threat of Nazism, writing in *Peace News* in August 1940 that he did not believe that 'a Hitlerian Europe would be quite so terrible as most people believe it would be' and even confiding to his journal in 1941 that the Nazi social system was 'on the whole, better than ours: less corrupt, more truly communal and creative'.[158] (As Chapter 6 notes, however, at the same time Murry was also publicly urging the defence of freedom.) In *Trust or Perish* (1946) Murry still insisted that Britain must refrain from war and, if necessary, unilaterally disarm. But *The Free Society* (1948) expressed a radical change of perspective. He now saw Communism as a threat to freedom – justifying even a preventive war against it – and critiqued planning, nationalisation and Labour's policy of giving workers material benefits without demanding a new, 'responsible' freedom: here and in *Community Farm* (1952) he also fretted about the expanding welfare bureaucracy.[159]

Like Murry, Hodges at first doubted Mannheim's planning vision but came to accept it. But he was plagued by fears that democratic planning was a 'phantasy', and he turned in a more Marxist direction.[160] In June 1943, he presented a paper on 'Politics and the Moot', urging the group to stop 'evading' socialism – which went 'partly the same way' as they aimed to – by obsessing about natural law, 'talking about managers' and chasing 'the phantom of the Third Way'.[161] A choice had to be made, he argued, and a genuinely *socialist* commitment could 'give sense to the planners and vision to the moving masses'.[162] While his embrace of Communism did not derive from his Christianity, Hodges thought it better than Catholic authoritarianism or a Protestantism with the 'right ideals' but unrealistic politics.[163] Christianity's power lay in its 'archetypes', and Hodges envisioned a socialist 'collective commonwealth' on that basis.

By staying in the Moot and becoming one of its most prolific contributors, Hodges's critique had more impact than Murry's. The Moot may not have 'ignored' socialism, but it had, certainly, avoided taking a clear stance upon it. For instance, unlike other critiques of capitalism popular among Christians, such as 'Distributism' or 'Social Credit', the group did not debate private property (beyond insisting it be used 'responsibly'). Murry told Oldham the Moot's more Marxist members – especially himself ('the pacifist-socialist community crank') and Löwe ('an honest-to-God Communist') – had held back early on so as to not endanger the group's dynamic.[164] Oldham admitted 'socialism' reflected the group's view that 'no private interests should impede public interests', but he feared the term would 'scare off some valuable allies'.[165] Other members agreed with Hodges that Christians must be less naïve about power, but they thought he overstressed class struggle, wrongly discounted the possibility of reforming existing structures and, worryingly, exemplified a trend towards giving 'social justice' priority over freedom.[166] Mannheim insisted that a broad social revolution would endanger freedom, justifying his preference for 'revolution from above' even if he was not happy with the phrase itself.[167] After discussing Hodges's 'Politics and the Moot' paper, the Moot put greater stress on the control of 'great concentrations of capital' in 'the interests of the people', but it still rejected broad-based social revolution in favour of a democratic, reformist approach.[168] Hodges insisted, however, that a destructive revolution would only be avoided if 'political democracy' was prepared to 'declare unambiguously for economic democracy'.[169] He was later disillusioned by socialist acquiescence to 'the collectivist trend of the times': Russian Communism had become a 'terrible power-machine' and the Labour Party offered little except expanding bureaucracy.[170] True socialists, he argued, should reject 'the state machine', and he continued to stress a 'cultural revolution' over planning.[171]

A quite different politics – a conservatism influenced by pluralist-medievalist ideals of civil society – made Eliot deeply sceptical about planning. At the first Moot meeting, he saw Christianity's power in the 'local circles' and 'small groups' that were being undermined by mass society: 'welding people together without local distinction' through State planning could release 'terrible demonic forces in mass-hysteria'.[172] He rejected increasing State power and doubted Mannheim's progressive view of culture, sharing instead the views of Christopher Dawson and V. A. Demant.[173] While praising Mannheim's 'Planning for Freedom' paper for its 'courageous attack' on relevant problems, he doubted its 'analysis of inevitability' and saw Mannheim's main assumptions and his definitions of democracy, freedom and social progress as too vague. Mannheim's views were also 'thoroughly urban', ignoring human relations to nature.[174] Reviewing *Man and Society* in 1940, Eliot praised parts of Mannheim's 'substantial' and 'impressive' book, and he seemed to accept that mass society had come to stay: social techniques must be used 'for good' lest they be used 'for evil'. If there was an alternative, he (like Murry) saw it in the 'dark age attitude': 'waiting, perhaps for many generations, for the storm of the machine age to blow over; retiring, with a few of the best books, to a small self-contained community, to till the soil and milk the cow'.[175] Still, he valued Mannheim's diagnosis of the situation and call for an elite 'Order'. He doubted strongly, though, that culture and religion could be planned.[176]

From about the middle of the war, Eliot started finding more fault with planning in general and Mannheim's views in particular. He aired his misgivings in *Theology* in May 1943, in a review of *Diagnosis of Our Time*.[177] In August that year, he feared planning would bring forth something dangerous. Christianity's 'twilight', he wrote to Oldham, might lead not to a 'sensible materialism' but instead to 'a kind of reversion': 'When the planners have done their planning, they may be surprised to find people starting to sacrifice goats on rustic altars'.[178] Soon after, Eliot defined culture definitively as 'that which cannot be planned, except by God'.[179] In a

1944 letter to Oldham, he dismissed Hodges's socialism as merely a decision to 'plump for one kind of totalitarianism rather than another'.[180] In
March 1945, he wrote privately that Mannheim was 'a very good fellow' but
his ideas were 'dangerous'.[181] That month, Eliot wrote a spirited rebuttal of a
CNL supplement by 'Civis' urging Christians to support a full-employment
policy. Under the pseudonym 'Metoikos', Eliot denied any *Christian* aspect
to the (otherwise worthy) aim of reducing unemployment. If secular politics were to dictate Christian opinion, he warned, distinctions between
'eternal' and 'temporal' categories would crumble, 'and we shall be well
on the way to the religion of the State'.[182] Thus, early on, Eliot was somewhat open to aspects of planning for freedom. But his dislike of State
power – probably encouraged by Hodges's explicitly socialist redefinition
of planning and the emerging *reality* of a planned State – saw him increasingly alienated from the group on this issue.

Eliot has sometimes been seen as a dominant figure in the Moot; however, as the discussion about planning suggests, he was often on the margins
of or even outside its consensus. Indeed, he told Oldham that he valued the
Moot precisely for the '*significant disagreement*' he experienced there: he
had found people, as he put it, '*worth* disagreeing with'.[183] (He later wrote
that the members of a 'clerisy' were compelled into each other's company
'by the fact that they find each other the most profitable people to disagree
with'.[184]) At the opposite extreme, it has been argued that the Oldham group
was completely irrelevant to Eliot. This too is wrong. Eliot clearly used his
differences with it (through years of activity in the Moot, *CNL*, CCFCL
and CFC) to creative ends. He thought the Moot's 'variety' had given it its
'zest' and 'cohesion', and he claimed to have found 'an unexpectedly deep
and genuine sense of loyalty and kinship' that was 'so very fecundating': 'If
it has made as much difference to everyone as it has to me', he wrote, 'it
has justified itself fully'.[185] In 1943, he described Oldham's draft of Temple's
CNL supplement as 'a masterpiece of syncretism and selection': 'almost the
whole of the document seems to me wholly admirable'.[186] His participation
influenced both *The Idea of a Christian Society* (1939) and *Notes towards
the Definition of Culture* (1948).[187] Still, he rejected pursuing a programme
of State power, socialism and vague Christian 'principles'.

When Michael Polanyi joined the Moot in summer 1944, he brought
further anti-statist and anti-Marxist views to the group, this time from
a liberal position.[188] Mannheim had invited him to the group after long
discussions, in the knowledge that Polanyi disliked 'planning for freedom'.
(Philip Mairet later recalled a 'ding-dong battle' at the Moot between the
two men in 1944.[189]) Polanyi had what he called a '"radical" Keynesian
attitude' that foresaw the least possible amount of planning, seeing
Mannheim's views as akin to Communism's all-pervasive statism.[190] He

also doubted planning was as innovative as often claimed.[191] Rather than State coordination, Polanyi stressed 'dynamic orders of spontaneous formation and autonomous continuation' as the best response to totalitarianism: Mannheim's allowance for 'regions' of unplanned spontaneous creativity was, in his view, insufficient.[192] Complex societies needed not more planning but more 'individual initiative'.[193] Polanyi also critiqued Mannheim's view of culture for being relativist and based on social determinism (though Mannheim saw himself as *opposing* Marxist excesses here). For Polanyi, ideas had a fully independent power.[194] Like Eliot, Polanyi agreed with the need for 'clerisies', and he saw faith as a bulwark against totalitarianism.[195] But he uncompromisingly attacked Marxism's intellectual pervasiveness, including among Christians. He depicted planning as having arisen in nineteenth-century utopianism and culminating with the Russian Revolution: rather than an adaptation to social development (as Mannheim argued), planning derived above all from the will of specific groups of people who sought to 'take the place of God'.[196]

Polanyi took part in Oldham's ad hoc post-Moot meetings after Mannheim's death. By summer 1948, he was uncomfortable with Hodges's 'combination of Marxism and Biblicism', and he blamed Marxism's appeal on the mistaken view – which had been shared by Mannheim – that planning was 'inevitable': it was necessary, Polanyi insisted, to 'break the fascination with this empty slogan', since planning had proven to be 'almost wholly irrelevant'.[197] Marxism 'perverted' the content of 'Christian hopes'.[198] Marx had been right to attack unregulated capitalism but over-confident about planning: calamitous Russian famines had shown the need for market allocation of resources, for wages to be 'adequately graded' and for corporate profit-making.[199] One had to accept, Polanyi argued, that 'the condition of man is miserable' and social institutions could not be perfected: 'We shall have to resign ourselves once more', he wrote, clearly rejecting Mannheim's view, 'to the inevitability of such social evils as economic wastage, competitive struggle, inequality and oppression'.[200]

Conclusion

Presenting 'planning for freedom' to the Moot for the first time in January 1939, Mannheim urged analysing the 'social experiments' of Communism, Fascism and 'late Capitalism' in order to 'counteract' all of them.[201] His listeners, seeing totalitarian trends advancing throughout the West, broadly agreed. Christianity did not stress State planning, Fenn claimed, but rather 'small groups of people' and 'the absence of control'.[202] But Mannheim persuasively argued that if Christians did not use social techniques in line with their views of personality and community, others would command them for contrary purposes: planning for freedom was not 'necessarily Christian', but it at least was aimed to enable a modern Christian life.[203] It was a 'third way' between *laissez-faire* and totalitarianism, mixing secular sociology with the ecumenical insistence on, as Temple put it, a 'deliberate planning of life' to preserve freedom in mass society.[204] Society could be steered rather than rigidly controlled. While the group opposed excessive State power – Oldham urged Christians to 'resist encroachments by the State into fields best left to voluntary action' – planning nonetheless became part of its consensus.[205]

But the group exemplified Bliss's quip that 'even middle ways have two sides'.[206] Oldham, Moberly and Clarke were quickly convinced by Mannheim; others, like Vidler, Hodges, Murry and Eliot only more reluctantly, and in part temporarily, accepted his viewpoint. Anxieties about hubris were aired in the *CNL*: there were fears of uncontrolled or irresponsible State power and a concern that a failure to recognise human 'sin' could only lead to disaster.[207] Murry, Hodges and Eliot, for different reasons, later questioned or rejected the consensus around planning. Murry's pessimism about the State led him to focus on local community. Hodges insisted on *socialist* planning, a leftward pressure resisted by Eliot (who had long urged 'safeguarding Christianity itself, in our enthusiasm for society'[208]) and, after 1944, by Polanyi. But the group's dislike of *laissez-faire* and aim of 'social justice' enabled finding value even, at times, in Communism. Marxist atheism was denounced but so was acquiescence to an 'un-Christian' capitalism; liberalism's moral void made it appear there was something worthwhile in Communism's seemingly 'spiritual' unity. The group's post-war anti-Communist shift reflected a broader one by British Christians, but the WCC and parts of the Church of England resisted full absorption into the East–West conflict, seeing Marxism as only one symptom of a universal secularist dominance.[209] After the war, *laissez-faire* was critiqued, the welfare state cautiously welcomed and Europe encouraged to steer between American capitalism and Russian Communism. While by the end of the 1940s many Christians had become convinced 'Cold Warriors', the Oldham group sought to avoid the transformation of their faith into a 'politicised doctrine'.[210]

What enabled this mix of secular sociology and Christianity? First, all involved sought to re-establish a lost cultural unity. Mannheim thought a 'militant democracy' would inculcate and enforce 'basic virtues': liberalism would be rescued by a planned order explicitly oriented towards freedom. This echoed Oldham's aim of a 'common social philosophy', Maritain's goal of a 'minimal unity' and Eliot's notion of a culturally orienting 'idea'. Liberal Anglican traditions, too, accepted State direction in religion and culture, a position contrary to the more 'medievalist-pluralist' views of Eliot, Dawson and Demant.[211] Second, Mannheim's call to use social techniques for Christian purposes gave faith a clear role in industrial society, which group members welcomed. Third, Mannheim agreed that smaller groups were vital: a strong 'we-feeling' would emerge via local 'roots'.[212] Fourth, planning for freedom provided an alternative to Marxism, favouring a cross-class alliance over class struggle, a peaceful 'revolution from above' over violent social transformation and the power of 'values' over materialist social determinism.[213] Relatedly, planning for freedom's vagueness about private property helped bridge the group's political divisions, at least until Hodges pushed for a more socialist stance. This lack of focus on property ownership also limited the group's engagement with the alternative schemes for economic organisation at the time, whether 'Distributism' or 'Social Credit'. Moreover, there was little discussion of 'Keynesianism' or monetary policy, with most discussions revolving around broad categories such as 'statism', 'planning' and *laissez-faire*. Fifth, Mannheim, despite calling sociology 'perhaps the most secularized' approach to human life, saw Christianity as vital to solving the 'crisis of valuation'.[214] Its repertoire of psychologically vital symbolic and experiential resources – 'archetypes', 'paradigmatic experiences' and rituals – could shape values, generate commitment and give planning a 'spiritual' foundation. Vidler stressed this aspect in comments after Mannheim's death. Mannheim may not have been a Christian 'in any strict sense of the term', but he was also 'far from being a secularist': 'No one realised more keenly that there are depths in man's existence which neither science nor politics can plumb. He saw that the crisis of our time is at bottom moral, spiritual, theological.'[215]

Mannheim was only one of many advocates of planning in these years, and related ideas were discussed in the Moot and *CNL*. For example, Oldham saw in Mary Parker Follett's *Dynamic Administration* (1942) and T. N Whitehead's *Leadership in a Free Society* (1936) the 'germ of a philosophy' for a society 'both planned and free'.[216] He praised Peter Drucker's *The Future of Industrial Man* (1942) – which depicted centralised bureaucracy as both inevitable and dangerous – for stressing human imperfection and asserting the aim of re-establishing 'a self-governing social sphere' that was compatible with Christianity.[217] In the *CNL*, Basil Smallpeice linked James Burnham's *The Managerial Revolution* (1941) and Whitehead's *Leadership* to Mannheim's idea of a class of managers committed to specific values.[218] Other Christians also mixed faith and management theory.[219] Dawson rejected Mannheim's 'rational' planning; nonetheless, he argued similarly about the problem of a 'disintegrated and despiritualised' society and denied that cultural reintegration could be left solely to 'private initiative' or 'unplanned activities'.[220]

Even the phrase 'planning for freedom' was not unique to Mannheim.[221] Indeed, liberal Austrian economists such as F. A. Hayek and Ludwig von Mises also used it, though in an opposite sense. Hayek, for example, meant planning *for competition*, in which states would *introduce* markets where they did not already exist. He was scornful of arguments – including Mannheim's – that depicted planning as inevitable, and he rejected giving the State more power to achieve moral or social purposes (beyond extending the reach of competitive markets themselves).[222] Karl Popper distinguished Hayek's planning for freedom from Mannheim's: the latter was, in his view, 'collectivistic' and 'holistic', likely to bring 'tyranny' rather than freedom.[223] In contrast, Barbara Wootton's *Freedom under Planning* (1945), inspired by Mannheim, argued against Hayek and for the compatibility of planned and private activities towards a common goal.[224]

The Oldham group's discussions thus took part in a much broader argument about planning and freedom. Throughout the 1930s, liberal economic orthodoxy had weakened, allowing a 'middle-opinion' in favour of State planning to develop.[225] *Laissez-faire* became a common shorthand signifier for a failed version of capitalist liberal democracy. In 1940, even *The Times* saw 'the anarchic tendencies of *laissez-faire*' as 'obsolete'.[226] In a war in which State allocation of resources for a common purpose seemed vindicated, the language of planning, social justice and reconstruction became ubiquitous.[227] It has been said that a consensus emerged – extending 'from the Communist Party to the Butlerite wing of the Conservative Party' – on the need to avoid a return to the poverty, inequality and widespread social exclusion of the pre-war years; however, war-time unity on 'liberty, equality and democracy' concealed a sometimes wide divergence about what each of these terms practically meant, and there was substantial opposition to the planning consensus.[228] Hayek depicted Mannheim as an 'extreme' representative of a 'dominant' position during the war, and he suggested that he had imported 'Eastern' (i.e. German) ideas into Britain.[229] He denied extensive State planning could co-exist with democracy and critiqued Mannheim's claim that freedom needed redefinition in mass society.[230] There was also post-war resistance to planning even by some who, unlike Hayek, had once been sympathetic to it.[231]

Christians took part in debates about successfully combining planning and liberty in the 1930s and 1940s, and many became more accepting of the State. In his best-selling *Christianity and the Social Order* (1942), Temple demanded State guarantees of decent housing and living wages, worker contributions to corporate decision-making and the provision of annual paid holidays.[232] The SCM also tended in a 'socialist' direction.[233] The churches largely accepted the Beveridge plan as a contribution to fighting inequality and poverty but insisted on a strong voluntary sector and vigilance against irresponsible State power or dehumanising bureaucracy.[234] One of the BCC's first statements backed the Beveridge Report and denied that his plan would 'sap the springs of initiative and enterprise'.[235] The *Christian World* agreed.[236] The *Church of England Newspaper* thought the Church should back the reforms but without claiming them as explicitly 'Christian' (though it also gave voice to critics of this position).[237] The *Church Times* thought the plan should be 'cordially welcomed from the Christian point of view'.[238] The *British Weekly, Guardian,* and *Catholic Herald* were also in favour.[239] The Oldham group went further, seeing 'planning' not only as adjusting prices or labour markets or welfare provision but also as a tool for fundamental social renewal. But members also shared doubts about statist planning and welfare that were typical of Christian commentators in Britain at this time. In broad strokes, one can find in the discussions of the group evidence of a shift to the 'left' during the war (in the sense of a growing acceptance of State planning for the reduction of social inequalities) and to the 'right' in the immediate postwar years (driven by anti-Communism and a greater emphasis on the dangers of State power).

Mannheim became a point of reference for Christian discussions about planning even beyond the contexts of the Oldham group itself.[240] Both Temple and William Paton publicly cited Mannheim's idea of 'planning for freedom' as influences.[241] In *Christendom* in 1941, Maurice Reckitt praised Mannheim for grappling seriously and subtly with crucial problems. His main critique was that Mannheim lacked a recognisable 'doctrine of man' that would guide what planning was *for*; moreover, Mannheim ignored the spiritual aspects of human life, especially the existence of a divinely given natural order.[242] Two years later (and rather like Eliot, who was a participant in the Christendom Group), *Christendom* was taking a more critical view of planning and singled out Mannheim as exemplifying its potential dangers.[243]

Thus a stream of Christian opinion hostile to planning co-existed with its acceptance. While arguing that Christianity was essential to a 'recovery of the West', Michael Roberts warned against those Christian sociologists who had a 'passion' for planning that was 'no less extravagant than that of Hitler, Wells and Stalin'.[244] Some Christians critiqued the material emphasis in discussions of planning and social reconstruction. Labour peer Lord Elton complained that the 'better Britain' promised by the planners would bring only a more equitably distributed materialism: 'we can complacently look forward', he sardonically observed, 'to a better Britain founded upon the present statistics of irreligion, venereal disease, black-marketing, juvenile delinquency, theft, bigamy and divorce'.[245] (Even a supporter of the Beveridge Report such as Temple argued that the aim must not simply be more 'comfort' but rather 'responsible citizenship' and the 'development of the person in his community'.[246]) The goal of full employment was critiqued as misguided for failing to consider what work was *for* and reducing people to economic resources.[247] There was also fear of a vast army of social workers who would tell people how to live. In the *Church of England Newspaper*, the right-wing Tory MP Sir Waldron Smithers praised Hayek's 'epoch-making' *Road to Serfdom* as an antidote to the widespread enthusiasm for planning.[248] The editor of the *Catholic Herald* also praised Hayek's warnings about planning, even if he rejected his celebration of competitive markets and found that Hayek ignored natural law.[249]

The *Christian World* in 1948 well expressed a widespread Christian longing for a 'middle path' between the 'jungle' of capitalism's 'anarchic individualism' and the 'cage of Marxian Communism'.[250] This planning consensus was largely confined to elite (or at least solidly middle-class) opinion and remained at least somewhat controversial.[251] Some saw the welfare state as a first step towards bureaucratic totalitarianism. Churchill's – absurd – claim during the 1945 election campaign that Labour would introduce 'some form of Gestapo' as part of its welfare plans (if 'very humanely directed in the first instance') expressed such fears.[252] While there was broad agreement on the goals of reform and need for something between liberalism and the 'omni-competent state', ambivalence, tension, debate, and dissension remained. That 'middle ways' had, at least, 'two sides to them' (as Bliss had put it) was apparent in the Oldham group and in British intellectual culture at large with regard to the linked issues of economy, State and liberty. As the next chapter shows, the group's consensus about national identity was stronger, but it too developed in a drastically changing world situation.

Notes

1 Oldham, *Church, Community and State*, pp. 9–10.
2 *Ibid.*, pp. 7–8, 25. *Churches Survey Their Task*, pp. 87–129.
3 Grimley, 'Civil Society and the Clerisy', pp. 239–42.
4 LPL Lang 26, fos. 75–93, Karl Mannheim, 'Planning for Freedom', n.d. [discussed January 1939] (hereafter cited as Mannheim, 'Planning for Freedom').
5 Pemberton, 'Middle Way', p. 48; Daniel Ritschel, *The Politics of Planning: The Debate on Economic Planning in Britain in the 1930s* (Oxford: Clarendon Press, 1997), pp. 4, 20.

6 Mannheim, 'Planning for Freedom', p. 3.

7 Ibid., pp. 1, 3; Mannheim, Diagnosis, p. 1; and Moot Papers, M7, p. 265.

8 Mannheim, Diagnosis, p. 123.

9 Ibid., pp. 12–30.

10 Mannheim, 'Planning for Freedom', pp. 10, 14, 15.

11 Moot Papers, M4, p. 196 and M14, p. 508; Mannheim, Diagnosis, pp. 105, 138, 148–9.

12 Mannheim, 'Planning for Freedom', pp. 10, 14.

13 Ibid., pp. 1, 2, 5. Moot Papers, M8, p. 295. Mannheim, Man and Society, pp. 259–65.

14 Mannheim, Diagnosis, pp. 7, 49. Moot Papers, M4, pp. 194–5; Mannheim, 'Planning for Freedom', p. 10.

15 Mannheim, 'Planning for Freedom', p. 13. Mannheim, Diagnosis, pp. 4, 7, 25, 46–9, 52–3, 60–72.

16 Mannheim, 'Planning for Freedom', p. 14.

17 Ibid., pp. 4–5, 15; Mannheim, Diagnosis, pp. 70–1, 109, 123–4, 144.

18 Mannheim, 'Planning for Freedom', pp. 9, 10.

19 Mannheim, Diagnosis, p. 119. Mannheim, 'Planning for Freedom', p. 11. Mannheim, Man and Society, p. 264.

20 Mannheim, Diagnosis, p. 51; Moot Papers, M4, p. 199. See Colin Loader, The Intellectual Development of Karl Mannheim: Culture, Politics, and Planning (Cambridge: Cambridge University Press, 1985), pp. 149–77.

21 Mannheim, 'Planning for Freedom', pp. 6–7; Moot Papers, M3, p. 164; M17, pp. 585–8.

22 Moot Papers, M3, p. 149.

23 Mannheim, Diagnosis, pp. 48–9, 109.

24 Moot Papers, M3, p. 161; M17, pp. 585–8. Mannheim, Diagnosis, pp. 101–2.

25 Mannheim, Diagnosis, pp. 9, 11, 48, 51, 70–1, 119, 123, 126, 129–30.

26 Moot Papers, M19, p. 667; Mannheim, Diagnosis, p. 101.

27 Mannheim, Diagnosis, p. 100.

28 See ibid., pp. 15, 20, 24, 26, 47, 100, 101, 103, 120, 123, 129, 131, 135, 140.

29 Loader, Intellectual Development, pp. 159–61; Mannheim, Freedom, Power and Democratic Planning, pp. 288–9.

30 Mannheim, 'Planning for Freedom', pp. 12–13.

31 Ibid., p. 12.

32 Moot Papers, M9, pp. 334, 339; M12, pp. 419, 436; M13, pp. 451, 466; M15, pp. 530–2.

33 Mannheim, Diagnosis, pp. 142–3.

34 OA 14/1/23, H. A. Hodges, 'Christian Archetypes and Symbols', 22 June 1942, p. 2; OA 14/1/91, H. A. Hodges, 'What Is an Archetype?', 27 August 1945, p. 1.

35 Moot Papers, M15, pp. 530, 534. OA 14/1/91, H. A. Hodges, 'What Is an Archetype?', 27 August 1945, p. 3: 'We may agree that the archetypes exist and are found in the places where Jung says they are found, without being committed to his theory of their hereditary character, which raises serious difficulties and is at best unproven. Likewise we may agree with him about

their profound significance, without implying that he himself has understood it exhaustively.'

36 Mannheim, *Diagnosis*, pp. 134–5.
37 *Moot Papers*, M14, p. 507.
38 Mannheim, *Diagnosis*, pp. 106–8.
39 *Moot Papers*, M3, pp. 163–4.
40 Mannheim, *Diagnosis*, pp. 102, 106, 130. *Moot Papers*, M12, p. 421.
41 Mannheim, *Diagnosis*, pp. 126–8.
42 Mannheim, 'Planning for Freedom', p. 11; IOE MOO/47, letter from Karl Mannheim, n.d. [*c.* March 1941], p. 1.
43 OA 14/9/63, Walter Moberly, 'Short Notes on Mannheim and Hodges' Papers', n.d. [discussed April 1939].
44 *Moot Papers*, M3, pp. 165–6; M10, p. 367; M11, p. 397.
45 OA 13/7/46, 'Comments on Paper by Mannheim', n.d.
46 *Moot Papers*, M3, p. 165. OA 14/6/92, A. R. Vidler, 'Comments on Papers by Mannheim and Hodges', n.d. [discussed April 1939], pp. 1–2.
47 *Moot Papers*, M8, pp. 298, 313; M11, p. 397; IOE MOO/44, A. R. Vidler, 'Notes on Some Cultural Issues', p. 1.
48 *Moot Papers*, M20, p. 689.
49 A. R. Vidler, 'Comment on "Our Struggle"', *Theology*, 47:289 (July 1944), 151–4 (p. 153).
50 A. R. Vidler, review of Cook, *The State and Ourselves Tomorrow*, *Theology*, 49:309 (March 1946), 90–1.
51 CERC CCFCL 2/1/2, 'The Spiritual Front', 5 July 1940; LPL Lang 26, fos. 223–5, J. H. Oldham, 'An Initiative of the Churches towards a More Christian Society', rev., 8 July 1940, p. 2; W. Temple 6, fos. 79–83, 'A Fraternity of the Spirit', 7 March 1941, p. 6.
52 *Moot Papers*, M5, pp. 222–3; Oldham, *Resurrection*, pp. 18–19.
53 OA 13/6/33, H. A. Hodges, 'Fifteen Points of Agreement', 24 June 1943.
54 *CNL* 32L, 5 June 1940, pp. 1–2.
55 *CNL* 86S, 18 June 1941, J. H. Oldham, 'Predicament of Society and the Way Out', p. 2. Emphasis in original.
56 *CNL* 104S, 22 October 1941, Oldham, 'Planning for Freedom', pp. 2–3; *CNL* 174L, 24 February 1943, p. 2; *CNL* 174S, 24 February 1943, Oldham, 'Diagnosis of Our Time', pp. 1–4.
57 *CNL* 1S, 1 November 1939, Oldham, 'What Is God Doing?', p. 3; *CNL* 54L, 6 November 1940, p. 2; *CNL* 89L, 9 July 1941, pp. 1–2; *CNL* 116L, 14 January 1942, p. 1.
58 *CNL* 2L, 8 November 1939, pp. 1–2.
59 *CNL* 24L, 10 April 1940, p. 2.
60 *CNL* 41S, 7 August 1940, William Temple, 'Begin Now', p. 3.
61 *CNL* 275L, 11 December 1946, p. 15.
62 *CNL* 37S, 10 July 1940, V. A. Demant, 'Our Justification', p. 1. References to the 'machine-age' or 'machine-society': *Moot Papers*, M2, p. 85; M3, pp. 164–5; M5, p. 242; M7, pp. 253–4; M15, pp. 524–5.

63 Simon Blaxland-de Lange, *Owen Barfield: Romanticism Comes of Age* (Forest Row: Temple Lodge, 2006), pp. 144–5.

64 *CNL* 294S, 12 December 1945, Bishop of Sheffield [Leslie Hunter], 'The Church and the People', pp. 7–8.

65 *CNL* 267S, 21 August 1946, Violet Markham, 'The Man and the Machine', p. 8.

66 *CNL* 45S, 4 September 1940, J. H. Oldham, 'The Way Out', pp. 1–2; *Moot Papers*, M7, p. 278.

67 *CNL* 41S, 7 August 1940, William Temple, 'Begin Now', p. 1.

68 Murry, *Price of Leadership*, pp. 93–5, 98–9, 99–100; Lea, *John Middleton Murry*, pp. 289, 323.

69 OA 13/6/32, 'Elements of a Political and Social Faith', 11 September 1942, p. 1.

70 *Moot Papers*, M1, pp. 40, 49; M2, p. 114; M7, pp. 274, 275, 278; M17, p. 599.

71 *CNL* 180L, 21 April 1943, p. 6.

72 OA 14/5/1, J. M. Murry, 'Paper Read at the Moot, Sept. 23–6, 1938', p. 8; OA 14/5/13, J. M. Murry, 'The Agricultural Community and the Future of Society', 17 June 1943, p. 4.

73 *CNL* 239L, 25 July 1945, pp. 1–6; *CNL* 244S, 3 October 1945, David G. Peck, 'The Church and Countryside'. *CNL* 278L, 22 January 1947, p. 6.

74 Mannheim, *Diagnosis*, p. 145.

75 Eliot, *Idea of a Christian Society*, pp. 58, 61, 62, 64. See also McVey, 'Backgrounds', pp. 182–3.

76 OA 14/1/57, H. A. Hodges, 'Archetypes and Paradigms in a Future Society', 6 September 1943, p. 8.

77 *CNL* 24S, 10 April 1940, J. H. Oldham, 'Christianity and Politics', p. 3; *CNL* 85L, 11 June 1941, p. 2.

78 *CNL* 41S, 7 August 1940, William Temple, 'Begin Now', p. 3.

79 *Ibid.*, p. 1; *CNL* 190S, 8 September 1943, 'Responsibility in the Economic System', p. 3.

80 *CNL* 5S, 29 November 1939, Oldham, 'Preliminaries to the Consideration of Peace Aims', p. 3. *Churches Survey Their Task*, pp. 102–3.

81 Murry, *Price of Leadership*, pp. 151–2; *Moot Papers*, M1, p. 53.

82 *CNL* 27S, 1 May 1940, Hodges, 'What Difference Does Christianity Make?', p. 2.

83 OA 9/7/23, Oldham to Ehrenström, 27 May 1946, p. 4; *CNL* 253L, 6 February 1946, p. 4; *CNL* 263L, 26 June 1946, pp. 3–4; Morgan, *Barth Reception*, p. 186.

84 *CNL* 92S, 30 July 1941, W. G. Symons, 'Ecumenical Christianity and the Working Classes'. Oldham stated no previous supplement had aroused more interest: *CNL* 134L, 20 May 1942, p. 2.

85 *CNL* 253L, 6 February 1946, p. 4; *CNL* 341L, 6 July 1949, p. 213.

86 *CNL* 104S, 22 October 1941, J. H. Oldham, 'Planning for Freedom', p. 2.

87 Mannheim: *Moot Papers*, M16, p. 548.

88 *CNL* 88S, 1 July 1941, J. H. Oldham, 'The Predicament of Society and the Way Out. II', p. 5.

89 *CNL* 100L, 24 September 1941, p. 1.

90 *Moot Papers*, M1, p. 49; M16, p. 547. LPL Lang 26, fos. 65–74, Hodges, 'Towards a Plan for a New *Summa*', p. 9.

91 *CNL* 140L, 1 July 1942, p. 1. A reader saw 'a Christian source in Bolshevism', which had 'struck its roots in the soil of a deeply religious national spirit': *CNL* 306L, 3 March 1948, p. 6.

92 *CNL* 198S, 29 December 1943, William Temple, 'What Christians Stand for in the Secular World', p. 4.

93 *CNL* 189S, 25 August 1943, Reinhold Niebuhr, 'Russia and the Christian World', pp. 2–3.

94 *CNL* 223S, 13 December 1944, Oldham, 'Love and Life', p. 7; *CNL* 248L, 28 November 1945, pp. 6–8.

95 *CNL* 191L, 22 September 1943, pp. 3–4. *CNL* 323L, 27 October 1948, p. 5.

96 *CNL* 232L, 18 April 1945, p. 4.

97 *CNL* 280S, Ian Crombie, 'The Wholehearted Pursuit of Social Justice', p. 13. WGS, DA 43, Box 1, File: WCC Assembly Amsterdam '48, 'The Free Society' (draft), November 1947, p. 26.

98 *Churches Survey Their Task*, pp. 102–3.

99 UL BC MS 20c Moot, copy of letter from Christopher Dawson, n.d.; *CNL* 1S, 1 November 1939, J. H. Oldham, 'What Is God Doing?'.

100 *CNL* 7L, 13 December 1939, p. 1; *CNL* 45S, 4 September 1940, J. H. Oldham, 'The Way Out', p. 4.

101 *CNL* 24S, 10 April 1940, J. H. Oldham, 'Christianity and Politics', p. 2.

102 *CNL* 88L, 1 July 1941, p. 1.

103 *CNL* 89L, 9 July 1941, pp. 1–2.

104 *CNL* 91L, 23 July 1941, p. 1.

105 *CNL* 106S, 5 November 1941, E. Lampert, 'The Revelation of Russia', pp. 2–3.

106 *CNL* 199S, 12 January 1944, anon., 'The Future of Europe', p. 4.

107 *CNL* 311S, 12 May 1948, Josef L. Hromàdka, 'Between Yesterday and To-morrow'.

108 *CNL* 316S, 21 July 1948, 'The Church and Communism', pp. 11–13.

109 *Ibid.*, pp. 14–16.

110 OA 9/8/42, Every to Oldham, 4 September 1948; OA 9/8/45, Crossman to Oldham, 11 October 1948, p. 1.

111 Coupland, *Britannia, Europa and Christendom*, pp. 104–7, 166–7. Lucian N. Leustean, 'The Ecumenical Movement and the Schuman Plan, 1950–1954', *Journal of Church and State*, 53:3 (2011), 442–71 (pp. 464–5, 471).

112 Erhard Besier, Armin Boyens and Gerhard Lindemann, *Nationaler Protestantismus und ökumenische Bewegung: Kirchliches Handeln im Kalten Krieg (1945–1990)* (Berlin: Duncker & Humblot, 1999); Kirby, *Religion and the Cold War*.

113 *CNL* 237L, 27 June 1945, pp. 4–5.

114 *CNL* 240L, 8 August 1945, p. 4.

115 *CNL* 263S, 26 June 1946, anon., 'Christians in Politics: I. Christian Conservatism and Christian Radicalism'.

116 *Moot Papers*, M16, p. 561. On Beveridge's religious beliefs, see Harris, 'Enterprise and Welfare States', p. 185. Cf. Phillips, *Kingdom on Earth*, p. 283, which calls Beveridge 'a social Christian'.

117 Mannheim, 'Planning for Freedom', p. 9.

118 *Moot Papers*, M20, p. 698.

119 *CNL* 178S, 24 March 1943, J. H. Oldham, 'Christians and the Beveridge Report', p. 4.

120 *CNL* 184L, 16 June 1943, pp. 3–4; *CNL* 200L, 26 January 1944, p. 2.

121 *CNL* 217S, 20 September 1944, Violet R. Markham, 'Old Age Pensioners'.

122 *CNL* 190S, 8 September 1943, 'Responsibility in the Economic System'; *CNL* 207S, 22 March 1944, 'Responsibility in the Economic System – Government Regulation'; *CNL* 242S, 5 September 1945, 'Responsibility in the Economic System – III: The Question of Ownership'.

123 *CNL* 229S, 7 March 1945, 'Civis', 'Full Employment and the Responsibility of Christians', pp. 10, 16.

124 *CNL* 236S, 13 June 1945, Kathleen Bliss, 'Houses'.

125 *CNL* 259L, 1 May 1946, pp. 1–4; *CNL* 273L, 13 November 1946, pp. 1–6; *CNL* 273S, 13 November 1946, Kathleen Bliss, 'Planner's Paradise'.

126 *CNL* 203L, 8 March 1944, pp. 1–3. *CNL* 211L, 28 June 1944, pp. 3–4. S. J. D. Green, *The Passing of Protestant England: Secularisation and Social Change, c. 1920–1960* (Cambridge: Cambridge University Press, 2011), pp. 211–41.

127 *CNL* 203L, 8 March 1944, p. 2.

128 *CNL* 207S, 3 May 1944, Douglas Woodruff, 'Christians and a Free Society'. On Woodruff, see Villis, *British Catholics and Fascism*, pp. 57–76.

129 *CNL* 207L, 3 May 1944, pp. 3–4.

130 MSC, Oldham to editorial board, 13 April 1944 (including copy of letter from Symons); Oldham to Symons, 13 April 1944. Emphasis in original.

131 *CNL* 211S, 28 June 1944, A. D. Lindsay, 'Christians and a Free Society', p. 5.

132 *Catholic Herald*, 12 February 1943, pp. 1, 5.

133 A. R. Vidler, *Essays in Liberality* (1957), discussed in Loader, Intellectual *Development*, p. 158.

134 *CNL* 180L, 21 April 1943, p. 5.

135 *CNL* 228L, 21 February 1945, pp. 5–6. This was followed up in *CNL* 232L, 18 April 1945, pp. 4–6.

136 *CNL* 237L, 27 June 1945, pp. 2–4; *CNL* 253L, 6 February 1946, p. 4. Mannheim thought the Peckham Centre exemplified 'planning for freedom': *Freedom, Power and Democratic Planning*, pp. 252–3.

137 *CNL* 242S, 5 September 1945, 'Responsibility in the Economic System – III: The Question of Ownership', p. 5. Emphasis in original.

138 *CNL* 239S, 25 July 1945, N. A. Howell-Everson, 'Joint Consultation'; *CNL* 261S, 29 May 1946, L. John Edwards, MP, 'Some Reflections on Industrial Relations'. Edwards was a Labour MP and personal private secretary to Sir Stafford Cripps.

139 *CNL* 213L, 26 July 1944, p. 2.

140 *CNL* 274S, 27 November 1946, J. Middleton Murry, 'Can Democracy Survive?', pp. 11, 15.

141 OA 9/7/33, copy of letter from H. A. Hodges, 4 December 1946, p. 1.

142 *CNL* 333L, 16 March 1949, pp. 81, 82–3.

143 *Ibid.*, p. 82.

144 *Moot Papers*, M1, p. 53.

145 OA 14/5/1, J. M. Murry, 'Paper read at the Moot, Sept. 23–6, 1938', p. 8. *Moot Papers*, M2, pp. 67–74, 107.

146 *Moot Papers*, M3, pp. 165, 182–3; M9, p. 322.

147 *Theology*, 41:244 (October 1940), 245–9.

148 *Moot Papers*, M8, p. 303.

149 Murry argued democracy had been 'destroyed' by the war: Britain would try 'to go decorously Beveridge-National-Socialist', which would fail, bringing a 'Communist revolution': OA 9/5/3, Murry to Oldham, 15 June 1943, p. 1. The only option was 'to form a cell of good living in the decaying fabric of the old society': OA 14/5/13, Murry, 'The Agricultural Community and the Future of Society', 17 June 1943, p. 5.

150 *Moot Papers*, M8, pp. 296, 297, 313.

151 IOE MOO/129, 'Memorandum by J. M. Murry', n.d.

152 *Moot Papers*, M8, pp. 294–5.

153 *CNL* 132S, 6 May 1942, J. H. Oldham, 'Of these Stones', pp. 3–4.

154 *Moot Papers*, M17, p. 592.

155 IOE MOO/93, 'Letter from J. M. Murry', 14 September 1942, p. 2.

156 OA 9/6/83, 'Letter from J. Middleton Murry', 5 July 1944, p. 1.

157 *CNL* 223S, 13 December 1944, J. H. Oldham, 'Love and Life'; *CNL* 310L, 28 April 1948, pp. 7–8; *CNL* 310S, 28 April 1948, Daniel Jenkins, 'Mr. Murry and the Free Society'.

158 Ceadel, *Semi-Detached Idealists*, p. 421; Lea, *John Middleton Murry*, p. 278. See also *ibid.*, pp. 312–15.

159 Lea, *John Middleton Murry*, pp. 288–9. John Middleton Murry, *Trust or Perish* (London: Andrew Dakers, 1946). On Communism's threat: Murry, *Free Society*, pp. 13, 30, 47–8, 70, 99–112, 224. On his rejection of pacifism: *ibid.*, pp. 36, 37, 39–41 62–3, 75–86, 157–66. On Labour and bureaucracy: *ibid.* 254–5. See also Murry, *Community Farm*, pp. 207, 245–7; and Ceadel, *Semi-Detached Idealists*, 421–3.

160 *Moot Papers*, M18, p. 630.

161 OA 14/1/43, H. A. Hodges, 'Politics and the Moot', 9 June 1943, pp. 2–4.

162 *Ibid.*, pp. 4–5.

163 OA 14/1/71, H. A. Hodges, 'The Collective Commonwealth and the Christian', 22 January 1944, pp. 17–18.

164 OA 9/5/3, Murry to Oldham, 15 June 1943, pp. 1–2.

165 *Moot Papers*, M17, pp. 593–4.

166 *Ibid.*, M17, pp. 585–93.

167 *Ibid.*, M3, p. 164; M8, p. 295; M17, pp. 585–6.

168 *Ibid.*, M17, pp. 579–81.

169 OA 14/1/57, H. A. Hodges, 'Archetypes and Paradigms in a Future Society', 6 September 1943, pp. 8, 10.

170 *Ibid.*, p. 5; OA 14/1/71, H. A. Hodges, 'The Collective Commonwealth and the Christian', 22 January 1944, p. 7.

171 OA 9/7/33, copy of letter from H. A. Hodges, 4 December 1946, pp. 1, 6.

172 *Moot Papers*, M1, p. 55.

173 IOE MOO/35, 'Notes on Mannheim's Paper by T. S. Eliot', 10 January 1941, p. 2; Grimley, 'Civil Society and the Clerisy', p. 243.

174 UL BC MS 20c Moot, 'Comments on Papers by Mannheim and Hodges, by T. S. Eliot', n.d. [discussed April 1939], pp. 1–2.

175 *Spectator*, 7 June 1940, p. 782.

176 IOE MOO/68, 'Letter to Dr Oldham from T. S. Eliot', n.d., pp. 1, 3. Writing on Mannheim's 'Towards a New Social Philosophy' (19–22 December 1941), Eliot found his views 'very relevant' and later agreed with some of them: OA 14/6/14, 'Comments on Mannheim's Letter by T. S. Eliot', 24 November 1944.

177 T. S. Eliot, 'Planning and Religion', *Theology*, 46:275 (May 1943), 102–6.

178 OA 9/5/10, Eliot to Oldham, 21 August 1943, p. 3.

179 OA 14/6/13, 'Comments by T. S. Eliot on Michael Polanyi's notes on the clerisy', 22 November 1944, p. 2.

180 OA 9/6/67, Eliot to Oldham, 11 May 1944, pp. 1–2.

181 T. S. Eliot, letter to Allen Tate, 13 March 1945, quoted by Stefan Collini, *Absent Minds*, p. 319.

182 *CNL* 230S, 21 March 1945, 'Metoikos' [T. S. Eliot], 'Full Employment and the Responsibility of Christians'.

183 IOE MOO/35, notes on Mannheim's paper by T. S. Eliot, 10 January 1941, p. 2. Emphasis in original.

184 OA 14/6/10, 'Notes by T. S. Eliot on the Place and Function of the Clerisy', 10 November 1944, p. 3.

185 OA 9/5/17, extracts from letters from T. S. Eliot, 6 September 1943, p. 1. Spurr reduces Eliot's motivation to participate in the Moot and *CNL* to 'a sense of personal obligation' towards Oldham: Spurr, *'Anglo-Catholic in Religion'*, pp. 188–93, 190. However, Eliot's extensive participation in the *CNL*, CCFCL, CFC and Moot, and repeated emphasis on their value, suggest otherwise. The letters Spurr cites to stress Eliot's distance from the group come from a later period when he was, indeed, becoming more alienated from its approach.

186 OA 9/5/19, 'The Christian Witness in the Present Crisis', 6 October 1943, p. 11.

187 Collini, *Absent Minds*, pp. 319–20. Eliot, *Idea of a Christian Society*, pp. 85–7; *Moot Papers*, p. 15.

188 Mary Jo Nye, *Michael Polanyi and His Generation: Origins of the Social Construction of Science* (Chicago: University of Chicago Press, 2011), p. 185.

189 Kojecky, *T. S. Eliot's Social Criticism*, p. 155.

190 Mullins and Jacobs, 'Idea of the Clerisy', p. 150. This was not an unusual stance: Ritschel, *Politics of Planning*, p. 6. See Phil Mullins and Struan Jacobs, 'Michael Polanyi and Karl Mannheim', *Tradition & Discovery: The Polanyi Society Periodical*, 32 (2005), 20–43, esp. pp. 23, 24; and Struan Jacobs and Phil Mullins, 'Faith, Tradition, and Dynamic Order: Michael Polanyi's Liberal Thought from 1941 to 1951', *History of European Ideas*, 34 (2008), 120–31.

191 *Moot Papers*, M20, pp. 692–3.

192 Jacobs and Mullins, 'Faith', p. 131.

193 *Moot Papers*, M20, p. 701.

194 Stefania Ruzsits Jha, *Reconsidering Michael Polanyi's Philosophy* (Pittsburgh: University of Pittsburgh Press, 2002), pp. 23–4, 5.

195 OA 9/6/99, 'Letter from Michael Polanyi', 18 November 1944.

196 *Moot Papers*, M20, p. 700.

197 OA 9/8/33, 'Copy of a Letter from Professor Michael Polanyi', 25 June 1948, p. 2.

198 OA 14/6/42, Michael Polanyi, 'Forms of Atheism', 8 October 1948, p. 3.

199 *Ibid.*, p. 4.

200 *Ibid.*, p. 5.

201 *Moot Papers*, M3, p. 161.

202 *Ibid.*, M3, p. 166.

203 Mannheim, *Diagnosis*, p. 144.

204 *Guardian*, 11 July 1941, p. 330.

205 LPL W. Temple 6, fos. 79–83, J. H. Oldham, 'A Fraternity of the Spirit', March 1941, p. 6.

206 *CNL* 333L, 16 March 1949, p. 82.

207 *CNL* 110L, 3 December 1941, p. 1; *CNL* 138S, 17 June 1942, 'X', 'The Changing Organization of Industry'; 160S, 18 November 1942, George Every, 'Planning within Limits'.

208 OA 14/6/21, 'Comments on Middleton Murry's Paper by T. S. Eliot', n.d. [discussed September 1938], p. 3.

209 *Church of England Newspaper*, 20 August 1948, p. 3; 27 August 1948, p. 1.

210 Diane Kirby, 'Divinely Sanctioned: The Anglo-American Cold War Alliance and the Defence of Western Civilization and Christianity, 1945–1948', *Journal of Contemporary History* 35:3 (2000), 385–412.

211 Grimley, 'Civil Society and the Clerisy', p. 243.

212 Loader, *Intellectual Development*, p. 161.

213 See Mannheim, 'Planning for Freedom', esp. pp. 2–6; and *Moot Papers*, M17, pp. 585–8.

214 Mannheim, *Diagnosis*, p. 116.

215 Editorial, *Theology*, 50:321 (March 1947), 81–2.

216 *CNL* 132S, 6 May 1942, 'Of These Stones', p. 3. See also *Moot Papers*, M18, p. 637.

217 *CNL* 180L, 21 April 1943, pp. 1–4. Drucker saw 'the Christian concept of man's nature' as the basis of freedom: *The Future of Industrial Man* (Piscataway, NJ: Transaction, 1995 [1942]), pp. 110–11.

218 *CNL* 180S, 21 April 1943, Basil Smallpeice, 'The Managers of Industry'.

219 *Christian World*, 20 July 1944, p. 11.

220 IOE MOO/128, Christopher Dawson, 'Planning and Culture', n.d. [1941], pp. 3, 7.

221 E.g. *New Statesman and Nation*, 16 June 1945, pp. 383–4; 25 August 1945, pp. 132–3.

222 Paula Valderrama, ' "Planning for Freedom": Hayekian and Polanyian Policies in Latin America', *International Journal of Political Economy*, 41:4 (2012–13),

88–105. F. A. Hayek, *The Road to Serfdom: Text and Documents. The Definitive Edition*, ed. Bruce Campbell (Chicago: University of Chicago Press, 2007 [1944]), pp. 91–9.

223 K. R. Popper, *The Open Society and Its Enemies*, Vol. II (London: Routledge and Keegan Paul, 1980 [1945]), p. 336.

224 Or Rosenboim, 'Barbara Wootton, Friedrich Hayek and the Debate on Democratic Federalism in the 1940s', *International History Review*, 36:5 (2014), 894–918, esp. pp. 912–13.

225 Arthur Marwick, 'Middle Opinion in the Thirties: Planning, Progress and "Political Agreement"', *English Historical Review*, 79 (1964), 285–98; Pemberton, 'Middle Way'.

226 *The Times*, 1 July 1940, p. 5. Oldham praised this leading article in *CNL* 40L, 31 July 1940, p. 3.

227 Ritschel, *Politics of Planning*.

228 David Morgan and Mary Evans, *The Battle for Britain: Citizenship and Ideology in the Second World War* (London: Routledge, 1993), pp. 112, 127.

229 Hayek, *Road to Serfdom*, pp. 73–4, 109.

230 *Ibid.*, pp. 174–5.

231 Ivor Thomas, *The Socialist Tragedy* (London: Latimer House, 1949); John Jewkes, *Ordeal by Planning* (London: Macmillan, 1948).

232 John Kent, 'William Temple, the Church of England and British National Identity', in Richard Weight and Abigail Beach (eds.), *The Right to Belong: Citizenship and National Identity in Britain, 1930–1960* (London: I.B. Tauris, 1998), pp. 19–35 (pp. 25–6).

233 Hastings, *Oliver Tomkins*, p. 23.

234 Machin, *Churches and Social Issues*, pp. 134–43. E. R. Norman, *Church and Society in England, 1770–1970: A Historical Study* (Oxford: Clarendon Press, 1976), 372–77.

235 *Christian World*, 25 February 1943, p. 4. See also *Church of England Newspaper*, 5 March 1943, p. 1; *Guardian*, 26 February 1943, p. 75; *Spiritual Issues of the War*, 173 (25 February 1943), 2–3.

236 *Christian World*, 10 December 1942, p. 6; 25 February 1943, p. 4; 4 March 1943, p. 6; 11 March 1943, p. 5; 12 August 1943, p. 8.

237 E.g. Christians should 'support' the Beveridge Plan but be 'watchful and questioning at the same time'; *Church of England Newspaper*, 26 February 1943, p. 4.

238 *Church Times*, 11 December 1942, p. 670; 23 July 1943, p. 381.

239 *British Weekly*, 10 December 1942, p. 121; 17 December 1942, pp. 151, 153; 18 March 1943, p. 297; 7 December 1944, p. 131. *Guardian*, 11 December 1942, pp. 400, 401; 15 January 1943, pp. 20, 21. *Catholic Herald*, 4 December 1942, p. 4; 11 December 1942, p. 4; 18 December 1942, p. 4; 12 March 1943, p. 1.

240 E. C. Urwin, *Religion in Planned Society* (London: Epworth Press, 1942).

241 William Paton, *The Church and the New Order* (London: SCM, 1941), pp. 153, 156; F. S. Temple (ed.), *William Temple: Some Lambeth Letters* (London: Oxford University Press, 1963), pp. 91–2.

242 Maurice B. Reckitt, 'Plan and Society', *Christendom*, 11:41 (March 1941), 46–52.

243 'Beyond Planning', *Christendom*, 13:51 (September 1943), 89–92.

244 Michael Roberts, *Recovery of the West* (London: Faber and Faber, 1941), pp. 304–5; see a review in *Catholic Herald*, 1 August 1941, p. 6.

245 *Church of England Newspaper*, 9 March 1945, p. 1.

246 *Church of England Newspaper*, 5 February 1943, p. 4.

247 See 'Editorial: Anniversary – and After', *Christendom*, 13:51 (September 1943), 67–9 (p. 69); 'Notes and Comments', *Christendom*, 13:51 (September 1943), 70–2 (p. 71).

248 *Church of England Newspaper*, 16 June 1944, p. 1.

249 *Catholic Herald*, 30 June 1944, p. 3.

250 *Christian World*, 11 November 1948, p. 1.

251 David Kynaston, *A World to Build: Austerity Britain 1945–48* (London: Bloomsbury, 2007), esp. pp. 19–59, 69; Rodney Lowe, 'The Second World War, Consensus and the Foundation of the Welfare State', *Twentieth Century British History*, 1:2 (1990), 152–82 (pp. 175–8); Stapleton, 'Resisting the Centre'; Helen McCarthy, 'Leading from the Centre: The League of Nations Union, Foreign Policy and "Political Agreement" in the 1930s', *Contemporary British History*, 23:4 (2009), 527–42.

252 Kynaston, *A World to Build*, pp. 64–5. Clement Attlee had distinguished the Labour Party's programme from Communism and rejected the idea of a political police force in his book *The Labour Party in Perspective* (1937).

5

'The rock of human sanity stands in the sea where it always stood': nationalism, universalism and Europe

The last chapter showed how 'planning for freedom' helped the Oldham group map a middle way between *laissez-faire* capitalism and totalitarian collectivism and offer what most members saw as an alternative to Marxism. But confronting totalitarianism, particularly in its right-wing form, also required engaging with nationalism. The group had mixed feelings about national identity: it saw 'nationality' as a legitimate aspect of human community but rejected what it distinguished as 'national*ism*'. This led to an ambivalent patriotism and an interest in supranational categories, such as federalism, universalism, Christendom and the West, each of which, however, proved to be not entirely satisfactory. The post-war years also compelled members to define Britain's relationship to Europe in the context of an emergent superpower rivalry. The essential distinction between a legitimate 'nationality' and unhealthy 'nationalism' endured across dramatically changing political and military situations: the pre-war crisis and months of 'phoney war', the perilous years of 1940 and 1941 (the 'Battle of Britain'), and the improving fortunes of the Allies between 1942 and victory in 1945, as well as post-war reconstruction. The group's engagement with a specifically 'British' (or, often, 'English'[1]) identity had two main purposes: defining a distinctive national character relevant to social renewal and fitting national considerations into wider categories.[2] In this chapter, I will outline the Oldham group's consensus on national identity, particularly as defined at Oxford in 1937 and in the early discussions within the CCFCL and Moot. I will move on to changing articulations of national identity after the military disasters in late spring and summer 1940 and, then, in the period after the crisis had passed. A final section explores how British identity was imagined within larger contexts.

The Oldham group and the nation: from Oxford to Dunkirk

While Christianity has a complex relationship to national identity, there has tended to be what John Baillie called 'a positive relation between the

Church and at least *a* nation', particularly in the twentieth century.[3] But that relation was often contested. Inter-war ecumenism distinguished between a positive sense of belonging to the nation as a divinely legitimated community (often referred to as 'nationality') and 'nationalism' as its idolatrous perversion; however, tensions in the movement reflected theological traditions and often overlapping national allegiances. For example, whereas British Christians – like most Britons – supported the League of Nations, German Christians – like many Germans – were often hostile towards it.[4] British Christians, too, were often pacifist and supportive of 'appeasement' in the 1930s.[5] That decade cast nationalism's dangers in stark relief, with the rise of National Socialism, Fascist Italy's invasion of Abyssinia, the Spanish Civil War, Japanese expansionism and the League's ineffectiveness in all these crises. The German Protestant 'church struggle' between pro-Nazi *Deutsche Christen* and the oppositional Confessing Church, and the Nazi persecution of Jews and Catholics concerned many British Christians. Ecumenical activists, led by clergy such as Bishop George Bell, sought to keep German members included, which was not easy, since many Confessing Church members, while rejecting aspects of Nazism, were deeply nationalist.[6]

Nationalism was a central issue at the 1937 Oxford ecumenical conference on 'Church, Community and State'. A preparatory pamphlet by Oldham mixed accommodation and critique. He wrote that Germans were divided about harmonising 'the truth of national individuality' and 'the Christian Gospel'. Merely acknowledging divided opinion was common when conference reports sought to avoid taking a stand, but Oldham also asserted an 'irreconcilable conflict' between sacralising 'the racial and national soul' – as in Nazism – and the genuinely Christian view that 'all souls, individual and national, are judged by the Gospel'.[7] At a plenary lecture, Eliot argued it was 'sensible' neither to 'exalt' nation, race or class nor to seek to eliminate such differences.[8] Reaching such agreement was difficult. Moberly chaired a conference session at which the Germans' '*Blut und Boden*' views had been 'hotly contested' by American delegates, who saw nationalism as a 'temporary, provincial and undesirable concept'.[9]

The Oxford summary report and a volume on international relations reveal a careful balancing act. Nationality was assumed, like race, as a natural marker of difference, and nations were seen as a 'part of the God-given basis and structure of human life'.[10] A 'fundamentally healthy' form of 'nationality' was separated from a 'nationalism' linked with 'egotism', 'fear', 'hatred' and 'indifference'.[11] The German concept *Volk* was seen similarly. While accepted as a legitimate concept, its use by the Nazis was condemned: 'excessive deference to *Volk*' rejected God's desire for 'universal brotherhood'.[12] Any 'coldness or hostility' to other nationalities, 'ruthlessness' towards those who were seen as 'obstacles to the closing of the ranks' or rejection of 'cosmopolitan sympathies' was condemned.[13] The report also denied racial purity or superiority, and it denounced racism and anti-Semitism.[14] Accommodation, clearly, had its limits: ties of 'common blood, soil, tradition, culture and purpose' were accepted, but 'abuse' of this 'divine gift' was not. Defining national community through shared hatreds violated God's commandment of neighbourly love.[15] Still, even authoritarianism was seen as a form of 'reconstruction' that responded to a real problem of cultural 'disintegration', which had also made patriotism a 'dominant rallying and unifying force' from Japan to Ireland.[16] But while nations were God's way of diversifying human life, 'egotism' against other nations or against minorities was a 'sin', and the 'deification' of nation, race or class was condemned as 'idolatry'.[17]

In Britain, the mixture of national and religious identities was, broadly speaking, uncontroversial. There were longstanding national self-images as a Protestant nation, and there were various institutionalised national churches: in general, British Christians idealised 'a universal community, enriched by national difference' rather than one that would abolish such distinctions.[18] The twentieth century saw an enduring cultural linkage between Englishness and 'a tolerant, undemonstrative form of Protestantism'.[19] The inter-war Church of England claimed (with some success) to represent the Christian foundation of the national community, while the non-Anglican free churches also asserted their place in the national imagination and political arena.[20] Archbishop Temple favoured a clearly national 'fellowship' over a rootless 'internationalism', and, like him, prominent Anglicans such as V. A. Demant and George Bell saw nations as divinely legitimated repositories of human diversity.[21]

The Oldham group, clearly, was nationally focused. Eric Fenn prefaced his book *The Crisis and Democracy* (1938) with a letter to his son calling 'our belief in justice' one of 'our resources as a people': but while that tradition had 'dignity', Fenn nonetheless argued *modern* English life had departed from faith, threatening Britain's place in the world.[22] An ambivalent national identity was typical. Dawson argued that Christians should accept 'nationality' as long as it was not 'an exclusive ideal'.[23] In the *CNL* in November 1939, Oldham claimed genuine peace would come not from an *absence* of nations but rather a 'concourse' of them, each with a 'native health of its own' and willingness to serve others.[24] In 1941, he distinguished 'the truth and priceless educational values of nationality' from 'the deadly evil of national pride, exclusiveness and aggression'.[25] Nationalism was one of faith's two 'great rivals' (along with secularism): Christians valued 'loyalty to one's people' but not as the main purpose of life.[26] They should neither crave national importance nor 'belittle or ignore it'.[27] Expressing the diversity of creation and the work of generations, nationality deserved 'reverence'.[28] Indeed, the group was wary of an 'uprooted' detachment from any specific culture.[29] Polanyi saw 'national feeling' as the only sentiment in which a 'responsible devotion to a community' could be 'rooted'.[30] The ideal of a Christian-influenced 'nationality' thus marked the group's middle way between a 'rootless' internationalism and destructive nationalism. But the course of this middle way was affected by changing circumstances. In the war's first phase (until summer 1940), national loyalties were seen ambivalently. Oldham, for example, found fulsome words for national allegiance in the *CNL's* precursor issue in October 1939:

> The bonds which unite those who speak the same speech, love the same countryside and city streets, share the same historical memories and the same ways of life are drawn closer in time of calamity. Suffused with a common feeling we know how dear is the land that gave us birth and how precious is the tradition of our island race with its love of liberty and the reign of law, its struggles for justice, its adventures and creative achievements, its poetry and laughter, its tolerance and human kindness.[31]

Tolerance, the rule of law, self-initiative, willingness to compromise, parliamentarianism and an enduring (if submerged) Christian faith were seen as national traditions.[32] However, as a *CNL* reader put it, 'our own house badly needs repair'; indeed, in the early phase of the war, critiques of national *realities* were as insistent as the praise of national *ideals*.[33] The Christian and national causes were far from identical, Oldham maintained: any faith that identified with a society as 'secular and material' as Britain's could no longer be seen as Christianity.[34]

For this reason, the gap between democracy and totalitarianism was sometimes profoundly downplayed in the group. Shortly after the Oxford conference, Fenn had written 'there is nothing to choose between a dictatorship and democracy if both are godless'.[35] Within days of the war's outbreak, Oldham wrote to the Moot to express the fear that Britons would forget that 'anti-Christ' was not only among the Nazis but also 'in our own hearts'.[36] Vidler came under State scrutiny after a *Theology* editorial denied British moral superiority.[37] The *CNL* called the British a sinful people indifferent to their own 'crying evils'; the 'devil of self-righteousness' could not deny, for example, the 'dictated peace' that had enabled Hitler's rise or the widespread corruption in democratic nations.[38] Germany and Russia even had 'an idealism of a kind', whereas the British 'talked vaguely' of democracy and Christianity, 'content to repose as comfortably as the times allowed on the sofa of national tradition'.[39] With no creed, they had drifted, accepting mass unemployment, growing statism and a vacuous mass culture.

Niebuhr called Nazi racial theories exaggerated forms of a general decay.[40] A supplement argued Britain had the 'very same things in varying degree' that it condemned in Nazism.[41] A *CNL* reader compared the British media to Nazi propaganda, and an essay saw Germany as no less Christian than other nations: 'The Hitler movement is suburban, and suburbia is everywhere practically out of touch with the traditions of Europe, including the religious traditions.'[42] In the Moot, Oakeshott saw 'our ideas' – shaped by a ubiquitous materialism – as 'fundamentally the same as Hitler's.'[43] Shaw warned that Britain was as 'guilty' as others; Oldham thought a 'plutodemocratic' Britain should not be defended.[44] It must become *worthy* of victory and could not 'fall quietly back' into its pre-war life.[45]

Shifting views: 'The hopes of Europe have descended upon this island'

Against this background, the *CNL* issues responding to the evacuation of British and Allied forces at Dunkirk (26 May–4 June 1940) and the fall of France in late June testify – amid fears of invasion and defeat – to a revaluation of national heritage, clearer distinctions between totalitarianism and liberalism, closer links between religious and national identities, and a new emphasis on a national 'mission'. The distinction between *nationality* and *nationalism* continued, but it was recalibrated. For example, in late 1939, Oldham had declared that the gap between Britons' ideals and their empire's achievements made them seem hypocritical.[46] Christians should not, he had written then, pray for national victory ('as though the British Empire were in any sense God's favourite') but rather for the victory of *values* that they, despite their 'unworthiness and manifold shortcomings', might defend.[47] But by the end of June 1940, the empire's survival was seen as vital. Britons had not only created a free society – 'acknowledging the rights of the common man and cherishing the qualities of toleration, mercy and humanity' – they had spread it globally.[48] The terms 'Commonwealth' and 'Empire' were used almost synonymously, referring to a 'federation' with a 'substantial, even if imperfect, harmony of interests, ideals and aspirations.'[49] There was greed and injustice in imperial history but also 'devotion, idealism and self-sacrificing enterprise.'[50] Allegedly 'British' traits were praised: confidence, 'mutual trust', and an 'inborn sense of freedom and respect for the individual.'[51] Owen Barfield thought a British individualism could resist 'collectivism abroad, erected into an idol and run mad.'[52] Oldham stressed Britons' 'fundamental sanity' and their relatively strong degree of social integration.[53]

This revaluation of British tradition encouraged the belief in a divinely ordained national 'mission'. In July 1940, Oldham saw religious significance in the fact that the British Empire was freedom's last defence.[54] Britain's history called it to its unique 'destiny' to try to create 'a world-order'.[55] In October, he evoked (echoing Churchill) the 'miraculous deliverance' at Dunkirk.[56] Russian religious philosopher Georgy Fedetov suggested in the *CNL* that 'providence' had given the Commonwealth the role of opposing totalitarianism.[57] In May 1941, a *CNL* essay declared dramatically, 'The hopes of Europe have descended upon this island and there they will stay inseparably bound up with the fate of England.'[58] Oldham stressed the religious meaning of British traditions of 'public service, local initiative and voluntary effort', which could inspire 'new social structures', infuse 'fresh energies into the body politic' and give 'positive meaning' to resistance against tyranny.[59]

Nationalism remained worrying, even during the 'phoney war', and there were warnings against sacralising the nation, mistaking national interests for God's will or ignoring the need for national humility. The *CNL* thought there was too much 'complacency' regarding Britain's social and moral condition, and group members cautioned against assuming God was on Britain's side. In September 1939, Murry suggested Christian principles 'might only concur in defeat', and he decried Britons' 'unrealistic assumption of victory'.[60] Critiques of Britain's failings recurred, as did the view of totalitarianism as 'common to our civilisation as a whole'.[61] In December 1940, for instance, Oldham quoted a *CNL* reader's assertion that Britons were not immune from the global spread of 'un-Christian civilisation'.[62] Nazism had originated in a 'spiritual evil' that was 'common to western civilisation': the inclination to 'barbarism' was signalled in Britain by 'the growth of the gangster type', 'the search for sensation and thrills' and 'the breakdown of sex conventions'.[63]

Britain thus still needed to *change*, bringing its national purposes in alignment with social justice. Oldham thought it not enough to defend Britain as it was: 'we must *create* the good', he wrote, that could reshape the future. This meant a new social covenant 'between leaders of industry and industrial workers, between machine workers and cultivators of the soil, between richer and poorer nations, between more advanced and less advanced peoples'.[64] Claiming that serving the nation meant dedication 'to the fulfilment of God's purposes', he asked for *which* Britain the nation fought: the 'selfish', 'materialistic' one of 'unfair privilege and social injustice', or one prioritising 'human values' that allowed each citizen 'the chance of fulfilling the purpose of his existence as a son of God?'.[65] The war allowed British heritage to inform a belief in Britain's global significance. Demant argued that 'the fate of the civilised world' would be decided in 'the soul of the British people'.[66] Drawing the right lesson would enable a 'messianic consciousness' of Britain's importance to Europe and the world.[67] Oldham saw Britain's 'high mission' in creating a living example of a national society that upheld the values that totalitarianism denied.[68] Britain's cause could, he stated, be made 'juster and stronger'.[69]

The national *mission* was paired, however, with national *humility*. Quoting from Mairet's *New English Weekly*, Oldham recommended 'the way of penitence':

> the British spirit, torpid as it often is, may yet become 'manifest once more as the human spirit which cannot deny the liberty of the individual, nor the covenant of social justice, nor even the reverence due to Nature, however it may neglect or sin against them'. If that happens, it may yet be found that 'the rock of human sanity stands in the sea where it always stood, in sinful, repentant but yet faithful Albion'.[70]

'Repentance' meant a 'costly break with what has been wrong' in order to reach 'the gateway to a new life'. Repentance and atonement were given a transformative political potential. Freedom, it was insisted, also had to be defended at home, even against public opinion: discrimination against conscientious objectors, for example, was seen to violate the British 'tradition of toleration, good humour and fair play'.[71] Such depictions claimed a 'true' English spirit had been corrupted by materialism, capitalism and mass society but, equally significantly, could be recovered through a broad commitment to national renewal.

While urging humility and repentance and remaining suspicious of unhesitating nationalism (Oldham, for example, thought a Christian's national devotion could never be 'unqualified'[72]), the *CNL* from the summer of 1940 more actively promoted a Christian patriotism. Oldham called upholding freedom of speech a 'patriotic duty'.[73] A 'common spirit of patriotism, prudence and adventure' would build, he claimed, 'the civilisation of the future'.[74] As guest editor in August 1940, Eliot suggested Britain's relative lack of violent political divisions offered a 'solid basis for unity in patriotism'.[75] A year later, he called patriotism a 'natural virtue' and a 'permanent feeling, which for better as well as worse cannot be exorcised': 'It includes the attachment to natural as well as to constructed surroundings, to place as well as to people, to the past as well as to the future; the attachment of a people to its own culture, and to its ability to make that specific and voluntary contribution to Christendom and to the world'.[76] He warned here, though, that such feelings could turn to the vices of 'nationalism, imperialism in the bad sense, collective pride and collective cupidity'; they could be 'a cloak for individual or sectional selfishness'. Similarly, Oldham saw that the natural virtue of 'love of country' might be 'perverted to evil ends'. Patriotism, he wrote, should not be ignored but rather had to be filled 'with a Christian meaning'.[77] Quoting Archbishop Lang, he said Britons

Figure 6 T. S. Eliot, 1948, by John Gay

'should strive so to be patriots as not to forget we are Christians'.[78] In 1942, Oldham called it a 'patriotic duty' to fight 'unreasoning hate', even towards Germans.[79] Polanyi later stressed patriotism's positive qualities, arguing that Fascist totalitarianism had robbed patriotism of its 'humane and honourable attributes', making it merely 'a theory of violence'.[80]

Britishness after the crisis

With the entries into the war of the USSR and USA in 1941 and a gradual turning tide after 1942, the group's evocations of national distinctiveness became more restrained and expressed concerns about a declining commitment to social renewal. National traditions continued to be praised (if less lavishly); humility and repentance were advocated; and a British 'mission' was reframed in the context of American–Soviet rivalry. In 1942, Mannheim still stressed Britain's historic task of developing a democratic, planned social order.[81] In autumn that year, Oldham called

the nation a 'great moulding force' with an 'encompassing web of tradition and custom'.[82] While not a specifically Christian entity, it was a reality
Christians must consider: echoing Demant and Temple, Oldham saw 'true'
internationalism not in the 'the antithesis between, but the fulfilment of a
true nationalism'.[83]

Moot meetings in October 1943 and January 1944 saw intense
discussions of patriotism, reconstruction and a national mission.
Oldham, Mannheim, Clarke and Hodges demanded fundamental social
change. Oldham argued that Britain could not keep 'blindly fighting'
for the sake of tradition but must 'awaken the sense of a new England
arising from the old'.[84] Mannheim suggested that the end of the war
would bring 'chaos' but also a new 'pattern of life' that might be shaped
by Christian principles and the British revival of 'the citizen tradition'. What was needed was not 'jingoism' but the pursuit of a national
mission, the prevention of 'Fascism from within' and the encouragement of moral 're-equipment'.[85] Hodges thought this also required a
theological reformation.[86] (The group preferred 'moral re-equipment'
over 'moral rearmament', a term used by Frank Buchman's 'Oxford
Group Movement'.[87]) Jenkins urged discovering the values needed for
planning in 'the national tradition'.[88] Clarke insisted nationalism could
be defeated by using the national 'instinct' to guide reforms in education, local government and race-relations.[89] There was, he said, a key
role for the English, even if the term 'mission' was 'dangerous and arro-
gant'; in the future, Europe would look to Britain as a model for social
reconstruction.[90] But there were also warnings. Miller saw post-war
democracy endangered if Britons were to see Churchill as the 'Father
of the People': Christians must reject power-worship and political
centralisation.[91]

The *CNL* continued to praise what it called national virtues. In 'char-
acteristically British fashion', Oldham wrote, the national consensus
for social change – while 'revolutionary' – had not benefited political extremes. The British were, he wrote, 'recovering the excellences
of their own tradition'.[92] 'The Englishman's Utopianism', wrote George
Every, 'is practical and scientific'.[93] Dorothy L. Sayers saw this practical
English spirit in the refusal to surrender to 'horrid fantasies or millen-
arian vapourings' and in staying focused on immediate problems: 'doing
the next thing', as she put it.[94] The British were depicted as less 'cruel'
than other nations (if potentially more 'callous').[95] In 1944, Oldham
highlighted Britain's strong 'voluntary principle'.[96] Bliss saw 'English'
ideals regarding 'personal relationships', 'voluntary effort' and 'self-
help' as an antidote to tyrannical bureaucracy.[97] After victory in Europe,
she argued that 'ordinary people' had found a new appreciation for the

common law and other traditional bulwarks of freedom, in contrast to the 'cynical' inter-war years. The popular legitimacy of Britain's institutions was 'a possession of priceless worth' that central Europe lacked.[98] In 1946, she again praised a 'national tradition' of tolerance.[99] Vidler thought Britain had avoided totalitarianism not through its present virtues but rather through its 'old traditions'.[100] In 1948, Murry wrote of the British 'genius' for compromise and freedom, locating these skills in a tradition reaching back to the seventeenth century; even in his former advocacy of Communism, he observed, his 'conscience as an Englishman' had compelled him to repudiate revolutionary violence.[101]

Emphasis on a British 'mission' continued well after the passing of the post-Dunkirk crisis. At the start of 1942, Oldham urged Britons to promote 'liberty, toleration and respect for the individual' and resist 'unregulated power'.[102] He praised

> the dogged quality of our people, bred in us by we do not know what influences of environment, climate and history – the quality of showing our best when our backs are to the wall, the capacity to lose every battle but the last. This heritage and tradition, which is a gift from the past – in the religious view a gift from God – is a reservoir from which we may certainly draw 'renewed accessions of strength'.[103]

In May 1942, he saw the need for a philosophy of a planned-but-free society through which Britain could 'save itself by its exertions and the world by its example'.[104] As noted, Mannheim's *Diagnosis of Our Time* (1943) identified Britain's distinctively religious character and ability to combine conformity with individualism as its contribution to the world.[105]

But there were doubts about how far Britain's example could benefit others. In November 1946 Murry thought its traditions and institutions – such as parliamentarianism, a disinterested civil service and the rule of law – might allow it to 'muddle through', but their very distinctiveness limited their transferability.[106] Britain's 'liberal tradition', Oldham claimed, was specific, and it would be 'folly' to think it might be 'transplanted overnight to Russia or the Balkans'.[107] Still, Britain had a crucial role to play. Returning there in 1947 after years spent in India, the missionary and theologian Lesslie Newbigin described it as a society 'deeply-rooted' in Christian views about individuality and responsibility that was seeking to apply them to modern life. This effort, he continued,

> is surely the most important political happening in the whole world. An attempt is being made to create a kind of social and economic organisation which will combine the measure of rational control without which modern society must disintegrate into chaos, with the measure of personal freedom without which society cannot remain human.[108]

In 1948, Murry thought British 'patriotism' could create consensus on the need for what he called the 'free society'.[109] Britain's national mission gave it responsibility *for* Europe without it being entirely *in* Europe.

The *CNL* emphasised social renewal, national humility and the universal nature of the western crisis. Oldham argued the war was not a binary conflict between the forces of 'death' and 'life': there were 'forces of life' in Germany and 'forces of spiritual decay and death' in Britain.[110] The war was not simply 'a great Christian cause'.[111] In April 1945 he again warned against identifying the Church with the nation's secular aims, claiming there were some whose religion was not Christianity but rather 'Church-of-Englandism'.[112] (Here one recalls Archbishop Fisher's comment that Churchill's own religiosity was that 'of the Englishman', sustained by a belief in a God 'with a special care for the values of the British people'.[113]) Imminent victory posed the danger of national egotism. In September 1944, Oldham warningly called Germany a 'portent' of a false culture across the entire West.[114] In January 1945, he insisted Britain and America were not 'immune from the canker which is eating into the vitals of European society'.[115] In March, he praised Lewis Mumford's *The Condition of Man* (1944) for showing how the Allies were infected by the same evil they were fighting.[116] The revelation of the horrors of the concentration camps confirmed the war's justification, but the 'dividing line in the real struggle' was not, Oldham said, 'straight and clear'.[117] Bliss saw the 'German technocrats' as a logical result of the West's materialism.[118] In August 1945 Oldham urged Britons and Germans to admit their 'common sin': Germany, having experienced 'the terrible power of demonic forces', might even help Britain overcome national self-righteousness, particularly in the emerging atomic age.[119] The *CNL* praised the Nuremberg trials but thought them one-sided: 'are there no crimes', Bliss asked, 'for which the victors ought to be brought to the bar of judgment?'.[120]

This concern to avoid simple dichotomies and resist western triumphalism (which would also deny the need for social reforms) was also applied to the Soviet Union. Immediately after the war, the *CNL* sought a balanced view.[121] Bliss pointed to Russian ruthlessness and oppression in Eastern Europe, but she also warned against a partisan western media that condemned Russian methods while saying little about black-marketeering and other crimes by British and American troops.[122] One side should not be indulged, she wrote, and the term 'Anglo-Saxon' should not come to mean 'anti-Russian'.[123] The *CNL* commented on an article by Berdyaev that praised Russian community life (influenced by Orthodoxy) over the 'depersonalized and mechanized' West: 'dehumanization', Bliss stated, was as real in Western Europe or America as it was in the Soviet Union.[124]

She also urged that the relationship with Russia should be based upon understanding, a commitment to peace and honest mutual criticism.[125]

It is striking that the continental immigrants in the group – Löwe, Mannheim and Polanyi – reinforced its positive views of British national character. Although he had been at first bewildered by Britain after arriving in 1933, Löwe, like Mannheim, quickly came to admire it.[126] He argued, most notably in *The Price of Liberty: An Essay on Contemporary Britain* (1937), that the English (he tended to use 'English' rather than 'British') were uniquely skilled at what he called 'spontaneous conformity' or 'spontaneous collectivism': i.e., forming cohesive social units without State direction. They thus offered a model for 'a new Western civilisation'.[127] Their conformity consisted in a social code based on 'self-restraint' and 'common decency and fairness'.[128] Secularised elements of English Protestantism, he claimed, encouraged such social agreement.[129] Britain showed that freedom's (necessary) limitation need not be externally *imposed* but might emerge organically from below: the Englishman's dictator, Löwe wrote, 'is installed in his heart'.[130] He thought the battle between Fascism and democracy would be decided in Britain, whose educational system (unlike Germany's) had found a way to meld mass education with democracy.[131] Though not Christian, Löwe's views were amenable to religious perspectives, and Oldham recommended *The Price of Liberty* in the *CNL*.[132] Löwe praised seventeenth-century England's self-image as 'a missionary country which felt a responsibility for humanising and civilising the world', urging that the United States and Britain had to become willing to 'police the world and to defend international order'.[133]

Mannheim, too, saw English traditions of liberty, self-organisation, compromise and tolerance as crucial to 'planning for freedom', and he shared the group's sense of national 'mission'.[134] British culture had inculcated helpful 'blended attitudes', combining conformity with spontaneity and enabling planning to be allied with a respect for privacy.[135] (This paralleled Dawson's distinction of the English 'national temperament' from Prussian 'drilled obedience' or Slavic 'mass mysticism', which had each enabled variants of totalitarianism to emerge.[136]) But Mannheim decried Britons' reluctance to think seriously and their preference for 'muddling through'.[137] The British 'tragedy', Mannheim argued, was 'the absolute hatred of ideas': 'anybody who thinks is suspect'.[138] (It should be noted that native Britons associated with the group – Temple, Hodges and Oldham – held similar views.[139]) Overall, however, Mannheim contributed to a strongly positive view of Britishness. After his death, Vidler memorialised him in *Theology*: 'Since he came to England he had assimilated to an extraordinary degree the English tradition', he wrote, 'and had discovered, as few Englishmen have, the strengths and the weaknesses of contemporary English society'. 'Like many continentals', he continued, 'he believed that Great Britain has a unique responsibility for the future welfare of mankind'.[140]

Polanyi had similar perspectives to Löwe and Mannheim. Before Polanyi attended the Moot in June 1944, Oldham had drawn attention to his article 'The English and the Continent'.[141] There, Oldham summarised, Polanyi argued that, uniquely in Europe, English social progress had been driven by 'religious sentiment' rather than rationalism and anti-clericalism: its culture was 'based on the principles of toleration and freedom under the reign of law, and guided by standards of decency in both individual and social relations'.[142] This moral strength had eroded, but it returned after Dunkirk. Polanyi argued that English patriotism had 'recalled' the USA, the Dominions and all of Europe to 'their common moral traditions'.[143] (Mannheim thought that Britain had been less affected by secularisation than most other western countries to begin with.[144]) Polanyi told the Moot that, whereas he had once found national identity 'reactionary' and less real than class, he was struck by the cross-class presumption in Britain 'that we should somehow get on together', which provided a solidarity that worked against tyranny or civil war.[145] In either case, Christianity had saved Britain from descending into totalitarianism.[146]

Universalism, Christendom and federalism

While trying to fuse Christian principles with national traditions, the Oldham group also considered ways of relativizing British identity through supra-national imagined communities and institutional structures. Various larger contexts – from distinctly religious to explicitly secular – were addressed: Christian universalism, ideals of 'Christendom', forms of federalism, 'Anglo-Saxon' cooperation and the post-war UN. These were not alternatives to a renewed *national* society but rather seen as larger communities into which it could be embedded.

The Oxford conference had stressed that the 'universal' fellowship of Christianity opposed the elevation of nation or race as 'the ultimate authority over human life'.[147] Universalism derived from God's unitary sovereignty, unlike an 'internationalism' pieced together from separate state sovereignties.[148] The Moot shared Lex Miller's view (echoing Oxford's conclusions) that Christians had 'a dual citizenship and a dual calling', which should counteract sacralised nationalisms.[149] Eliot stressed the need for 'a visible and authoritative centre of allegiance outside of the nation'.[150] The 'irreconcilable opposition' between universal human fellowship and the 'deification' of particularised identities was stressed from the *CNL*'s first issue, and national or racial bigotry was condemned.[151] Christianity, Oldham stated, recognised that 'the fundamental thing in an individual is not his nationality but his humanity'.[152] What he called 'common humanity' trumped racial or national differences.[153] On the other hand, it was important that Christian universalism should not be confused with what Fenn called 'an abstract international idealism' that merely ignored the power of national loyalty.[154]

At Oxford, Christian universalism was described not only as an ideal but also as a 'fact': the Church was a 'supra-national society', opposing 'disruptive nationalism and aggressive imperialism'.[155] The *CNL* urged Christians to promote a 'widening of sympathies' via their membership in a 'universal society', and it reported on war-time fellowship efforts in Britain among various (often refugee) Christian groups.[156] William Paton claimed Christians' 'universal fellowship' enabled them to support what was 'sane and decent in the spirit of the nation', offering a model of brotherhood based not on utopianism but on common moral obligations and commitments.[157] Ecumenism signified a faith-based world community, 'the dialectical antithesis' of a 'fissiparous' nationalism.[158] But Oldham urged Christians not to 'forfeit' their local solidarities, since a 'deracinated ecumenical clique' would be weak: 'all Churches have pasts, and cultures, and national traditions', and 'the Christians who form these Churches are Americans and Japanese, capitalists and trade unionists, almost infinitely diverse in matters of culture, taste, thought forms, language and social background'.[159] Rooted diversity, in this view, was the basis of true universalism.

The term 'Christendom', when used to refer (globally) to all Christians, expressed this universalism; however, the word also evoked a specifically European ideal of transnational loyalty. What Philip Coupland calls the 'myth of Christendom' depicted medieval Europe as a society in which Christianity was the main cultural 'point of reference', 'state and society were one' and 'Europe was united under the moral authority of the Church': 'Christendom' thus became a shorthand for a lost (but recoverable) European unity. The popularity of this image has waxed and waned, but the early twentieth century saw its resurgence.[160] In Britain, the term was given inter-war prominence by the 'Christendom Group' of Anglo-Catholic thinkers, and, as noted, Maritain's vision of a 'new Christendom' infused the Oldham group's language.[161] At war's outbreak, Oldham urged the Moot to work towards 'a reborn Christendom', and he envisioned a 'restoration' or 'resurrection' of Christendom in his 1940 book with the latter title.[162] In *God's Judgment on Europe* (1940), Vidler decried the destruction of Christendom (i.e. a 'common European culture') by secularisation and liberalism.[163] He took a similar view in *Secular Despair and Christian Faith* (1941): the breakdown of the 'medieval synthesis' had been necessary, but it had also unleashed the modern crisis.[164] Others, too, saw a 'rebirth' of

Christendom as a goal.[165] Christendom's geography was vague and variable, referring at times to Europe or 'the West'. (The latter was also vaguely defined, being distinguished from Asia, Nazi Germany and Russia.[166])

Thus, 'Christendom' evoked not so much a political map as the structural subordination of politics to religion: i.e. 'God enthroned above the nation'.[167] It did not mean *denying* the nation. As Eliot put it in the Moot, Christendom 'cannot be the abolition of national, racial, local or cultural differences' but must rather be 'their transcendence in a unity and harmony of different elements'.[168] Moreover, it was not always Eurocentric: Europe was seen as a product of Christianity, but its catastrophe meant Christianity's renewal might begin in China, India or Russia.[169] At Christmas 1945, Daniel Jenkins called for Christendom to re-emerge where 'it first had birth', and thereafter Bliss claimed 'a new Christendom in Europe' – i.e. a belief 'that power can be restrained by law' – was not a 'wild dream'.[170] Christendom, it was thought, might give a context for national development and international relations; however, an institutional structure was never specified, and Christendom remained a political ideal rather than anything remotely resembling a concrete policy.

More institutionally focused, Federal Union (FU) was a popular movement proposing the amalgamation of national sovereignties into a higher, federal entity. Founded after the Munich crisis, and given influential expression in the American journalist Clarence Streit's book *Union Now* (1939), the movement's very name became a buzzword. However, it was rent by divisions between 'Atlanticists' and 'Europeanists', and among socialists, liberals and conservatives.[171] Prominent Christians both supported and opposed it.[172] The Oldham group was ambivalent. It shared the federalist critique of nationalism. Essays in *CNL* in 1940 by Löwe, Fedetov and Temple urged constructing a supranational political unit, saw an emerging 'new commonwealth' and favoured federalism.[173] Baillie told the Moot that FU, which was popular among Scottish clergy, had sought his support, but he remained doubtful.[174] Hodges credited federalists for at least recognising significant trends, such as growing global interdependence.[175]

But the group tended to think that federalism addressed a *spiritual* crisis with purely *organisational* solutions. Oldham called it 'sheer delusion' to believe that any 'improvement of machinery' would suffice: there needed to be 'some body of commonly accepted ideas about the ends for which society exists'.[176] Federalism seemed to promise only the rearrangement of the same flawed modernity. In his contribution to a wide-ranging essay collection on FU published early in 1940, Murry criticised its advocates for a 'utopian' desire to reorganise modern societies without fundamentally changing them. He argued that an extensive economic collectivism and – using language common to the Oldham group – 'some prior and widespread agreement upon the true ends of human life' would be necessary preconditions to a successful federalism: here, he insisted that only a 'Christian dynamic' could create a new democracy.[177] In April 1940 Oldham told the Moot that FU was 'the wrong thing', and in a 1941 broadcast he argued that it, or any other 'World-State', would improve nothing while accelerating the exhaustion of the earth's resources.[178] (Mairet similarly accused FU of ignoring the capitalist exploitation of people and nature.[179]) Changing military realities proved decisive in such discussions. In 1941 and 1942, German victories throughout Europe swept aside federalist ideals.[180] Social transformation became even more a central concern. Löwe insisted that when British leaders discussed federalism they became lost in 'tedious' details, ignoring the need for 'radical' social change.[181] Murry, reiterating his earlier critique, read federalist economics as either 'world free-trade in a new guise' or a dangerous 'World-State', neither of which he could support.[182] A united Europe remained a goal within the group, but interest in federalism faded.

Scepticism about federalism – and the shifting realities of the war – increased the group's stress on the 'Anglo-Saxon' or 'English-speaking' nations.[183] At first referring to the Dominions, this concept gained relevance with US entry into the war. Moot members urged Britain to 'unite the Anglo-Saxon world on a new basis' (Mannheim) and stressed cultural bonds, such as traditions of 'empirical' philosophy (Dawson) or limited State power (Polanyi).[184] Murry had written an article for the *Adelphi* (which had been censored), urging Britain to seek a 'new united states of Anglo-Saxon peoples' and a 'new kind of democracy'.[185] Polanyi thought religion's role in the public life of anglophone countries had kept the secular 'leviathan' at bay.[186] But humility was needed: the 'prevailing Anglo-Saxon attitude towards other races', Oldham wrote, was akin to the Nazi notion of a *Herrenvolk* (master race) and in need of 'fundamental change'.[187] The group was also doubtful about American influence. Its intellectual exchange with American Protestants had revealed significant theological and cultural differences.[188] Mannheim even saw American psychology as 'Fascist in its excitability'.[189] In late 1944 Oldham told Visser 't Hooft that he had come to the conclusion that America was 'leagues away' from Britain.[190]

Such doubts about America fed, privately and publicly, into the group's sense of national 'mission' and Britain's unique responsibility for Europe. Another 'middle way' emerged. In 1943, Mannheim asserted that Britain must lead a 'progressive Europe', since 'America is too far and Russia is too near'. In 1944, he called Britain 'the only culture left which represents the European tradition': Russia was a 'new venture' while America had abandoned European traditions.[191] This paralleled Hodges's claim that *both* Communism and capitalism were destroying Europe's traditional culture.[192] In the *CNL*, Oldham argued that Britain could mediate between the Soviets and Americans, 'enforcing a rule of justice over Europe', and its Commonwealth prepared it for a significant international role.[193] In mid 1945, Barbara Ward claimed that the British people's empiricism, tolerance and political maturity gave them a unique responsibility to find a 'synthesis' of the Russian and American 'extremes' and develop a compromise between 'complete socialism and complete *laisser faire* [*sic*]'.[194]

The relationship to Europe, however, was complex. In late 1947, Bliss argued Britons could no longer see themselves as a detached island or think only of 'cultivating our own patch' in economics, politics and culture. Britain had often taken up and 'tamed' continental impulses, she argued, stressing that Britain's 'steadying hand' was having a positive impact on the current European situation. But Britain was distinct from Europe. It was 'not shut up exclusively to the continent' but – via its Commonwealth – 'open to the world'; also, Christianity's influence across its political spectrum was unique.[195] She suggested that the influence of adherents of Christian socialism in Parliament was distinct, and she insisted that continental Christian Democratic parties were alien to Britain's political system.[196] The *CNL* highlighted a meeting promoting a 'Western Union' in May 1948, but, although favouring European cooperation, Bliss ultimately urged a *global* rather than a *European* perspective.[197]

There were similar doubts, though, at the global level. As with FU, the *CNL* welcomed the UN, founded in late October 1945, while at the same time questioning its value. Early documents from the CCFCL had called for a new international 'machinery for conference and cooperation' but also for an 'ethos of inter-state relations'.[198] The group found this latter element lacking in the UN. In May 1945, Bliss stressed that Christians thought world peace could only be built by 'those who learn to discipline themselves to act responsibly in their relations with others'.[199] Picking up this theme against the background of negotiations setting up the UN in August that year, Oldham emphasised that institutions alone could not guarantee peace, since only a few nations – especially the USA and USSR – held true power.[200] After Parliament ratified the UN Charter, Bliss stressed that it would not be 'an infallible guarantee of peace': it could be a boon to peace and cooperation only 'if the nations choose to use it'. There was, she thought, no purpose in planning a new world order if the 'convictions' it would require eroded.[201] (A 1946 BCC conference agreed that the churches should support the UN but stressed that real security required 'Christian values'.[202]) Post-war power politics seemed to exemplify a spiritual crisis. On the eve of the UN's founding, the *CNL* thought it was probably 'doomed to failure without a radical revolution in men's minds'.[203]

Related discussions, such as those on controlling atomic weapons, also brought out the group's opposition to a 'World-State', and preference for improving relations *among* sovereign nations and social renewal *within* them.[204] There was no shared cultural basis for a world state based on constitutionalism, and any other form was undesirable.[205] This emphasis on *culture* made the group concerned about the formation of the United Nations Educational, Scientific and Cultural Organization (UNESCO). Both privately and in the *CNL*, Oldham worried the organisation would advocate a 'secularist ideology'.[206] (Visser 't Hooft urged churches to work with UNESCO so as to influence it but told Oldham he feared it might become a tool for a 'radical secularisation of the world' comparable with that desired by Nazi ideologue Alfred Rosenberg.[207]) The cultural mission of UNESCO made it relevant to Christians, but its potential for spreading anti-religious views made it seem hostile to them.[208] Christian influences on the Universal Declaration of Human Rights were, nevertheless, celebrated, even if the *CNL* doubted its power.[209]

Conclusion

National identity was a recurring issue in the Oldham group, as it sought both to emphasise the legitimacy of *nationality* (in opposition to a 'rootless' internationalism) and to resist *nationalism* (in the face of aggressive, sacralised understandings of national belonging). In the context of war, navigating this middle way involved, first, a Christian patriotism combining a love of national traditions with national 'humility' and an ethic of 'service' to other nations, and, second, efforts to embed national sovereignty and identity in supra-national contexts. This tension between nationality and nationalism was a stable aspect of the group's consensus, reflecting a distinction and vocabulary also employed in other Christian contexts.[210] An emphasis on a legitimate patriotism that grew out of local customs and relationships – and that avoided aggressive nationalism – had been, for example, a key part of G. K. Chesterton's thought from the turn of the century; his ideas had, in turn, influenced Christopher Dawson, among others.[211] Use of the term 'nationality' to denote that which belonged to a particular 'national' culture was also common in the Christian press.[212] However, a changing world situation brought significant shifts within this framework. Between Oxford 1937 and the summer of 1940, stress was placed on Britain's collective *failure* to embody Christian principles, and the moral difference between liberalism and totalitarianism was, at times, blurred. The war sharpened this distinction, and the group was virtually unanimous in supporting the war effort. The Dunkirk evacuations and the beginning of the 'Battle of Britain' in the summer of 1940 brought a markedly positive revaluation of national traditions and a vision of Britain's providential 'mission' to save European civilisation. Rather than a rejection of 'Christian nationhood' in the service of a Christian internationalism – a position adopted by some Christians affiliated with the ecumenical movement – what emerged was an embrace of a 'true' Christian nationality aimed at opposing a false, idolatrous nationalism.[213]

Here, evocations of 'Christian civilization' and patriotic images of 'England' were neither separate nor contradictory.[214] Many of the themes employed in the group's rhetoric matched those of British political leaders of the inter-war and war years, such as Stanley Baldwin's and Winston Churchill's emphases on the innate qualities of the British people, such as 'their sense of community and fair play' and their 'instinct for decency, justice and the rule of law'.[215] National beleaguerment and the resulting public spirit seemed to offer space for a 'revolutionary' creed of fellowship and community, one that was famously expressed in some of George Orwell's war-time writings.

The appeal to Englishness by the Oldham group was also strategic, as it was thought that 'some movement of a distinctively English model' would have more appeal.[216] Strongly positive views of British (or 'English') traditions also came from the group's continental members. But this patriotism stressed that Britain must 'repent' for its own sins. A stress on repentance was common among Christians, such as in a joint statement by the Church of England, Church of Scotland and Federal Council of Evangelical Free Churches in September 1939.[217] However, the *Christian World* argued that the demand for penitence should not extend to suggesting that Britain's own lapses gave it no right to combat far worse sins.[218] Other Christians – including C. S. Lewis – warned against a surfeit of repentance, lest crucial moral distinctions between Nazism and the democracies should be lost.[219] The group's thinking ultimately reflected typical elements of British liberal internationalist thinking, not least a concern about the destructive nature of nationalism (though this did not lead to a pacifist conclusion).[220]

While the Oldham group moved towards the nation in 1940, the nation was moving, at least rhetorically, towards Christianity. The war was widely described as a defence of 'Christian civilisation'.[221] The image of a fight against 'evil', or Britain as a 'Christian nation' fighting the Nazi 'devil', it has been argued, 'moved to the heart of national discourse'.[222] In a similar way to the Oldham group, the *Church of England Newspaper* praised the British Empire or Commonwealth as a model for world federation and the voluntary self-limitation of national sovereignty.[223] At times, Christians argued their faith could give an added, 'spiritual' quality to service to the nation, but many saw a danger of a sacralised nationalism and the instrumentalisation of genuine religious feeling by the State. Efforts by leading Labour Party politician Stafford Cripps to fuse patriotism, social renewal and Christianity, for example, were criticised in the Oldham group as 'making religion the handmaid of politics'.[224] Church leaders such as Bell and Temple also warned against the Church becoming 'the State's spiritual auxiliary'.[225] Some also pointed out that Christians were not alone in the war: 'Mohammedans, Buddhists, Hindus, Parsees, Jews and other non-Christians, are fighting on the side of a good against evil', a leading article in *Nature* observed: 'The good is a common factor of all the higher religions'.[226] But the Christian churches were seen as vital to rebuilding a Europe in which other institutions had been destroyed or discredited.[227] Bliss described them 'as the chief remaining support in a disintegrating society' and 'the foundations of a new life'.[228]

While the shift by Oldham and his companions towards patriotism and emphases on national traditions and character were not unusual in war-time Britain, their stress on 'service', 'humility' and 'realism' departed from dominant patriotic narratives that emphasised 'heroic, populist and uto-pian constructions of national identity and citizenship'.[229] In line with other Christian circles, they portrayed social renewal as a prerequisite to victory and saw Britain's distinct post-war role as melding Christian and demo-cratic principles to act as a model for the rest of Europe. There were similar-ities with German Lutheran theologian Dietrich Bonhoeffer's understanding of Christian patriotism.[230] Like Bonhoeffer, the Oldham group emphasised the 'real and particular' against the 'conceptual and intangible', stressing the positive elements of a concrete national heritage.[231] Like Niebuhr and other American Christians, the Oldham group's members embraced a 'cautious patriotism', allowing public support of one's own nation while maintaining an independent standpoint on the war's meaning and conduct.[232] Their patri-otism was self-critical, relative and conditional: 'true' patriotism, in their view, required humility, repentance and service towards others. There were many versions of this point of view. The editor of the *Catholic Herald*, to take but one example, argued in 1940 that 'the candid and realist Christian critic is the true British patriot'.[233] With Britain's improving strategic situation from 1942, evocations of Britain's 'mission' became less prophetic and more focused on mediating between the Soviet Union and the United States. But even after the defeat of National Socialism and Fascism, the *CNL* remained suffused with a sense of crisis. The post-war order was still threatened by totalitarianism – in the form of Soviet Communism – and the democracies were plagued by the idealisation of scientific-technological power (including, now, that of the atom), the lack of a true system of values and the predominance of national self-aggrandisement and capitalist greed.

In addressing their age's opportunities and threats, the Oldham group considered not only how the nation should be imagined but also how Britain might be embedded in larger cultural or political contexts. A Christian universalism, emphasising the unity of all humankind as divinely created beings, was a consistent part of their worldview. Its institutional meaning, however, remained vague. The same can be said of 'Christendom' ideals, which described less a geographically specific (and ultimately medieval) European unity than the aim of placing politics under the authority of faith. Plans for supra-national institutions that would either pool sovereignty (federalism) or coordinate collective security (the UN) were much discussed. However, while Marxists condemned federalists for ignoring class conflict, and federalists, in return, criticised Marxists' lack of attention to sovereignty, the Oldham group thought *both* overlooked the 'spiritual' dimension of the world crisis. Committed to international cooperation, the group was nonetheless sceptical about organisational solutions to problems that, in its view, actually required fundamental cultural transformations. As had been the case at Oxford 1937, both dangerous varieties of nationalism and false forms of internationalism were condemned. The group's strong attachment to the nation as a meaningful, religiously legitimated form of community also made it sceptical about plans for a 'World-State', especially one that would promote secularism.

Still, there was a certain Europeanisation of the group's thinking in the course of the war. If specifically 'English' values and traditions – and a national 'mission' – had predominated in the dark days of 1940 and 1941, what followed saw an effort to locate these traditions (and that mission) within a positive vision for 'the Western democracies' in contrast to either Hitler's or Stalin's 'New Order'.[234] The 'European heritage' was valued, since it had been deeply influenced by Christianity, whereas Nazism was seen as its 'betrayal'.[235] In May 1945, Oldham called for re-embracing the 'imperishable values' of what he called 'our tradition'; but 'our' here referred not to something uniquely *British* but rather to comments by Bishop George Bell in the House of Lords about the 'four spiritual traditions' of *European* civilization.[236] Nonetheless, European ideals competed with emphases on western, Anglo-Saxon and transatlantic cultural unities, and a continuing fixation on Britain's imperial and Commonwealth relations. There was a broader ecumenical Christian shift, also visible in the group, away from Europe and towards 'the West' as a vehicle for Christian values and social reconstruction, even though the inter-war period had seen sustained critiques of the West's loss of its Christian roots.[237] The war was pivotal here. 'The Christian civilization of the West', declared Daniel Jenkins in the *CNL* in December 1945, 'has decisively shattered the most murderous attempt ever yet made upon its life, and many of its leaders have not unimpressively re-affirmed its Christian basis'.[238] Eliot advocated both European unity and the need for national diversity: 'It seems difficult enough, in the future before us, to achieve any European unity; it seems difficult enough, on the other hand, for each nation to preserve its distinct and traditional culture: what we have to attempt seems more difficult than either, because it is *both*.'[239]

The Protestant churches were ambivalent about early steps towards European unification, reflecting both their national orientations but also fears (especially at the grassroots level) of Europe as a *Catholic* project.[240] The interest of leading British clergy in continental political cooperation dimmed after the war: there was still 'enthusiasm for "Europe United"' in the British churches, but it proved to be a 'passing moment'.[241] Even for Christians, it has been observed, 'sovereignty was dear to an Empire that stood alone against Fascism', and, with the increasing division of Europe between two superpowers, bold plans to supersede the nation were abandoned.[242] In 1948, the Archbishop of York declared federalism in a Europe divided between East and West to be beyond 'the realms of practical politics' and 'a sheer waste of time'.[243] After what has been called the 'great British federalism boom of 1939–1940', Christian social thought again focused on the nation-state, even if international cooperation continued to be seen as vital.[244] Just as 'planning for freedom' had responded to left-wing totalitarianism, so a Christian patriotism seemed to answer the idolatry of the extreme right. As with planning, this was a patriotism with a purpose beyond national survival: it was deeply connected to an ideal of 'freedom'. It is to a closer analysis of this central concept for the Oldham group that the next chapter turns.

Notes

1 On use of 'English' as a synonym for 'British', see Peter Mandler, *The English National Character: The History of an Idea from Edmund Burke to Tony Blair* (New Haven: Yale, 2006), pp. 148, 194, 205.

2 On 'national character': Peter Mandler, 'The Consciousness of Modernity? Liberalism and the English National Character, 1870–1940', in Martin Daunton and Bernhard Reiger (eds.), *Meanings of Modernity: Britain from the Late-Victorian Era to World War Two* (Oxford: Berg, 2001), pp. 119–44; and Matthew Grimley, 'The Religion of Englishness: Puritanism, Providentialism and "National Character", 1918–1945', *Journal of British Studies*, 46:4 (2007), 884–906.

3 *Moot Papers*, M20, p. 706. Emphasis in original.

4 Barnes, *Nazism, Liberalism, and Christianity*, p. 58.

5 Catherine Anne Cline, 'Ecumenism and Appeasement: The Bishops of the Church of England and the Treaty of Versailles', *Journal of Modern History*, 61 (1989), 683–703; Andrew Chandler, 'Munich and Morality: The Bishops of the Church of England and Appeasement', *Twentieth-Century British History*, 5:1 (1994), 77–99; A. J. Hoover, *God, Britain and Hitler in World War II: The View of the British Clergy, 1939–1945* (Westport, CT: Praeger, 1999), pp. 1–6.

6 Barnes, *Nazism, Liberalism, and Christianity*, pp. 96–101; Richard J. Evans, *The Third Reich in Power* (New York: Penguin, 2005), 220–33; Matthew D. Hockenos, 'Pastor Martin Niemöller, German Protestantism, and German National Identity, 1933–1937', in Wood, *Christianity and National Identity*, pp. 113–30. On Bell: Cline, 'Appeasement', pp. 696–8; Hastings, *A History*, p. 342; Andrew Chandler, *George Bell, Bishop of Chichester: Church, State, and Resistance in the Age of Dictatorship* (Grand Rapids, MI: William B. Eerdmans, 2016), pp. 52–8.

7 Oldham, *Church, Community and State*, pp. 12–13.

8 *The Times*, 17 July 1937, p. 18.

9 *Moot Papers*, M20, p. 704.

10 *Churches Survey Their Task*, p. 70. E.g. 'nation': *ibid.*, pp. 13, 21, 24, 40, 58, 59, 84. On race: *ibid.*, 72–3. Thompson, *God and Globe*, pp. 120–44, esp. pp. 130–1.

11 *The Universal Church and the World of Nations* (Chicago: Willett, Clark, 1938), p. 3; *Churches Survey Their Task*, pp. 30–1.

12 *Churches Survey Their Task*, pp. 71–2, 76, 229.

13 *Ibid.*, p. 194.

14 *Ibid.*, pp. 33, 74, 184, 226, 228, 231, 235, 238.

15 *Ibid.*, p. 202.

16 *Ibid.*, pp. 68, 192.

17 *Ibid.*, p. 58.

18 Coupland, *Britannia, Europa and Christendom*, p. 5; Philip Coupland, 'Britain, Europe and Christendom in Mid-Twentieth-Century British Christian Thought', *Political Theology*, 6:3 (2005), 367–91 (p. 370).

19 Grimley, 'Religion of Englishness', p. 885. See also Wolffe, *God and Greater Britain*, pp. 5–19.

20 Grimley, *Citizenship*; Catterall, *Labour and the Free Churches*.

21 Keith Robbins, 'Avoiding the Challenge? British Churches, British Society and European Integration, 1947–1949', in Duchhardt and Morawiec, *Die europäische Integration und die Kirchen*, pp. 5–20 (p. 7). Coupland, *Britannia, Europa and Christendom*, p. 5.

22 Fenn, *Crisis and Democracy*, pp. 14–15.

23 Dawson, *Religion and the Modern State*, p. 138.

24 *CNL* 1S, 1 November 1939, J. H. Oldham, 'What Is God Doing?', p. 2.

25 *CNL* 72L, 12 March 1941, p. 2.

26 *CNL* 83L, 28 May 1941, p. 2; *CNL* 164S, 16 December 1942, J. H. Oldham, 'Christmas 1942', p. 2.

27 *CNL* 199L, 12 January 1944, p. 1.

28 *CNL* 204L, 22 March 1944, p. 1.

29 *Moot Papers*, M14, p. 508 (Mannheim); M1, pp. 44–5 (Farmer); M13, p. 456 (Oldham).

30 Polanyi quoted in *CNL* 194S, 15 December 1943, J. H. Oldham, 'The Obligations of Our Heritage', pp. 3–4.

31 *CNL* 0S, 18 October 1939, J. H. Oldham, 'What Is a Christian News-Letter?', p. 2.

32 *CNL* 5S, 29 November 1939, J. H. Oldham, 'Preliminaries to the Consideration of Peace Aims', p. 3.

33 *CNL* 13S, 24 January 1940, 'Our Readers Contribute', p. 2.

34 *CNL* 21L, 20 March 1940, p. 2.

35 Eric Fenn, *That They Go Forward: An Impression of the Oxford Conference on Church, Community and State* (London: SCM, 1938), p. 30.

36 OA 9/2/34, Oldham to members of the Moot, 6 September 1939, p. 1.

37 See Vidler, *Scenes*, pp. 114–16.

38 *CNL* 0S, 18 October 1939, J. H. Oldham, 'What Is a Christian News-Letter?', p. 2; *CNL* 11S, 10 January 1940, J. H. Oldham, 'Christianity and Political Justice', p. 3.

39 *CNL* 13S, 24 January 1940, J. H. Oldham, 'Our Members Contribute', p. 2.

40 *CNL* 14L, 31 January 1940; Niebuhr, 'Wrong Answers', p. 2.

41 *CNL* 17S, 21 February 1940, 'X', 'The Reality of the Christian Life', p. 2.

42 *CNL* 24L, 10 April 1940, p. 1; *CNL* 80S, 7 May 1941, anon., 'The Nazi Creed', p. 3.

43 *Moot Papers*, M2, p. 106.

44 *Ibid.*, M4, pp. 193–4.

45 *CNL* 11L, 10 January 1940, p. 1.

46 *CNL* 5S, 29 November 1939, J. H. Oldham, 'Preliminaries to the Consideration of Peace Aims', p. 2.

47 *CNL* 7L, 13 December 1939, p. 3.

48 *CNL* 35L, 26 June 1940, p. 1.

49 *CNL* 36L, 3 July 1940, pp. 1–2. See similar arguments in *Church of England Newspaper*, 22 January 1943, p. 4; and *Guardian*, 5 May 1944, p. 155.

50 *CNL* 36L, 3 July 1940, p. 2.

51 *CNL* 39L, 24 July 1940, p. 2.

52 *CNL* 39S, 24 July 1940, Owen Barfield, 'Effective Approach to Social Change', pp. 3, 4.

53 *CNL* 39L, 24 July 1940, p. 2.

54 *CNL* 36L, 3 July 1940, p. 1. Emphasis in original.

55 *Ibid.*, p. 2.

56 *CNL* 49L, 2 October 1940, p. 1.

57 *CNL* 33S, 12 June 1940, G. Fedetov, 'A Russian Voice', p. 2.

58 *CNL* 80S, 7 May 1941, anon., 'The Nazi Creed', p. 7.

59 *CNL* 88S, 1 July 1941, J. H. Oldham, 'The Predicament of Society and the Way Out – II', p. 4.

60 *Moot Papers*, M5, p. 228.

61 *CNL* 45S, 4 September 1940, J. H. Oldham 'The Way Out', p. 1.

62 *CNL* 60L, 18 December 1940, p. 3.

63 *CNL* 77L, 16 April 1941, p. 3; *CNL* 82L, 21 May 1941, p. 1.

64 *CNL* 36L, 3 July 1940, p. 2. Emphasis in original. See also *CNL* 37L, 10 July 1940, p. 2.

65 *CNL* 37L, 10 July 1940, p. 2.

66 *CNL* 37S, 10 July 1940, V. A. Demant, 'Our Justification', p. 1.

67 *Ibid.*, p. 2.

68 *CNL* 38L, 17 July 1940, pp. 1–2.

69 *CNL* 39L, 24 July 1940, p. 2.

70 *CNL* 40L, 31 July 1940, p. 3.

71 *CNL* 41L, 7 August 1940, p. 3.

72 *CNL* 37L, 10 July 1940, p. 1.

73 *CNL* 39L, 24 July 1940, p. 1.
74 *CNL* 42L, 14 August 1940, p. 1.
75 *CNL* 44L, 28 August 1940, p. 3.
76 *CNL* 97L, 3 September 1941, p. 4.
77 *CNL* 121L, 18 February 1942, p. 3.
78 *CNL* 84L, 4 June 1941, p. 1.
79 *CNL* 117L, 21 January 1942, p. 3.
80 BC, BAI 1/7/2 (3 of 3), Michael Polanyi, 'Science and the Modern Crisis', 14 November 1944, p. 4.
81 *CNL* 135L, 27 May 1942, pp. 1–2.
82 *CNL* 157L, 28 October 1942, p. 1.
83 *Ibid*. This notion reappeared in *CNL* 222L, 29 November 1944, p. 2.
84 *Moot Papers*, M18, pp. 647–8.
85 *Ibid*., M18, pp. 628, 648–9.
86 *Ibid*., M18, p. 649.
87 *Ibid*., M2, p. 92 n. 27.
88 *Ibid*., M19, p. 677.
89 *Ibid*., M18, p. 653.
90 *Ibid*., M18, pp. 629, 643; M19, p. 672.
91 *Ibid*., M18, p. 648.
92 *CNL* 63L, 8 January 1941, p. 2.
93 *CNL* 160S, 18 November 1942, George Every, 'Planning within Limits', p. 4.
94 *CNL* 216L, 6 September 1944, pp. 1–2.
95 *CNL* 181L, 5 May 1943, p. 4.
96 *CNL* 203L, 8 March 1944, p. 3.
97 *CNL* 213L, 26 July 1944, p. 2.
98 *CNL* 235L, 30 May 1945, p. 2.
99 *CNL* 291L, 6 August 1947, p. 6.
100 Vidler, *Free University*, p. 14.
101 Murry, *Free Society*, pp. 114–16, 132, 213.
102 *CNL* 115L, 7 January 1942, p. 3–4.
103 *CNL* 122L, 25 February 1942, p. 1.
104 *CNL* 132S, 6 May 1942, J. H. Oldham, 'Of These Stones', p. 3.
105 Mannheim, *Diagnosis*, pp. 51, 126.
106 *CNL* 274S, 27 November 1946, J. Middleton Murry, 'Can Democracy Survive?', p. 15.
107 *CNL* 275L, 11 December 1946, p. 13.
108 *CNL* 298S, 12 November 1947, J. E. L. Newbigin, 'Some Thoughts on Britain from Abroad', pp. 10–11.
109 Murry, *Free Society*, pp. 114–16, 262–3.
110 *CNL* 112L, 17 December 1941, p. 1.
111 *CNL* 129L, 15 April 1942, p. 1.
112 *CNL* 232L, 18 April 1945, p. 3.
113 Andrew Chandler, review of Wolffe, *God and Greater Britain*, *English Historical Review*, 110 (1995), 948–50 (p. 948).

114 *CNL* 216L, 6 September 1944, p. 4. *CNL* 217L, 20 September 1944, p. 2.
115 *CNL* 225L, 10 January 1945, p. 5.
116 *CNL* 229L, 7 March 1945, p. 1.
117 *CNL* 233L, 2 May 1945, p. 2.
118 *CNL* 242L, 5 September 1945, p. 3.
119 *CNL* 241L, 22 August 1945, p. 12; *CNL* 269S, 18 September 1946, J. H. Oldham, 'The Control of Atomic Energy', p. 10.
120 *CNL* 271L, 16 October 1946, pp. 3–4.
121 *CNL* 241L, 22 August 1945, p. 5.
122 *CNL* 248L, 28 November 1945, p. 1.
123 *Ibid.*, p. 1.
124 *Ibid.*, p. 7.
125 *Ibid.*, pp. 9–10.
126 Adolph Lowe, *The Price of Liberty: An Essay on Contemporary Britain*, 3rd edn (London: Hogarth Press, 1948 [1937]), p. 10. Loader, *Intellectual Development*, pp. 152–3.
127 Lowe, *Price of Liberty*, pp. 10, 14–15, 26, 40–4. Mathew Forstater, 'Adolph Lowe on Freedom, Education and Socialization', *Review of Social Economy*, 58:2 (2000), 225–39 (pp. 227–8).
128 Lowe, *Price of Liberty*, pp. 13–14, 15, 26.
129 *Ibid.*, p. 19.
130 *Ibid.*, p. 25.
131 *Ibid.*, p. 40. See Forstater, 'Adolph Lowe', pp. 230–1.
132 *CNL* 5L, 29 November 1939, p. 3.
133 *Moot Papers*, M1, p. 43.
134 *Ibid.*, M11, p. 390; M16, p. 557. Mannheim, *Diagnosis*, pp. ix, 11.
135 Mannheim, *Diagnosis*, pp. 51, 126. See also *ibid.*, pp. 11, 129–30. *Moot Papers*, M19, pp. 668, 673.
136 IOE MOO/88, Dawson, 'Freedom and Vocation', n.d. [intended to be discussed in December 1941, actually discussed in September 1942], p. 8.
137 *Moot Papers*, M11, pp. 382–3.
138 *Ibid.*, M11, pp. 388–9.
139 *Birmingham Post*, 25 June 1938, and *Daily Sketch*, 25 June 1938, in CCFCL 12/1/1. *CNL* 17L, 21 February 1940, p. 2. *Moot Papers*, M10, p. 354.
140 *Theology*, 50:321 (March 1947), 81–2.
141 *CNL* 194S, 15 December 1943, J. H. Oldham, 'The Obligations of Our Heritage'. Original article: Michael Polanyi, 'The English and the Continent', *Political Quarterly*, 14:4 (1943), 372–81.
142 *CNL* 194S, 15 December 1943, J. H. Oldham, 'The Obligations of Our Heritage', pp. 2–3.
143 *Ibid.*, p. 3.
144 Mannheim, *Diagnosis*, p. 101.
145 *Moot Papers*, M20, p. 708.
146 BC, BAI 1/7/2 (3 of 3), Michael Polanyi, 'Science and the Modern Crisis', 14 November 1944, p. 5

147 See, e.g., *Churches Survey Their Task*, pp. 31–4, and 13, 40, 50, 77, 83–4, 168–70.

148 *Ibid.*, pp. 58, 168–9.

149 *Moot Papers*, M18, p. 649.

150 IOE MOO/123, T. S. Eliot, 'Notes on Social Philosophy', n.d. [possibly summer 1942], p. 2.

151 *CNL* 0S, 18 October 1939, J. H. Oldham, 'What Is a Christian News-Letter?', p. 2.

152 *CNL* 57S, 27 November 1940, J. H. Oldham, 'The Demand for a Christian Lead', p. 4.

153 *CNL* 165L, 23 December 1942, p. 3.

154 Fenn, *That They Go Forward*, p. 61.

155 *Churches Survey Their Task*, pp. 169, 173–4.

156 *CNL* 0S, 18 October 1939, J. H. Oldham, 'What Is a Christian News-Letter?', pp. 2–3. On international fellowship services, see *CNL* 67L, 5 February 1941, p. 2; and *CNL* 86L, 18 June 1941, pp. 1–2.

157 *CNL* 10S, 3 January 1940, William Paton, 'The World-Wide Christian Society', pp. 3–4.

158 *CNL* 116S, 14 January 1942, Revd Geoffrey Curtis, 'The Week of Prayer for Christian Unity', p. 1.

159 *CNL* 222L, 29 November 1944, p. 2.

160 Coupland, *Britannia, Europa and Christendom*, p. 21.

161 Oliver, *Church and Social Order*, pp. 118–39; *Moot Papers*, p. 659n.20. Wollenberg, *Christian Social Thought*, pp. 31–2.

162 Oldham, *Resurrection of Christendom*, pp. 33, 34, 40, 41, 45, 46, 52, 55, 63.

163 Vidler, *God's Judgment on Europe*, pp. 17–18.

164 Vidler, *Secular Despair*, p. 12.

165 E.g. LPL W. Temple 7, fos. 291–306, 'The British Churches and European Christian Institutions', n.d. [probably spring 1944], p. 2. See also Coupland, 'Britain, Europe and Christendom', pp. 380–7.

166 *Churches Survey Their Task*, p. 191. *CNL* 248L, 28 November 1945, pp. 1, 7.

167 *CNL* 129L, 15 April 1942, p. 2.

168 IOE MOO/35, 'Notes on Mannheim's Paper by T. S. Eliot', 10 January 1941, p. 1. See also Paul Robichaud, 'Eliot's Christian Sociology and the Problem of Nationalism', in Benjamin G. Lockerd, ed., *T. S. Eliot and Christian Tradition* (Madison, NJ: Fairleigh Dickinson University Press, 2014), pp. 207–15.

169 *CNL* 186L, 14 July 1943, p. 1.

170 *CNL* 250S, 26 December 1945, Daniel Jenkins, 'Christmas Has Happened', pp. 10–11; *CNL* 253L, 6 February 1946, p. 4; *CNL* 252L, 23 January 1946, p. 2.

171 On the 'Federal Union boom', see Coupland, *Britannia, Europa and Christendom*, pp. 22–7. See also Ceadel, *Semi-Detached Idealists*, pp. 385–9, 400–3, 410, 415–18.

172 William Paton, William Temple and George Bell tended to support it; the Bishop of Gloucester (Arthur Headlam), chair of the Church of England's Council on Foreign Relations, opposed it; and the Anglican Wartime Committee criticised FU's failure to address economic issues. See Coupland,

Britannia, Europa and Christendom, pp. 23–6, 36, 38; Zeilstra, *European Unity in Ecumenical Thinking*, pp. 157–8, 172, 174; and *Guardian*, 27 October 1939, p. 654.

173 *CNL* 29S, 15 May 1940, Adolf Löwe, 'Social Transformation and the War', p. 5; *CNL* 33S, 12 June 1940, G. Fedetov, 'A Russian Voice', p. 2; *CNL* 41S, 7 August 1940, William Temple, 'Begin Now', p. 1.

174 *Moot Papers*, M5, p. 227.

175 OA 14/1/43, [H. A. Hodges], 'Politics and the Moot', 9 June 1943, p. 10.

176 *CNL* 6L, 6 December 1939, p. 3. *CNL* 5S, 29 November 1939, J. H. Oldham, 'Preliminaries to the Consideration of Peace Aims', p. 3.

177 J. Middleton Murry, 'Pre-Conditions of Federal Union', in M. Chaning-Pearce, ed., *Federal Union: A Symposium* (London: Jonathan Cape, 1940), pp. 155–63.

178 *Moot Papers*, M8, pp. 295–6; Oldham, *Root of Our Troubles*, p. 15.

179 *CNL* 35S, 26 June 1940, Philip Mairet, 'Man, Nature and War', p. 3.

180 *CNL* 63L, 8 January 1941, p. 2. See also *Guardian*, 10 January 1941, p. 19; and *CNL* 138L, 17 June 1942, p. 1. Ceadel, *Semi-Detached Idealists*, pp. 410, 415–18.

181 IOE   MOO/62, 'Copy of Letter from Adolf Löwe to Dr Oldham', n.d. [1941], p. 2.

182 OA 14/5/13, J. M. Murry, 'The Agricultural Community and the Future of Society', 17 June 1943, p. 2.

183 *CNL* 75L, 2 April 1941, p. 2; *CNL* 115L, 7 January 1942, p. 1; *CNL* 116L, 14 January 1942, p. 2; *CNL* 142L, 15 July 1942, p. 1.

184 *Moot Papers*, M9, p. 317; M10, p. 355; M20, p. 709.

185 In summer 1940 Murry's 'Adelphi Centre' and farmhouse were searched. Suspicious documents (including a draft article by Niebuhr) were confiscated. *Moot Papers*, M9, p. 318; Lea, *John Middleton Murry*, p. 280.

186 BC, BAI 1/7/2 (3 of 3), Michael Polanyi, 'Science and the Modern Crisis', 14 November 1944, p. 5.

187 *CNL* 124L, 11 March 1942, p. 2. Later, however, the *CNL* referred to the 'backward African races, which have been swept into the fierce currents of modern civilisation': *CNL* 297L, 29 October 1947, p. 3.

188 See *CNL* 186S, 14 July 1943, Henry P. Van Dusen, 'British and American Approaches to the Peace', p. 2.

189 *Moot Papers*, M18, p. 628.

190 OA 9/6/97, Oldham to Visser 't Hooft, 13 November 1944.

191 OA 9/5/36, Mannheim to Oldham, 25 October 1943, p. 3; OA 9/6/101, 'Letter from Karl Mannheim', 20 November 1944, p. 7.

192 OA 9/7/33, 'Copy of Letter from H. A. Hodges', 4 December 1946, p. 3.

193 *CNL* 115L, 7 January 1942, pp. 1–4. *CNL* 116L, 14 January 1942, p. 1.

194 *CNL* 240S, 8 August 1945, Barbara Ward, 'The Fate of Europe', p. 7.

195 *CNL* 300L, 10 December 1947, pp. 7–9.

196 See *CNL* 263L, 26 June 1946; *CNL* 281L, 19 March 1947, pp. 4–5; *CNL* 318L, 18 August 1948, p. 9.

197 *CNL* 311L, 12 May 1948, pp. 2–3.

198 CERC CCFCL 2/1/1, memo, 'The Churches and the International Crisis', n.d. [discussed September 1939].

199 *CNL* 235L, 30 May 1945, p. 4.

200 *CNL* 241L, 22 August 1945, p. 4.

201 *CNL* 242L, 5 September 1945, pp. 1, 3.

202 *The Times*, 8 January 1946, p. 7.

203 *CNL* 244L, 3 October 1945, p. 2.

204 *CNL* 269S, 18 September 1946, J. H. Oldham, 'The Control of Atomic Energy', pp. 9–12.

205 *Ibid.*, p. 9.

206 OA 9/7/28, Oldham to Visser 't Hooft, 28 October 1946, p. 1.

207 OA 9/7/30, Visser 't Hooft to Oldham, 8 November 1946, pp. 1–2.

208 *CNL* 274L, 27 November 1946, p. 1.

209 *CNL* 329L, 19 January 1949, p. 18.

210 V. A. Demant, 'Europe: Its Predicament and Its Future', *Christendom*, 13:49 (March 1943), 9–16 (p. 11).

211 Joseph R. McCleary, *The Historical Imagination of G. K. Chesterton: Locality, Patriotism, and Nationalism* (Abingdon: Routledge, 2009).

212 See, e.g., *Guardian*, 1 May 1936, p. 310; 4 May 1945, p. 176. *Christian World*, 22 June 1944, p. 5. *Church Times*, 19 May 1939, p. 539. *Church of England Newspaper*, 15 October 1943, p. 4; 16 February 1945, p. 12; and 8 February 1946, p. 12.

213 Thompson, *God and Globe*, pp. 2, 14–15.

214 Richard Weight, *Patriots: National Identity in Britain, 1940–2000* (London: Macmillan, 2002), p. 28.

215 Morgan and Evans, *Battle for Britain*, p. 21. Kevin Myers, 'National Identity, Citizenship and Education for Displacement: Spanish Refugee Children in Cambridge, 1937', *History of Education*, 28:3 (1999), 313–25 (pp. 313–14).

216 *Moot Papers*, M10, p. 354.

217 *British Weekly*, 7 September 1939, p. 377; *Christian World*, 21 September 1939, p. 2.

218 *Christian World*, 21 September 1939, p. 6.

219 C. S. Lewis, 'Dangers of National Repentance', *Guardian*, 15 March 1940, p. 127. A leading article called 'much of this talk of a "common guilt" ... sheer morbid nonsense': *Christian World*, 8 May 1941, p. 4.

220 David Edgerton, *Warfare State: Britain, 1920–1970* (Cambridge: Cambridge University Press, 2006), pp. 48–58.

221 Robbins, 'Christian Civilisation'; Hoover, *God, Britain and Hitler*, pp. 97–120; Lawson, *Church of England*, pp. 11–15.

222 Lawson, *Church of England and the Holocaust*, p. 11. See also Coupland, *Britannia, Europa and Christendom*, pp. 16–17.

223 *Church of England Newspaper*, 14 June 1940, p. 1; 12 May 1944, p. 12.

224 LPL W. Temple 11, fo. 208, Oldham to Temple, 14 November 1942. See also W. Temple 11, fo. 194 Oldham to Temple, 11 October 1942; and W. Temple 11, fo. 195, draft letter from *CNL* no. 156, 21 October 1942. *Moot Papers*, M17, p. 601.

225 Parker, 'Reinvigorating Christian Britain', pp. 65–73, quote at p. 67.

226 'Religious Instruction in the Schools', *Nature*, 150:3811 (14 November 1942), 559–60.

227 *CNL* 144S, 29 July 1942, Barbara Ward, 'Christian Co-operation and Europe'; *CNL* 181S, 5 May 1943, J. H. Oldham, 'The Church in Europe'; *CNL* 225S, 10 January 1945, George Bell, 'The Churches and European Reconstruction'; *CNL* 243L, 19 September 1945, pp. 2–5; *CNL* 243S, 19 September 1945, Henry Carter, 'The Human Situation in Europe'; *CNL* 246L, 31 October 1945, pp. 1–4.

228 *CNL* 250L, 26 December 1945, p. 6.

229 Rose, *Which People's War?*, pp. 18–19, 24.

230 Stephen Backhouse, 'Nationalism and Patriotism', in Nicholas Adams, George Pattison and Graham Ward (eds.), *Oxford Handbook of Theology and Modern European Thought* (Oxford: Oxford University Press, 2013), pp. 41–60 (p. 44).

231 Keith Clements, *A Patriotism for Today: Dialogue with Dietrich Bonhoeffer* (Bristol: Bristol Baptist College, 1984), p. 87. Stephen Backhouse, 'Patriotism, Nationhood and Neighbourhood', *Modern Believing* 53:4 (2012), 398–407 (p. 400).

232 Gerald L. Sittser, *A Cautious Patriotism: The American Churches and the Second World War* (Chapel Hill: University of North Carolina Press, 1997).

233 *Catholic Herald*, 5 July 1940, 4.

234 *CNL* 118L, 28 January 1942, 1.

235 *CNL* 202L, 23 February 1944, 1.

236 *CNL* 234L, 16 May 1945, 1. These were 'the humanist tradition', 'the scientific tradition', 'the tradition of the rule of law' and 'the Christian religion'; *ibid.*, 1

237 Zeilstra, *European Unity in Ecumenical Thinking*, 205; Thompson, *God and Globe*, 2.

238 *CNL* 250S, 26 December 1945, Daniel Jenkins, 'Christmas Has Happened', p. 9.

239 T. S. Eliot, 'The Social Function of Poetry', *Adelphi*, 21:4 (1945), 152–61 (p. 160).

240 Leustean, 'Ecumenical Movement', pp. 458–9, 460–1, 468–9.

241 Robbins, 'Avoiding the Challenge?', p. 20.

242 Zeilstra, *European Unity in Ecumenical Thinking*, 206. Lucian Leustean, *The Ecumenical Movement and the Making of the European Community* (Oxford: Oxford University Press, 2014), pp. 177–8.

243 *Church of England Newspaper*, 25 June 1948, p. 4.

244 Coupland, *Britannia, Europa and Christendom*, 86, and 46–7, 60–1, 80–2.

6

'A new order of liberty': freedom, democracy and liberalism

Previous chapters have touched on the issue of freedom in the contexts of the Oldham group's views on 'planning' and the links its members saw among Christianity, Englishness and liberty. This chapter looks more directly at how the group understood 'freedom', an issue to which it returned, whether privately or publicly, perhaps more than any other. I will first examine group members' views of 'freedom', particularly in relation to faith. I then turn to their considerations of how such conceptions of freedom might be translated into social and political practice, an issue that raised ambivalences, prerequisites and limits with regard to individualism, democracy and tolerance. A third section then turns to whether the Oldham group's ideas themselves can be seen as 'totalitarian'. I will conclude that claims the group sympathised with (and even propagated) 'totalitarian' ideology fail to appreciate how the defence of personal freedom and an ideal of pluralism were at the heart of its efforts. Nevertheless, despite its commitment to freedom, the group was indeed ambivalent about the prospects for democracy in a mass society.

Defining freedom: 'true' and 'false'

Defences of 'freedom' and 'liberty' recurred in CCFCL and CFC memoranda, Moot discussions and *CNL* articles. At a 1937 meeting, the churches were urged to work against social and political tendencies 'to standardise and stereotype' thought and 'to suppress individuality'.[1] The need to preserve freedom was stressed in every meeting of the Moot. Vidler asserted that personal liberty for even 'irregular' or 'nonconformist' behaviour had to be protected.[2] Shaw saw the Moot as seeking 'a new order of liberty'.[3] In 1941, Oldham argued that the future depended entirely on 'the preservation of freedom'.[4] On the radio, Murry counselled Christians to work for a 'free society', and he later urged them to create anti-totalitarian institutions, condemning the Soviet rejection of objective morality.[5] The *CNL* regularly defended freedom. Oldham suggested Finnish resistance to Soviet invasion in early 1940 might help re-establish 'Christian liberty' in Russia itself.[6] He claimed Christians sought 'a community of free men bound to one another in mutual loyalty and trust', decrying Nazism's abolition of independent centres of 'political cohesion'.[7] He saw 'vital Christian interests' in preserving freedom.[8] The need, another *CNL* essay put it, was 'free men for a free society'.[9] In the *CNL* in 1943, Temple declared freedom to be 'fundamental to Christian civilisation'.[10]

The group defined what it saw as true freedom in the light of a divinely created human nature; it also attacked 'debased' or 'spurious' definitions of democracy and freedom (such as the 'freedom to maintain privilege').[11] Genuine liberty was *Christian* liberty, based on the middle axioms of responsible freedom and the acceptance of dependence in human life. Oldham expressed a key group consensus by defining 'freedom' as the ability to influence one's social environment, something that had been lost in large-scale industry and mass society. Communities were disappearing in which 'men in association with their neighbours take decisions directly affecting their own lives, are bound to one another in a system of acknowledged obligations and responsibilities and are consciously dependent on one another for mutual help'.[12] Responsibility had also declined. Moberly thought it had become so diffused as to be 'nonexistent': life seemed utterly determined by financial, industrial and political systems.[13] Both the State and capitalism, Oldham argued, could prevent people from becoming 'responsible agents' in the service of others.[14] This had serious consequences. 'Let freedom and responsibility go', he insisted, 'and Christianity as a life in this world goes with them'.[15] Hodges, too, thought modern people were often compelled to act unfreely.[16] Freedom's *loss* had in part resulted from efforts to *create* it. Science's emancipatory aims had called forth 'vast, mechanical, impersonal forces' that, Oldham claimed, deprived many 'of real existence as persons'. The results were disillusion, weakened social conventions, declining standards of work, and indifference to destruction and waste as long as others paid for it: 'On the shifting sand of irresponsible individuals', he concluded, 'it is impossible to found a democratic society'.[17] Irresponsibility was common in 'wide circles' of society.[18]

Such concerns were shared by all of the key members of the group. Modern threats to responsible freedom – and ways of defending it – ran throughout Mannheim's writings. Similar themes shaped Baillie's report for the Church of Scotland's commission on the war's religious meaning.[19] Vidler referenced related notions in *Theology*.[20] Murry's communitarian views were based on maintaining liberty, from complaints in *The Price of Leadership* (1939) about freedom's loss in the 'vast aquarium of technical civilization', via the argument in *Adam and Eve* (1944) that true freedom meant a personal responsibility to be 'experienced throughout a man's working life', to his complaint in *The Free Society* (1948) about the loss of scope for individual decision-making.[21] Despite many political shifts, Murry advocated what he once called 'the maximum of responsible freedom' (even if, as noted in Chapter 4, he at times sorely misjudged the nature and threat of Nazism).[22] The *CNL* stressed the link between freedom and responsibility into the post-war period, and a 1947 CFC pamphlet saw life's very aim as 'the growth of persons in freedom and responsibility'.[23] Oldham developed the idea of 'the responsible society' as a better route to social justice than (socialist) statism: he preferred '*responsible* society' to '*free* society' in order to distinguish it from '*laissez-faire* liberalism'.[24] The idea of the 'responsible society' shaped ecumenical social thought from the late 1940s to the mid 1960s, when some saw it as too supportive of the status quo.[25]

In the eyes of group members, Christian freedom was also defined by service and an awareness of dependence on others and on God. Christians, Oldham argued, believed 'men should be liberated from themselves for the single-minded service of God and their fellow-men'.[26] But modernity had altered the 'texture of human life' so as to deny this dependence.[27] The modern claim of absolute human independence was 'man's fundamental sin', causing 'unhappiness, strife and suffering' and leading society to be 'shaken to its foundations'.[28] The admission of dependence was seen as distinctively Christian, opposed to all other main schools of modern thought. But Oldham believed thinkers from diverse traditions were starting to realise that a person 'existed only in relations, dependent at every point of his existence on nature, his fellow-men and God'.[29] The *CNL* published an essay by Emil Brunner condemning freedom's misinterpretation as 'unconditional absolute independence' and arguing that Christian views of 'responsible love' were opposed to *either* individualism or collectivism.[30]

Although the group was critical of what it often referred to as 'liberal' individualism, it also defended traditional 'liberal' freedoms of conscience, expression and assembly. A memo laying out the *CNL's* aims stressed such liberties.[31] In the Moot, Hodges argued that people needed certain rights, liberties and responsibilities to achieve genuine personhood.[32] Hetherington admitted that – despite its shortcomings – liberalism had been 'the most fruitful social discovery of the last 500 years'. It had established key values: protection against arbitrary State action; freedom of worship; the freedoms of assembly, speech and press; the free choice of schools and of employment.[33] Vidler insisted liberal freedoms were necessary, even if many had been twisted into 'an extravagant perversion'.[34] Moot visitor Geoffrey Vickers saw respect for diversity as 'the central liberal value which we want to carry over into the new age'.[35] Mannheim critiqued leftists who dismissed liberalism: inequality certainly made its freedoms 'incomplete', but they nonetheless remained fundamental.[36] Murry later described Mannheim's aim as uniting 'Christian elements in the Liberal Tradition' with 'liberal elements in the Christian Tradition' to influence those controlling increasingly powerful social techniques.[37] In 1940, Oldham cited Murry and Temple to argue that freedom of conscience – including the freedom 'to obey God' – was essential.[38] The 'Anglo-Saxon political tradition' was based on respecting individual and group rights.[39] The 'planners', he told the Moot, must not interfere with religion, and the freedom to obey God's will as a guide to social life had to be protected.[40] Finally, the need for a pluralist tolerance in order to harmonise competing aims and interests was stressed. Mannheim, too, emphasised that planners would have to leave an 'unplanned sector' and make 'a deliberate choice of diversity in society'.[41] True freedom would enable the 'free-lance citizen' to escape from 'the mould of society'.[42]

After the war, the freedoms of opinion, speech, worship and assembly were contrasted to Soviet tyranny. The gratitude due to the Russian people should not, Oldham argued, limit the insistence on human rights and freedom, such as access to information and the right to criticise the powerful.[43] He insisted that Britain and its 'daughter commonwealths' had ideas and practices vital to democracy and that rights and freedoms were 'essential Christian values'.[44] In 1946, he wrote that Christians must protect democratic institutions that had subjected political power to principles of justice.[45] Democracy and the freedoms of expression and association were at the heart of Murry's vision of 'the free society'.[46]

However, liberal freedoms alone were neither a bulwark against totalitarianism nor a route to a Christian society. Political freedoms were seen as insufficient without social justice and a consensus on the purpose of freedom. Civil liberties were, Oldham stressed, only 'half the picture', and weakened by poverty and inequality.[47] Baillie agreed with Maritain's description of liberal humanism as 'barren wheat and starchless bread': it gave freedom without saying what it was for.[48] Group members praised Arthur Koestler's *The Yogi and the Commissar* (1945) for warning that western civilisation had forgotten the values it should defend.[49] After the war, the CNL positioned itself as an open-minded voice in the East–West divide. Its commitment to social justice convinced most of the group to support the welfare state and to find some virtues in Communism, but it also stressed freedom over equality, particularly when some Christians argued for Communism's emancipatory potential. A supplement by Josef Hromàdka – a Czech Lutheran pastor who had greeted Communism as a progressive advance – was published, but Bliss distanced the CNL from his analysis in the introductory letter.[50] After the 1948 Amsterdam WCC conference, where Hromàdka had spoken, she noted readers had both praised and criticised his views.[51] A call by Oldham for personal liberty in Russia brought a published response arguing that social justice should take priority over freedom.[52]

The group saw freedom threatened during the war not only by the enemy but also by the British State.[53] Some restrictions were needed, Oldham agreed: Britons had had, he wrote (referring here to the deputy prime minister), 'to surrender our liberties to Mr. Attlee in order to avoid having to surrender them to Hitler, knowing that we can get them back from Mr. Attlee, though not from Hitler'.[54] Even so, those freedoms were unlikely to return in the same form, and the *CNL* critiqued limits on civil liberties.[55] Even amid fears of invasion, it called free speech 'a patriotic duty', urging readers to fight a 'black-out of mind'.[56] Oldham thought the public's 'robust common sense' and the free press would limit efforts to make 'everybody a watchman of everybody else'.[57] But he decried the penalising of unpopular opinions, such as denying employment to conscientious objectors. 'War hysteria is a monster to be controlled', he wrote, 'not humoured like a dictator'.[58] By the end of the war, the overall view was one of relief: in the summer of 1945, Bliss praised the outgoing Parliament for having 'mobilized the nation for war without enslaving it'.[59]

Christianity seemed the long-term answer to secular liberalism's weakness. Faith clearly needed freedom, but freedom, it was argued, also needed faith. Fenn insisted that 'the very basis of democracy is destroyed once faith in God decays'.[60] Murry claimed democracy could not exist without Christianity.[61] The relationship to God, Oldham wrote, gave an inviolable status, 'a citadel of personal life' that 'society may not invade'; only rights anchored in religion could resist 'the encroachments of the community and the State'.[62] In the *CNL*, Owen Barfield agreed, arguing people could be free because 'God speaks to and through the individual, *and for no other reason*'.[63] Without God's 'unconditional demand', Oldham insisted, the political order would be shaped only by competition and 'the reign of force'.[64] All liberties, he argued, were 'grounded in the liberty to worship and obey God'; Dawson, similarly, thought 'spiritual liberty' was essential to its political form.[65]

This relationship had, however, eroded. Europe's crisis, Murry claimed, came from 'a mutual outbidding of apostate Christian societies' that were all in the process of abandoning Christian principles; the only truly free society, he argued, would be 'a specifically Christian society'.[66] Oldham often insisted on reviving the Christian view of human dignity. Responsibility to God remained 'the basis and buttress of all liberty'.[67] At the start of 1941, Oldham saw democracy based on eternal principles that were at the heart of all great revealed religions.[68] Six months later, he agreed with philosopher John Macmurray that only religion offered a standpoint from which to defend freedom.[69] In March 1943, he saw no proof that 'the spirit of toleration' that democracy needed could 'grow from any but a religious root'.[70] In late 1944, he claimed that British and American liberties sprang from 'religious roots', something 'more ultimate' than politics alone.[71]

'Atomistic' individualism was contrasted with a communitarian personalism. In the Moot, Hodges called for a social critique based on the Christian understanding of 'personality'.[72] Citing Brunner's *Man in Revolt* (1937), Oldham decried a modern preference for 'unrestrained individualism' over community responsibility.[73] Employing his trademark motto – 'real life is meeting' – in the *CNL*, he insisted that the 'isolated individual' did not exist: 'we are persons only in our relation with other persons'.[74] The modern ideal was the individual as a kind of 'Robinson Crusoe': this, Oldham stated, was 'a pure myth'.[75] In 1940, he claimed true freedom was not the 'freedom to do exactly what we choose' or 'to pursue our own ends and selfish interests regardless of others'. Such goals had a place in resisting 'tyranny, injustice and privilege', but, on their own, they would produce only 'a welter of competing selfishnesses'.[76] Modern individualism made people think they were free but in fact it made it easier for them to be, as Mannheim put it, 'herded into masses'.[77] Oldham thought Britain was degenerating into a mass civilisation as dangerous to freedom 'as any form of dictatorship'. 'Modern dangers' meant cultural development could no longer be left to chance: a 'middle course' was needed between 'rigid central control' and 'liberal individualism'.[78]

The distinction between the 'individual' (isolated and unrestrained) and the 'person' (embedded in 'organic' relationships and conscious of responsibilities to others) was crucial. 'As a Christian', Murry commented in a radio broadcast, 'I believe in the value of the individual person, provided he is a person'.[79] Citing Maritain, Oldham argued in 1941 that a democracy could not be based on individuals but must draw strength from 'persons living in community'.[80] Temple's December 1943 *CNL* supplement likewise called for moving from a 'democracy of the individual' to a 'democracy of the person', stressing the role of 'lesser groupings': 'the family, the school, the guild, the trade union, the village, the city, the county'.[81] The 'humanist' stress on individuals, Oldham argued, had to be replaced by a religious view of persons 'existing only in relation to other persons', a relation that was 'bounded and limited by God and neighbour'.[82] Reviewing Erich Fromm's *The Fear of Freedom* (1941), Vidler agreed with its thesis, as he put it, that freedom was an 'ambiguous gift': the post-Renaissance period had seen the birth of the 'individual', freed from traditional authorities, but that figure had become 'isolated, lonely, insecure, rootless; when he becomes aware of this he is frightened, and is ready for submission to new kinds of bondage'.[83] The view that atomised individualism led to new forms of mass conformity was well established in the Oldham group, and modern egoism had been condemned at Oxford 1937; however, works such as Fromm's helped to reinforce them. A *CNL* reader's letter decried individualism's degeneration into 'libertinism' and stressed the need for democracy to maintain a 'delicate balance of privileges and obligations'.[84] Liberalism's failure to base individual rights in a realistic view of human nature had, Oldham argued, left it vulnerable.[85] Even the family existed in broader relations: it might be 'very nice to draw the curtains and shut the door', wrote Moira Symons in the *CNL* early in 1948; however, family 'is never an end in itself' but part of the 'organic whole' of the life of society.[86]

Enabling freedom: ambivalences, prerequisites and limits

Oldham group members defined a 'true' liberty in accordance with Christian principles of responsible freedom, dependence and service. Liberal rights were valued but seen as insufficient: rights, they argued, had to be anchored in faith. 'Atomistic' individualism was condemned in favour of an 'organic' personalism. Understanding how the group planned to implement these principles means also accounting for ambivalences, prerequisites and limits in its thinking about freedom. These included an insistence on common values and revived community, which raised in turn the thorny question of how to deal with dissent.

In 1940, Oldham saw 'free men, free nations, a community of nations freely cooperating' as necessary elements of a new order. He insisted, however, that one must know the 'purposes' for which this freedom should be used.[87] Here, liberalism had failed. Baillie expressed a core view of the group when he wrote that 'modern man' had won 'the long battle for freedom' but could not answer the question 'free for what?'.

> Almost overnight, his freedom came to seem to him a hollow and empty thing, and also a bewildering and perplexing thing. Hardly had he fought his way out into the open before he began to look for guidance, for a strong hand to lead him, for an authoritative voice to tell him whither he ought to go and what he ought to do – and even what he ought to think. He was thus a ready victim to the first bogus guides that came his way, so long as only they spoke in accents of sufficient authority and self-assurance.[88]

The 'bogus guides' included totalitarian movements and, more broadly, secularism.

One prerequisite for a genuine 'democracy of the person' was thus an agreement on norms and aims: democracy, Oldham wrote, needed a 'common basis of interests, habits and aspirations' or a 'common social purpose' based on 'natural virtues'.[89] Binding 'common convictions' could not be 'changed from election to election' but would have to be 'settled once for all, either by consent or by civil war'; Oldham – building on Löwe's idea of British 'spontaneous conformity' – stressed the need for 'spontaneous consent'. 'Spontaneous', indeed, became a key term for the group, but it was argued that true spontaneity required specific forms of unity in which to freely develop.[90] Oldham praised Löwe's view that order 'presupposes a community of purpose' and 'conformity in habits'.[91] Responsibility was related to such common values. A *CNL* essay on 'educating for a free society' was typical, stressing that unity could only arise among people who felt responsible for each other, enabling them to 'co-operate spontaneously'. A free society was 'a fellowship in which each can find the opportunities for living his own life', but ensuring that freedom did not lead to people 'enslaving or stultifying each other or themselves' required a consensus on 'what matters most': 'Freedom is specific, and it is not possible without a *specific* common faith in *specific* human values.'[92]

With 'organic' community's erosion, what remained in society were, on the one hand, isolated individuals and, on the other, enormous enterprises and powerful states. True freedom, however, required a healthy community existing *between* these extremes. A truly Christian society would thus distribute responsibility, avoid centralised power and give intermediate groups autonomy.[93] In the *CNL*, Temple stressed that personhood developed in small groups whose participants felt they could influence their 'quality and activity'.[94] The 'voluntary principle' must be recovered, the 'spontaneous initiation and conduct of activities by individuals and groups independently of the State and free from State control'.[95]

Local self-organisation was thus crucial. Oldham saw 'spontaneous, creative initiative' as vital to creating a 'New Christendom'.[96] The *CNL* praised examples of war-time local initiative. But it also aired concerns that this capability was declining. In early 1940, Oldham quoted a reader's claim that the 'civic revival' at the start of the war had dissipated into 'apathy and cynicism': the English, the correspondent claimed, 'have little idea of governing themselves beyond grousing at things they dislike'.[97] Still, Oldham argued that national traditions retained 'the art of self-government', and 'British liberty' was grounded in independence from the centralised State.[98] Clarke emphasised the need for 'organic groupings'.[99] One *CNL* essayist argued that 'spontaneous sociability' had to be especially encouraged in the suburbs, 'that last stronghold of isolationism'.[100]

The emphasis on 'spontaneous', 'organic' community involved the group in wider debates. In early February 1940, for example, the Moot discussed a promotional campaign by H. G. Wells for his book *The Rights of Man*, which called for a 'World Government'. Oldham asked V. A. Demant to respond, leading to a paper read at the Moot. Demant critiqued Wells's conception of rights as detached from 'organic' social relations: leaving citizens only a direct relation to the (global) sovereign, he asserted, would weaken 'all intermediate loyalties'. Demant saw rights threatened by the loss of 'organic' relations, the decline of faith and the failure of education to 'direct the emotions'. The Moot broadly agreed.[101] But some saw his paper as unrealistic. Moberly appreciated its stress on 'the organic' but insisted that industry and the powerful State could not be reversed; Murry found Demant's language 'baffling', especially his equating of 'organic' with medievalism and 'inorganic' with modern democracy.[102] He disliked Wells's secularism but thought he at least understood society.

More to the group's taste was a July 1941 *CNL* supplement by G. D. H. Cole – an atheist and non-Marxist libertarian socialist – titled 'Democracy Face to Face with Hugeness'. Cole argued that mass society overwhelmed people's capacities for social relationships, leaving them susceptible to irrationality.[103] Parliamentary democracy had been endowed with a fatal flaw from the beginning: 'Jacobins and Benthamites alike', Cole suggested, had defined it 'atomistically', with millions of votes 'mystically' forming a General Will.[104] People had thus been 'torn' from the small groups in which 'true' democracy flourished: trade unions, cooperatives, friendly societies and local government. There was a need for 'democratic ways of living for little men in big societies', i.e. 'a host of little democracies' where 'the spirit of neighbourhood and personal acquaintance' could live. This would enable 'real democracy' instead of its 'atomistic perversion'.[105] Oldham later used similar terms to assert that the individual – 'torn from his roots in an organic social life' – had become 'an isolated atom in a largely formless mass, swayed by mass emotions', and he linked Mannheim's and Cole's views on social 'hugeness' and mass psychology.[106] Such concerns about irrational 'masses' were commonplace, and Cole's essay later became a touchstone in the *CNL*.[107]

Murry, similarly, sought a new model of community life based on living out the 'Christian idea of mutual responsibility' in small, personal groups.[108] He knew this solution was not open to all. Thus, in a 1940 broadcast he suggested that totalitarianism had a 'positive side' and might be the 'only refuge' for 'the ordinary democratic man'.[109] But, as noted in Chapter 4, Murry grew sceptical of State planning and later repudiated his earlier, rosier view of the potentials of totalitarianism. His book *Adam and Eve* (1944), which Oldham reviewed critically but sympathetically, argued that community could only be 'real' in small groups of personal acquaintances who recognised their 'mutual dependence'. His chief example was 'the farming community'.[110] But people had to be *prepared* to live this kind of life, which he explained in a two-part article, 'Educating for Chaos', in early

1941. Murry was pessimistic about the post-war world, foreseeing an era of 'barbarisation', 'economic, social and moral anarchy' and 'much sporadic violence and lawlessness'. In this dystopian context, children had to be taught to act 'creatively' and self-sufficiently.[111] Sex roles were complementary: a boy should be a 'good all-rounder, in the provision of the primary necessities of life'; girls would need 'all those primary skills which will make them the fitting helpmates and co-partners of pioneers'.[112] Alongside technical proficiency, 'educating for insecurity' would inculcate moral purpose. 'From being a cog in a vast machine that is running down', Murry wrote, the technically skilled individual 'can transform himself into the fly-wheel of a smaller machine whose operations are governed by a hierarchy of real human values'.[113] Oldham approved of this vision as a means to resist 'the new absolutism'.[114] It embodied the group's aim of encouraging an outlook that was both self-reliant and other-centred. The *CNL* similarly supported youth training initiatives, such as the 'County Badge' scheme or the 'Grail movement' for Catholic girls and young women.[115]

Still, despite critiques of mass culture's disintegrative tendencies, the *CNL* offered occasional respites from cultural pessimism. A reader letter in 1941 insisted that 'mass' life still contained many 'dynamic self-determining, vigorously independent atoms' and viable, small-scale communities.[116] Possibilities for social renewal *within* the mass was a common theme in the group. Notably, the problem of 'mass man' was not confined to workers. 'Mass psychology', Oldham argued, 'pervades all classes'. Indeed, if anything, the urban or suburban middle classes posed the greatest difficulties: the working-classes possessed vibrant local institutions, whether trade unions or the cooperative movement.[117] Bliss, too, critiqued a Christian tendency to see 'industrial populations' as undifferentiated 'masses'. She cited a French study that had found 'within the masses, small communities – the working group of men in a factory, the young people who go hiking together or frequent a particular club or dance hall'.[118]

However, there was an obvious tension between the Oldham group's advocacy of liberty, autonomy and tolerance and its demand for a cultural consensus. What about those who rejected that consensus? This raised the problems, as it was sometimes put, of 'heresy' and the 'dissenter'.[119] Some made clear that tolerance had its limits. In 1939, Eliot insisted a Christian society 'can only be realised when the great majority of sheep belong to one fold'.[120] A similar principle had motivated his notorious insistence in *After Strange Gods* (1934) that, in a necessarily 'homogeneous' population, 'any large number of free-thinking Jews' would be 'undesirable' and 'a spirit of excessive tolerance is to be deprecated'.[121] But Mannheim, too, stressed that planning required a strong consensus and a degree of homogeneity. Toleration was desirable, but *laissez-faire* liberalism, in his view, 'mistook neutrality for tolerance'.[122] That democracy need not 'tolerate the intolerant' was a position (and language) shared by Mannheim, Maritain and Murry.[123] The main aim was clearly *voluntary* agreement, which Mannheim argued would require 'a revival of religion'; otherwise – as in Germany – an unmoored culture would lead to 'submission and dictatorship'.[124] In August 1942, Hetherington thought effective planning implied 'social control': plans that were questioned 'in principle' could not be implemented, and some freedoms of property and contract law would have to be limited.[125] A 'political and social faith', a Moot paper argued, would not only value freedom but also accept the 'subordination of individual and sectional interests to the common good' and the suppression of 'anti-social liberties'.[126] Oldham wrote that the liberal equation of toleration with neutrality had only worked so long as a latent agreement on 'unquestioned values, standards and ways of behaviour' had prevailed; with that agreement eroded and democracy under attack, he wrote, one could not argue that all viewpoints had 'equal rights'.[127]

It was expected that a Christian society could rely on persuasion rather than force in inculcating a new consensus.[128] Löwe thought it would use 'human and psychological treatment' to convince the 'dissenter' to realise that 'the principles of Christian order were the only possible ones for society'; still, the 'heretic' would have to be 'dealt with'.[129] Oldham agreed but insisted a Christian society must allow 'the maximum field for thought and freedom'.[130] Mannheim believed that 'drastic repressive measures' would be used only in 'marginal' cases. Britain's tradition offered the option of a 'popular self-discipline'. Various methods were appropriate to different 'spheres', from an 'authoritative imposition of values' to 'freedom of choice'.[131] (Murry, for example, stressed the need for post-war, working-class *self*-discipline to avoid workers abusing their new position of strength.[132]) Encouragement and education would peacefully produce a new consensus. The few remaining dissenters would, it was implied, be treated humanely. Moberly insisted there should be no 'suppression of dissent'.[133] Echoing Mannheim, he argued that only 'neutrality' rather than toleration was to be abandoned. The issue came down to a new emphasis:

> We don't want forcibly to suppress the Fascist or Bertrand Russell, but to make it clear that they are 'dissenters', and that our society as a whole is standing for something other than their ideals. If they want to withdraw their children from ethical teaching to which they are conscientiously opposed, it is for them to contract *out* and not for the democrat to contract *in*.[134]

Reacting to Clement Attlee's 1948 decision to remove Communist Party members from the civil service, Bliss stressed the issue's complexities. It would be 'the height of folly', she wrote, for democracies to 'tolerate the intolerant'; but while Communists may be 'enemies of a free society', one should prefer persuasion to a 'purge'.[135] The issue remained complex.

A 'Christian totalitarianism'?

The foregoing exploration of the Oldham group's understanding of freedom enables a clearer consideration of its susceptibility to what might be called 'Christian totalitarianism'. The group clearly sought to learn from totalitarian movements and systems; at times, it suggested a religiously inspired totalitarian system might be a viable (if not the preferred) goal. Some Moot members themselves were discomforted by anti-democratic tendencies in some discussions. Other critiques have gone further. Graeme Smith has labelled Oldham's own aims 'totalitarian'.[136] He focuses on Oldham's work for Oxford 1937, such as the preparatory pamphlet *Church, Community and State*. In it Oldham stated that it was 'conceivable' that 'the aims of an authoritarian state might be inspired by, or in large measure consistent with, the Christian view of life'. This statement, Smith claims, shows that Oldham was 'sympathetic to totalitarianism, if in its Christian form'.[137] Context, however, is vital. As noted in Chapter 1, the conference had sought to accommodate many political views, partly to keep the German churches on board. Oldham used this pamphlet to map out the terrain of Christian *debate* rather than to state firm conclusions (let alone his own preferences). Even here, he linked freedom, democracy and Christianity. He defined the totalitarian State as one

> which lays claim to man in the totality of his being; which declares its own authority to be the source of all authority; which refuses to recognize the independence in their own sphere of religion, culture, education and the family; which seeks to impose on all its citizens a particular philosophy of life; and which sets out to create by means of all the agencies of public information and education a particular type of man in accordance with its own understanding of the meaning and end of man's existence.

It was, in short, a State that also declared itself to be 'a Church', whose claims were based on 'certain ultimate beliefs regarding the nature and destiny of man'.[138] As defined here, Oldham clearly argues *against* a totalitarian State.

Mark Thomas Edwards has offered a wider critique of 'authoritarian tendencies' among ecumenical Protestants during the war, focusing on the United States but citing Oldham and his circle as contributing to 'totalising discourses'.[139] However, Edwards equates totalitarianism as a *political* system with a purportedly 'totalising' *cultural* ideology – nostalgic and medievalist in nature – that was intended to rebuild a new 'Christendom'.[140] 'God's totalitarianism', for Edwards, consisted of 'efforts to revitalise an imagined Judeo-Christian consensus', a process in which he sees a 'subtle rejection of religious and cultural pluralism'.[141] As I have noted, the Oldham group had certainly criticised liberalism's moral 'neutrality', but its insistence on a value consensus was accompanied by emphases on freedom, tolerance and decentralised political power. However all-encompassing Christian principles might be, their *political* manifestations would – it was argued – stay within democratic bounds. Edwards, curiously, even sees Eliot as advocating 'a kind of Christian social engineering'.[142] Although Eliot (like Dawson) had sympathies with some authoritarian movements, contempt for 'progressive' egalitarianism and a willingness to associate with some people more clearly associated with Fascism, he (also like Dawson) emphasised local community, cultural diversity, a moderate nationalism and parliamentarianism.[143] Similarly, claims that Oldham was 'anti-modern' is excessive: he may have condemned aspects of modernity, but he – like most of his collaborators – also sought to define a faith appropriate to a socially, politically and economically 'modern' age.[144] Edwards and Smith raise important questions about Christian social thought, but they fail to acknowledge the insistent (if not always consistent) support for freedom, tolerance and diversity in transatlantic ecumenism, as well as the widespread view that Parliament and the rule of law would be essential in any desirable Christian order. Still, there were times in the group's private discussions where more authoritarian options were considered, and a closer look at its thinking about 'Christian totalitarianism' will round off this chapter's consideration of its committed (if still sometimes ambivalent) support for democracy.

The group's closest brush with support for authoritarianism came during a few exchanges during the first four Moot meetings, from April 1938 to April 1939, in which 'theocracy', 'Christian dictatorship', a 'Christian totalitarian State' and a 'totalitarian Christian Order' were all discussed. Here, totalitarian trends seen as inherent in the West more broadly – such as increasing State power and 'mass' culture – were frequently presented as *inevitable*.[145] The first Moot meeting saw intensive discussion along these lines.[146] Even in the democracies, a new 'integration of the community' was inescapable, Löwe argued, though whether it would be shaped by 'pagan' or Christian impulses was still undecided. Mass society's relentless advance meant a 'Christian totalitarian state' might emerge, but he saw a possibility that Britain could maintain its 'spontaneous conformity'. Where states made 'religious claims' as a sacralised focus of identity the resulting community, Dawson said, would be totalitarian. He compared totalitarian Christianity to the Kingdom of God: it was, he quipped, 'a very long range policy'. Baillie saw restoring clear *distinctions* among Church, community and State as one option, but another was a 'Christian dictatorship' or 'theocracy' to express a 'Christian spirit'. Moberly thought Christians could accept political dictatorship but not an 'all-embracing community', i.e. a competing political 'Church'. Murry and Eliot, however, criticised acceptance of totalitarian trends. Murry thought Christianity would lose its 'inward dynamic' in totalitarianism; Eliot agreed, adding that Christianity could not accept a totalitarian replacement. Murry thought Löwe and Dawson underestimated the 'terrific hiatus' between the Kingdom and existing society. Eliot went further: 'the best thing a Christian totalitarian state could do', he asserted, 'would be to abdicate': faith depended on 'local circles and small groups'. Oldham found the thought of a Christian totalitarianism appalling and distinguished it sharply from 'planning': 'The Church need not be dismayed if the State demanded conformity in certain regions', he claimed, 'but there were certain fields that could not admit conformity without suicide'.

Oldham asked Murry for an essay on this for the second meeting. In 'Towards a Christian Theory of Society', Murry insisted – agreeing with Mannheim and Löwe, and departing from his earlier views on the

Figure 7 John Middleton Murry, 1934, by Howard Coster

State – that a vast increase in State power was 'indispensable' to the modern 'machine-society'. Christians had to abandon their fears about this. He admitted he was proposing 'a kind of theocracy', but he insisted it would retain key freedoms.[147] Building on the nineteenth-century views of Samuel Taylor Coleridge and of Thomas and Matthew Arnold, Murry argued the State and the Church must 'draw together': the State would become 'an enlarged Church' and 'instrument for realising the Kingdom of God' by undertaking what had previously been Church tasks – 'education, care of the sick, provision for the poor' – and by 'materialising' Christian ideals of brotherhood through political equality.[148] This would be, Murry wrote (in language taken up by Eliot), the 'idea' of 'a Christian and national and democratic society' led by an elite 'clerisy'.[149] The goal was 'civilisation with freedom'.[150]

Reactions to Murry's ideas were mixed. Löwe agreed that a Christian society depended upon reconnecting Church and society and using Christian moral principles to counteract 'amoral forces of efficiency, expediency and self-interest'.[151] Mannheim thought that Murry rightly stressed that Christianity could not be purely personal and individualist if its social vision were to remain viable. The options might be seen as a 'Christian dictatorship' or a 'theocracy', but Mannheim preferred a democratic alternative that would enable a 'new kind of freedom', and he remained unsure where Murry's views on this score lay.[152] Hodges agreed with Murry that Christianity's influence would have to be expressed through people in their daily lives. But he thought it was 'utopian' to aim at converting the community to Christianity: Christians would never be numerous enough to dominate the State, and they would have to make their claims in a contested, and largely secular, public sphere.[153] Eliot thought Murry was correct that the State would necessarily play a much greater role, and he saw 'great value' in his concept of a 'national Christian society'; however, he also thought it necessary to maintain distinctions between a Christian State and Christian community and to insist on timeless elements in the faith appropriate to *any* society.[154] Some responses were more critical. Dawson opposed the idea of the State and the Church drawing together, preferring an 'autonomous spiritual society' separate from the State.[155] Farmer thought that Murry, and others, exaggerated the inevitability of the 'omni-competent State'; Newbigin agreed with Murry that the State would have to grow in power, but he denied it could be Christianised.[156] Vidler suggested that Murry underestimated the radical corruption of human society (which would hinder its Christianisation).[157] Baillie believed Murry came too close to arguing that Christianity implied a specific social and political order. Noting that Murry had previously rejected Löwe's 'Christian totalitarianism', Baillie saw Murry's 'Christian society' as nonetheless taking a very similar form.[158]

Murry clarified that a Christian society simply meant 'a society more effectively permeated by Christian values'. It would be a 'theocracy' only in the sense of having 'a preponderance of Christian men in governing groups', but their aims would be democratic, namely:

> to safeguard democracy against the aberrations of democracy; to defend and extend wherever possible enclaves of relative economic and social autonomy – in the village community, in the independent corporation, the vocational association; to increase to the utmost the opportunities of genuine personal responsibility without which the flowering of Christian personality must be stunted; to use the release of energies under a machine-economy in order to combat the psychological pressures of mass-organization, and to create a counter-process to cultural uniformity.[159]

Oldham took a position close to Murry's but with a different emphasis. He agreed that taming the State required it to be 'consciously inspired by Christianity' so that individuals could submit to it without 'self-degradation'.[160] But he sought to differentiate more clearly between Church and society, while still hoping that the latter could be Christianised by the former. Murry reiterated that a Christian society would protect democracy and ensure 'the provision of the maximum number of autonomous spheres'. The Moot agreed, but Moberly was concerned about the 'benevolent despotism' towards which all this seemed to lead.[161]

Indeed, in *The Price of Leadership* (1939) Murry proposed a 'democratic totalitarianism'. Assuming that some form of totalitarianism was inevitable (democracy in its present form was, he wrote, 'doomed'), he explored how it could be made benign. However, he employed a somewhat eccentric and narrow definition of 'totalitarianism', referring not to what he called the 'deplorable' existing regimes but rather merely to the monopolisation of political power by one party. Britain's current 'National' Government – consisting of politicians of all major parties – was a nucleus, he argued, for a 'democratic totalitarianism': it might never be defeated but it could still remain sensitive to public opinion. Civil rights and due process would remain as long as the ruling class was 'reasonable', 'accustomed to democratic forms' and non-'militarized'.[162] That year, Eliot used a similar term; however, for him 'totalitarian democracy' was not a positive goal but rather 'a state of affairs in which we shall have regimentation and conformity, without respect for the needs of the individual soul; the Puritanism of a hygienic morality in the interest of efficiency; uniformity of opinion through propaganda, and art only encouraged when it flatters the official doctrines of the time'.[163]

The third and fourth meetings continued to discuss such issues, but they saw a marked shift away from 'Christian dictatorship' and towards, as Chapter 4 explained, a consensus around Mannheim's ideal of 'planning for freedom'. Mannheim clearly aimed to resist a totalitarian 'enforced unanimity'.[164] Baillie stressed that a 'new Christendom' would have Christian leadership and inspiration but contain 'a very large diversity of men and of views'. He found that Maritain, for example, offered something 'half way between a liberal and a totalitarian order', even if some might see it as an 'authoritarian state'.[165] From this point onward, however, a more consistent emphasis on defending 'freedom' and 'democracy' is apparent in the group. Moberly saw these terms as vital in highlighting the 'concrete issue' between them and totalitarianism: 'If there were war tomorrow', he argued in April 1939, 'we should feel that we were fighting for some kind of individual freedom and some kind of decency'. He sought what he called a 'middle way' between totalitarianism and Britain's 'false' freedom.[166] Mannheim called democracy 'the most important phrase', since totalitarianism showed what freedom's absence meant. However, he defined democracy not as a chaos of 'everybody deciding about everything' but rather as the potential for social advancement and leadership regardless of economic class.[167] Hodges, likewise, saw the English tradition as based upon 'constitutional government' instead of direct democracy, a distinction with which Mannheim agreed.[168]

In later meetings during the war, the group lined up more clearly behind the term 'democracy'. Succumbing to totalitarianism, Moberly stated, 'would lead to a new Dark Age'.[169] 'We all want to avoid Fascism', Mannheim later insisted.[170] In spring 1941, he called for a 'militant democracy' to win the war and the resulting peace. 'Our democracy is like a sleeping beauty', he commented, 'sleeping and sleepy, in a state that corresponds to older stages of society'; if reformed, however, democracy might be a step towards a Christian society and a 'Third Way'.[171] In the *CNL*, Dawson warned of the danger of a Christian totalitarianism, to which he saw true Christianity inherently opposed.[172] In the Moot in June 1943, some participants stressed defending freedom even against growing political demands for social justice. Social justice, as Chapter 4 made clear, was important to the group, but there were also fears its advocates were taking freedom for granted.[173] Mannheim criticised Marxist assumptions that democracy was 'a sham' because capitalists allegedly owned the State or that the proletariat was the only progressive class. This rhetoric only succeeded, Mannheim said, in turning managers against the workers and vice versa, when what was needed was a cross-class movement. The democratic State was, he insisted, 'still "ours" to a degree which Marxists overlooked'.[174] But in October 1943, Hodges insisted that centralised power would increase unless restrained by 'strong forces in the body of the people', which he claimed did not exist. He glumly concluded that Fascism might be inevitable, meaning that a spiritual recovery would have to be organised from within (and in opposition to) totalitarianism.[175] Miller thought Mannheim's vision itself would require a 'dictatorship' to overcome capitalist resistance to redistributive planning and restrain monopolies.[176] Even at a time when the war was slowly turning in the Allies' favour, Mannheim saw only a 'five per cent chance' of avoiding totalitarianism, though he argued it was still worth fighting for. 'There was no safety even with democracy', he conceded, but insisted there was at least 'a chance for freedom'.[177] This position shaped the group's consensus, emphasising the aim of freedom while accepting the likely *inevitability* of at least some totalitarian trends (which, it was hoped, might be steered in a more benign direction).

Conclusion

The Moot agreed upon the need for 'planned freedom', but the nature of that freedom remained unclear. Assertions of 'democracy', Oldham wrote in 1944, 'may cover divergent and even totally opposed systems of life', some that were as tyrannical as any dictatorship.[178] There were, indeed, competing definitions in circulation (Eliot called democracy a 'doubtful term'[179]), but it was clear that group members thought that freedom was necessary for a Christian life. In 1941, Oldham wrote:

> The fight to-day is for the status and dignity of man, for the freedom of the human person, for the possibility of human community. What has to be preserved and re-established in face of deadly assault is the substance of man's humanity – the values of personal, social and political freedom, of social obligation and responsibility, of neighbourliness and fellowship. These are not values peculiar to Christianity, but they are the presuppositions of a society in which the Christian message can have significance.[180]

The Christian had a dual view of the State and freedom, he argued in an early *CNL*: 'The high task to which we are summoned is a double one – to protect the freedom of the human spirit against illegitimate encroachments on the part of the State and at the same time to use the power of the State so to shape society as to foster the growth of Christian freedom.'[181] True freedom, he stated in 1945, needed responsibility that was rooted in the 'capacity to know and obey the will of God'.[182] The modern question, he said in 1948, was

> whether we, and, what is more important, our children's children, are going to live as free persons in relation with other persons in mutual responsibility and obligation, or whether our lives are going to be increasingly shaped and

determined by impersonal forces and subjected to the central direction of
a group of organisers or social engineers or commissars. The answer to the
question is given in the last resort by what we fundamentally believe about
what man, in his essential nature, is.[183]

'Christian freedom' meant responsibility and awareness of human dependence on God, nature and other people. The group defended individuality
against totalitarian *Gleichschaltung* but preferred communitarian personalism to 'atomised' individualism. It shared the view expressed at Oxford
1937 that the 'personalism' of Christianity must not be confused with –
and, indeed was 'the very opposite of' – 'individualism'.[184] Its thinking was
also in line with C. S. Lewis's war-time assertion that 'a Christian must
not be either a Totalitarian or an Individualist'.[185] It agreed with Niebuhr
that democracy must be based on an understanding of human flaws and
defended against 'mass' culture.[186] In a way similar to A. D. Lindsay, it
distinguished 'Christian individualism' based upon true individual personhood from 'scientific individualism' based on the 'mass'.[187] It insisted
that freedom must be framed by a true understanding of life in community. Here, the group channelled personalist streams of thought that were
widespread in Europe and gave them a Protestant and British colouring.
Certain oppositions were prominent: the 'person' was preferred over the
'individual'; an 'organic' freedom was stressed over an 'atomistic' chaos; and
'spontaneous' action was praised but seen as dependent upon a 'common'
framework of values and norms.

The group's claims that true freedom needed transcendent belief and
that rights needed to be anchored in faith were not uncommon at this
time.[188] The view that Christian culture 'undergirded national identity and
democratic ways of life' was widely shared in 1930s and 1940s Britain.[189]
In 1940, the Anglican *Guardian* praised foreign secretary Lord Halifax for
asserting that British respect for the individual sprang from a belief in an
'immortal soul'.[190] In 1944, Temple claimed Christianity as democracy's
source: 'If I am a creature with a life-span of sixty or seventy years, I cannot
count for anything over against the nation or the State. But if I am a child
of God, destined for eternal fellowship with Him, I have therein a dignity
with which the State can make no comparable claim. It is here that man's
dignity resides, in a region where all are equal.'[191] The *Church of England
Newspaper* insisted British democracy was Christian: 'If England is the
mother of Parliaments, let Englishmen remember that the Church is the
mother of England. She is, in other words, the mother of the mother of
Parliaments.'[192] F. R. Barry, Bishop of Southwell, thought freedom would be
doomed without Christian underpinnings, as 'economic individualism' had
made the individual 'the slave of impersonal processes which he could not

understand nor control.'[193] 'Christian democracy', the *Church Times* argued in 1947, turned religious claims into the political insistence that individuals had rights no state could overrule.[194] The Oldham group was far from alone in asserting that true freedom had a Christian basis that was particularly well anchored in British traditions, an argument that appeared in both Anglican and free church guises.[195] But doubts about some Christian traditions were also expressed. Murry critiqued Puritanism for infecting Christianity with individualism; Oldham thought 'Protestant individualism' had no future in a mass society, and Roman Catholicism tended towards authoritarianism or 'obscurantism'.[196]

While freedom was clearly praised, there were some doubts expressed in the group about the specific relation between Christianity and democracy. Hodges, for example, stressed that democracy, rights and equality could, in fact, be rooted 'in humanist soil' and had not hitherto played a part in Christian traditions: 'Christ and the Apostles', he observed in the Moot, 'never took part in a general election'.[197] Mackinnon similarly noted in the *CNL* that Christianity had largely developed in un-free societies.[198] At times, the group's critique of 'mass democracy' and individualism echoed those of distinctly illiberal thinkers – whether authoritarian Catholics or 'Neo-Tories' – who rejected parliamentary government.[199] The *CNL* praised the dynamism and 'social purpose' in totalitarianism, something that in the late 1930s seemed to be lacking in liberal societies; meanwhile, Oldham suggested that Christianity needed its own 'storm-troops', *Mein Kampf* or activist 'Order' modelled on totalitarian parties.[200] Eliot's political journey from the 1920s through the 1940s included, at times, support (or at least sympathy) for anti-democratic movements and regimes.[201] A religious society, he argued in 1939, would not be 'an ecclesiastical despotism', but it would also not be a 'democracy'.[202] Guest-editing the *CNL*, he praised Christian-oriented Portuguese authoritarianism.[203] (Portuguese dictator António de Oliveira Salazar received an honorary degree from Oxford University in 1941 and was praised in the Christian – especially Catholic and Anglo-Catholic – press.)[204] As noted, Murry sometimes downplayed the totalitarian threat.[205]

All the same, the group explicitly sought a pluralist society and a strong civil society as defences against totalitarianism. Even Dawson – who thought 'democracy' was not only insufficient as a Christian goal but also alien to 'aristocratic and individualist' English political practices – argued during the war that what could broadly be called the 'Christian-liberal-democratic-western tradition' should be defended to maintain 'the integrity and freedom of personality'.[206] Eliot, similarly, saw democracy's justification lying less in 'its actual or potential achievements' than in 'the failures and misdemeanours of despots and oligarchs'.[207] Within the group parliamentary government was never seriously questioned. Parliament, Hetherington argued, had proved a 'remarkably good piece of machinery'.[208] Oldham (like Mannheim) insisted that planning would remain subject to 'an intelligent and alert public opinion' and 'a democratically chosen Parliament'.[209] Democracy – primarily in the sense of accountability to elected representatives and, ultimately, the people – was to endure, but it was also to be revived by a new spirit and rejuvenated by vital communities. Here was a mixture of planning and personalism that proved a stable element of the group's thought.

The group considered whether the decline of liberal democracy made a 'Christian totalitarianism' inevitable, but this conclusion was rejected. Christianity itself might be described as, in some way, 'totalitarian' (i.e. as governing *all* aspects of life and identity), but the group saw it as *politically* best suited to a pluralist, decentralised democracy. Describing Christianity as 'totalitarian' was not unusual, even among Christians. In a short book on Oxford 1937, Eric Fenn wrote that 'the Church is no stranger to totalitarianism, for it must itself make a total claim upon man'; indeed, he insisted that 'the Church itself has an ineradicable totalitarian principle within it'.[210] In 1940, the *Christian World* published two articles by different authors titled 'Totalitarian Christianity': each suggested that totalising political ideologies could only be met by an equally 'total' faith.[211] Another argued 'the Church must have a totalitarian message that can be pitted against these other totalitarian claims'.[212] Bishop Bell claimed Britain would only prevail 'if we give the Christian religion ... the same place in our lives, and in our political and social system, as they give the Nazi religion in theirs'.[213] But, here 'total' meant a deeply felt *worldview* rather than a form of *government*. Oldham may have admired the ability of Nazi and Communist movements to work towards a common purpose, but he clearly thought that the chosen purposes towards which they aimed were wrong and that comparable Christian efforts would seek freedom.[214] Thus, despite group members' critiques of individualism and democracy, they cannot be seen as 'God's totalitarians': they were committed to freedom, civil liberties, a broad pluralism and local community, even if they did see a need for a strong cultural consensus on values to be encouraged and defended by the State. Certainly, however, for some prominent observers, the goals of 'equality' or 'social justice' were already threatening to put Europe, as F. A. Hayek influentially put it, on *The Road to Serfdom* (1944).[215] Indeed, Hayek saw Mannheim as a key example of a dangerous planning consensus that aimed to orient society on specific ethical principles.

In its doubts about mass democracy, the group was far from alone, and varieties of 'constrained democracy' became common in the emergent post-war states of Western Europe.[216] The Oldham group saw freedom, democracy and liberalism as related but distinct. Freedom was consistently praised and given Christian content. Democracy was generally regarded positively but also seen ambivalently because of its perceived degradation in 'mass' society; however, if renewed through a Christian spirit and vibrant forms of local community, it was viewed as the form of governance best aligned with faith. Liberalism, however, was depicted more negatively, linked with 'atomistic' forms of individualism, a valueless moral neutrality and a purely secular-materialist worldview. Nonetheless, there were aspects of liberalism – in particular civil rights and an ethic of tolerance – that were seen as worthwhile. But while the Oldham group was committed to human rights, its members saw them not as abstract principles but rather as elements of a just social order based upon a true understanding of human nature and the social relationships it required.[217] For example, one of the definitions that Oldham gave to democracy was 'a society in which human meeting was possible'.[218]

The Christian contribution to human-rights thinking in the 1930s and 1940s has received increasing attention in the last couple of decades.[219] Samuel Moyn has stressed the impact of Christianity on human-rights thinking, but he has also described this influence as mainly 'conservative', as it was based upon communitarian ideals, questioning of 'atomistic' individualism and critiques of the Soviet Union.[220] There were, certainly, prominent conservative versions of Christian liberty. Dean Inge saw 'discipline' as central to 'Christian Freedom': 'Christianity', he wrote, 'promises to make us free; it never promises to make us independent. We are members one of another; we cannot march to heaven alone.'[221] But as the example of the Oldham group shows, while communitarianism and anti-Communism certainly played a part in Christian thinking, such views were compatible both with more politically 'left' perspectives and critiques of liberal capitalism. This version of 'third way' thinking was not simply a cover for political reaction but, from the perspective of its advocates, aimed to address both the radically new totalitarian abolition of freedom and the disintegrative effects of liberalism's untethered individualism. It was seen as an urgently needed form of liberation from a dehumanising modernity.

While group members agreed on the features of 'true' freedom (responsibility, dependence, tolerance, value consensus and community) some differed on the State's role: most accepted Mannheim's concept of 'planning for freedom', but some, as Chapter 4 showed, were sceptical, such as Eliot, Dawson and, later, Polanyi. Murry vacillated, at first urging a melding of State and Church, then rejecting this approach for a localist communal project. Some left-wing members of the group (such as Hodges and Miller) came to place social justice ahead of freedom as the essential aspect of a Christian society, a move that others found dangerous. There was agreement that *laissez-faire* led to social disintegration and that totalitarianism was a nightmare, but there was less certainty about realistic alternatives. No clear boundary between 'fundamental' values – which in the group's view required a society-wide consensus – and the realm of free individual conscience was drawn, and the extent to which dissent from a Christian social consensus could be accepted was left unresolved. Ultimately, however, the group was confident that Christian norms, British libertarian traditions and careful planning could remould core cultural assumptions without tyranny. As the next chapter shows, a Christian elite and educational policy played important roles in such plans.

Notes

1 CERC CCFCL 1/1/1, meeting at Lambeth Palace, 24 November 1937, p. 3.
2 IOE MOO/44, A. R. Vidler, 'Notes on Some Cultural Issues', n.d. [discussed April 1941], pp. 1–2.
3 IOE MOO/51, letter from Gilbert Shaw, n.d. [*c*. March 1941], p. 1.
4 LPL Temple 6, fos. 79–83, J. H. Oldham, 'A Fraternity of the Spirit', 7 March 1941, pp. 4, 7.
5 John Middleton Murry, 'Ends and Means', *Listener*, 23 May 1940, pp. 1014–15. *CNL* 87L, 25 June 1941, p. 4; *CNL* 284S, 30 April 1947, J. Middleton Murry, 'The Free Society', p. 15.
6 *CNL* 13L, 24 January 1940, p. 2.
7 *CNL* 38L, 17 July 1940, p. 1.
8 *CNL* 143L, 22 July 1942, p. 1.
9 *CNL* 110S, 3 December 1941, Edward Raven, 'Free Men for a Free Society', p. 1.
10 *CNL* 198S, 29 December 1943, William Temple, 'What Christians Stand for in the Secular World', p. 4.
11 *CNL* 312S, 26 May 1948, J. H. Oldham, 'Mr. Murry on the Free Society – II', p. 11; *CNL* 284S, 30 April 1947, J. Middleton Murry, 'The Free Society', p. 8.
12 *CNL* 86S, 18 June 1941, J. H. Oldham, 'The Predicament of Society and the Way Out', pp. 1, 2.
13 Walter Moberly, 'The Christian Faith and the Common Life', *Contemporary Review*, 153 (May 1938), 555–62.
14 *CNL* 3L, 15 November 1939, p. 2.
15 *CNL* 135L, 27 May 1942, p. 2.
16 LPL Lang 26, fos. 65–74, H. A. Hodges, 'Towards a Plan for a New *Summa*', n.d. [discussed January 1939], p. 5.
17 *CNL* 86S, 18 June 1941, J. H. Oldham, 'The Predicament of Society and the Way Out', pp. 1–3.
18 *CNL* 102L, 8 October 1941, pp. 1–2.
19 Clements, 'Oldham and Baillie', pp. 45–59.
20 See 'Planning for What?', *Theology*, 45:266 (August 1942), 65–70.
21 Murry, *Price of Leadership*, pp. 99–100; John Middleton Murry, *Adam and Eve: An Essay towards a New and Better Society* (London: Dakers, 1944), pp. 47–8.

22 IOE MOO/127, John Middleton Murry, 'Notes on Social Philosophy', n.d. [discussed July 1940], p. 1.

23 OA 20, 'The Christian Frontier', 1947.

24 Paul Abrecht, 'From Oxford to Vancouver: Lessons from Fifty Years of Ecumenical Work for Economic and Social Justice', *Ecumenical Review*, 40 (1988), 147–68 (p. 151).

25 Odair Pedroso Mateus, 'José Míguez Bonino and the Struggle for Global Christian Unity in the 1970s', in Katharina Kunter and Annegreth Schilling (eds.), *Globalisierung der Kirchen: Der ökumenische Rat der Kirchen und die Entdeckung der Dritten Welt in den 1960ern und 1970er Jahren* (Göttingen: Vandenhoeck & Ruprecht, 2014), pp. 237–54 (p. 240).

26 Oldham, *Resurrection of Christendom*, p. 13.

27 *CNL* 88S, 1 July 1941, J. H. Oldham, 'The Predicament of Society and the Way Out. II', p. 4.

28 Oldham, *Root of Our Troubles*, pp. 21–2. *CNL* 212S, 12 July 1944, J. H. Oldham, 'Christianity and Power', p. 6.

29 IOE MOO/83, J. H. Oldham, 'The Religious Foundations of the Frontier', 19 July 1942, p. 5.

30 *CNL* 302S, 7 January 1948, Emil Brunner, 'Man and Technics – Whither?', p. 14.

31 LPL Lang 26, fos. 160–1, 'The Task of the Council in War Time', 19 September 1939, p. 2.

32 OA 14/2/12, H. A. Hodges, 'Comments on Middleton Murry's Paper', n.d. [discussed September 1938], p. 5.

33 IOE MOO/85, H. J. W. Hetherington, 'Prolegomena to Planning: The Essential Freedoms', 28 August 1942, pp. 1–2.

34 Vidler, *God's Judgment on Europe*, p. 16.

35 *Moot Papers*, M8, pp. 306–7.

36 LPL Lang 26, fos. 75–93, Karl Mannheim, 'Planning for Freedom', n.d. [discussed January 1939], pp. 5–6.

37 *Moot Papers*, M7, p. 287.

38 *CNL* 54L, 6 November 1940, pp. 1–2.

39 *CNL* 115L, 7 January 1942, p. 2.

40 *Moot Papers*, M13, p. 452. *CNL* 192L, 6 October 1943, p. 2.

41 *Ibid.*, M20, p. 696.

42 *Ibid.*, M18, p. 636.

43 *CNL* 241L, 22 August 1945, p. 5.

44 *CNL* 260L, 15 May 1946, p. 5.

45 *CNL* 269L, 18 September 1946, p. 3.

46 *CNL* 284S, 30 April 1947, J. Middleton Murry, 'The Free Society', p. 8.

47 *CNL* 75L, 2 April 1941, p. 2.

48 LPL Lang 26, fos. 52–64, John Baillie, 'Paper on *True Humanism*', n.d. [for M3, January 1939], p. 6.

49 Bliss: *CNL* 235L, 30 May 1945, pp. 2, 3; Oldham: *CNL* 241L, 22 August 1945, p. 2; Dawson: *Blackfriars*, 26 (1945), 366–71.

50 *CNL* 311S, 12 May 1948, Josef L. Hromàdka, 'Between Yesterday and To-morrow'.

51 *CNL* 322L, 13 October 1948, pp. 5–8.

52 *CNL* 280S, 5 March 1947, Ian Crombie, 'The Wholehearted Pursuit of Justice'.

53 *CNL* 3L, 15 November 1939, pp. 1–2.

54 *CNL* 32L, 5 June 1940, p. 1.

55 *CNL* 3L, 15 November 1939, p. 1; *CNL* 6L, 6 December 1939, p. 4.

56 *CNL* 39L, 24 July 1940, p. 1. On the 'black-out of mind', see also 0S, 18 October 1939, p. 3 and 25L, 17 April 1940, p. 1. See also comments by Iredale: *Moot Papers*, M9, p. 318.

57 *CNL* 40L, 31 July 1940, p. 2.

58 *CNL* 41L, 7 August 1940, p. 3.

59 *CNL* 237L, 27 June 1945, p. 1.

60 Fenn, *That They Go Forward*, pp. 30–1.

61 Murry, *Price of Leadership*, p. 180.

62 Oldham, *Resurrection of Christendom*, p. 12; *CNL* 35L, 26 June 1940, p. 2.

63 *CNL* 39S, 24 July 1940, Owen Barfield, 'Effective Approach to Social Change', p. 4. Emphasis added.

64 *CNL* 218L, 4 October 1944, pp. 2–3.

65 *CNL* 3L, 15 November 1939, p. 2; IOE MOO/88, Christopher Dawson, 'Freedom and Vocation', n.d. [discussed December 1941], p. 4.

66 Murry, *Price of Leadership*, pp. 180–1.

67 *CNL* 31L, 29 May 1940, p. 1.

68 *CNL* 69L, 8 January 1941, p. 1.

69 *CNL* 87L, 25 June 1941, pp. 3–4.

70 *CNL* 175L, 3 March 1943, p. 2.

71 *CNL* 221L, 15 November 1944, p. 3. *CNL* 223L, 13 December 1944, p. 6.

72 OA 14/2/12, H. A. Hodges, 'Comments on Middleton Murry's Paper', n.d. [discussed September 1938], p. 1.

73 *CNL* 45S, 4 September 1940, J. H. Oldham, 'The Way Out', p. 3.

74 *CNL* 112S, 17 December 1941, J. H. Oldham, 'All Real Life Is Meeting', p. 3.

75 IOE MOO/83, 19 July 1942, Oldham, 'The Religious Foundations of the Frontier', p. 7.

76 *CNL* 54L, 6 November 1940, p. 2.

77 LPL Lang 26, fos. 75–93, Karl Mannheim, 'Planning for Freedom', n.d. [discussed January 1939], p. 15.

78 LPL W. Temple 6, fos. 79–83, Oldham, 'A Fraternity of the Spirit', 7 March 1941, p. 4.

79 Murry, 'Ends and Means', p. 1015.

80 *CNL* 88S, 1 July 1941, J. H. Oldham, 'The Predicament of Society and the Way Out. II', p. 3.

81 *CNL* 198S, 29 December 1943, William Temple, 'What Christians Stand for in the Secular World', p. 5. This passage was quoted in *The Church and the Planning of Britain: Report of the Social and Industrial Commission of the Church Assembly, 1944* (London: Church Assembly, 1944), p. 28.

82 *CNL* 199L, 12 January 1944, p. 4.

83 *Theology*, 46:271 (January 1943), 21–2 (p. 21).

84 *CNL* 225L, 10 January 1945, p. 3.

85 *CNL* 237S, 27 June 1945, J. H. Oldham, '*Prospect for Christendom*', p. 10.

86 *CNL* 303S, 21 January 1948, Moira Symons, 'Home and Community', p. 9.

87 *CNL* 40L, 31 July 1940, p. 3.

88 LPL Lang 26, fos. 52–64, John Baillie, 'Paper on Maritain's *True Humanism*', p. 6.

89 *CNL* 5S, 29 November 1939, J. H. Oldham, 'Preliminaries to the Consideration of Peace Aims', p. 4; *CNL* 108S, 19 November 1941, J. H. Oldham, 'The Need for a Fresh Approach to Christian Education', p. 2.

90 See, e.g., *CNL* 143L, 22 July 1942, p. 1. Mannheim, *Diagnosis*, pp. 11, 51, 123–4. *Moot Papers*, M3, p. 146; M11, p. 387; M12, pp. 410, 422; M20, p. 705.

91 *CNL* 211L, 28 June 1944, p. 4.

92 *CNL* 14S, 31 January 1940, anon., 'Educating for a Free Society', pp. 1–2. Emphasis in original. The supplement began as IOE MOO/13, 18 December 1939, Geoffrey Vickers, 'Education, War, Change'.

93 Oldham, *Resurrection of Christendom*, pp. 30–1.

94 *CNL* 198S, 29 December 1943, William Temple, 'What Christians Stand for in the Secular World', pp. 4–5.

95 *CNL* 104L, 22 October 1941, p. 1; *CNL* 103L, 15 October 1941, pp. 1–2; *CNL* 104L, 22 October 1941, p. 1; *CNL* 121, 18 February 1942, pp. 1–2.

96 *CNL* 3L, 3 January 1940, p. 3.

97 *CNL* 17L, 28 February 1940, pp. 1–2.

98 *CNL* 24S, 10 April 1940, J. H. Oldham, 'Christianity and Politics', p. 2.

99 *Moot Papers*, M7, p. 280.

100 *CNL* 226, 24 January 1945, Gladys Keable, 'Community in Suburbia', p. 5.

101 IOE MOO/19, V. A. Demant, 'Christian Faith and the Rights of Man', n.d. [discussed February 1940], pp. 3–4. *Moot Papers*, M7, pp. 258, 262, 276.

102 *Moot Papers*, M7, pp. 274, 276.

103 *CNL* 90S, 16 July 1941, G. D. H. Cole, 'Democracy Face to Face with Hugeness', pp. 1, 2.

104 *Ibid.*, p. 2.

105 *Ibid.*, pp. 3, 4.

106 *CNL* 86S, 18 June 1941, J. H. Oldham, 'The Predicament of Society and the Way Out', p. 2. *CNL* 104S, 22 October 1941, J. H. Oldham, 'Planning for Freedom', p. 3.

107 LeMahieu, *Culture for Democracy*, pp. 107–21.

108 OA 14/5/22, J. M. Murry, 'Comments on Maritain's *True Humanism*', n.d., p. 1.

109 Murry, 'Ends and Means', p. 1014.

110 Murry, *Adam and Eve*, pp. 205, 208. *CNL* 223S, 13 December 1944, J. H. Oldham, 'Love and Life'.

111 J. Middleton Murry, 'Educating for Chaos', *Adelphi* 17:5 (February 1941), 155–62 (pp. 155, 160).

112 Boys: *ibid.*, pp. 160–1. Girls 'must know how to cook with the French housewife's *savoir vivre*, and how to look after their own babies'; J. Middleton Murry, 'Educating for Chaos (II)', *Adelphi* 17:6 (March 1941), 203–11 (p. 203).

113 Murry, 'Educating for Chaos (II)', pp. 209–10.

114 *CNL* 77L, 16 April 1941, p. 3.

115 *CNL* 38L, 17 July 1940, p. 2; 47L, 18 September 1940, p. 1; 50L, 9 October 1940, p. 4; *CNL* 87L, 25 June 1941, p. 3.
116 *CNL* 89L, 9 July 1941, p. 3.
117 See, e.g., *CNL* 92S, 30 July 1941, W. G. Symons, 'Ecumenical Christianity and the Working Classes'.
118 *CNL* 337L, 11 May 1949, pp. 145–9.
119 *Moot Papers*, M2, p. 87.
120 Eliot, *Idea of a Christian Society*, p. 46.
121 Eliot quoted in Christopher Ricks, *T. S. Eliot and Prejudice* (London: Faber and Faber, 1988), p. 41. See also Anthony Julius, *T. S. Eliot, Anti-Semitism and Literary Form* (Cambridge: Cambridge University Press, 1995), pp. 162–7.
122 Mannheim, *Diagnosis*, pp. 7–8.
123 LPL Lang 26, fos. 75–93, Karl Mannheim, 'Planning for Freedom', n.d. [discussed January 1939], p. 14; Mannheim, *Diagnosis*, 49; UL BC MS 20c Moot, copy of letter from M. Jacques Maritain, 14 April 1939, p. 2; *Moot Papers*, M13, p. 454. Murry, *Free Society*, p. 113.
124 *Moot Papers*, M12, p. 422; M14, p. 484.
125 IOE MOO/85, H. J. W. Hetherington, 'Prolegomena to Planning: The Essential Freedoms', 28 August 1942, p. 1.
126 OA 13/6/32, 'Elements of a Political and Social Faith', 11 September 1942.
127 *CNL* 108S, 19 November 1941, J. H. Oldham, 'The Need for a Fresh Approach to Christian Education', p. 1.
128 *Moot Papers*, M4, pp. 210–11; M12, p. 409.
129 *Ibid.*, M2, pp. 87, 91.
130 *Ibid.*, M2, p. 91.
131 *Ibid.*, M14, p. 509.
132 *CNL* 274S, 27 November 1946, J. Middleton Murry, 'Can Democracy Survive?', pp. 11, 14. Murry, *Free Society*, pp. 253–67.
133 *Moot Papers*, M14, p. 512.
134 IOE MOO/121, Sir Walter Moberly, 'Religious Education in Our National Schools', n.d., pp. 1–2. Emphasis in original.
135 *CNL* 308L, 31 March 1948, pp. 4–5.
136 Graeme Smith, 'Christian Totalitarianism: Joseph Oldham and Oxford 1937', *Political Theology* 3:1 (2001), 32–46. The questionable claims of Smith (and of Edwards, noted below) about the 'totalitarian' nature of Oldham and other Oxford 1937 participants have been recently reiterated in Greenberg, 'Decolonization', pp. 340–1.
137 Oldham, *Church, Community and State*, p. 14. Smith, 'Christian Totalitarianism', pp. 41–2.
138 Oldham, *Church, Community and State*, pp. 9–10.
139 Edwards, 'God's Totalitarianism', pp. 286, 293–4.
140 Edwards denies that implying liberal religion 'was akin to or even a slippery slope towards the technocratic nightmares of the Third Reich and Supreme Soviet'; however, he argues that 'what began as and remained an

anti-totalitarian, liberal religious ideology, *if ever fully instituted, would have proven little better than the real thing*. *Ibid*., p. 287. Emphasis added.

141 *Ibid*., pp. 287, 292.

142 *Ibid*., p. 297.

143 Coupland, 'Anglican Peace Aims', pp. 107–10. On Dawson see Bernhard Dietz, 'Christliches Abendland gegen Pluralismus und Moderne: Die Europa-Konzeption von Christopher Dawson', *Zeithistorische Forschungen/Studies in Contemporary History*, 9 (2012), 491–7; and Lockerd, 'Beyond Politics'.

144 Smith, 'Christian Totalitarianism', p. 35.

145 *Moot Papers*, M1, pp. 52, 54; M2, pp. 73–4, 86.

146 The following quotes are from *Moot Papers*, M1, pp. 51–7.

147 LPL Lang 25, fos. 315–25, J. M. Murry, 'Towards a Christian Theory of Society', n.d. [September 1938], pp. 1, 9, 10.

148 *Ibid*., pp. 9–10.

149 *Ibid*., p. 9.

150 *Ibid*., p. 7.

151 OA 14/4/43, Löwe, 'Comments on Middleton Murry's Paper', n.d. [September 1938], pp. 1–2.

152 OA 14/3/54, Karl Mannheim, 'Comments on Middleton Murry's Paper', n.d [September 1938], pp. 1–2, 4.

153 OA 14/2/12, H. A. Hodges, 'Comments on Middleton Murry's Paper', n.d. [September 1938], p. 4.

154 OA 14/6/21, T. S. Eliot, 'Comments on Middleton Murry's Paper', n.d. [September 1938]. Eliot distinguished here among a 'Christian state', a 'Christian community', and a 'community of Christians', a division crucial to his book *Idea of a Christian Society*. Eliot, *Idea of Christian Society*, pp. 26–7, 28, 31, 34 36–7.

155 OA 14/4/32, Christopher Dawson, 'Comments on Middleton Murry's Paper', n.d. [September 1938], pp. 1–4.

156 OA 14/8/29, H. H. Farmer, 'Comments on Middleton Murry's Paper', n.d.; OA 14/8/51, Revd Lesslie Newbigin, 'Comments on Middleton Murry's Paper', n.d. [September 1938].

157 OA 14/6/91, A. R. Vidler, 'Comments on Murry's Paper', n.d. [September 1938].

158 OA 14/7/10, John Baillie, 'Comments on Middleton Murry's Paper', n.d. [September 1938].

159 OA 14/5/1, John Middleton Murry, 'Paper Read at the Moot, 23–26 September 1938', p. 12.

160 LPL Lang 25, fos. 305–14, J. H. Oldham, 'The Problems and Tasks of the Council on the Christian Faith and the Common Life', n.d. [September 1938], p. 3.

161 *Moot Papers*, M2, pp. 86–8.

162 Murry, *Price of Leadership*, pp. 45–46, 56, 58.

163 Eliot, *Idea of Christian Society*, p. 23.

164 LPL Lang 26, fos. 75–93, Karl Mannheim, 'Planning for Freedom', n.d. [discussed January 1939], p. 13.

165 LPL Lang 26, fos. 52–64, John Baillie, 'Paper on Maritain's *True Humanism*', n.d. [discussed January 1939], p. 10.
166 *Moot Papers*, M4, pp. 193, 194, 198.
167 *Ibid.*, M4, p. 194.
168 *Ibid.*, M4, p. 195.
169 *Ibid.*, M10, p. 360.
170 *Ibid.*, M8, p. 293.
171 *Ibid.*, M11, pp. 385, 388, 391–2.
172 *CNL* 107L, 12 November 1941, p. 2.
173 *Moot Papers*, M17, pp. 592–3.
174 *Ibid.*, M17, p. 587.
175 *Ibid.*, M18, p. 630.
176 *Ibid.*, M18, p. 631.
177 *Ibid.*, M18, pp. 631, 636.
178 *CNL* 221L, 15 November 1944, p. 2.
179 OA 14/6/16, T. S. Eliot, 'A Commentary', n.d., p. 3.
180 *CNL* 108S, 19 November 1941, J. H. Oldham, 'The Need for a Fresh Approach to Christian Education', p. 2.
181 *CNL* 3L, 15 November 1939, p. 2.
182 *CNL* 228L, 21 February 1945, p. 7.
183 J. H. Oldham, 'A Free and Tolerant Society', *Question: A Journal* 1:1 (1948), 8–25 (p. 8).
184 *Churches Survey Their Task*, p. 40. 'Christianity is emphatically a social religion. Its teaching is directed to men, not as units isolated from their fellows, but as members of groups and communities.' *Ibid.*, p. 109.
185 C. S. Lewis, *Mere Christianity* (New York: Macmillan, 1952), pp. 159–60. This quote was originally published in *Beyond Personality* (1945).
186 *CNL* 234L, 16 May 1945, pp. 2–3.
187 A. D. Lindsay, 'Christian Individualism and Scientific Individualism', in *Democracy, Should It Survive?* (London: Dennis Dobson, 1946), pp. 118–26.
188 Moyn, *Christian Human Rights*, pp. 124–5.
189 Rob Freathy, 'The Triumph of Religious Education for Citizenship in English Schools, 1935–1949', *History of Education: Journal of the History of Education Society*, 37:2 (2008), 295–316 (p. 303).
190 *Guardian*, 19 April 1940, p. 191.
191 William Temple, *The Crisis of the Western World and Other Broadcast Talks* (London: George Allen & Unwin, 1944), pp. 15–19 (p. 17).
192 *Church of England Newspaper*, 7 December 1945, p. 12.
193 F. R. Barry, *Church and Leadership* (London: SCM, 1945), p. 33.
194 *Church Times*, 20 June 1947, p. 368
195 Catterall, *Labour and the Free Churches*, p. 3.
196 Murry, *Price of Leadership*, pp. 37–38. *Moot Papers*, M7, p. 279; M10, p. 360.
197 OA 14/2/12, H. A. Hodges, 'Comments on Middleton Murry's Paper', n.d. [M2, September 1938], p. 5.

198 *CNL* 310S, 28 April 1948, Donald MacKinnon, 'Mr. Murry on the Free Society', p. 13.

199 Villis, *British Catholics and Fascism*; Bernhard Dietz, trans. Ian Copestake, *Neo-Tories: The Revolt of British Conservatives against Democracy and Political Modernity (1929–1939)* (London: Bloomsbury Academic, 2018).

200 *CNL* 24S, 10 April 1940, J. H. Oldham, 'Christianity and Politics', p. 4; *CNL* 37S, 10 July 1940, V. A. Demant, 'Our Justification', p. 1. *CNL* 45S, 4 September 1940, J. H. Oldham, 'The Way Out', p. 1; *CNL* 85L, 11 June 1941, p. 1. *Mein Kampf: Moot Papers*, M3, p. 145 (see also comments by Löwe, *ibid.*, p. 151) and LPL Lang 26, fos. 94–97, Oldham to Lang, 4 January 1939, p. 2. 'Storm troops': IOE MOO/2, 'A Reborn Christendom', August 1939, p. 19; IOE MOO/32, 'Topics for the Next Meeting of the Moot by Karl Mannheim' [*c.* December 1940], pp. 7–8. On the 'analogy of the "Party"': LPL Lang 26, fos. 194–203, 'The Spiritual Front', n.d. [sent to Lang 29 June 1940], pp. 5–6; a later version had replaced such analogies with references to an 'elite': IOE MOO/26, 'The Spiritual Front', 5 July 1940, pp. 3–4. In 1941, the University Catholic Federation of Great Britain stated the goal of training students 'to become "Storm Troopers of Catholicism"': *Catholic Herald*, 22 August 1941, p. 1. See Oldham's comments on learning from the 'new movements in Europe': LPL Temple 6, fos. 79–83, Oldham, 'A Fraternity of the Spirit', 7 March 1941, p. 1.

201 See, e.g., Kojecky, *T. S. Eliot's Social Criticism*, pp. 58–69.

202 Eliot, *Idea of a Christian Society*, pp. 42, 57, 94. See also McVey, 'Backgrounds', pp. 179–80, 182.

203 See *CNL* 42L, 14 August 1940, p. 3.

204 For praise of Salazar see *Guardian*, 14 June 1940, p. 287; 2 May 1941, p. 207; 8 January 1943, p. 13; 15 January 1943, p. 19; 3 November 1944, p. 389. *Catholic Herald*, 19 January 1940, p. 6; 2 May 1941, p. 3; 16 May 1941, p. 4.

205 Ceadel, *Semi-Detached Idealists*, p. 421; Lea, *John Middleton Murry*, p. 278.

206 IOE MOO/88, Dawson, 'Freedom and Vocation', n.d. [for M13, December 1941], p. 1; *CNL* 107L, 12 November 1941, pp. 1–2. See Villis, *British Catholics and Fascism*, pp. 105–16, esp. p. 114.

207 *CNL* 141L, 8 July 1942, p. 3.

208 IOE MOO/85, H. J. W. Hetherington, 'Prolegomena to Planning: The Essential Freedoms', p. 2.

209 *CNL* 104S, 22 October 1941, J. H. Oldham, 'Planning for Freedom', p. 3. Mannheim: *Moot Papers*, M20, p. 696. I agree with Kurlberg's critique of Edwards's claim that the group was totalitarian; however, I disagree with his view that 'the Moot was irrefutably undemocratic' or that a 'majority' of its members 'rejected universal suffrage': Kurlberg, 'Resisting Totalitarianism', p. 527.

210 Fenn, *That They Go Forward*, pp. 25, 29.

211 *Christian World*, 11 January 1940, p. 7; 28 November 1940, p. 10.

212 *Christian World*, 15 August 1946, p. 11.

213 *Church of England Newspaper*, 12 July 1940, p. 4.

214 LPL Temple 6, fos. 79–83, Oldham, 'A Fraternity of the Spirit', 7 March 1941, p. 1.

215 Hayek, *Road to Serfdom*, esp. pp. 100–56.

216 Müller, *Contesting Democracy*, pp. 5–6, 128–9. Conway, 'Rise and Fall'.

217 Annabel Brett, 'Human Rights and the Thomist Tradition', in Pamela Slotte and Miia Halme-Tuomisaari (eds.), *Revisiting the Origins of Human Rights* (Cambridge: Cambridge University Press, 2015), pp. 82–101.

218 *Moot Papers*, M14, p. 515.

219 Nurser, 'Ecumenical Movement'; John Nurser, *For All Peoples and All Nations: Christian Churches and Human Rights* (Geneva: WCC Publications, 2005).

220 Moyn, *Christian Human Rights*. See an insightful discussion and critique in P. Mackenzie Bok, 'Did the Christians Ruin Rights?', *New Rambler*, posted 15 February 2016, http://newramblerreview.com/book-reviews/history/did-the-christians-ruin-rights (accessed 5 February 2017).

221 *Church of England Newspaper*, 31 March 1944, p. 1.

7

'The democratizing of aristocracy': egalitarianism and elitism

The Oldham group had as a goal a society of free and responsible persons in service to God and their fellows. Its participants saw Britain as an amoral 'plutocracy' that betrayed the nation's Christian traditions, and they urged changes in the economy and in society to encourage 'social justice'. Breaking the power of 'privilege' was thus a prerequisite for a more Christian society. From such priorities came a strong egalitarian commitment to reducing disparities in wealth and opportunity. On the other hand, the group saw in the undifferentiated social 'mass' a threat to moral and intellectual standards. A few participants departed from the egalitarian, redistributionist consensus, and even those who did not sought to maintain certain traditional hierarchical distinctions regarding the quality of cultural production and to protect educational structures that had tended to serve a privileged minority. These tensions between egalitarianism and elitism were most apparent in discussions of the need for a culturally guiding elite in a new, planned society and of educational reform. This chapter thus focuses on a final 'middle way' in the group, that running between egalitarianism and elitism.

Egalitarian aims

The society towards which the Oldham group strived would reduce but not eliminate inequality. Here, ecumenical and sociological ideas mingled. The Oxford 1937 report insisted that the economy, like all of life, was under Christ's judgement, making violations of 'fellowship' by deep class differences unacceptable.[1] Alongside greed, irresponsible power and the denial of 'vocation', inequality was seen as a symptom of liberal capitalism. The report attacked 'indefensible inequalities of opportunity' with regard to wealth, education, health and leisure, and it observed that most people faced 'environmental evils' from which a privileged minority escaped.[2] Christianity neither demanded 'identical provision' nor disallowed differential rewards, but an economy that systematically violated 'dignity' and obscured 'common humanity' by 'emphasizing the external accidents of birth, or wealth, or social position' was, the report argued, 'anti-Christian'.[3] Taking, as usual, a moderate position, the report rejected either a 'complacent defence of exclusive privilege' on the right or what it called an 'unteachable and self-righteous fanaticism' on the left: it urged equal opportunity, care for the disabled, both the 'duty' and the 'right' to work, and the protection of natural resources.[4]

Karl Mannheim's critiques of capitalist inequality and arguments for a 'redistributive economy' resonated with such Christian aims of sharing wealth and fighting unjust privilege. Mannheim saw reducing inequality as vital to his goal of reinforcing pluralist democratic societies against totalitarianism. A new social unity could only be achieved through a 'basic security' based on 'a redistribution of profit'.[5] The planned society would bring a 'more even distribution of wealth and less accumulation in a few hands', with more going to 'workers and industrial classes'. He thought a revival of religion could inspire a willingness for 'self-sacrifice' in meeting this goal.[6] The Sermon on the Mount, he argued, might be 'retranslated' as a political system 'based on equality of opportunity'.[7] Planning would allow capitalism's inequalities to be counteracted by democratically controlled investment controls and 're-distribution schemes': the 'existing stratification' could be modified by taxation, 'maintaining an element of competition, only with less inequality'.[8]

Complaints about inequality, poverty and unemployment as well as calls for redistributive policies were often made in the group.[9] In the Moot, Oldham claimed that 'the redistribution of wealth' would be a 'crucial issue' in a Christian society, warning against 'strong City influences determined to hold on to their power at any cost'; Murry, meanwhile, insisted there should be 'no privilege for country, class or individual'.[10] Moot visitor Geoffrey Vickers thought the Moot's core aim was to address inequality, and his *CNL* essay on this point was influential in the group.[11] Hetherington saw one of the 'desperately wrong' things in British society as the 'wide inequality of income for equally honest effort'.[12] There was no single measure of equality, but Vidler defined the real goal as 'the best equality of treatment of the greatest number' with the least amount of 'coercion'.[13] The wartime spirit of unity and the growth in State controls, Löwe said, pointed the way towards a more equal society.[14] Clarke thought no progress could be made without addressing the class system, particularly in education (discussed below), but he admitted that 'a real facing of this issue would blow up Oxford'.[15] Educational equality required significant economic redistribution: otherwise, 'the whole thing would break down'.[16]

Figure 8 Alexander Roper Vidler, 1949, by Elliott & Fry

In questioning the class system, however, the group's consensus downplayed class struggle. As Chapter 4 made clear, this had much to do with Mannheim's view that social revolutions were likely to end in totalitarianism. A cross-class movement of 'progressive elements' among managers, technicians, civil servants, the middle class and workers was preferred.[17] Difficulties in this approach were acknowledged, and, ultimately, the middle classes were seen as the main force for change, especially through a strategy of 'revolution from above'.[18] A *CNL* supplement from late 1945 criticised a report by the Church of England's Commission on Evangelism for ignoring 'the mentally and practic-ally alert minority who influence opinion and initiate action'.[19] Hodges, how-ever, argued that simply ignoring the 'class war' was not a viable strategy: if it were a real feature of capitalist society, as he thought it probably was, then Christians would have to face it.[20]

The group's egalitarian impulses were genuine but clearly emphasised equality of *opportunity*: it was accepted that differences in wealth – even large ones – would remain. Still, while relative inequality was seen as inevitable, forms of absolute poverty were to be attacked by State efforts at wealth redistribution through taxation.[21] The concern was expressed, though, that too much of what they viewed as the wrong kind of egalitarianism was dangerous, referring to declining standards and an erosion of individual diversity in an undifferentiated social 'mass': in essence, a mere 'levelling down' rather than a genuine growth in opportunity and quality. The following two sections consider further this mixture of egalitarianism and elitism by looking, first, at the idea of a Christian (or at least Christian-influenced) 'elite' and, second, at the group's views on education.

A new elite: thinking about a 'clerisy'

The group agreed that a distinct group – an 'elite', 'order' or 'clerisy' – could play an important role in guiding cultural renewal. The concept of a 'clerisy' originated with poet and philosopher Samuel Taylor Coleridge in works such as *On the Constitution of Church and State* (1830), in which he had argued a pluralist society required a 'national clerisy', i.e. a 'learned Christian order consisting of clergy and schoolteachers' that would 'educate the public'.[22] The aim was to maintain Christian cultural influence. Related ideas were developed by Thomas and Matthew Arnold. Clerisy concepts were rediscovered in the inter-war years by those seeking to strengthen 'Christian civil society' against 'mass' culture. Mannheim's planning ideas were more statist, but his stress on freedom and non-State actors opened his approach to Christian principles: any planned society, after all, needed planners, who might form the basis of a Christian clerisy or 'Order', a view that Mannheim shared with Oldham. Many in the group advocated an elite, including Oldham himself; Polanyi; and the educators Oakeshott, Clarke and Moberly. However, the most developed arguments came from Eliot, Murry and Mannheim. The following sections will concentrate on their ideas about an elite, considering its justifications, membership, tasks and limits.

Justifications

Among intellectuals, a suspicion of crowds, masses and mobs reached back to the eighteenth century and grew in the early twentieth century. Between the wars, mass communication, the growth of commercialised leisure and the success of totalitarian movements meant the 'masses' were depicted as lacking individuality and vulnerable to manipulation.[23] In a radio broadcast in early 1940, Moberly argued that extending voting rights had not brought 'wider responsibility and more genuine democracy'; instead, Britons were 'in danger of acquiring too much of the psychology of the mob': 'the mentality of the casual street crowd is just what gives the dictator his chance; a little flighty and eager for sensation, uncritical and easily moved, and above all irresponsible'.[24] In 1941, Oldham, in a *CNL* essay, asserted that 'mass psychology pervades all classes', but he focused on the better-off:

> It is characteristic of the members of the wealthy, cosmopolitan crowd who in time of peace in London, New York, Paris, Vienna or Tokyo wear the same clothes, drink the same cocktails, perform the same dances to the same music, and respond in identical ways to the same stimuli. It is no less characteristic of the suburban masses, detached from any cultural or religious tradition, suffering from intolerable boredom, seeking satisfaction in any new thrill or sensation and ready to be led away by the lure of a counterfeit religion.[25]

Such a mass culture justified a new cultural leadership in the form of an 'elite' or 'clerisy'.

Murry introduced the idea of the clerisy to the Moot in September 1938, arguing that State and Church must 'draw together' to embody a Christian spirit in social life. Here, he adopted Coleridge's view of the clerisy as a 'national church' or 'permanent class' responsible for education.[26] In *The Price of Leadership* (1939), he saw the new elite shaped by three kinds of inevitability: all people needed a faith, all societies had a ruling class and all societies were becoming more totalitarian.[27] Marxists had too closely linked 'ownership' and 'administration': it was a 'fantasy' to think abolishing capital obviated the need for a ruling class. The 'equalitarian' left (such as Labour) had, he complained, failed to educate an 'alternative ruling class', leaving it dependent upon the existing one.[28] In a May 1940 broadcast he argued that only an elite and not a 'huge urban democracy' could control 'machine-civilisation' to 'human and Christian ends'. Oldham called this view 'profound and unanswerable'.[29] In *Adam and Eve* (1944), Murry suggested that Christianity was 'a religion of an élite' during periods of 'transition between one life-epoch and another'.[30]

Eliot had similarly long decried what he saw as a 'deterioration' of modern society and mass culture. In the 1920s, he had warned against the 'large crawling mass', and he saw his epoch as 'singularly stupid', insisting that it had been left to 'the small number of intelligent people of every race or nation' to maintain culture.[31] In 1928, he claimed 'real' democracy was always 'restricted', requiring 'limitation by hereditary rights and responsibilities' so that it could flourish.[32] Such thinking recurred in *The Idea of a Christian Society* (1939) and a late 1944 Moot paper titled 'On the Place and Function of the Clerisy'. In his book, Eliot argued that industrialism created 'bodies of men and women – in all classes – detached from tradition, alienated from religion and susceptible to mass suggestion: in other words, a mob'.[33] One part of his vision of an alternative Christian society was what he called 'the Community of Christians', a clerisy-like elite with responsibility for maintaining cultural standards.[34]

Murry's and Eliot's views derived from nineteenth-century Christian thought, but elites were equally important to Mannheim's secular sociology. In *Ideologie und Utopie* (1929), he had argued that only a 'socially unattached intelligentsia' could synthesise competing ideologies.[35] In *Man and Society* (1940) he insisted that all historical conflicts were decided by small groups, since the masses were shaped by 'creative minorities'.[36] His vision of 'planning for freedom' reserved key roles for elites, and Mannheim agreed with Oldham that an 'Order' could 'mobilise and integrate' new thought.[37] But he saw a troubling 'negative democratization' in western elites: a loss of internationalism (because of rising localism and nationalism), an overproduction of intellectuals (causing their 'proletarianization') and a decline of 'intellectual culture'.[38] In September 1939, he blamed 'cultural decline' on 'the disintegration of the leading élites'.[39] Disdaining 'the snobbish condemnation of the masses which is so widespread nowadays', he nonetheless warned against 'deteriorative tendencies in liberalism and democracy'.[40] 'Elite' was, he admitted, an 'unfortunate word'; still, it correctly denoted 'the few who ran the show in any society [and] mattered politically'.[41] These views influenced Oldham: 'a fundamental change', he wrote in a CCFCL memorandum in 1940, 'must begin with a few', urging that the 'first step' to be undertaken was 'the formation of an elite'.[42]

Membership

An elite or clerisy was justified as a countervailing force to cultural disintegration, 'mass' psychology and intellectual disorientation. But who would form it? The group agreed that it should not be synonymous with the *economic* elite: it would be selected on the basis of *capability* rather than *wealth*. The term 'elite' was also flexible and broad: a 1946 *CNL* essay defined it as the professions – 'clergy, lawyers and doctors' – as well as the 'higher technicians in industry', secondary school teachers, statesmen and 'the vast majority of the higher Civil Service'.[43] However, there were various emphases within this consensus.

In *The Idea of a Christian Society*, Eliot called his version of the clerisy the 'Community of Christians', which would exist alongside the 'Christian State' and 'Christian Community'. A 'nebulous' body of 'indefinite' outline, it would instead contain 'the consciously and thoughtfully practising Christians, especially those of intellectual and spiritual superiority'; unlike Coleridge's clerisy, it would not include all teachers or clergy but would contain laity in 'various occupations'.[44] In 1944, he explained that clerisies had existed throughout history but were 'the most difficult of all élites to distinguish and define'. The highest-level clerisy included all who 'originate the dominant ideas, and alter the sensibility, of their time', including philosophers, scientists, artists, writers, playwrights and musicians: George Bernard Shaw, for example, was 'a middle-grade cleric' and Noël Coward was among 'the lowest dregs of clerisy'.[45] Eliot insisted a clerisy should be an '*élite* and not a *class*', its membership deriving not from birth but 'by virtue of individual superiority developed by training'. Although clerisies tended to derive from dominant classes, they should be independent (even 'critical' or 'subversive') of the powerful.[46] The cleric, Eliot argued, 'should, to some extent, be able to look upon, and mix with, all classes as an outsider; just as he should, to some extent, get out of his own century. ... He should also have a supra-national community of interest with clerics of other nations; so as to work against nationalism and racialism (provincialism) as he does against class'.[47] Eliot wanted a single clerisy; Mannheim (and Polanyi) were open to groups of specialists.[48]

Murry's model was Thomas Arnold's early-nineteenth-century educational experiment at Rugby, an elite secondary school. There, Murry wrote, Arnold had tried to make Christianity relevant to industrial society and 'create an élite of Christian men'. Murry credited Arnold's efforts with much of the previous century's social progress: 'He set', Murry wrote, 'the leaven of a new spirit working in the new ruling class'.[49] That class had, however, still been defined by wealth. Rather than an economic elite, the mass society needed an administrative class educated to rule by a more equal educational system in which pupils were selected only by ability. Political partisanship and religious chauvinism had no place here: the 'Christian brotherhood' could have members from 'every political party', and they need not even be consciously Christian. They would constitute 'a fraternity of whole men, truly thinking for the common weal – "tendering the whole" in the spirit of Christ'.[50]

Introducing 'planning for freedom' to the Moot, Mannheim stressed that a democracy needed a principle of 'selection' of 'the best in the community without distinction of wealth or class'.[51] Traditional education had formed an 'individualised' elite that had been suited to a democracy run by a wealthy minority: it had to be adapted to mass society.[52] In 1940, he argued that leading roles could not be played by either the Communists (who were too extreme) or the 'traditional elite' (which was too 'inelastic'). Instead, a 'sect' within the 'old leadership' could become 'a new type of elite more responsive to the needs of modern democracy'.[53] The planned society needed a functional elite on rational lines, oriented to its ultimate values and consisting not only of Christian clergy and laity but also of 'representatives of secular thought'.[54] Society required 'responsible governing groups', and Mannheim argued oligarchy was best prevented by enabling 'the access of the gifted from the lower ranks into the leading positions'.[55] Details were sketchy, but this sort of thinking clearly shaped the group's consensus.

Tasks

As with the selection criteria for the proposed elite, its precise tasks remained vague. However, it was agreed that it would be responsible for guiding the formulation and implementation of a common 'social philosophy' that was supposed to govern social life. Eliot saw the 'Community of Christians' – working with a renewed education system and in the context of a 'common culture' – as capable of forming 'the conscious mind and conscience of the nation'.[56] He also referred to the need for an 'elite of thought, conduct and taste' that would produce 'something of a common mind about the questions of the day'.[57] The 'Community of Christians' would not, itself, exercise political power, but it would influence, guide and restrain those who did, forming, it has been described, a 'back-cloth of Christian ethical principles against which the political drama would be played'.[58] Polanyi agreed with much of Eliot's 1944 paper on the clerisy, seeing its 'first function' as keeping the 'great heritage of mind' in the West alive and helping to transmit it to future generations.[59] Mannheim's response to Eliot's paper likewise stressed the task of the clerisy as helping 'to maintain a high level of culture' after the war.[60]

Murry oriented his 'ruling-class' on Thomas Arnold's 'dream' of a Christian 'Order' in modern society that 'publicly acknowledged their Christian allegiance': they would pursue their 'secular' occupations with a clearly Christian inspiration.[61] Its purpose would be 'vivification' of the democratic and egalitarian aspects of 'a Christian commonwealth', in particular the education of citizens as to 'their obligations and privileges as members of a Christian community'.[62] This brotherhood would 'educate itself for responsible leadership', its influence deriving partly from its example of 'a self-discipline in living and a taxing of oneself for the cause'. It would examine 'the total situation', defend 'realms of responsible freedom' against 'collectivism' and counteract a trend towards specialisation in education 'which creates physical and mental hobbledehoys'.[63]

The idea of a small elite body exerting pressure on other institutions was also in Mannheim's concept of planning for freedom, which foresaw an 'Order' that would 'revitalise the social body' and 'spread the spirit'. It would develop new social ideas and 'persuade organised bodies like the Churches and the Civil Service to accept the new ideas and the practical proposals which are necessary in an age of democratic change'.[64] It would not exercise political power but would rather be 'a combatant order which forms an integral part of the social organism like its nervous system, coordinating its activities and spiritualising its aims'.[65] Mannheim saw analogous elements in the totalitarian parties (though he clearly wanted a group motivated by ideals of 'militant democracy') or among the Jesuits, who had 'tried to revitalise society, at once preserving its spiritual traditions and bringing about a rebirth'.[66] He insisted that 'elite groups in our society' – among them the Moot and 'enlightened civil servants' – would have to use social techniques in democratic ways.[67] He adopted a technocratic approach in *Man and Society*, urging that much State action should be 'non-political' and handled by experts. The elite would help to 'plan' intellectual life through education and by 'guiding and leading emotional development'.[68] In *Diagnosis of Our Time*, he argued that Christian attitudes had to be integrated into society via 'a body somehow similar to the priests' that would ensure adherence to a shared social philosophy.[69]

Limits

All of the group's main theories of an elite, clerisy or 'Order' stressed that it would be 'democratically' selected – in the sense of being drawn from all social classes – and foresaw its role as influencing political institutions rather than exercising power directly. The emphasis was on *cultural* rather than political leadership. But the planned institutional structure remained undefined; moreover, suggestions that an elite would form a 'ruling class' or 'ruling group' implied a political role. How would abuses of power be avoided? In an early Moot discussion, Vidler saw the necessity for 'institutional safeguards of the distribution of power'; Oldham, similarly, emphasised that 'society must reserve a large sphere for freedom, thus limiting the range of action of the ruling group'.[70] Given the vagueness with which the composition, tasks and institutional structure of the elite was defined, the issue of the limits to be placed on its power is one of the more difficult questions to answer. However, there were indications.

Eliot emphasised that the Community of Christians would primarily *criticise* political power. It was concerned with 'the organisation of values, and a direction of religious thought which must inevitably proceed to a criticism of political and economic systems'.[71] He was aware, though, that 'any organisation is always in danger of corruption'.[72] He saw the various institutions of a 'Christian society' exercising a mutually limiting and controlling function over each other, and such power as would be vested in the

Community of Christians was that of moral and social critique, positive personal example, and public persuasion.

In the Moot, Murry had called for the State and Church to 'draw together', raising more concretely the issue of political power.[73] In the discussion on the paper, Moberly cited Niebuhr's warning that power, while necessary, was 'inherently corrupting', and, therefore, 'abuse by the governing group was certain'. Murry reiterated his contention that a Christian society would aim for the 'maximum number of autonomous spheres', offering protection from State power; however, he also believed that 'the quality of the Christian men' who participated would mean they would even act 'in opposition to their own power'.[74] He expanded upon this in a radio broadcast, arguing that no elite could be trusted 'unless it is inspired and purified by a selfless love of Christ': '[g]iven a body of real Christians – Christians prepared to live according to a severe standard of austerity and frugality, and to accept responsibility – much might happen'.[75] Thus, Murry thought limits on power might emerge organically from the faith of the elite itself.

While Mannheim, too, was relatively vague about the mechanisms to constrain the planners or elite, he emphasised they would be responsible to Parliament and the public will.[76] He saw 'parliamentary control' of society's laws (and the 'control of controls by democratic methods') as 'the great achievement of the liberal age'; 'with modifications', he argued, it should continue in a planned society.[77] Mannheim's experience in Britain convinced him that a powerful elite could co-exist with a fundamentally tolerant and dynamic liberal social order. He also believed that the key limitation of that elite's power would be a politically active populace enabled through improved education.[78] This was a perspective that Oldham shared, arguing in an early issue of the *CNL* that Britain had largely failed to create 'a population capable of exercising the rights of free citizens.[79] Oldham touched on a recurring issue in the group: the necessity for a fairer, more extensive and more effective system of education. Here, too, elitist assumptions were rarely far from the surface, and while specific arguments for an 'Order' faded in the group, the need to form an elite remained central to its thinking about education.

Education: 'the democratizing of aristocracy'

Education was a key topic for the Oldham group, particularly access to it, the universities' role in forming a new 'elite' and the need for a coherent philosophical foundation for teaching. Oldham and Fred Clarke – who was director of the University of London's Institute of Education and a former professor of education in South Africa and Quebec – had long been involved in ecumenical thinking about education. Both wrote essays for Oxford 1937's report on it.[80] They stressed that education, in the present 'crisis' of mass society, should encourage, as Clarke put it, the 'freely creative personality'.[81] Given that education was embedded in a global diversity of political systems – from totalitarianism to liberal democracy – the Oxford summary report offered few conclusions other than calling for freedom of conscience and specifying challenges to Christian education: secularisation, a radical faith in human autonomy, social disintegration, weakening 'family ties', expanding State power and new forms of media (especially cinema and radio broadcasting).[82] The report urged Christians to develop a theology 'relevant to current life', connect to youth movements, elaborate a philosophy of education, and maintain religious instruction in school and family.[83]

Education was discussed in the Moot, its subgroup on education, the CCFCL, the CFC and the *CNL*.[84] One recurrent theme was the need to increase access to education. (More adult education was also specifically advocated.[85]) A CCFCL memo insisted that a 'just order' was impossible without 'substantial equality of educational opportunity'; a Christian society would educate 'all alike as *persons*' in line with 'a positive social philosophy' with strongly Christian elements.[86] Oldham told Archbishop Lang that a 'greater equalisation of opportunity' was essential, but he voiced concern that the post-war left might rely upon 'mechanical methods' and a 'strict regimentation of education' in pursuing this goal.[87] Expanding educational access in the *wrong* manner would threaten quality. The 'middle way' here envisioned maintaining elite educational structures but detaching access to them from wealth.

In discussing religion and education it should be stressed that the Oldham group did not mainly mean instruction about Christianity. The churches at this time were pressing for more 'religious education' (which was indeed established in all State schools in the 1944 Education Act).[88] While the group was not hostile to this aim, it stressed not the teaching of religious themes in a separate class but rather, as Clarke put it, rethinking 'our whole educational philosophy' in the light of faith.[89] Similar points were put in different ways. Shaw saw education as 'a moulding of the individual to a certain end which must be life in a social world'.[90] For Hodges, 'Christian education' meant not only teaching religion but also teaching 'everything else in a Christian spirit'.[91] Eliot argued for a 'Christian doctrine of education in general'.[92] Oldham had talked this way since the early 1930s.[93] But the group doubted that State schools would be able to propagate the 'minority' faith of Christianity.[94] Translating Christian ideas in ways acceptable to secularists – as discussed in Chapter 3 – was thus key. Marjorie Reeves, in the *CNL*, saw religious education as based upon 'fundamental experiences' that formed a 'common basis of education' with humanists while also 'preparing the ground for specific Christian truth'.[95]

Examples from early in the group's existence show a typical mixture of egalitarianism and elitism. In *The Price of Leadership* (1939) Murry praised the 'public' schools (i.e. private, elite institutions) and the ancient universities, but he argued that they should be opened to meritocratic admissions. Murry, himself a former scholarship boy, praised the *form* of Britain's elite education but critiqued its monopolisation by the *economic* ruling class. He urged a 'democratization' of the public schools.[96] There should no longer be different educations for the 'rich man's son' and the 'poor man's son'; this was so even if only a small number of either would receive the 'ruling-class' education, since Murry foresaw an accompanying expansion of vocational training.[97] He wanted 'a public-school education for everybody who would profit by it', a position he distinguished both from the status quo and from those seeking to 'destroy' the public schools and replace them with the 'specious uniformity' of working-class education.[98]

Similar emphases appeared that year in a paper by Clarke applying Mannheim's planning ideas to education, a version of which was published as the influential *CNL*-Book *Education and Social Change* (1940).[99] Clarke argued that in a 'collectivized social order', the division between elite 'cultural' education and popular 'practical' education could not be sustained, as technical knowledge had to be used in line with common values.[100] Only in this way could one avoid 'cultural corrosion' and the 'lapse into a ghastly Brave New World of technicized titillation'.[101] Typical for the group, while not calling for a classless society, Clarke saw class in 'functional' terms and separated educational quality from economic privilege.[102] A new 'popular philosophy of education' would unify 'the values of culture and usefulness'.[103] He broadly, though not uncritically, approved of the 1938 Spens Report on secondary education, the last pre-1944 Government report, which had supported a still elitist but more meritocratic system.[104] Clarke thought that selection oriented towards creating a new 'ruling class' would remain, but it would no longer allow 'segregation' based solely on 'social grounds'.[105] The goal was a 'systematic *sorting* by criteria of aptitude and ability as distinct from prerogatives of class': the '*democratizing of aristocracy*' would preserve 'aristocratic quality and temper and standards' while employing democratic selective criteria.[106] The public schools would become 'generally accessible' while conserving their 'essential values', even if their 'aristocratic humanism' had to be adapted to a 'modern industrial democracy'.[107] Mannheim saw Clarke's paper as a promising basis for education in a planned society.[108]

In a paper circulated to the Moot (published anonymously in the *CNL* in January 1940), Geoffrey Vickers similarly stressed the need to 'unify the educational system', 'extend the educational period' and 'deepen the educational purpose'. Unification meant overcoming English education's extreme inequality. Universities had to become 'open to ability irrespective of money', making reform of primary and secondary education essential: the public schools also should take 'the best of each year's youth irrespective of wealth'.[109] Vickers thought opening the public schools to a wider social base would be opposed not only by the privileged but also by those on the left who rejected any form of educational stratification.[110] Along with equal access (and a longer period of secondary schooling), he urged a holistic curriculum combining intellectual, physical and moral capabilities and focusing on the development of 'character'. Freedom, after all, required instilling capacities for 'self-government'.[111]

At the Moot's seventh meeting, in February 1940, Löwe and Moberly gave papers on the universities. Moberly's appeared anonymously in the *CNL* in 1946 and fed into his book *The Crisis in the University* (1949).[112] Both called for broadening access to education and a philosophy to orient it.[113] They cited David Paton's *Blind Guides?* (1939), which had depicted higher education as beset by cultural decay. Moberly relied upon John Henry Newman's 'idea of a university', developed during the 1850s. Education, they agreed, had to be more than technical skills. Moberly said it must provide a *Weltanschauung*; for Löwe, 'cultural knowledge' and the capacity to interpret 'the meaning, structure and evolution of the world as a whole' were essential.[114] Oxford and Cambridge had long offered the right *kind* of education in their curricula and 'corporate life' but were too socially exclusive.[115] Conversely, the modern universities that taught the majority of students were more democratic but gave no idea of how to live life, failing to provide students with 'compelling convictions' amid the modern 'chaos of values'.[116] Their curricula suggested faith could not contribute to 'real' knowledge or even to ethics.[117] In a 'great act of abdication', Moberly wrote, modern universities failed to integrate knowledge 'in some plan of life':

> If you want a bomb the chemistry department will teach you how to make it, if you want a cathedral the department of architecture will teach you how to build it, if you want to keep your body in health the physiological and medical department will teach you how to do so. But if you ask whether and why you should want bombs or cathedrals or healthy bodies the university is content to be dumb and impotent.[118]

Löwe thought the group had to explain the position of the 'educated man' in the new social order so as to define a 'new intellectual elite'.[119] Modern universities needed a 'corporate life' on the Oxford or Cambridge model; yet, their closeness to the working world could also mould a new synthesis.[120] Löwe and Moberly believed 'democratisation' would ensure selection of the best students and strengthen the planned order's legitimacy. But Moberly warned against lowering standards in the process.[121] The Moot welcomed the papers, noting similarities and differences. Both wanted to adapt what Moberly called 'the Oxford and Cambridge tradition' to democratic society, but they differed on strategy.[122] Löwe thought an 'experimental college' could demonstrate new techniques; Moberly focused instead on the 'conversion' and interconnection of existing small groups at universities.[123]

Mannheim's earliest contributions on planning in the Moot in 1939 had made similar arguments for the importance of 'education for freedom', which would help create the 'fundamental set of rules and moral codes' essential to tackling liberalism's disintegrative tendencies. Rather than a purely religious education, this would mean a 'collaboration between history, philosophy, empirical sociology and psychology' that could 'give the individual a broader outlook and help him to realise his place in our society' and reduce 'dependence on mass emotion'.[124] (Education's 'principal aim', he wrote, 'is usually to achieve a basic social conformity'.[125]) In 1942, contributions to the Moot's education group expressed similar views. Mannheim saw education as vital to a transition away from *laissez-faire*, and he urged reducing inequality by extending 'the basis of social selection'.[126] Another paper, by H. C. Dent – editor of the *Times Education Supplement* and, with Clarke, member of the 'All Souls Group' of educational reformers – argued that defenders of democracy would have to learn to use education as effectively as had authoritarian and totalitarian movements. Dent called British education 'highly undemocratic' and 'the very essence of inequality of opportunity'; moreover, its 'basic philosophy' was oriented not towards democracy but rather towards an 'acquisitive and competitive' society where 'the prizes are privilege, power and the well-filled purse'. Democratisation required a holistic curriculum emphasising educational 'quality' as well as its 'quantity', and imparting not only knowledge but also 'the elements of healthy and happy living in community'.[127]

The Oldham group not only discussed education policy but also tried to influence it. Oldham met with R. A. Butler (the Secretary of State for Education) and Lord Halifax in 1940 to discuss how education might keep 'pagan' forces at bay.[128] Moot member Walter Oakeshott was involved with another Christian circle around the publisher Geoffrey Faber that advised Butler. Mannheim's ideas also inspired that group, from which emerged an ambitious educational scheme involving State control, a technical curriculum, organised youth movements and the inculcation of Christian doctrine. But when Butler presented it to the Conservative Party's Central Council in September 1942 it was rejected as 'Christian Fascism', ultimately pushing Butler towards the more moderate bill that was eventually passed and that received the royal assent in August 1944, becoming widely known as the Butler Act.[129] It established universal secondary education, raised the school-leaving age, aimed to equalise educational provision, and introduced religious education and morning prayers in all State schools. Clarke was in regular contact with Butler and involved in many initiatives for educational reconstruction.[130] Through policy consultations and public lectures and articles, he contributed to the Act itself as well as its public and professional reception.[131]

The *CNL* publicly backed Butler's Education Bill. In May 1943, Oldham urged Christians not only to support it but also to agree on educational values, develop 'a new synthesis between school and employment' and encourage a more 'meaningful' approach to work.[132] Arguing in October 1943 that the Bill responded to the 'gross and scandalous injustice' of unequal opportunity, he found it 'shocking' that some Christians threatened to derail it were their denominational interests to be insufficiently served.[133] In November, he called for fulfilling the Act's promises on educational quality.[134] Even when passed, the Act, as Clarke stressed, was only 'a beginning, not an end'.[135] A *CNL* essay by Michael Clarke (former headmaster at Repton and a secretary of the CFC) called for the public schools to honour their promise of 'education for all according to capacity' and to create a 'new aristocracy of service independent of wealth'.[136] The *CNL* also urged that teaching be made a more attractive profession.[137] In 1947, however, it noted that the first report of the Central Advisory Council for England (set up by the Education Act) had found 'unresolved perplexities' and 'bewilderment' about the purposes of education, as well as widespread 'moral confusion' caused by relativism and the rise of scientific worldviews.[138] But a follow-up article in 1948 expressed a 'sober hope' that the place of religious education could be improved.[139]

Amid post-war social reconstruction, the group's focus on university reform continued. Introducing a *CNL* essay in February 1946, Bliss called on universities to develop a 'synthesis' of 'the old classical-Christian tradition' and science.[140] The anonymous essay itself was a version of Moberly's Moot paper from six years earlier.[141] Since the Butler Act had (in theory) created a more equal school system, the focus was now on the universities. They were considered in light of Bruce Truscot's recent, influential books comparing Oxford and Cambridge – 'Oxbridge' – with modern 'redbrick' universities.[142] Training an 'elite', Moberly argued, was one of the universities' 'essential tasks', an ideal that Oxbridge embodied.[143] Redbrick universities, which lacked a tutorial system and were plagued by 'uninspiring' environments, had fallen 'woefully short' on this, but they had in their favour a proximity to 'the realities of a vigorous provincial and

industrial life' and a less narrow, privileged student body.[144] All universities had to address 'fundamental questions' and inculcate a 'philosophy
of life', neither privileging nor ignoring Christianity.[145] In October 1946,
Bliss – commenting on a series of short SCM books, several authored by
group members – argued that the universities had to unify various forms
of knowledge.[146] In 1948, she admitted that few students were interested
in seeing the universities in Christian terms.[147] The universities appeared,
Daniel Jenkins concluded more grimly, to be 'failing disastrously' as 'cultural centres in our civilisation'.[148] Moberly's *The Crisis in the University*
(1949), which grew out of discussions in the CFC and SCM, also stressed
the universities' inability to stand for 'civilised values'.[149] They failed to ask
key questions, maintained a false 'neutrality', imparted fragmented knowledge, left materialist presuppositions unquestioned and neglected spiritual
issues. Knowledge had to be reintegrated, guided by 'universal', 'western'
and 'British' values, each with a Christian 'ingredient'.[150] Moberly, as chair
of the University Grants Committee, also supported Master of Balliol A. D.
Lindsay's experimental University College of North Staffordshire, founded
in 1949 (now Keele University), which aimed to combine education for
citizenship, technical knowledge, humanistic values and Christian inspiration.[151] In one of the last issues of the *CNL*, Bliss admitted that turning
modern universities into Oxbridge 'replicas' was impossible, but she
emphasised that underneath their 'privilege' there was 'something perhaps
indispensable' to 'the true university'.[152]

The repeated stress within the Oldham group on the value of elitist educational models derived from a consistent concern – shared widely among
the group's participants – that the pursuit of class *equality* might cause
educational *quality* to suffer. Eliot was particularly adamant on this point.
He admitted that the erosion of religious influence meant the State had
a role to play in 'the education of the people'. Values and standards had
declined – the British, he complained, 'do not even know what to eat and
drink: their minds are too lazy' – and there was a need to re-educate 'the political classes'.[153] Eliot also agreed that education had an integrative function
in the face of growing cultural fragmentation, even praising the secular
educational movement of 'humanism' (represented in the USA by Irving
Babbitt and in the UK by F. R. Leavis) for recognising this problem. But he
insisted Christianity *alone* offered a true alternative to totalitarian education, even if he warned against Church and State becoming intertwined
through 'centralisation and standardisation'.[154] In the *CNL*, Eliot linked
freedom of thought to the educational problem of providing 'people who
can think freely – and wisely'.[155] He saw most people, however, as unable
to think either 'freely' or 'wisely', expressing a broader concern about the
dangers of 'mass' cultural uniformity.[156] 'I hope', Eliot wrote while guest

editor of the *CNL* in the summer of 1942, 'that we shall not consciously or unconsciously drift towards the view that it is better for everybody to have a second-rate education, than for only a small minority to have the best'.[157] Eliot dissented from the churches' democratising ambitions and defended the class system as an element in transmitting traditional culture.[158] In *Notes towards the Definition of Culture* (1948) he argued that 'the headlong rush to educate everybody' was 'lowering our standards' and hindering the transmission of 'the essentials of our culture': 'destroying our ancient edifices to make ready the ground upon which the barbarian nomads of the future will encamp in their mechanised caravans'.[159] Families were crucial 'transmitters of culture', and to preserve different 'levels' of culture 'there must be groups of families persisting, from generation to generation, each in the same way of life'.[160] Classes defined those 'ways of life', and – so Eliot's argument went – had to be maintained to preserve cultural diversity. Compared to the group's consensus, Eliot was more committed to elite hierarchies, more accepting of class disparities and less willing to adapt education to modern society.[161] Still, he shared the group's main consensus that an educational, intellectual and political elite, while necessary, should not be synonymous with an economic elite, even if later in the post-war period he may have become more comfortable with the idea of 'cultural leadership' being exercised by a 'traditional governing class'.[162]

Conclusion

The Oldham group's consensus saw economic equality as a goal of (indeed, as a prerequisite for) a more Christian society. Stress was placed on creating equal chances rather than outcomes; however, given Britain's class system, it was agreed that a substantial redistribution of resources was needed to realise the principles of equality of opportunity and meritocratic advancement. The aim of 'social justice', again, helped overcome anxieties about State power. Still, elitism continued to influence the group's thinking out of a fear that – in a 'mass' society – a cultural levelling *down* had to be avoided. The group's elitist assumptions, doubts about 'mass' society and strategy of 'revolution from above' led it to focus on a 'small creative minority', as Hodges put it, or 'the few' who, Oldham thought, would lead a Christian social revival.[163] The group thus carried on an intense, if unresolved, discussion about the role an elite, a 'clerisy' or a 'Community of Christians' would play in a Christian society, and they considered how traditional elements of elite education could be maintained while no longer being monopolised by the wealthy.

Here was another kind of 'middle way': rather than seeing democratic and 'aristocratic' principles as opposed, the group sought to fuse them. Oldham believed 'democratic' elements were essential to a Christian society, namely, the possibility of human 'meeting', the settling of differences through discussion and the broad distribution of political power. But he insisted that they must be 'combined with the aristocratic principle of listening to the counsel of the wisest'.[164] Eliot similarly argued that 'aristocracy' and 'democracy'·were not antithetical: 'in the long run', they were 'even necessary to each other'.[165] Mannheim sought an elite that was meritocratic in its selection, technocratic in its tasks and democratic in its subservience to parliamentary sovereignty. He, like the group generally, urged democratising rather than abolishing ideals such as 'aristocracy' or 'the gentleman': 'gentlemanly' ideals, he thought, could be adapted to a new situation. Clarke – who argued that 'the only security for democracy was that it should form its own aristocracy' – agreed that British ideals of the gentleman could preserve 'excellence' in a mass society threatened by pursuit of a mythical, absolute equality.[166] Clarke's *Freedom in the Educative Society* (1948) was based on Mannheim's idea that education had to create an elite to 'leaven' a planned society.[167] In the *CNL*, Oldham praised F. C. Happold's *Towards a New Aristocracy* (1943), which recounted his experiences as headmaster of Wordsworth's School in Salisbury, and endorsed his conclusion that 'No democracy can exist unless it has within itself an aristocracy sufficiently powerful and informed to direct general opinion'.[168] Moot guest participant Philip Mairet had earlier published *Aristocracy and the Meaning of Class Rule* (1931), arguing for an intellectual elite – not defined by wealth – to counter liberal failings. The *CNL* opposed allowing wealthy students simply to 'buy their way in' to public schools: 'If 75 per cent of the population at a public school are there by virtue of wealth, the tone of these schools is bound to be set by the 75 per cent'.[169] Still, education had to create an elite capable of administering a complex, and more egalitarian, modern society.

British political tides were broadly flowing towards more egalitarianism in the late 1930s and 1940s. The argument for creating a new society in which 'economic reconstruction' would stress 'equitable distribution' even reached the reliably conservative editorial page of *The Times*: 'The new order', it observed in July 1940, 'cannot be based on the preservation of privilege, whether the privilege be that of a country, of a class, or of an individual'.[170] At the end of that year, the Oxford Conference's call for abolishing inequalities was reiterated in *The Times* by Anglican, Roman Catholic and free church leaders endorsing and extending the pope's 'Peace Points'.[171] There was a trend towards ideals of 'developmental democracy', in which the State was seen to have a legitimate (if still limited) role in ensuring equal access to education in order to enable people to contribute to community life.[172] The war brought forth several educational reform plans built on a 'radically progressive' consensus.[173] Here, too, equalitarian aims joined elitist assumptions. The aim of a 'technocratic cadre of expert planners' was common in social thought.[174] The self-image of senior civil servants and experts as 'Platonic guardians' enabling and protecting 'civilisation' was part of the 'liberal elitism' that shaped the wider mind-set in Europe's post-war 'constrained democracies'.[175]

Some Oldham group participants went further in their fears of an undifferentiated social mass. In his influential book *Beyond Politics* (1939), Christopher Dawson had argued for an organisation, like a 'party', to shape cultural development, suggesting it would be formed, as a *Guardian* review summarised, from 'a purified aristocracy, not of birth but of training', and recruited largely from the public schools.[176] Dawson feared that democracy too readily accepted a 'lowering down of standards to a level which is acceptable to everybody'; moreover, he argued it would not be enough to 'equalize' the 'machine order', since that would only mean 'equality in slavery'. A more fundamental re-ordering of society was necessary.[177] But this would not necessarily be more 'democratic': the 'English' tradition, he insisted, was less democratic than constitutionalist and parliamentarian and was, moreover, 'aristocratic and individualist'. 'Modern democracy', he argued, was born in the French Revolution, which had become 'definitely totalitarian'.[178] As I have shown, a sense that egalitarianism was moving towards an undifferentiated 'mass' was widespread. The *CNL* commented on the 'decline of the middle classes' with reference to a series of articles in the *Economist*, agreeing with its complaint that the middle classes were threatened by a radical 'egalitarianism which dislikes any kind of social difference'.[179]

In this wider discussion marked by competing impulses towards egalitarianism and elitism, the Oldham group participated in a discussion about the relationship of education to a 'new order', with the passage of the Education Act of 1944 playing a central role. (In mid 1946, Bliss noted that 'Two years ago no sphere of the national life was more constantly under discussion than that of education.'[180]) The Oldham group was not alone in arguing that a Christian-influenced educational philosophy was needed. *The Times* and several MPs responded positively to Church insistence that secularisation had to be countered via Christian influence in education, helping to shape the religious clauses of the Education Act.[181] Christian educationalists established a strong position in the 1930s and 1940s, arguing for using faith to reshape educational priorities: the tradition of creating 'Christian gentlemen' pioneered by Thomas Arnold was reborn in a new form.[182] Board of Education officials saw State education as a tool for reshaping mass society, a view reinforced by the emphasis on Britain's Christian identity and traditions during the war. This stance was by no means confined to Conservatives: in 1947, Labour's minister of education, George Tomlinson, allowed the *CNL* to reprint a radio broadcast in which he emphasised Christianity's role in the education of youth.[183]

Some prominent voices (such as the literary critic F. R. Leavis) called for universities to remain detached from social change to preserve tradition; others (such as the Marxist scientist J. D. Bernal) thought they should engage with society to steer it.[184] An emphasis on education for 'citizenship' – stressing 'character' and active political participation – grew in reaction to the experience with Nazism.[185] In many such visions, science and the humanities would be complementary: the former was utilitarian; the latter oriented people in society.[186] Like the psychiatrist and philosopher Karl Jaspers, who was featured in the *CNL*, the group saw here a bulwark against social atomisation and nihilism.[187] Education would guide a transition away from the false individualism of the mass to a true freedom of 'persons' in community. Education had to be decoupled from class inequalities, even if traditional *forms* of Britain's elite education (in the public schools and at Oxford and Cambridge) would be preserved to enable a new elite to apply Christian insights to modern life.

In this context, the cultural 'neutrality' of the universities was still seen as a problem, as was noted in post-war SCM pamphlets on university education written by Oldham group members. Hodges claimed it had been 'among the causes which helped to bring about the evil we deplore.'[188] (He had earlier condemned the replacement of the ethos of the Renaissance with a 'utilitarian' education 'infected by the prevailing ethic of success.'[189]) Baillie complained that 'never in any culture has intellectual life so much lacked a sense of direction as in the Western world during the last several generations': western universities had declined into 'a condition of complacent disinterestedness.'[190] The idea that education should (but had failed to) impart a coherent moral framework for western civilisation was widespread.[191] However, the *CNL* argued for pluralist and 'free' universities, insisting that Christianity should not be imposed on students. In this sense, Christians had to press for 'neutral' or even 'non-Christian' universities, Oldham stated.[192] Bliss insisted the faith had to 'vindicate itself in free and open debate.'[193] (Pointing to Christians' own history of 'intolerance and persecution', conservative historian Herbert Butterfield argued in the *CNL* in 1949 that the churches should be 'thankful that, if society is not Christian, it is at any rate not yet wholeheartedly anything else.'[194]) A *Theology* editorial, however, was careful to distinguish Moberly's call in *The Crisis in the University* for 'free' and 'open' universities from 'the neutrality or indifference about the fundamental human problems with which it has been confused.'[195]

The Oldham group's elitist tendencies were distinct from the social critiques of William Temple, A. D. Lindsay, or George Bell, which derived from a Christian socialist tradition. Indeed, the group has been seen as 'unapologetically elitist' and Oldham's 'elitist conception of "the living Church"' has attracted criticism.[196] On the other hand, as I have shown, this elitism co-existed with a commitment – shared by most group participants – to an egalitarian reshaping of British society. Matthew Grimley has helpfully described the group's elitism as 'constructive.' Unlike the period's merely aesthetic or artistic elitism (which was also mostly secular), the Oldham group had an alternative social order in mind that would maintain Christian – indeed, even broadly 'humanist' – standards in a mass society.[197] Nearly all of the core members of the group had studied at Oxford or Cambridge, and many had had public school educations: they aimed to open such paths to a wider number of intelligent young people. And for all the group's critiques of 'mass' society, precisely those members who most urged a cultural elite also celebrated elements of popular culture. Mannheim took an optimistic view of 'popularisation', arguing it should be possible to find 'new forms for the dissemination of the substance of culture without diluting it', citing both jazz and the works of Noël Coward.[198] Eliot, who railed against the levelling effects of mass culture, also stressed the value of 'authentic' forms of popular culture; moreover, he did not reject mass culture as such, even appreciating some of its products.[199] He saw forms of 'independent lower-class culture' (such as music hall) as allied with aristocratic 'high-art' against shallow, commercialised and middle-class culture. One key aspect in its favour, for Eliot, was the strongly ritualised and participatory element in traditional lower-class culture, which generated 'communal solidarity' and distinguished it from the more 'passive' culture of the middle class.[200] In various ways, then, the 'middle way' taken by the Oldham group between egalitarianism and elitism reflected a central British social debate in the years around the Second World War and shaped the form taken by post-war reconstruction.

Notes

1 *Churches Survey Their Task*, pp. 60, 87–129.
2 *Ibid.*, pp. 60, 104–9.
3 *Ibid.*, pp. 105–6.
4 *Ibid.*, pp. 111, 116–17.
5 *Moot Papers*, M20, p. 667.
6 *Ibid.*, M11, pp. 385–6.
7 *Ibid.*, M14, p. 506.

8　*Ibid.*, M17, p. 587; M20, p. 696.

9　E.g. *ibid.*, M4, p. 194; M10, p. 354; M11, p. 387; M14, p. 506; M16, p. 563; M20, p. 696.

10　*Ibid.*, M9, pp. 320–2.

11　*Ibid.*, M8, pp. 306–7.

12　*Ibid.*, M11, p. 387.

13　*Ibid.*, M16, p. 568.

14　IOE MOO/25, Adolf Löwe, 'Social Transformation and the War', n.d. [discussed April 1940].

15　*Moot Papers*, M13, p. 473.

16　*Ibid.*, M18, p. 644.

17　*Ibid.*, M3, p. 164; M17, p. 587.

18　*Ibid.*, M2, p. 116; M7, p. 287; M20, p. 687.

19　*CNL* 245S, 17 October 1945, anon., 'The Conversion of England', p. 10.

20　*Moot Papers*, M17, pp. 577–8, 595.

21　*Churches Survey Their Task*, p. 103.

22　Grimley, 'Civil Society and the Clerisy', p. 236.

23　LeMahieu, *Culture for Democracy*, pp. 107–9.

24　Walter Moberly, 'The Shadow of Insecurity', *Listener*, 9 May 1940, 933–4 (p. 933).

25　*CNL* 86S, 18 June 1941, J. H. Oldham, 'The Predicament of Society and the Way Out', p. 2.

26　LPL Lang 25, fos. 315–25, John Middleton Murry, 'Towards a Christian Theory of Society', p. 7.

27　Murry, *Price of Leadership*, pp. 45, 46, 49, 51, 78–9.

28　*Ibid.*, pp. 26, 42–3.

29　Murry, 'Ends and Means', p. 1015; *CNL* 31L, 29 May 1940, p. 3.

30　Murry, *Adam and Eve*, p. 48.

31　Kojecky, *T. S. Eliot's Social Criticism*, pp. 47, 53.

32　*Ibid.*, p. 91.

33　Eliot, *Idea of a Christian Society*, p. 21. OA 14/6/10, 'Notes by T. S. Eliot on the Place and Function of the Clerisy', 10 November 1944.

34　Eliot assumed readers were familiar with Murry's idea of the clerisy: Eliot, *Idea of a Christian Society*, p. 74.

35　John Heeren, 'Karl Mannheim and the Intellectual Elite', *British Journal of Sociology*, 22:1 (1971), 1–15; Iris Mendel, 'Mannheim's Free-Floating Intelligentsia: The Role of Closeness and Distance in the Analysis of Society', *Studies in Social and Political Thought*, 12 (2006), 30–52.

36　Mannheim, *Man and Society*, p. 75.

37　IOE MOO/32, Karl Mannheim, 'Topics for the Next Meeting of the Moot', n.d. [*c.* December 1940]; Loader, *Intellectual Development*, p. 239 n. 21.

38　Mannheim, *Man and Society*, pp. 93–5, 99, 100, 102, 104, 105.

39　IOE MOO/11, 'Sociology of Education, Preliminary Remarks by Karl Mannheim', n.d. [September 1939], p. 6.

40　Mannheim, *Man and Society*, p. 106.

41　*Moot Papers*, M14, p. 514.

42 LPL Lang 26, fos. 194–203, 'The Spiritual Front', n.d. [June 1940], pp. 6, 7.

43 *CNL* 253S, 6 February 1946, 'The Future of Our Universities', pp. 1, 5.

44 Eliot, *Idea of a Christian Society*, pp. 35, 37, 42.

45 OA 14/6/10, 'Notes by T. S. Eliot on the Place and Function of the Clerisy', 10 November 1944, p. 2. 'If you are going to refuse Coward the title of cleric you will have to draw a line somewhere and you will not find it easy to draw.' *Ibid.*, p. 4.

46 *Ibid.*, pp. 1, 3. Emphasis in original.

47 *Ibid.*, p. 3.

48 Grimley, 'Civil Society and the Clerisy', p. 243.

49 Murry, *Price of Leadership*, p. 87.

50 Murry, 'Ends and Means', p. 1015.

51 Mannheim, 'Planning for Freedom', p. 10.

52 Mannheim, *Man and Society*, pp. 113–14.

53 Loader, *Intellectual Development*, p. 152.

54 Mannheim, 'Planning for Freedom', p. 12.

55 Mannheim, *Diagnosis*, p. 71.

56 Eliot, *Idea of a Christian Society*, p. 42.

57 *Ibid.*, pp. 77, 88.

58 Kojecky, *T. S. Eliot's Social Criticism*, p. 221.

59 OA 9/6/99, 'Letter from Michael Polanyi', 18 November 1944, p. 1.

60 OA 9/6/101, 'Letter from Karl Mannheim', 20 November 1944, p. 1.

61 Murry, *Price of Leadership*, p. 114.

62 *Ibid.*, pp. 139–40.

63 Murry, 'Ends and Means', p. 1015.

64 Mannheim, 'Planning for Freedom', p. 12.

65 *Ibid.*

66 *Ibid.*

67 *Moot Papers*, M8, p. 295.

68 Mannheim, *Man and Society*, pp. 359–66; *Moot Papers*, M10, p. 362.

69 Mannheim, *Diagnosis*, p. 119.

70 *Moot Papers*, M2, pp. 89–90.

71 Eliot, *Idea of a Christian Society*, p. 6.

72 *Ibid.*, p. 48.

73 Murry, 'Towards a Christian Theory of Society', p. 9.

74 *Moot Papers*, M2, pp. 86, 89, 90.

75 Murry, 'Ends and Means', p. 1015.

76 Mannheim, *Man and Society*, p. 339.

77 *Ibid.*, pp. 330, 340, 344–66.

78 Loader, *Intellectual Development*, pp. 173–4, 176.

79 *CNL* 13L, 24 January 1940, p. 3.

80 Fred Clarke, 'The Crisis in Education', and J. H. Oldham, 'Some Concluding Reflections', in *Church, Community, and State in Relation to Education* (London: George Allen & Unwin, 1938), pp. 3–26, 213–34; Dennis Bates, 'Ecumenism and Religious Education between the Wars: The Work of J. H. Oldham', *British Journal of Religious Education* 8:3 (1986), 130–9.

81 Clarke, 'Crisis in Education', p. 4.

82 *Churches Survey Their Task*, pp. 138–42.

83 *Ibid.*, pp. 130–66.

84 Clements, *Faith on the Frontier*, p. 414. William Taylor, 'Education and the Moot', in Richard Aldrich (ed.), *In History and in Education: Essays Presented to Peter Gordon* (London: Woburn, 1996), pp. 159–86 (p. 166).

85 *CNL* 213S, 26 July 1944, Ernest Barker, 'The Education of All Adults'; *CNL* 226L, 24 January 1945, pp. 1–3.

86 LPL Lang 26, fos. 223–5, J. H. Oldham, 'An Initiative of the Churches towards a More Christian Society', rev., 8 July 1940, p. 1. Emphasis in original.

87 LPL Lang 26, fos. 173–4, Oldham to Lang, 4 April 1940.

88 Parker, 'Reinvigorating Christian Britain', pp. 73–9.

89 IOE MOO/55, Fred Clarke, 'Some Notes on Religious Education', April 1941, p. 1.

90 *Moot Papers*, M4, p. 199.

91 OA 14/2/12, H. A. Hodges, 'Comments on Middleton Murry's Paper', n.d. [discussed September 1938], p. 3.

92 IOE MOO/58, T. S. Eliot, 'Paper on Religious Education' [1941], p. 1.

93 Bates, 'Ecumenism and Religious Education', 134–6.

94 IOE MOO/121, Moberly, '"Religious Education in our National Schools": Notes by Sir Walter Moberly', n.d. [probably late 1941].

95 *CNL* 200S, 26 January 1944, Marjorie Reeves, 'Religious Education', pp. 1, 4–5.

96 Murry, *Price of Leadership*, p. 58.

97 *Ibid.*, pp. 17, 58–9.

98 *Ibid.*, pp. 21.

99 See *Moot Papers*, M6, pp. 245–7.

100 IOE MOO/7, Fred Clarke, 'Notes on English Educational Institutions in the Light of the Necessities of Planning for Freedom in the Coming Collectivised Regime', 21 August 1939, pp. 1–2, 3–4, 6, 21.

101 *Ibid.*, p. 25.

102 *Ibid.*, p. 19.

103 *Ibid.*, p. 25.

104 Joan Simon, 'The Shaping of the Spens Report on Secondary Education 1933–38: An Inside View', *British Journal of Educational Studies*, 25:1 (1977), 63–80 and 25:2 (1977): 170–85.

105 Fred Clarke, *Education and Social Change: An English Interpretation* (London: Sheldon Press, 1940), pp. 30, 44.

106 *Ibid.*, p. 45. Emphasis in original.

107 *Ibid.*, pp. 56–57, 61, 63. *Moot Papers*, M18, p. 644; M13, p. 473. He later reconsidered the Act's 'cultural–vocational distinction', seeing unified, 'multi-lateral' schools as more democratic; Brian Simon, *Education and the Social Order, 1940–1990* (London: Lawrence and Wishart, 1991), p. 49.

108 IOE MOO/10, Mannheim, 'Some Remarks upon F. Clarke's Paper "English Educational Institutions"', n.d. [September 1939], p. 1.

109 IOE MOO/13, Vickers, 'Education, War, Change', n.d., p. 1.

110 *Ibid.*, p. 4.

111 *Ibid.*, p. 5. *CNL* 14S, 31 January 1940, [Geoffrey Vickers], 'Educating for a Free Society', p. 6. Vickers's supplement was 'widely discussed' and influenced efforts towards reform by the Board of Education early in the war: McKibbin, *Classes and Cultures*, p. 221.

112 *CNL* 253S, 6 February 1946, 'The Future of Our Universities'.

113 IOE MOO/18, Adolf Löwe, 'Some Notes on University Education', n.d. [discussed February 1940] (hereafter 'Some Notes'); MOO/16, Walter Moberly, 'The Universities', n.d. [discussed February 1940] (hereafter 'The Universities').

114 Löwe, 'Some Notes', p. 2.

115 Moberly, 'The Universities', pp. 9–10; Löwe, 'Some Notes', pp. 2–3, 4.

116 Moberly, 'The Universities', pp. 8–10, 14; Löwe, 'Some Notes', pp. 6–8.

117 Moberly, 'The Universities', pp. 12, 14.

118 *Ibid.*, p. 13.

119 Löwe, 'Some Notes', pp. 8, 10, 16.

120 Moberly, 'The Universities', p. 18.

121 Löwe, 'Some Notes', pp. 18–19; Moberly, 'The Universities', pp. 18–19.

122 *Moot Papers*, M7, pp. 256–61, esp. pp. 256, 257.

123 Löwe, 'Some Notes', pp. 23–4. *Moot Papers*, 258–9. Moberly, 'The Universities', p. 22. Moberly's idea fed into a CCFCL memorandum: LPL Lang 26, fos. 194–203, 'The Spiritual Front', n.d. [circulated June 1940], pp. 7–8.

124 Mannheim, 'Planning for Freedom', pp. 13–16.

125 Mannheim, *Man and Society*, p. 278.

126 IOE MOO/73, Mannheim, 'The Diagnosis of Our Time (Syllabus)', n.d. [*c.* January 1942], p. 2.

127 IOE MOO/81, H. C. Dent, 'Reform in Education', 16 May 1942, pp. 1–4. Frank W. Mitchell, *Sir Fred Clarke: Master-Teacher, 1880–1952* (London: Longmans, 1967), pp. 111–12.

128 LPL Lang 26, fo. 182, memo by Lang, n.d.; fo. 186, Lang to Butler, 6 June 1940; fo. 187, Butler to Lang, 7 June 1940; fos. 190–3, Oldham to Lang, 29 June 1940.

129 Harris, 'Enterprise and Welfare States', pp. 191–2.

130 Mitchell, *Sir Fred Clarke*, pp. 112–16. David Crook, 'Universities, Teacher Training, and the Legacy of McNair, 1944–94', *History of Education*, 24:3 (1995), 231–45; Gary McCulloch, 'The Standing Conference on Studies in Education: Sixty Years On', *British Journal of Educational Studies*, 60:4 (2012), 301–16; Gary McCulloch, 'Fred Clarke and the Internationalisation of Studies and Research in Education', *Paedagogica historica*, 50:1–2 (2014), 123–37.

131 Hsiao-Yuh Ku, 'Education for Liberal Democracy: Fred Clarke and the 1944 Education Act', *History of Education*, 42:5 (2013), 578–97. Clarke, however, criticised the tripartite system set up by the Act, believed selection should take place at thirteen rather than eleven years of age and insisted the public schools be integrated into the national educational system rather than maintaining their traditional privileges.

132 *CNL* 182L, 19 May 1943, pp. 4–5.

133 *CNL* 193L, 20 October 1943, pp. 1–2.

134 *CNL* 195L, 17 November 1943, p. 3.

135 Ku, 'Education for Liberal Democracy', p. 582.

136 *CNL* 215S, 23 August 1944, Michael Clarke, 'Education and the Social Order', pp. 5–8.

137 *CNL* 221S, 15 November 1944, Kathleen Bliss, 'Teach? Not Likely!'.

138 *CNL* 291L, 6 August 1947, pp. 2, 4.

139 *CNL* 326L, 8 December 1948.

140 *CNL* 253L, 6 February 1946, pp. 2–3.

141 Moberly, 'The Universities'.

142 'Bruce Truscot' was the pseudonym of Edgar Allison Peers, professor of Spanish studies at the University of Liverpool. His books *Redbrick University* (1943), *Redbrick and These Vital Days* (1945) and *First Year at the University* (1946) popularised the terms 'redbrick' (which he coined) and 'Oxbridge' (which he did not).

143 *CNL* 253S, 6 February 1946, 'The Future of Our Universities', pp. 1, 5.

144 *Ibid.*, pp. 7–9.

145 *Ibid.*, p. 16.

146 *CNL* 272L, 30 October 1946, p. 2.

147 *CNL* 303L, 21 January 1948, pp. 3–4.

148 *CNL* 319L, 1 September 1948, p. 6.

149 Walter Moberly, *The Crisis in the University* (London: SCM, 1949), pp. 22–3.

150 *Ibid.*, pp. 106–47. See *CNL* 339L, 8 June 1949, pp. 179–83; and *CNL* 339S, 8 June 1949, Michael Foster, 'Notes on Some Implications of University Reform'.

151 Grimley, 'Civil Society and the Clerisy', p. 245.

152 *CNL* 339L, 8 June 1949, p. 180.

153 IOE MOO/123, Eliot, 'Notes on Social Philosophy', n.d. [*c*. July 1940], p. 1.

154 T. S. Eliot, 'The Christian Conception of Education', in *Malvern, 1941*, pp. 201–13.

155 *CNL* 43L, 21 August 1940, p. 1.

156 Kojecky, *T. S. Eliot's Social Criticism*, pp. 198–9.

157 *CNL* 141L, 8 July 1942, p. 3.

158 Kojecky, *T. S. Eliot's Social Criticism*, p. 207.

159 Eliot, *Notes towards the Definition of Culture*, p. 108.

160 *Ibid.*, p. 48. See also Kojecky, *T. S. Eliot's Social Criticism*, pp. 210, 216.

161 IOE MOO/58, Eliot, 'Paper on Religious Education' [1941], p. 1.

162 Kojecky, *T. S. Eliot's Social Criticism*, pp. 194–6, 200–1. Collini, *Absent Minds*, p. 316.

163 *CNL* 183S, 2 June 1943, H. A. Hodges, 'The Problem of Archetypes', p. 1; LPL Lang 26, fos. 194–203, 'The Spiritual Front', n.d. [*c*. June 1940], p. 6.

164 *Moot Papers*, M14, p. 515.

165 Letter from T. S. Eliot, *Christendom*, 13:55 (September 1944), 216. Eliot shared the views of Ford Madox Ford and T. E. Hulme 'that an aristocratic elite was necessary to ensure progress or a moral order, as well as to prevent a Hobbesian war of all against all'; McVey, 'Backgrounds', p. 181.

166 IOE MOO/11, Mannheim, 'Sociology of Education', n.d.; *Moot Papers*, M14, pp. 510, 514. Hodges thought the gentlemanly ideal ignored the reality of class struggle: *Moot Papers*, M16, p. 547.

167 Fred Clarke, *Freedom in the Educative Society* (London: University of London Press, 1948), pp. 48, 50.

168 *CNL* 210L, 14 June 1944, pp. 2–3.

169 *CNL* 218L, 4 October 1944, p. 4.

170 *The Times*, 1 July 1940, p. 5. See *Moot Papers*, M9, p. 321.

171 *The Times*, 21 December 1940, p. 5.

172 C. B. Macpherson, *The Life and Times of Liberal Democracy* (Oxford: Oxford University Press, 1977); Hsiao-Yuh Ku, 'Fred Clarke's Ideals of Liberal Democracy: State and Community in Education', *British Journal of Educational Studies*, 61:4 (2013), 401–15.

173 Simon, *Education and the Social Order*, pp. 34–8.

174 Grimley, 'Civil Society and the Clerisy', p. 233.

175 Ian Loader, 'Fall of the "Platonic Guardians": Liberalism, Criminology and Political Responses to Crime in England and Wales', *British Journal of Criminology*, 46 (2006), 561–86; Müller, *Contesting Democracy*, pp. 5–6, 128–9. See also Julia Stapleton, 'Political Thought, Elites and the State in Modern Britain', *Historical Journal*, 42 (1999), 251–68.

176 *Guardian*, 17 March 1939, p. 166.

177 IOE MOO/88, Christopher Dawson, 'Freedom and Vocation', n.d. [1941], p. 5.

178 *CNL* 107L, 12 November 1941, pp. 1–2.

179 *CNL* 309L, 14 April 1948, p. 2.

180 *CNL* 267L, 21 August 1946, p. 1.

181 Peter Gosden, 'Putting the Act Together', *History of Education*, 24:3 (1995), 195–207 (p. 202).

182 Freathy, 'Triumph', p. 297. Myers, 'National Identity'.

183 Myers, 'National Identity', pp. 324–5; *CNL* 300S, 10 December 1947, George Tomlinson, 'Freely Ye Have Received, Freely Give'.

184 Loader, *Intellectual Development*, pp. 163–4.

185 Derek Heater, 'The History of Citizenship Education in England', *Curriculum Journal*, 12:1 (2001), 103–23 (p. 106); Freathy, 'Triumph'.

186 Loader, *Intellectual Development*, 164–5.

187 *CNL* 247S, 14 November 1945, Karl Jaspers, 'The Renewal of the University'.

188 H. A. Hodges, *Objectivity and Impartiality* (London: SCM, 1946), 10–11; Vidler, *Free University*.

189 LPL Lang 26, fos. 65–74, H. A. Hodges, 'Towards a Plan for a New *Summa*', n.d. [discussed January 1939], pp. 9–10; IOE MOO/63a, Hodges, 'Christian Thinking Today' [July 1941], p. 2.

190 Baillie, *Modern University*, p. 19.

191 Walter Lippmann, 'Man in Modern Education', in *Democracy, Should It Survive?* (London: Dennis Dobson, 1946), pp. 62–9; *Theology*, 50:322 (April 1947): 153–4.

192 *CNL* 274L, 27 November 1946, p. 7.

193 *CNL* 291L, 6 August 1947, p. 6.

194 *CNL* 333S, Herbert Butterfield, 'The Christian and History: I. The Christian and Academic History', p. 91.

195 *Theology*, 52:347 (May 1949), 160–2.

196 Kurlberg, 'Resisting Totalitarianism', p. 527; Hastings, *Oliver Tomkins*, p. 33.

197 Grimley, 'Civil Society and the Clerisy', p. 233.

198 *CNL* 227S, 24 January 1945, Karl Mannheim, 'The Meaning of Popularisation in a Mass Society', p. 8. Jazz and Noël Coward, Mannheim argued, showed 'genuineness may exist on lower as well as on higher levels'; *ibid.*, pp. 8–9.

199 Morgan and Evans, *Battle for Britain*, pp. 88–91. Jeroen Vanheste, *Guardians of the Humanist Legacy: The Classicism of T. S. Eliot's Criterion Network and Its Relevance to Our Postmodern World* (Leiden: Brill, 2007), pp. 226–30.

200 David Chinitz, 'T. S. Eliot and the Cultural Divide', *PMLA*, 110:2 (1995), 236–47, esp. pp. 238–40.

8

Conclusion

After the Second World War, John Baillie, in *What Is Christian Civilisation?* (1945), expressed a key conviction of the Oldham group. As a review of the book noted, Baillie saw the problems of the age as rooted in the 'disturbance of the traditional intellectual outlook' and the 'simultaneous disturbance of the traditional social life of the community'.[1] There were many urgent efforts, like Baillie's, to rethink Christianity amid the 'disturbances' of the 1930s and 1940s: the crisis of liberalism, the rise of totalitarianism, the growth in State power, a destructive war and the many problems of post-war rebuilding. The world was setting a new agenda, and many Christians responded not only as citizens but also as members of a faith community who believed they possessed unique, 'spiritual' resources to heal a damaged culture. 'The crucial question which has engaged my thoughts', Oldham wrote privately in May 1941, 'has been the question of what Christianity means, and can mean, in the modern world'.[2]

The Oldham group's discussions revolved around views of human nature and the purposes of social life. The core argument was that people had to be enabled (and encouraged) to live as free, responsible beings in service to God and their neighbours, and in awareness of their dependence on God, other people and nature. These simple-sounding principles led to a complex, ambivalent interaction with social realities and with predominant political and philosophical worldviews. The group's aims required rebuilding genuine forms of 'community' so as to counteract what group members saw as a long-term secularisation marked by 'materialism' and belief in human 'self-sufficiency'. The group aimed to defend freedom against both liberalism's 'disintegrative' tendencies and totalitarian oppression. Oldham, citing Niebuhr, believed that democracy expressed 'the nature of man as a spiritual, free and social being'.[3] But one had to maintain the possibility of 'personal moral decision' in ever more bureaucratic and industrialised contexts and seek, as G. D. H. Cole put it in the *CNL*, 'democratic ways of living for little men in big societies'.[4] But neither the State nor industry as such was rejected: despite a few key dissenters, the group adopted a vision of 'planning' combined with large regions of free and 'spontaneous' social interaction.

No detailed blueprint of a Christian society emerged, but a group consensus was defined by various 'middle ways' that steered a course amid the age's extremes.

- Group members rejected a secularised 'liberal' theology that reduced faith to ethics and sought the Kingdom on earth as well as a 'continental' Protestantism that drew a radical distinction between human and divine categories. While some Catholic perspectives were influential, political Catholicism was generally seen as too medievalist and authoritarian. 'Middle axioms' were defined so as to connect absolute religious principles to an ambiguous and increasingly complex social life.
- Oldham's idea of a 'frontier' between faith and secularity represented both a meeting place and a boundary. It encouraged Christians to influence society in accordance with their beliefs while accepting the 'autonomy of the secular' and working with open-minded secularists. But it was insisted that in this process Christians had to stress the distinctive wisdom and power inherent in their faith.
- Mannheim's notion of 'planning for freedom' offered a path between a fragmented *laissez-faire* capitalism and an oppressive holism, such as collectivist Marxism. Christianity would provide values to guide the planners and 'spiritual' resources for social transformation.
- 'British' or 'English' traditions were seen as vital, and the group encouraged a 'Christian patriotism' characterised by self-criticism, humility and service to other nations. This would, it was argued, avoid either the aggressive 'nationalism' apparent in Fascism and National Socialism or the allegedly rootless, shallow 'internationalism' of the political left.
- Condemning both 'atomistic' liberal individualism and statist collectivism, the group praised a *personalist* freedom that was densely embedded in community. While critical of 'mass' democracy, it valued civil rights and parliamentary government, clearly rejecting the option of a 'Christian totalitarianism'.
- The group sought a more egalitarian society while holding elitist assumptions. It saw a Christian elite, possibly an educative 'clerisy', as part of a new society. It also stressed broadening access to education while maintaining many structures of the existing hierarchical system.

Some of these aims matched broader tendencies in British political discussion, but within the Oldham group they were distinctively combined and underlain by Christian principles. While the group was influenced by Anglican and free church traditions, elements of neo-Thomism, forms of personalism and sociological theories, its overall position cannot be described under any single political programme or intellectual or religious tradition. The rhetoric of 'revolution' was common in its discussions; however, the group's aims were in fact often presented as *variations* of existing tendencies and established ideals. It sought, for example, a 'true' freedom rather than a 'false' individualism; a 'Christian' patriotism rather than destructive 'nationalism'; planning *for freedom* rather than planning *for oppression*; and holistic education rather than fragmented, amoral and 'materialistic' knowledge.

The core members upon whom I have focused contributed to the group's collective dynamics, but they also trod individual paths through the years considered. Oldham brought people together, shaped the group's agenda and expressed points of consensus in private memoranda or the pages of the *CNL*. (Bliss called him an 'enabler' with a capacity for 'thinking things together', a view that Vidler shared.[5]) His views remained largely constant, but Mannheim moved him towards a more positive view of the State's role in the new order. Over time, his initially relentless focus on the formation of an 'Order' subsided (most probably a result of the fruitlessness of the discussions in this direction), though similar principles remained in the group's continuing focus on an 'elite'. The Moot, in turn, strengthened Mannheim's belief that Christianity offered a 'spiritual' response to cultural disintegration, introducing a new element into his war-time writing. Baillie contributed to the group's theological sensibilities, querying others' suggestions about relations between faith and society, subtly introducing aspects of continental Protestantism or, with more success, explaining how Jacques Maritain's Catholicism could appeal across confessional divides. His experiences in the group influenced his reports for the Church of Scotland on the war's meaning, which similarly employed 'middle axioms', a stress on lay action and notions of Christian 'anthropology'.[6] Bliss quickly rose from Oldham's assistant to editor of the *CNL*. She adapted the existing assumptions and viewpoints of the *CNL* to post-war conditions, and traces of her participation in the group are apparent across her post-war career, including in her 1969 book *The Future of Religion*.[7] Hodges became one of the Moot's most prolific members, developing the idea of 'archetypes' and their role in a 'collective commonwealth'. He turned in a clearly socialist direction by the middle of the war, urging the group to criticise more directly private property and market economics and to recognise class conflict. Vidler gradually moved away from his profound pessimism about the survival of liberal society in the late 1930s, coming to see a role for planning and the State in creating a more egalitarian society.[8] Murry continued his eccentric intellectual path through the 1930s and 1940s. At first advocating a 'national church', he soon rejected planning for freedom, insisting that only local models of communal living could respond to the crisis of modernity. After the war, he abandoned both his previous pacifism and Marxism and took a more sober view of the potential for rural communes. Finally, Eliot's *Idea of a Christian Society* (1939) was influenced by his early exchanges in the group, and he initially expressed a cautious openness towards Mannheim's ideas. But by the middle of the war he doubted planning for freedom, becoming a critic of the welfare state and its accompanying egalitarian educational reforms, views he expressed in *Notes towards the Definition of Culture* (1948).

Wider connections

The Oldham group was part of a wider Christian intellectual world. For example, while sharing the aim of a 'clerisy' with the Oldham group, the circle around *Christendom*, a journal of 'Christian sociology', held many divergent views.[9] (Eliot was a member of both groups.) In 1941, Vidler wrote that the Christendom Group had 'done more intensive and concerted thinking' on the social order 'than any other body of English Christians'; still, they were 'a rather confined group' out of touch with 'the general run of Anglican thinkers'.[10] In 1943, Oldham suggested that, apart from his own projects, only the Christendom Group and the Iona Community (an experiment in Christian living led by Church of Scotland minister George MacLeod) had both 'a definite purpose' and 'appreciable influence'; but neither was, in his view, 'strong enough to challenge and lead the Church as a whole'.[11] He praised the essay collection *Prospect for Christendom* (1945),[12] but while Oldham's circle was broadly ecumenical and open to secular ideas, the Christendom Group was decidedly and consistently Anglo-Catholic, aimed to replace rather than incorporate secular knowledge, and expressed more discontent with cultural plurality. Among those around *Christendom* it is also possible to find more sympathies with some aspects of Fascism (at least into the early period of the war) and a far more consistent anti-Communism.[13]

There were many other connections with the wider Christian world in Britain. The Oldham group worked with the SCM through publications and public lectures. Dawson was a key figure in the Catholic-led 'Sword of the Spirit' movement and an intellectual circle around the *Dublin Review*.[14] Vidler, as editor of *Theology* and warden of St Deiniol's Library, participated in many Anglican-led activities and discussions. Murry had his own, pacifist networks through *Adelphi*, *Peace News* and the 'Adelphi Centre'. Bliss, Eliot, Mairet and Oldham were part of the 'Society of St Anne's', in Soho, founded by Moot member Gilbert Shaw and including Dorothy L. Sayers, V. A. Demant, Donald MacKinnon, Maurice Reckitt and Theodora Bosanquet (of the journal *Time and Tide*).[15] Eliot, Hodges and Vidler spoke at Archbishop Temple's high-profile 'Malvern' conference (but later distanced themselves from it).[16] Alexander Miller was a deputy leader of the Iona Community.[17] Oldham was on committees organised by the Church of England and BCC and he organised events on an ad hoc basis (such as midday addresses at the church of St Mary Woolnoth in London in 1940).[18] The group was also part of the international ecumenical network. The Geneva offices of the WCC-in-formation were a 'nerve-centre' for exchanges between Britain and the German resistance.[19] The *CNL* reprinted (usually anonymously) letters from correspondents in occupied Europe. Communications were easier with the USA, such as with Niebuhr's *Christianity and Crisis*, which acted as a partner to *The Christian News-Letter*.

These Christian efforts took place in an even wider media context. Christian newspapers and journals of course addressed religious viewpoints on the war and society, but so did more secular media. *The Times* and the *Manchester Guardian* regularly carried statements by senior clergy and gave Christian views on the war and post-war rebuilding. (A prominent joint statement by British Protestants backing and extending the pope's 'peace points' was published in *The Times* in December 1940.) In early 1941, the *News Chronicle* opened a series of articles on 'God and the War', with contributions from prominent authors, religious leaders and thinkers.[20] One of Britain's premier science journals, *Nature*, argued repeatedly for cooperation between Christianity and science in building a new society.[21] The BBC produced many religious radio commentaries and series, and politicians of all major parties used Christian imagery in describing the war and the rebuilt society to follow. Christianity was certainly not unquestioned: a prominent, vocal cadre of atheists had emerged during the inter-war period, and critiques of religious social views came both from the left and the right. Still, in the 1930s and 1940s distinctions between 'religious' and 'secular' could be vague and Christian perspectives were seen as of broad interest. Thus, the Oldham group was offering its ideas to a public accustomed to encountering Christian ideas and language in the press, on the radio and on the book stalls.

Larger contexts

Christianity helped build the twentieth century through its influence on concepts, movements and institutions. Developing this point requires a middle way all its own. Religious ideas (like any others) should be seen as independent variables and not simply products of 'real' underlying economic relations; but religious ideas (like any others) must also be understood in the social contexts from which they emerge. One way of reconstructing both aspects is to focus on specific political projects, as I have done in this book.[22] Religion is an evolving field of claims – about the nature of reality, the meaning of life, the goals of social interaction and many other things – that is structured by constellations of social, cultural, political and institutional power and also developed by particular actors in relation to specific theological traditions. By examining the Oldham group's arguments about faith and society, I have tried to appreciate both agency and context in a case with wider significance for the twentieth-century historiography of Christian social thought, the Second World War, modernity and secularisation.

Religion and society: 'a faith by which to live'

The Oldham group brought Christians (and a few non-Christians) together to work out the social meaning of their faith and develop strategies to implement it. Christianity's inherent tension between *engaging with* and *withdrawing from* society has been solved in many ways, and the twentieth century saw countless varieties of Christian social thought. Some idealised, and were implemented in, forms of authoritarian corporatism.[23] Other Christians were attracted to (or at least sympathised with) Fascism or Nazism.[24] Conversely, many others saw the authoritarian and totalitarian regimes of the 1920s and 1930s as a threat not only to a 'democratic' but also to a 'Christian' social order. Early-twentieth-century British Christianity was strongly influenced by the 'social Gospel', Christian socialism and varieties of moral activism.[25] In the inter-war period, there were intense discussions in the ecumenical movement about faith's social relevance. Reflecting upon these debates, and attempting to bring them forward in the radically changing circumstances of the 1930s and 1940s, the Oldham group critiqued what it saw as various wrong answers to the question of how Christianity and society should interact, whether 'liberal' visions of building the Kingdom on earth, evangelical individualism, authoritarian Catholicism or 'continental' Protestantism's radical separation of human society and divine will.

The context of world events and the perception of a deep cultural malaise played a crucial role in motivating Christian responses. Inter-war totalitarian movements and regimes posed a vast new challenge. Radically different visions of how Christians should react emerged amid what have been called the 'culture wars' of Europe's 'transwar' period.[26] There were some insistent calls for Christians to 'return to the catacombs' or go 'underground' to keep Christianity alive, some of which were occasionally heard in the Moot but which were gener-ally contested in the *CNL*.[27] The Oldham group's consensus was that the faithful should openly fight totalitarian trends and actively seek to reshape society. At the heart of the matter was 'culture', i.e. values and norms and how they were derived. 'Every human society needs a faith by which to live', Oldham argued in 1940, complaining that Britain lacked 'a faith clear and strong enough to set against the pagan faiths of Nazism and Communism as a dynamic and integrating power in society'.[28] 'At the root of everything', he wrote at war's end, 'is a *clash of ultimate beliefs*'.[29] Similarly, the Anglican *Guardian* insisted in 1940 that 'what men think and believe is going to regulate their social action': 'current events are proving everywhere that beliefs matter'.[30] The aim of reshaping values can be seen in light of what has recently been called 'cultural sover-eignty', i.e. forms of self-assertion by groups seeking to define and articulate their identities or beliefs in both thought and action.[31] Here, the goal was not directly to take on political power but rather to articu-late and assert a *cultural framework for living* that could be translated into everyday social practice. Christianity was seen as a resource for reorganising social interaction, restoring 'community' and reshaping a range of institutions both within and beyond the State. Indeed, the key institutions of State sovereignty (such as Parliament or the civil service) were left largely untouched in the group's visions of a new society. What mattered was the culture within which those institutions operated: the goals towards which they worked and the assumptions they made about the human beings upon (and through) whom they acted. Of course, it was hoped that such cultural changes would also gradually create a new political reality, but the approach was relatively indirect. Rogers Brubaker has, similarly, recently described religion as a 'mode of social organising' and a way of grounding political 'claims' aimed at changing public life.[32] Many mid-century Christians focused on culture rather than politics per se, on the principle that, as V. A. Demant put it in the *CNL*, 'if there is a sickness in the culture, no aims moral or political, however strongly held, can be achieved'.[33] This approach was similar to that of inter-war non-conformist socialists who focused on defining central principles and aims in line with Christian traditions rather than venturing into the more detailed realm of social policy itself.[34]

The aim to make Christian values culturally sovereign was expressed in various ways, such as Eliot's overarching 'idea' of a Christian society or Oldham's 'common social philosophy'. There are various conceptual resonances here. One might think of the more recent idea of a *Leitkultur* – a 'guiding' or 'leading' culture – demands for which have grown in several European countries amid fears of cultural drift and fragmentation. The term has, however, been co-opted by extreme nationalists, the opposite of what the Oldham group sought.[35] Some might hear echoes here of cultural 'hegemony', but the group – despite some participants' Marxist sympathies – did not see culture in socially determinist terms and aimed not to maintain the dominance of any particular class. 'Identity' might seem key to the group, and, indeed, the concepts of 'commonality', 'connectedness' and 'groupness' that Frederick Cooper and Rogers Brubaker have rescued from more amorphous understandings of 'identity' were integral to its plans.[36] But while the Oldham group was mainly Protestant, British and relatively elite, its aims relied little on denominational, national or class allegiance: it sought a 'unity' based not on *belonging* but on an *agreement* about values that was, in theory, open to people of many backgrounds, including non-Christians.

The Oldham group was part of a broader effort by twentieth-century Christians to renew liberal democracy. To this end, the group developed particular strategies: pursuing a 'revolution from above' by an elite 'Order', generating a community-based cultural 'leaven' through small groups ('cells'), and engaging in a dialogue with the public about human nature and the social order. After the war, this model – circles of Christian intellectuals meeting with experts, businessmen and senior civil servants – was picked up by others, and they have been described, generally, as 'Oldham groups'.[37] But this strategy was also typical of an era in which it was thought that small elites could efficiently work the levers of the 'planned' society. Christian efforts to gain cultural influence later shifted, as a more fragmented, complex, egalitarian, pluralist and secularised post-war society emerged.

Arguably, at no point in the twentieth century was the critical engagement by British Christians with the fundamentals of the liberal, capitalist social order more intense than in the 1930s and 1940s. Late-nineteenth and early-twentieth-century Christian contributions to the 'social question' had focused on alleviating poverty and 'moral' issues, from drink to prostitution. From the 1960s, issues of sexuality, family, lifestyle and the 'permissive society' became central issues in the public debates around faith and society.[38] Between these periods – from the 1920s to the 1950s – war; totalitarianism; economic dislocations; the rise of welfare states; and a chronic, pervasive sense of crisis focused Christian attention on the foundations of the social order, particularly the meaning of freedom.[39] These distinctions are not absolute: Christian concerns about sex, morality and family endured throughout the century, and capitalism, imperialism and poverty have remained key Christian topics since the 1960s. However, the 1930s, the Second World War and post-war reconstruction brought a remarkable and distinctive outpouring of Christian social thought. The Oldham group's struggles to take into account the ambiguities and grey zones of everyday social life while also identifying and upholding what it saw as timeless and essential elements of faith reveal some of the key fault lines and argumentative strategies of such thinking.

Christianity, war and social reconstruction: 'the crisis of civilization and all that'

Indeed, truly understanding British responses to inter-war crises and the enormous social changes of the Second World War means accounting more fully for those reactions of a religious variety. Christianity played a greater role at the time than it has in the subsequent memory or historiography of the war, although this has been recently changing.[40] During the war, countless books offered a Christian view on the war's meaning. Some – such as George Bell's *Christianity and World Order* (1940) and William Temple's *Christianity and Social Order* (1942) – were bestsellers. The SCM put out a popular series of 'crisis booklets', and, at the request of the MOI, the Society for the Propagation of Christian Knowledge published pamphlets under the title 'The Church and the War'.[41] The MOI issued its own weekly newsletter, *The Spiritual Issues of the War*. Both the Catholic-led 'Sword of the Spirit' movement and cross-denominational 'Religion and Life Weeks' offered nation-wide events, lectures and exhibitions examining the war from a Christian perspective.[42] Local organisations contributed as well: the Cambridge United Council of Christian Witness, for example, organised a 'New Order' exhibition on Christianity's post-war role.[43]

Christian perspectives overlapped with non-Christian ones but also had their own emphases, assumptions and conclusions: interpreting the war as a 'spiritual' crisis, seeing a need for British 'repentance', insisting on a moral military strategy and aiming to orient post-war reconstruction on specifically religious principles. The sense of living in an interregnum between one dying epoch and another still being born was common in the 1930s and 1940s and fitted well with Christian concepts of death and resurrection. In the confrontation with totalitarianism, 'liberal democracy' – a term joining two traditions that had not been necessarily synonymous – came to be seen as 'the most authentic expression of the Western tradition' or even 'a constitutive feature of the West itself'.[44] The feverish reconceptualisation of liberalism in the crucible of crisis and war gave an opening for Christians to insert their faith into the predominant reimaginings of the post-war 'new order'. And, as recent research has shown, Christians were in fact often successful in helping to shape the language and landscape of post-war politics, both in domestic and in international contexts (even if they were not able to determine them).[45]

Many Christians brought a distinctive perspective to the war's meaning in Britain. 'We certainly have no lack of diagnosis', the Bishop of Southwell (a supporter of the CCFCL) observed in 1945, noting several common varieties of social commentary: 'It is the end of economic man, the end of Liberalism, or of Capitalism, or Nationalism, of Western hegemony, of a class-society, and many other things.' He argued that 'beneath all these upheavals' was something 'simpler and more profound':

> The most important and characteristic truth may be that what is per-ishing in agony is the non-religious phase of modern history, the attempt to develop western civilisation on materialist or positivistic bases. The post-Renaissance chapter is ending. The humanistic experiment has failed. The attempt to build a culture of human values on the assumption that man is the measure of all things and without religious presuppositions, has broken down in failure and disillusionment. Hitler cashed in on man's despair, and the glowing hopes of the French revolution have ended in a revolution of destruction.[46]

The Oldham group shared the analysis of a totalitarianism born in secu-larisation and a 'true' freedom that had to be anchored in faith. Amid the war's flurry of social blueprints – one journal noted that 'the air has been thick from the start' with visions of post-war rebuilding – many Christians saw an opportunity to rejuvenate not only the nation but also the churches.[47] 'Surely', wrote Labour peer and historian Lord Elton in the Anglican *Guardian* in 1940, 'we may hope that one of the results of this war will be regeneration through suffering, victory not only over the enemy, but over ourselves, so that not only the Christian standards of con-duct, which a small but vocal minority has so violently assailed, but the full Christian faith from which they once sprang, will steadily revive'.[48] Ecumenical Christian thinking during the war focused on maintaining individual dignity in the face of State power, asserting the 'sacredness of personality' and promoting 'brotherly fellowship' on both community and international levels.[49]

In retrospect, the Christian moral narrative served the Allied cause well.[50] There were contemporary hopes that this would be so. In October

1942, a leading article titled 'The Church as a Social Force' appeared in the science journal *Nature*.[51] Britain's enemies, it observed, had been strengthened by their 'enthusiastic belief in the Nazi and Fascist doctrines which their leaders have inspired'. In a similar way to the Moot and *CNL*, it then argued that such 'perverted' beliefs required 'a like enthusiasm and intense conviction on our part': 'The religious faith of the Nazi must be countered with one equally strong and equally capable of fostering devotion and loyalty and commanding sacrifice.'[52] The churches were seen by many as having a key role to play.

But cultural pessimism extended beyond the defeat of Nazism. 'We have become weary of reading', *Theology* observed in 1947, 'and hesitant about recommending, books that deal with the crisis of civilization and all that.' 'There have been too many of them', the commentator continued: 'They go over the same ground again and again, one pausing longer at this point, another at that point. But everything that can be said seems to have been said *ad nauseam*.'[53] There was, indeed, no shortage of post-war jeremiads. They were often linked to a search for 'immutable ethical foundations for right political conduct' that would be amenable to Christian concepts.[54] A 1947 series in the *British Weekly*, for example, examined a widespread assumption that something had 'gone wrong with civilisation', and that one age had died but the next was yet to be born. The 'real crisis' was one of values: 'men have lost the old faith they once lived by', it insisted, and 'the next phase of history must come with a rebirth of those things of the spirit that alone can give us the real peace and freedom that we lack.'[55] The Oldham group contributed to a sense of both cultural decay and renewal, showing the intensity, complexity and depth of Christian reactions to the war.

The group's post-war decline – signalled by the *CNL*'s shrinking membership – also revealed wider trends. Adrian Hastings suggested that the Christian intellectual ferment of the 1930s and 1940s subsided because the problems it had arisen to face were addressed: 'Fascism was defeated, the Welfare State adopted and the relationship with Communism was stabilised through the establishment of the Iron Curtain and acceptance of the Cold War as a social commonplace.'[56] The world set the agenda, and the agenda moved on. Christians did not *stop* thinking about the meaning of the war, but their emphases shifted with the waning of 'secular pressure': 'When the pressure was relaxed', Hastings observes, 'the vigour of church concern with the secular speedily declined.'[57] The Britain that emerged from the war was not the one the Oldham group had sought, but they had helped create it by contributing to a consensus on social renewal, state welfare and educational reform. There had been a growing sense of beleaguerment among the inter-war churches. In much of Europe, this had fed a right-wing political resurgence, fed in part by the strength of left-wing anti-clericalism.[58] In Britain, however, the political results were less clear, given that both the left and right had Christian roots and the power of political Catholicism (and anti-clericalism) was marginal: there was no clear-cut British division into Protestant, Catholic and Socialist 'milieux' as there was, for example, in inter-war Germany.[59] For similar reasons, no 'Christian Democratic' political movement emerged there as it did in much of continental Europe.

The crisis of modernity: 'the spiritual disintegration of the West'

Nonetheless, the 1930s and 1940s saw an intense religious response in Britain to modernity. For Oldham group members, the key problems of the 'modern' world were not machines, industry, cities, or mass communications as such but rather the *cultural* abandonment of a true understanding on human life from which one might judge morality, generate identity, develop values and orient social practices. This is what their repeated references to cultural 'disintegration' meant. In Britain, Christians – Church leaders such as Bell and Temple, as well as intellectuals and activists such as Dawson and Oldham – were among the earliest to employ the concept of the 'totalitarian state' in the 1930s, seeing in it a threat to Christian values.[60] The 'spiritual disintegration of the West' became, for Christians, an explanation for the crises they were experiencing.[61] For many, secular liberalism seemed to have reached a dead end. But the Oldham group was not *anti*-modern: it was, instead, *critical of* the paths modernity had taken, insisting both that Christianity could adapt to an industrial, urban and scientific modernity and that modernity could be steered in a more Christian direction. Even those who had sympathised with anti-modern or authoritarian politics (such as Dawson and Eliot) believed that Christianity could thrive if people changed the way they *thought*, though they stressed more traditional and unchangeable elements of the faith in this process.[62]

A longing for 'community' and opposition to scientific 'materialism', 'atomistic' individualism and capitalist 'plutocracy' extended from democratic forms of guild socialism to variants of Fascism. The Oldham group can be clearly distinguished from anti-democratic circles and movements. Roger Griffin has called Fascism an authoritarian nationalist 'palingenetic' movement, i.e. one with the aim of social renewal and rebirth.[63] The Oldham group also had 'palingenetic' aims and myths, but it was anti-racist, anti-nationalist, non-militarist and committed to parliamentary government. While making some similar complaints about modern society as did far-right 'Neo-Tories', the Oldham group never questioned, as the Neo-Tories did, parliamentary democracy.[64] This consistent emphasis also distanced them from authoritarian variants of Catholicism.[65] Its attacks on 'materialism' or the dominance of a relentless, mechanical rationality do not make the group anti-modern: indeed, efforts to counteract modernity's excesses should be seen as part of modernity itself.[66] By celebrating science but urging its orientation on spiritual values, praising freedom and tolerance but insisting on non-relative standards of judgement, and accepting industry and urbanism but seeking to maintain 'organic' community in their midst, the Oldham group helped to formulate Christian responses to the modern age. Many other groups and thinkers were seeking to mould Christian perspectives at this time, but the support the group received from the Protestant establishment, its integration in influential international networks and relatively high-profile public projects – whether in the form of the *CNL*, radio broadcasts or books – arguably gave it a particularly important place within that broader context.

It has been recently argued that Christian contributions to human-rights thinking resulted from a sudden and 'epoch-making reinvention of conservatism' in the 1930s and 1940s, with conservative Catholic and Lutheran thinkers seen as having introduced lingering right-wing assumptions into understandings of human rights.[67] However, one can overstate the conservatism of Christian influences; moreover, talking about 'rights' is only one way of talking about human freedom, and there has been a long, if still perhaps ambivalent, history of grounding claims to liberty, an independent 'civil society' and even individual rights, in religious languages and concepts.[68] Many liberal and left-wing Christians in the ecumenical movement pursued a politics of anti-racism, anti-imperialism and anti-totalitarianism across the 1920s and 1930s, based not least upon religious views of human nature.[69] Christian personalism and other forms of emancipatory Christian social visions flourished during the war, proposing versions of freedom that were embedded in conceptions of duties, moral constraints and community well-being.[70] In the common-law tradition of the United Kingdom, there was an established language of discussing the 'liberties of the subject', and the language of 'human rights' only became established in the 1960s.[71] Christian Democracy in its continental – mainly Catholic and conservative – form did not catch on in post-war Britain; however, a book titled *Towards Christian Democracy* (1945) did appear there, written by the prominent *socialist* politician Stafford Cripps.

But even some who had long pressed for a greater Christian social influence found that the intermixture of religion and politics threatened to undermine faith's true nature. As Maurice Reckitt, of the Christendom Group, complained in 1943:

The sad truth would seem to be that in spite of innumerable conferences and study circles, we have still to develop any sustained habit of specifically Christian thinking. What there is of this, moreover, is predominantly devoted to themes prescribed by the secular fashions of the moment: the League of Nations, Federal Union, the Beveridge Report. It is not applied to the discovery of what are the essential problems in the contemporary situation and the true Christian approach to the understanding of them.[72]

A fear of the dangers of secularism was certainly shared by the Oldham group, even if they were more willing to enter into a constructive (though still critical) engagement with it.

Secularisation: 'the inherent possibilities of our society'

The philosopher Charles Taylor has diagnosed within modernity a 'move from a society where belief in God is unchallenged and indeed, unproblematic, to one in which it is understood to be one option among others, and frequently not the easiest to embrace'.[73] It was apparent to the Oldham group's members that they lived in just such a society. Writing in the *Contemporary Review* in 1938, for instance, Moberly insisted that the 'common assumptions of social and industrial life, of education and social service' had become secular: it was the Christian, not the atheist, who was seen as 'slightly peculiar'.[74] For Oldham's group, as for Taylor, an 'immanent' theory of knowledge and understanding of life – one without room for transcendence – had become culturally sovereign in the West.[75] Many of the faithful in the 1930s and 1940s thought a 'post-Christian' West was approaching (or already at hand).[76] The view that Christians were a 'minority' (and *active* Christians a *tiny* minority) became a commonplace in the group, feeding the seemingly paradoxical insistence on working *with* and even learning *from* secularism in seeking a more Christian society. The group's ambivalent understanding of 'the secular' as a shared social space, a beneficial body of knowledge and a dangerous cultural foe shows the complexity of the Christian engagement with twentieth-century secularity.

Whether the group's diagnosis regarding secularisation was right or wrong cannot be extensively addressed in a work of intellectual rather than social history. However, there are signs of faith's continuing vitality in mid-twentieth-century Britain and suggestions that the Second World War may even have caused a growth in popular religiosity that lasted through the 1950s.[77] Indeed, Callum Brown, considering both quantitative evidence of attitudes, church attendance and religious practice, as well as the resurgence in traditional views on gender and the family, has suggested that Britain was a more religious nation between 1945 and 1958 than at any time since the late Victorian period.[78] Still, an assumed secularisation shaped the worldviews of many Christians, though their reactions varied.

Oxford economist Denys Munby, in his influential book *The Idea of a Secular Society* (1963), distanced his period from the Christian anxieties of a previous generation. Munby (a practising Anglican) responded to Eliot's *The Idea of a Christian Society* (1939). He defined the 'neutral' liberal society as one that did not promote or 'identify with' a particular religion. It was pluralist, tolerant and rationalist, and it strove towards no particular overarching aim other than the expansion of freedom, choice and prosperity. He argued that this form of social order was better at serving human needs than any oriented on specific religious or political ideas.[79] Munby located Eliot's pessimism about the liberal order – one that had been shared by the Oldham group – firmly in the context of the 1930s, when there had been 'good grounds ... for believing that "neutral societies" were doomed to disappear before the crusading zeal of Communism and Fascism'. By the 1960s, however, despite the threats of atomic war and Communism, it was 'less easy to be pessimistic about the inherent possibilities of our society'. Thus: 'In spite of the theological prophecies that a people without God will perish, in spite of the condemnations of moralists who point to the allegedly growing laxity of sexual morals and the supposed increase in neuroses, our society has shown signs of vigour that would hardly have been believed in the thirties.'[80] It had, in short, become easier to see secular liberalism in a more positive light, especially in contrast to societies (such as those on the other side of the Iron Curtain) that placed dogma above individual choice. Munby wrote that the Church itself 'seems to be acclimatizing itself as it has acclimatized itself to most previous forms of society'.[81] It has, in fact, been recently argued that there were pronounced trends in British Christianity towards 'self-secularisation' in the 1960s, replacing a Christian social vision with (often left-wing) political theory. Theological impulses drove this shift towards a more 'secular' religion, famously formulated in Britain by Bishop John Robinson's controversial best-seller *Honest to God* (1963) – which argued for 'religionless Christianity' – and noticeable in shifts in the SCM's activism.[82]

The Oldham group had similarly believed that Christianity had to be rethought for a modern age, doubted the churches' political effectiveness and examined faith in the context of everyday *action*. There were connections between group participants and later trends: Oldham wrote appreciative letters to Robinson in the midst of the *Honest to God* debate, and parts of Oldham's *Life Is Commitment* (1953) had presaged Robinson's themes ten years before. In addition, several group members stayed active with the SCM and WCC, and some helped develop new theological streams.[83] Vidler's contribution to the hotly debated *Soundings* collection in 1962, for example, argued that 'religionless Christianity' had already been inherent in F. D. Maurice's nineteenth-century theology.[84] But significant differences are also apparent. In the 1930s and 1940s, the Oldham group sought neither to dissolve Christianity into social action nor to dismiss orthodox or institutionalised faith: indeed, the group wanted to *serve* the churches and to *defend* supernatural and transcendent elements of faith that it claimed had been ignored by a tepid theological 'liberalism'. While, in retrospect, the group's commitment to a 'social faith' and its possible exaggeration of the extent to which Britain was 'post-Christian' may have presaged later 'self-secularising' trends – even ultimately contributing to a self-fulfilling prophecy of religious decline – this was far from its aim.[85] Religion, in its view, need not be *adapted to* but should rather be made *relevant for* modernity (a subtle distinction they nevertheless saw as crucial), enabling the latter's transformation and maintaining the former's transcendental essence.

Evaluations

In the decade before the Second World War, some British Christians concluded that, while totalitarianism offered wrong answers to the purpose of human social life, secular liberalism offered none at all.[86] They thus increasingly sought a response to what was seen as a new, two-front political challenge. When an epochal global war began, they (with relatively few exceptions) threw themselves wholeheartedly into a defence of a liberal and capitalist system that many continued to see, at best, ambivalently. For all their belief in a deep similarity between totalitarian and *laissez-faire* societies and their conviction that mass culture and industrial capitalism hindered living a Christian life, it seemed clear that a victory for Nazism in the war (or of Soviet Communism after 1945) would herald the end of Christianity as a viable social force. Moreover, some of the guiding principles of the Oldham group's aims included decentralised politics, pluralism, the reigning in of 'irresponsible' economic and social power, healthy community life, parliamentarianism, and the dignity of the person. For all its alleged weaknesses and outrages, secular liberalism at least held out the potential for Christian action. Defeating totalitarianism was thus seen as a necessary but insufficient step towards a Christian society, a minimal consensus upon which a wide swathe of British Christianity, whatever its other debates, could agree. The effect was that Christian individuals and institutions contributed to a British consensus on social reform and renewal that ultimately strengthened liberal democracy in the hour of its greatest peril.

The Oldham group was an important part of those broader Christian efforts to rethink liberal society in the context of crisis and war, its role enhanced by its high-profile connections in key Christian intellectual networks and active strategies of public engagement. A post-war editorial in *Theology* praised the group's main periodical publication as 'an organ which has faithfully and steadily expressed the workings of the Christian conscience both in its assurances and in its perplexities': 'the first thing anyone should do who wishes to estimate the quality and range of Christian witness in Britain during the war', it concluded, 'is to study the volumes of the *C.N.L.*'[87] Indeed, the group produced a rich body of ideas about the value of the person, the need for community, the potentials (and perils) of the State and the meaning of culture. Undoubtedly, its visions of a new, free social order were shot through with limits, ambiguities, gaps and contradictions that many today will find questionable, appalling or even dangerous. Given the enormity of the issues it addressed – totalitarian regimes, global war and massive transformations of social life – others may see its efforts simply as inconsequential or even faintly ridiculous. The Moot's 'rarefied' intellectual discussions have been called 'abstract and totally theoretical', and Oldham's plans for changing the world 'delusory'.[88] Even well-disposed observers have doubted the group's significance and stressed that the Moot's aims 'were never realized'.[89] It has been argued that, at best, Oldham's group 'lost the argument' but made an 'intriguing, if doomed attempt to preserve religion, hierarchy and common culture in the context of a modern mass society'.[90]

The group itself was sometimes doubtful about whether defeat by totalitarianism could be avoided, but its members remained doggedly convinced that an attempt should be made and that Christianity could contribute to victory. What made them think so? They lived in an age when one might imagine that small groups with large ideas could change the world: the examples of Communism, Fascism and National Socialism seemed to demonstrate this point. The group was also part of a relatively small elite of largely Oxbridge-educated intellectuals, academics, social critics, politicians and civil servants who defined the political society that mattered. It was in such circles that policy ideas were developed and implemented, particularly in an age of 'planning'. Finally, as committed Christians they believed that faith could not only figuratively move mountains but also divert, God willing, the course of history. This conviction carried on past the 'end' of the Oldham group: in September 1950 – rather more than a year after the last issue of the *Christian News-Letter* – Oldham wrote to Vidler to say that he had been struck in a new and profound way by the need for Christians to respond to the threat of atomic war. As previously, his aim was to enlist both the powerful (e.g. Government ministers) and the populace ('the press too is of crucial importance') to overcome the influence of atheism and the assumption that humankind's fate was solely in its own hands. 'Only God', Oldham insisted, 'can avert war'.[91] Still, he foresaw (here recalling his earlier search for an 'Order') the need for 'a body of men who will in the name of God raise the standard of revolt against acceptance of things as they are and keep that banner unfolded'. Something *like* the *CNL* was also needed. Looking back, Oldham commented that 'one of the most distinctive things about the *CNL* was that it tried during the war to do justice to the truth in both belligerency and pacifism'.[92] The main battle, as ever, would be fought in the realm of ideas.

Certainly, in the 1930s and 1940s, the Oldham group was mostly concerned with political *thought* rather than *action*. But by placing the discussions of the Moot in a broader set of organisations and projects I have sought to avoid depicting its members merely as elite intellectuals engaged in purely speculative discussion about an imagined Christian society. Via the CCFCL and the longer-lived CFC the group sought to influence both the churches themselves and also sympathetic members of Britain's economic, academic, media and political elites. The *CNL* – the group's most successful and publicly visible effort – offered a remarkable distillation of international, cross-denominational Christian commentary on numerous issues of urgent political and social relevance. Nevertheless, compared to its ambitions the group remained chronically under-funded and short-staffed. It failed to issue even a clear programmatic manifesto, and it wielded no direct political power. And, of course, no 'Christian society' of the sort envisioned in internal documents, Moot discussions or the pages of the *CNL* emerged in Britain after 1945. However, these are not critiques unique to this group, nor do they make its efforts historically uninteresting. Most social visions remain, after all, unrealised, and most political projects fail; nonetheless, understanding the roads not taken is important. The group's diversity of opinion and the resulting vagueness of some of its ideas may even have helped it avoid a pitfall faced by the more theologically and politically coherent Christendom Group, susceptible as it was to questionable theories and fads, such as 'Distributism' (Chesterton and Belloc – key advocates of this approach – were hardly mentioned in the *CNL* or in Moot discussions) or C. H. Douglas's 'social credit' scheme.[93] Nor was the group prone to excessive optimism about the potential support for explicitly Christian ideas. Its assumption that Christians were (and would probably remain) a minority in a pluralist, secular and even 'post-Christian' society – thus making it necessary to translate Christian ideas into more secular terms – give its general approach a continuing relevance that other 'Christian sociologies' of the era might lack.

The search for 'middle ways' was the Oldham group's recurrent priority across many topics, and, as I have shown, this approach could be not only fruitful but also reasonable in view of the often violent political extremes on offer. However, there are also many points where a contemporary observer might disagree with the conclusions the group reached, just as did many of the group's contemporaries. By its very nature, the intellectual strategy of the 'middle way' invites attacks from both of the sides between which it seeks to navigate. Both the origins and social positions of group members and also the intellectual strategy they used to address the issues of their day thus created 'blind spots' in their views of the world situation.

From one perspective, political conservatives and religious traditionalists might argue that the Oldham group went too far in the direction of ecumenism and social progressivism. Ecumenical approaches can, at times, disregard precisely those features of particular denominational traditions that, for many of their adherents, are central to their faith. Where the ecumenist may see a 'convergence' of religious perspectives or propose a 'synthesis' as a force for renewal, others may see a questionable compromise and a sapping of communal strength that might otherwise derive from a clear doctrine and distinct identity. We have seen such critiques within the Oldham group (from Eliot, for example), and they were directed at ecumenical groups throughout the twentieth century. Similarly, for much of its existence the Oldham group saw at least points of agreement with Marxism, and its overall consensus strongly supported a large-scale expansion of State planning. As shown in Chapter 4, political conservatives and many American Protestants condemned the 'left-wing' economic policies recommended by the WCC after the war, which were broadly in line with the ideas of the Oldham group. Indeed, even within the Moot there were strong liberal and conservative critiques of the planning consensus.

From the opposite perspective, some will see the Oldham group as fundamentally conservative, even reactionary, with regard to its basic acceptance of capitalism. For all its rhetoric of aiming for 'revolutionary' social transformation, the Oldham group failed, for example, to demand a more fundamental revision of the economic order (with regard, say, to property rights or the dominance of market relations) and it continued to accept a substantial amount of social inequality. Within the group, Hodges and Murry expressed the most left-wing discontent with the failure of their colleagues to adopt a more clearly socialist position. The group also had little direct contact with socialism as a political movement, such as with Christian socialist MPs in Parliament. There is some suggestion, as noted in Chapter 1, that the *CNL* was regarded sceptically by Labour leaders. Given the periodical's ambivalent stance on socialism, this is perhaps unsurprising.

Furthermore, two issues have been little emphasised in this book: gender and empire. Neither of these topics had a very high priority in the group's discussions; however, they were not absent, and given their salience in contemporary historiography some discussion is in order. I would argue that the group's stance on gender issues could be described, for its time and Christian context, as ambivalently progressive; nonetheless, it (unsurprisingly) included strongly traditional elements. Many women were involved in Christian activism – several of whom wrote for the *CNL* – and the group clearly and consistently argued that women had vital roles to play, both publicly and privately, in creating a more Christian society: in the Moot, Mannheim referred to women as 'the most oppressed class in history', and the *CNL* took a stance against the cliché that 'a woman's place is in the home'.[94] Nonetheless, while there was support for women having a more active place in public life – for example in 'public service'[95] – the *CNL*, often in articles by women, clearly linked their role to the domestic sphere, child-rearing and family (and expressed concern about changes in modern society, such as rising divorce rates).[96] Fears about declining sexual morality (and the war-time scourge of the 'good-time girl') were also aired.[97] In contrast, the pioneering spirit and drive for social reconstruction were often depicted as more 'manly' virtues.[98] While women were not explicitly excluded in discussions around an elite 'clerisy', it seems to have been assumed that that institution itself would be primarily male. Nonetheless, it is clear that all of the fundamental middle axioms that the group claimed should orient human life – responsibility, freedom, community, service and dependence – applied to both men and women equally, and contributions from both sexes were deemed essential to the creation of a more Christian society.

Its views of British national identity and of Britain's role in the world might also seem to cast the group as clearly 'conservative'. For all its critiques of modern Britain, the Oldham group's discussions and writings were infused with elements of an idealised British (often 'English') national mythology. (Though it should not be forgotten that lead roles in this idealisation were played by its immigrant members.) This romanticised view of the nation's past contributed to one of the largest absences in the group's discussions over the period covered in this book: empire. The British Empire had reached its peak in the inter-war period, it was essential to Britain's war effort and there were initial moves towards decolonisation in the immediate post-war years. However, there were relatively few references to the colonies or the Empire in the Moot, in memoranda of the CCFCL and CFC, or in the *CNL*. The topics were present, above all in the *CNL*'s coverage of world events, but they were not prioritised in the way that the topics of the previous chapters clearly were. Much of the commentary that was made specifically concerned the welfare and freedoms of Christians in colonial areas.[99]

The participants were positively disposed towards the Empire, but they were not, on the whole, opposed to decolonisation (to the extent that they expressed a view one way or the other in the period under consideration). In the 1920s, Oldham had worked to encourage the principle of 'trustee-ship' in colonial policy, aimed at protecting the interests of the colonised and preparing them for self-rule.[100] (This position built upon an ideal of 'stewardship' that was an integral and long-extant element in liberal imperialism.) Eliot, too, was critical of the effects of westernisation on non-western populations.[101] The *CNL* published comments arguing that significant reforms were needed to combat racist tendencies in the Empire.[102] However, the group tended to see the Empire, for all its past crimes, as having developed into a relatively benign and remarkably diverse partnership. As discussed in Chapter 5, the group praised the Commonwealth and Empire as models for global governance. At a meeting of the Moot, Fred Clarke argued that the Empire 'worked' because 'different national groups felt their cultural and familiar values had been taken into account and so they could live at peace in the same political system'.[103] Vidler even suggested that 'the British Empire might be a necessary part of God's purpose for mankind'.[104] Above all, the group emphasised maintaining 'goodwill' and finding peaceful resolutions to conflicts between colonisers and colonised, thereby presenting a clear alternative to totalitarianism. India was the most pressing case during the group's existence. Oldham publicly urged that the way be opened to Indian independence, though he also expressed a preference for a continuing 'partnership' within the Commonwealth.[105] The *CNL* praised the efforts of the British Government to mediate between Hindus and Muslims in India in the run-up to partition.[106] In 1949, however, Oldham issued a clear warning about Islam: it 'has always been intolerant of other religions', he wrote, 'and Moslem countries are less open than formerly to influences which might lead them to mitigate their intransigence'.[107]

Imperial issues, however, were secondary in the group's discussions: its concerns lay mainly within Europe. Despite recent claims – based on WCC sources – that ecumenical social thought was obsessed with imperial issues from the 1880s to the 1960s (moving from a pro-Empire to a firmly anti-colonial stance) and that by the 1930s the 'love affair between ecumenicals and empire had come to an end', this clearly did not apply in the British case.[108] Oldham and his colleagues were typical of British ecumenists, stressing that, while 'the actual achievement of the British Empire is only a very partial embodiment of the ideals we profess', it was still something valuable.[109] Indeed, the Oldham group shared a continuing belief in a national civilising 'mission' that extended to Europe and the world as a whole rather than specifically to Britain's colonies. The crimes of Empire were condemned, but the *idea* of Empire was accepted (if allied with moral principles), a long-term survival of ideals of 'liberal imperialism'. In the 1950s and, especially, 1960s, decolonisation moved firmly onto the British ecumenical agenda. But the late 1930s to the end of the 1940s mark a clear interlude in which the most pressing crises were framed as European and western problems that were largely divorced from imperial considerations.

Naturally, the group's conclusions were shaped by its members' distinct and individual standpoints. Their own social positions – white, (predominantly) male and (mostly) middle-class – may have played a role in setting their priorities. However, groups with similar memberships have taken radically different stances; indeed, some participants in the Oldham group, not least Oldham himself, had earlier been intensely focused on African and Asian issues. I suggest that the group's main concerns – both the topics on which they focused and those that they (at least substantially) ignored – flowed far more from their ideas than from their identities. The fundamental problems of modernity, as they saw it, lay in Europe and 'the West'. It would be there, and only there, that solutions might be found.

Oldham group participants had post-war influence in the contexts of organised Christianity, State education and the wider public sphere. Oldham was in his mid seventies when he disbanded the Moot in early 1947 and the *CNL* ceased publication in 1949, but he remained a respected senior figure in ecumenical Christianity. His notion (developed across the war) of the 'responsible society' became a guiding concept in the WCC for nearly two decades.[110] Combining 'middle axioms' with expert consultation provided a model for post-war Christian activists.[111] Kathleen Bliss was one of the most 'dynamic and creative figures' in the post-war British ecumenical movement, serving on many WCC committees.[112] The CFC, which was led by Moberly and Vidler, became an important post-war vehicle for encouraging 'lay responsibility in society' and a key 'networking forum'.[113] From the 1940s through the 1960s, Vidler – not least as editor of *Theology* – was a leading, if at times controversial, Anglican intellectual.

It was in the field of education that group members such as Moberly, Clarke, Oakeshott and Hetherington had the most concrete impact.[114] They responded to and participated in an attempted 're-Christianising' of British education in the 1930s and 1940s driven by the conviction that totalitarianism could only be met by a religiously grounded democratic faith.[115] Connections were formed between group members, especially Clarke and Oakeshott, and Secretary of State for Education R. A. Butler while he was

Figure 9 Joseph H. Oldham, 1945

in the process of drafting and passing what became the 1944 Education Act.[116] Bliss reported that after the Act's passage, Butler had stated 'You have to read the C.N-L. – it's a source.'[117] A group set up by the SCM to consider post-war universities was led by Baillie and included Hodges and Moberly.[118] Moberly also took part in a CFC working group composed of university teachers and, based on a 1940 Moot paper, produced *The Crisis in the University* (1949), which generated substantial discussion among educators.[119] Clarke became the first chair of the Central Advisory Council for Education for England (set up by the 1944 Education Act), in which position he supervised a 1947 report on 'School and Life' ('The Clarke Report'). Moot influence was also apparent in Clarke's *Freedom in the Educative Society* (1948) and Marjorie Reeves's *Growing Up in a Modern Society* (1946).[120] Bliss was the first general secretary of the Board of Education of the Church of England, from 1958 to 1966.

More broadly, through active networking and publication activities, the members of the Oldham group participated in shaping the war-time and early post-war consensus about social reform. Adrian Hastings has suggested that the 1930s and 1940s saw 'by far the strongest body of thought and action' by British Christians since the late nineteenth century, and he has highlighted in this context activities related to and following on from the Oxford Conference.[121] The Oldham group was at the centre of this broader field. 'If the churches were not leading society at this point', Hastings concludes, 'they were at least keeping level with its more progressive developments'.[122] Indeed, the 'Christian social conscience' contributed to what has been called 'middle opinion' in 1930s and 1940s Britain, which aimed at 'peace in Europe' and 'social reconstruction at home'.[123] More specifically, it has been argued that the group was 'part of the social capital or network that bound together members of the establishment' and helped to 'crystallise' a 'structure of feeling' around social planning, sociology, citizenship and egalitarianism, thus paving the way for post-war planning and new versions of national identity.[124] Although it has been claimed that the enthusiasm for pursuing a 'reconciliation' between religion and science may have broadly declined by the outbreak of the Second World War, there was still a great deal of effort in this direction, driven by the perceived need for a renewed post-war society.[125]

That post-war society, up to the present day, has seen continuing discussion by Christians and non-Christians alike about the role of faith in what is now seen as both a more secular and a more multi-faith Britain. Issues that preoccupied the Oldham group – the relationship between faith and plurality, Christianity's public role in a secular society, the ethics of capitalism (and its alternatives), the impact of new communications technology, the sources and boundaries of national identity, the significance of globalisation, the relevance of 'the West' and the meaning of 'community' – have continued to be the focus of Christian clergy, thinkers and activists, whether in British, European or transatlantic contexts.[126] While many secularists have celebrated (and sought further to encourage) the loss of Christian authority, even some non-Christians have raised concerns about the loss of religion as a 'moral resource' in contemporary Europe, particularly as tensions within the process of European unification and the increasing influence of globalised market relations have grown. In response to what seems to some a continuing vitality of religion, a variety of observers, by no means all of them Christians, have introduced the idea that we are entering (or soon will be) a 'post-secular' period.[127] The answers that the Oldham group provided to the role of faith in modern social life were, clearly, of their time and place. The questions they asked, however, seem still to be very much alive.

Notes

1 *Theology*, 49:308 (February 1946), 50–1.

2 MSC, Oldham to Symons, 29 May 1941, p. 1.

3 *CNL* 234L, 16 May 1945, p. 2.

4 Clements, 'Oldham and Baillie', 52; *CNL* 90S, 16 July 1941, G. D. H. Cole, 'Democracy Face to Face with Hugeness'.

5 Bliss, 'Legacy', 18–23, pp. 18, 19. Vidler, *Scenes*, p. 118.

6 Clements, 'Oldham and Baillie'; and 'John Baillie'.

7 Kathleen Bliss, *The Future of Religion* (London: Penguin, 1972 [1969]).

8 Vidler, *Scenes*, p. 119.

9 Lyon, 'Idea of a Christian Sociology'; Coupland, 'Anglican Peace Aims', pp. 99–120.

10 *Church of England Newspaper*, 24 January 1941, p. 7.

11 LPL W. Temple 11, fos. 210–20, 'A Common Christian Strategy', n.d. [sent to Temple in March 1943], p. 1.

12 *CNL* 237S, 27 June 1945, J. H. Oldham, '*Prospect for Christendom*', p. 10.

13 Coupland, 'Anglican Peace Aims'.

14 Michael J. Walsh, 'Ecumenism in War-Time Britain: The Sword of the Spirit and Religion and Life, 1940–1945', *Heythrop Journal*, 23 (1982), 243–58, 377–94; Coupland, *Britannia, Europa and Christendom*, pp. 20–1.

15 Alzina Stone Dale, *T. S. Eliot: The Philosopher Poet* (Wheaton, IL: Harold Shaw, 1988), pp. 155–6.

16 *The Times*, 14 January 1941, p. 5; *Church of England Newspaper*, 17 January 1941, p. 5.

17 *Moot Papers*, p. 29.

18 *Guardian*, 30 August 1940, p. 422.

19 Clements, 'Oldham and Baillie', pp. 55–6; Clements, *Faith on the Frontier*, pp. 397–8. Clements, *A Patriotism for Today*, pp. 159–60.

20 For the 'God and the War' series, see *News Chronicle* between 27 January and 15 February 1941.

21 *Nature*, 138:3479 (4 July 1936), 1–3; supplement for 14 January 1939, 68–70; 145:3670 (2 March 1940), 329; 150:3808 (24 October 1942), 469–72; 162:4120 (16 October 1948), 589–91.

22 Chappel, 'Beyond Tocqueville'.

23 Müller, *Contesting Democracy*, pp. 103–4, 108–12; Michael Burleigh, *Sacred Causes: The Clash of Religion and Politics, from the Great War to the War on Terror* (New York: HarperCollins, 2007), pp. 123–213.

24 Villis, *British Catholics and Fascism*; Linehan, 'Fascist Clerics'; Richard Steigmann-Gall, *The Holy Reich: Nazi Conceptions of Christianity, 1919–1945* (Cambridge: Cambridge University Press, 2004). Coupland, 'Anglican Peace Aims'.

25 Lyon, 'Idea of a Christian Sociology', p. 227; Hastings, 'British Churches', p. 4; Ian S. Markham, *Plurality and Christian Ethics* (Cambridge: Cambridge University Press, 1994), pp. 32–3. Peter Catterall, 'The Distinctiveness of British Socialism? Religion and the Rise of Labour, c. 1900–39', in Matthew Worley

(ed.), *The Foundations of the British Labour Party: Identities, Cultures, and Perspectives 1900–39* (Farnham: Ashgate, 2009), pp. 131–52; Alan Wilkinson, *Christian Socialism: Scott Holland to Tony Blair* (London: SCM, 1998).

26 Paul Hannebrink, 'European Protestants between Anti-Communism and Anti-Totalitarianism: The Other Interwar *Kulturkampf?*', *Journal of Contemporary History*, 53:3 (2018), 622–43.

27 See, e.g., *CNL* 51S, 16 October 1940, Richard Russell, 'The Rebuilding of Europe', p. 4; *CNL* 62L, 1 January 1941, p. 1; *CNL* 78S, 23 April 1941, anon., 'Present Conditions in the Evangelical Church in Germany', p. 3. Temple claimed advocating a 'spiritual return to the catacombs' would be a 'shirking of responsibility': *CNL* 198S, 29 December 1943, William Temple, 'What Christians Stand for in the Secular World', p. 2. Vidler foresaw an 'underground' movement, as did Eleanora Iredale: *Moot Papers*, M3, pp. 147, 148. Visser 't Hooft and Oldham, *Church and Its Function in Society*, pp. 172–3 admitted that in some contexts the Church might need to 'seek refuge in the catacombs'.

28 LPL Lang 26, fos. 194–203, 'The Spiritual Front', June 1940, p. 1.

29 *CNL* 241L, 22 August 1945, p. 6. Emphasis in original.

30 *Guardian*, 20 September 1940, p. 455.

31 Feindt, Gißibl and Paulmann, *Kulturelle Souveränität*.

32 Rogers Brubaker, 'Religion and Nationalism: Four Approaches', *Nations and Nationalism*, 18 (2012), 2–20, esp. pp. 4–5.

33 *CNL* 257S, 3 April 1946, V. A. Demant, 'The Incompetence of Unaided Virtue or the Mischief of Ideals', p. 5.

34 Catterall, *Labour and the Free Churches*, pp. 216–19.

35 Bassam Tibi, *Europa ohne Identität? Die Krise der multikulturellen Gesellschaft* (Munich: Bertelsmann, 1998); Stefan Manz, 'Constructing a Normative National Identity: The *Leitkultur* Debate in Germany, 2000/2001', *Journal of Multilingual and Multicultural Development*, 25:5–6 (2004), 481–96.

36 Frederick Cooper and Rogers Brubaker, 'Identity', in Frederick Cooper (ed.), *Colonialism in Question: Theory, Knowledge, History* (Los Angeles: University of California Press, 2005), pp. 59–90, esp. pp. 75–7.

37 Forrester, *Beliefs, Values and Policies*, pp. 17–22.

38 Itzen, *Streitbare Kirche*; Phillips, *Contesting the Moral High Ground*.

39 Hastings, 'British Churches', pp. 4–13; Catterall, *Labour and the Free Churches*, pp. 4, 211, 215–16.

40 See Parker and Lawson, *God and War*, pp. 5–6.

41 *Guardian*, 20 January 1939, p. 39; 10 March 1939, p. 151; 5 April 1940, pp. 164–5.

42 *Guardian*, 4 April 1941, p. 167; 25 April 1941, p. 204.

43 *Guardian*, 18 April 1941, p. 192.

44 Bell, 'What Is Liberalism?', p. 704.

45 E.g. Kirby, 'Divinely Sanctioned'; Conway, 'Rise and Fall'; Nurser, *For All Peoples and All Nations*; Thompson, *God and Globe*; James Chappel, 'The Catholic Origins of Totalitarianism Theory in Interwar Europe', *Modern Intellectual History*, 8:3 (2011), 561–90; Müller, 'Towards a New History of Christian Democracy'.

46 Barry, *Church and Leadership*, p. 30.

47 'Reconstruction: End and Means', *The Round Table: The Commonwealth Journal of International Affairs*, 31:121 (1940), 25–39. Cited and discussed by Oldham in *CNL* 63L, 8 January 1941, p. 2.

48 *Guardian*, 30 August 1940, p. 418.

49 Zeilstra, *European Unity in Ecumenical Thinking*, p. 201.

50 Richard Overy, *Why the Allies Won* (London: Pimlico, 2006 [1995]), pp. 347–85.

51 *Nature*, 3808:150 (24 October 1942), 469–72.

52 *Ibid.*, p. 469.

53 *Theology*, 50:328 (November 1947), 361–2.

54 Müller, *Contesting Democracy*, pp. 128–9.

55 *British Weekly*, 20 March 1947, p. 323.

56 Hastings, 'British Churches', p. 5.

57 *Ibid.*, p. 9.

58 Todd Weir, 'The Christian Front against Godlessness: Anti-Secularism and the Demise of the Weimar Republic 1928 to 1933', *Past and Present*, 229:1 (2015), 201–38.

59 *Ibid.*, pp. 206–7.

60 Huttner, *Totalitarismus und säkulare Religionen*, pp. 265–322.

61 Ivor Thomas, 'Crisis in the Western World', *The Times Literary Supplement*, 29 July 1944, 366, 369. Thomas was a member of the CFC.

62 While Dawson did not 'sympathise with fascism, he *empathised* with it': Villis, *British Catholics and Fascism*, p. 105 (emphasis in original). See also Dietz, 'Christliches Abendland'.

63 Roger Griffin, 'Studying Fascism in a Postfascist Age: From New Consensus to New Wave?', *Fascism*, 1 (2012): 1–17.

64 Dietz, *Neo-Tories*.

65 Villis, *British Catholics and Fascism*; Pasture, 'Christian Fatherland'. Roger Griffin, 'The "Holy Storm": "Clerical Fascism" through the Lens of Modernism', *Totalitarian Movements and Political Religions*, 8:2 (2007), 213–27.

66 Veldman, *Fantasy*, pp. 1–3; Sterenberg, *Mythic Thinking*, pp. 1, 3–4.

67 Moyn, *Christian Human Rights*, p. 67.

68 Larry Seidentop, *Inventing the Individual: The Origins of Western Liberalism* (London: Allen Lane, 2014); Nick Spencer, *Freedom and Order: History, Politics and the English Bible* (London: Hodder and Stoughton, 2011); Nicholas Wolterstorff, *Justice: Rights and Wrongs* (Princeton: Princeton University Press, 2008); Annabel Brett, *Liberty, Right, and Nature: Individual Rights in Later Scholastic Thought* (Cambridge: Cambridge University Press, 1997); Brett, 'Human Rights and the Thomist Tradition'.

69 Thompson, *God and Globe*, pp. 1–23; Terence Renaud, 'Human Rights as Radical Anthropology: Protestant Theology and Ecumenism in the Transwar Era', *Historical Journal*, 60:2 (2017), 493–518.

70 See Bok, 'Did the Christians Ruin Rights?'.

71 Peter Catterall, '"Efficiency with Freedom"? Debates about the British Constitution in the Twentieth Century', in Peter Catterall, Wolfram Kaiser and

Ulrike Walton-Jordan (eds.), *Reforming the Constitution: Debates in Twentieth-Century Britain* (London: Cass, 2000), pp. 1–42.

72 *Christendom*, 13:51 (September 1943), 67–9.

73 Charles Taylor, *A Secular Age* (Cambridge, MA: Belknap Press of Harvard University Press, 2007), p. 3.

74 Moberly, 'The Christian Faith and the Common Life', p. 556.

75 Taylor, *A Secular Age*, pp. 15–16.

76 For the use of 'post-Christian', see *Church of England Newspaper*, 7 January 1944, p. 8; *Catholic Herald*, 27 October 1944, p. 3; editorial, *Christendom*, 13:54 (June 1944), p. 165; *Christian World*, 15 August 1946, p. 11; *Guardian*, 22 March 1946, p. 139; *CNL* 0L, 18 October 1939, p. 1; *CNL* 250S, 26 December 1945, Daniel Jenkins, 'Christmas Has Happened', p. 11. *CNL* 255L, 6 March 1946, p. 3; *CNL* 278L, 22 January 1947, p. 7; *CNL* 294L, 17 September 1947, p. 3. OA 9/8/45, Crossman to Oldham, 11 October 1948, p. 2. Murry: 'we have now entered on a post-Christian phase of European history'; John Middleton Murry, *The Betrayal of Christ by the Churches* (London: Andrew Dakers, 1940), p. 144. Nils Ehrenström, *Christian Faith and the Modern State: An Oecumenical Approach* (London: SCM, 1937), p. 13.

77 Parker, *Faith on the Home Front*.

78 Brown, *Death of Christian Britain*, p. 5.

79 D. L. Munby, *The Idea of a Secular Society and Its Significance for Christians* (London: Oxford University Press, 1963), pp. 14–35.

80 *Ibid.*, p. 11.

81 *Ibid.*

82 Brewitt-Taylor, 'Invention of a "Secular Society"?'; and 'From Religion to Revolution'.

83 Clements, *Faith on the Frontier*, p. 465. See Oldham's letters to David Edwards, editor of SCM Press, and to Robinson: LPL MS 3541, Oldham to Edwards, 27 March 1963 and 2 April 1963; Oldham to Robinson, 13 April 1963.

84 Duncan B. Forrester, 'Some Thoughts on "Religionless Christianity"', *Indian Journal of Theology*, 13:1 (1964), 11–19.

85 Brewitt-Taylor, 'From Religion to Revolution'; Peter Catterall, 'Church Decline, Secularism and Ecumenism', *Contemporary Record*, 5:2 (1991), 276–90.

86 Huttner, *Totalitarismus und säkulare Religionen*, p. 293.

87 *Theology*, 48:305 (November 1945), 241–3 (p. 242).

88 Jackson, *Red Tape and the Gospel*, p. 265; Hastings, *Oliver Tomkins*, p. 34.

89 Clements, *Faith on the Frontier*, pp. 353, 385.

90 Grimley, 'Civil Society and the Clerisy', p. 247.

91 MSC, Oldham to Vidler, 30 September 1950, p. 4.

92 *Ibid.*, p. 3.

93 Oliver, *Church and Social Order*, pp. 136–7; Elford and Markham, *Middle Way*, pp. 96–9; Coupland, 'Anglican Peace Aims', p. 106.

94 *Moot Papers*, M10, p. 348; *CNL* 194L, 3 November 1943, pp. 1–3.

95 *CNL* 122S, 25 February 1942, Henry Brooke, 'Private Duty and Public Service'.

96 *CNL* 168S, 13 January 1943, Kathleen Bliss, 'War and the Family'; *CNL* 202S, 23 February 1944, Kathleen Bliss, 'Families in Future'; *CNL* 218S, 4 October 1944, Nell Jenkins, 'The Family in Society'; *CNL* 231S, 4 April 1945, David R. Mace, 'The Outlook for Marriage'; *CNL* 257L, 3 April 1946; *CNL* 277L, 8 January 1947, pp. 1–8; *CNL* 279L, 5 February 1947, pp. 1–9; *CNL* 292L, 20 August 1947, pp. 1–9.

97 *CNL* 184S, 16 June 1943, Kathleen Bliss, 'Sex Relationships in War-Time', p. 2.

98 *CNL* 121, 18 February 1942, p. 2.

99 *CNL* 28S, 8 May 1940, J. Z. Hodge, 'Christianity in India: A War-Time View'; *CNL* 131L, 29 April 1942, pp. 2–3; *CNL* 153, 30 September 1942, pp. 1–4.

100 Clements, *Faith on the Frontier*, pp. 211–50.

101 Eliot, *Notes towards the Definition of Culture*, pp. 64–5.

102 *CNL* 118S, 28 January 1942, Margaret Wrong, 'British Policy in Africa'.

103 *Moot Papers*, M7, p. 274.

104 *Ibid.*, M19, p. 678.

105 *CNL* 50L, 9 October 1940, pp. 1–3. See also *CNL* 98S, 10 September 1941, William Paton, 'Britain and India'; *CNL* 130L, 22 April 1942, pp. 1–2; *CNL* 189L, 25 August 1943, p. 3; *CNL* 290L, 23 July 1947.

106 *CNL* 261, 29 May 1946, pp. 5–6; *CNL* 290L, 23 July 1947.

107 *CNL* 340L, 22 June 1949, p. 198. Here, however, he made clear that by far the greatest threat to Christianity was Communism.

108 Greenberg, 'Decolonization', p. 336.

109 29 November 1939, J. H. Oldham, 'Preliminaries to the Consideration of Peace Aims', p. 2.

110 Abrecht, 'Lessons', p. 151. Mateus, 'Global Christian Unity', p. 240.

111 Forrester, *Beliefs, Values and Policies*, pp. 17–22.

112 Clements, *Faith on the Frontier*, p. 402.

113 Gerald H. Anderson (ed.), *Biographical Dictionary of Christian Missions* (New York: Macmillan Reference, 1998), p. 506. M. Marinetto, 'The Historical Development of Business Philanthropy: Social Responsibility in the New Corporate Economy', *Business History*, 41:4 (1999), 1–20 (pp. 3–4).

114 See *Moot Papers*, pp. 15–16; Taylor and Reeves, 'Intellectuals in Debate', pp. 39–41.

115 Freathy, 'Triumph', esp. pp. 308–11, 314–15.

116 Taylor and Reeves, 'Intellectuals in Debate', pp. 39–41. McKibbin, *Classes and Cultures*, p. 221.

117 *CNL* 338L, 25 May 1949, p. 164.

118 Hastings, 'British Churches', p. 11.

119 Clements, *Faith on the Frontier*, p. 414. Harold Silver, *Higher Education and Opinion Making in Twentieth-Century England* (London: Woburn, 2003), pp. 41–5, 100–26. W. H. G. Armytage, 'From McNair to James', in David Hartley and Maurice Whitehead (eds.), *Teacher Education: Historical Aspects of Teacher Education from 1905 to 1990* (Abingdon: Routledge, 2006), pp. 356–71 (p. 357). Taylor, 'Education and the Moot', pp. 176–7, 179–81.

120 Taylor, 'Education and the Moot', p. 181.

121 Hastings, 'British Churches', p. 5.

122 *Ibid.*, p. 8.

123 Lord and Reeves, 'Themes of the 1930s', p. 4.

124 Steele and Taylor, 'Oldham's Moot', p. 197. See also Hastings, 'British Churches', pp. 8–9.

125 See Bowler, *Reconciling Science and Religion*, 3–4.

126 Alasdair MacIntyre, *After Virtue: A Study in Moral Theory* (London: Bloomsbury, 2007 [1981]); Roger Scruton, *Our Church: A Personal History of the Church of England* (London: Atlantic, 2012); Rowan Williams, *Faith in the Public Square* (London: Bloomsbury, 2012); Justin Welby, *Dethroning Mammon: Making Money Serve Grace* (London: Bloomsbury, 2017); Rod Dreher, *The Benedict Option: A Strategy for Christians in a Post-Christian Nation* (New York: Sentinel, 2017); Patrick Deneen, *Why Liberalism Failed* (New Haven: Yale University Press, 2018).

127 Jürgen Habermas, 'Faith and Knowledge', in Jürgen Habermas, *The Future of Human Nature* (Cambridge: Polity, 2003), 101–15; Jürgen Habermas, 'Notes on Post-Secular Society', *New Perspectives Quarterly*, 25 (2008), 17–29; Gorski *et al.*, *Post-Secular in Question*; May *et al.*, 'Religious as Political'.

Bibliography

Archives

BC   John Baillie Collection, University of Edinburgh
CERC   Church of England Record Office, London
IOE   Fred Clarke Papers, Institute of Education, University of London
LPL   Lambeth Palace Library, London
MSC   Martin Symons Collection, private archive of papers of W. G. Symons
OA   J. H. Oldham Papers, New College Library, Edinburgh (the 'Oldham Archive')
UL   Moot Papers, Brotherton Library, University of Leeds
WGS   W. G. Symons Papers, University of Birmingham

Newspapers and periodicals

Adelphi
British Weekly
Catholic Herald
Christendom
Christian News-Letter
Christian World
Church of England Newspaper
Church Times
Daily Mail
Economist
Federal Union News
Guardian
King-Hall News-Letter
Listener
Manchester Guardian
Nature

New Statesman and Nation
News Chronicle
Observer
Picture Post
Scotsman
Spectator
Spiritual Issues of the War
Theology
The Times
The Times Literary Supplement

Published primary sources

Arendt, Hannah. *The Origins of Totalitarianism*, 3rd edn. London: George Allen & Unwin, 1967 [1950].

Baillie, John. *What Is Christian Civilisation?* London: Oxford University Press, 1945.

Baillie, John. *God's Will for Church and Nation*. London: SCM, 1946.

Baillie, John. *The Mind of the Modern University*. London: SCM, 1946.

Barry, F. R. *Church and Leadership*. London: SCM, 1945.

Barth, Karl. *A Letter to Great Britain from Switzerland*. London: Sheldon Press, 1941.

Bliss, Kathleen. *The Future of Religion*. London: Penguin, 1972 [1969].

The Church and the Planning of Britain: Report of the Social and Industrial Commission of the Church Assembly, 1944. London: Church Assembly, 1944.

Church, Community, and State in Relation to Education. London: George Allen & Unwin, 1938.

The Churches Survey Their Task. London: George Allen & Unwin, 1937.

Clarke, Fred. *Education and Social Change: An English Interpretation*. London: Sheldon Press, 1940.

Clarke, Fred. *Freedom in the Educative Society*. London: University of London Press, 1948.

Cripps, Stafford. *Towards Christian Democracy*. London: George Allen & Unwin, 1945.

Dawson, Christopher. *Religion and the Modern State*. London: Sheed & Ward, 1938 [1935].

Dawson, Christopher. *The Judgement of the Nations*. London: Sheed & Ward, 1943.

Drucker, Peter F. *The Future of Industrial Man*. Piscataway, NJ: Transaction, 1995 [1942].

Ehrenström, Nils. *Christian Faith and the Modern State: An Oecumenical Approach*. London: SCM, 1937.

Eliot, T. S. 'Thoughts after Lambeth' (1931). In *Selected Essays, 1917–1932*, pp. 310–22. New York: Harcourt, Brace, 1932.

Eliot, T. S. *The Idea of a Christian Society*. London: Faber and Faber, 1939.

Eliot, T. S. *Notes towards the Definition of Culture*. London: Faber and Faber, 1962 [1948].

Eliot, T. S. *The Poems of T. S. Eliot*, Vol. I: *Collected and Uncollected Poems*, ed. Christopher Ricks and Jim McCue. London: Faber and Faber, 2015.

Eliot, T. S., *The Letters of T. S. Eliot*, Vol. VII: *1934–1935*, ed. Valerie Eliot and John Haffenden. London: Faber and Faber, 2017.

Fenn, Eric. *The Crisis and Democracy*. London: SCM, 1938.

Fenn, Eric. *That They Go Forward: An Impression of the Oxford Conference on Church, Community and State*. London: SCM, 1938.

Hayek, F. A. *The Road to Serfdom: Text and Documents. The Definitive Edition*, ed. Bruce Campbell. Chicago: University of Chicago Press, 2007 [1944].

Hodges, H. A. *Objectivity and Impartiality*. London: SCM, 1946.

Ingram, Kenneth. *Christianity: Right or Left?* London: George Allen & Unwin, 1937.

Jewkes, John. *Ordeal by Planning*. London: Macmillan, 1948.

Laski, Harold J. *Faith, Reason, and Civilisation: An Essay in Historical Analysis*. London: Victor Gollancz, 1944.

Lewis, C. S. *Mere Christianity*. New York: Macmillan, 1952.

Lindsay, A. D. 'Christian Individualism and Scientific Individualism'. In *Democracy, Should It Survive?*, pp. 118–26. London: Dennis Dobson, 1946.

Lippmann, Walter. 'Man in Modern Education'. In *Democracy, Should It Survive?*, pp. 62–9. London: Dennis Dobson, 1946.

Lowe, Adolph. *The Price of Liberty: An Essay on Contemporary Britain*, 3rd edn. London: Hogarth Press, 1948 [1937].

Malvern, 1941: The Life of the Church and the Order of Society. London: Longmans, 1941.

Mannheim, Karl. *Man and Society in an Age of Reconstruction: Studies in Modern Social Structure*. London: Kegan Paul, Trench, Trübner, 1942 [1940].

Mannheim, Karl. *Diagnosis of Our Time: Wartime Essays of a Sociologist*, 2nd edn. London: Kegan Paul, Trench, Trübner, 1943.

Mannheim, Karl. *Freedom, Power and Democratic Planning*. New York: Oxford University Press, 1950.

Mises, Ludwig von. *Omnipotent Government: The Rise of the Total State and Total War*. New Haven: Yale University Press, 1944.

Moberly, Walter, 'The Christian Faith and the Common Life', *Contemporary Review*, 153 (May 1938), 555–62.

Moberly, Walter. *The Crisis in the University*. London: SCM, 1949.

Munby, D. L. *The Idea of a Secular Society and Its Significance for Christians*. London: Oxford University Press, 1963.

Murry, John Middleton. *The Price of Leadership*. London: SCM, 1939.

Murry, John Middleton. *The Betrayal of Christ by the Churches*. London: Andrew Dakers, 1940.

Murry, John Middleton. 'Ends and Means'. *Listener*, 23 May 1940, 1014–15.

Murry, John Middleton. 'Pre-Conditions of Federal Union', in M. Chaning-Pearce, ed., *Federal Union: A Symposium*, pp. 155–63. London: Jonathan Cape, 1940.

Murry, John Middleton, *Adam and Eve: An Essay towards a New and Better Society*. London: Dakers, 1944.

Murry, John Middleton. *Trust or Perish*. London: Andrew Dakers, 1946.

Murry, John Middleton. *The Free Society*. London: Andrew Dakers, 1948.

Murry, John Middleton. *Community Farm*. London: Country Book Club, 1953.

Niebuhr, Reinhold. *The Children of Light and the Children of Darkness: A Vindication of Democracy and a Critique of Its Traditional Defense*. Chicago: University of Chicago Press, 2011 [1944].

Oldham, J. H. *Christianity and the Race Problem*. London: SCM, 1924.

Oldham, J. H. *Church, Community and State: A World Issue*. London: SCM, 1935.

Oldham, J. H. *The Resurrection of Christendom*. London: Sheldon Press, 1940.

Oldham, J. H. *The Root of Our Troubles: Two Broadcast Talks*. London: SCM, 1941.

Oldham, J. H., ed. *Real Life Is Meeting*. London: Sheldon Press, 1942.

Oldham, J. H. *Work in Modern Society*. London: SCM, 1950.

Oldham, J. H. *Life Is Commitment*. London: SCM, 1953.

Orwell, George. 'Notes on the Way'. In George Orwell, *The Collected Essays, Journalism and Letters of George Orwell*, Vol. II: *My Country Right or Left 1940–1943*, ed. Sonia Orwell and Ian Angus, pp. 30–3. London: Penguin, 1970 [1958].

Paton, William. *The Church and the New Order*. London: SCM, 1941.

Polanyi, Michael. *The Contempt of Freedom: The Russian Experiment and After*. London: Watts, 1940.

Polanyi, Michael. 'The English and the Continent'. *Political Quarterly*, 14:4 (1943), 372–81.

Popper, K. R. *The Open Society and Its Enemies*, Vol. II. London: Routledge and Kegan Paul, 1980 [1945].

Richardson, Alan. 'The Religious Situation of Wartime Britain', *Christianity and Society* (Autumn 1941), 8–17.

Roberts, Michael. *Recovery of the West*. London: Faber and Faber, 1941.

Temple, F. S., ed. *William Temple: Some Lambeth Letters*. London: Oxford University Press, 1963.

Temple, William. *Christianity and Social Order*. Harmondsworth: Penguin, 1942.

Temple, William. *The Crisis of the Western World and Other Broadcast Talks*. London: George Allen & Unwin, 1944.

Thomas, Ivor. *The Socialist Tragedy*. London: Latimer House, 1949.

The Universal Church and the World of Nations. Chicago: Willett, Clark, 1938.

Urwin, E. C. *Religion in Planned Society*. London: Epworth Press, 1942.

Vidler, A. R. *God's Judgment on Europe*. London: Longmans, Green, 1940.

Vidler, A. R. *Secular Despair and Christian Faith*. London: SCM, 1941.

Vidler, A. R. *Christianity's Need for a Free University*. London: SCM, 1946.

Vidler, A. R. *Scenes from a Clerical Life*. London: Collins, 1977.

Vidler, A. R. and W. A. Whitehouse. *Natural Law: A Christian Reconsideration*. London: SCM, 1946.

Visser 't Hooft, W. A. and J. H. Oldham. *The Church and Its Function in Society*. London: Allen & Unwin, 1937.

Wootton, Barbara. 'Freedom under Planning'. In Herbert Morrison, Barbara Wootton and Joan Robinson, eds., *Can Planning Be Democratic? A Collection of Essays Prepared for the Fabian Society*, pp. 37–54. London: Labour Book Service, [1944].

Secondary literature

Abrecht, Paul. 'From Oxford to Vancouver: Lessons from Fifty Years of Ecumenical Work for Economic and Social Justice'. *Ecumenical Review*, 40 (1988), 147–68.

Adam, Thomas. *Intercultural Transfers and the Making of the Modern World, 1800–2000*. Basingstoke: Palgrave Macmillan, 2011.

Adams, Guy B., John Forester and Bayard L. Catron, eds. *Policymaking, Communication, and Social Learning: Essays of Sir Geoffrey Vickers*. New Brunswick: Transaction, 1987.

Anderson, Gerald H., ed. *Biographical Dictionary of Christian Missions*. New York: Macmillan Reference, 1998.

Armytage, W. H. G. 'From McNair to James'. In David Hartley and Maurice Whitehead, eds., *Teacher Education: Historical Aspects of Teacher Education from 1905 to 1990*, pp. 356–71. Abingdon: Routledge, 2006.

Backhouse, Stephen. 'Patriotism, Nationhood and Neighbourhood'. *Modern Believing*, 53:4 (2012), 398–407.

Backhouse, Stephen. 'Nationalism and Patriotism'. In Nicholas Adams, George Pattison and Graham Ward, eds, *Oxford Handbook of Theology and Modern European Thought*, pp. 41–60. Oxford: Oxford University Press, 2013.

Barnes, Kenneth C. *Nazism, Liberalism, and Christianity: Protestant Social Thought in Germany and Great Britain, 1925–1937*. Lexington: University Press of Kentucky, 1991.

Barnett, Correlli. *The Audit of War: The Illusion and Reality of Britain as a Great Nation*. London: Macmillan, 1986.

Bates, Dennis. 'Ecumenism and Religious Education between the Wars: The Work of J. H. Oldham'. *British Journal of Religious Education*, 8:3 (1986), 130–9.

Bavaj, Riccardo. 'Intellectual History', version 1.0. *Docupedia-Zeitgeschichte* (13 September 2010), http://docupedia.de/zg/Intellectual_History.

Beaken, Robert. *Cosmo Lang: Archbishop in War and Crisis*. London: I.B. Tauris, 2012.

Bell, Duncan. 'What Is Liberalism?'. *Political Theory*, 42:6 (2014), 682–715.

Bennett, George. 'Paramountcy to Partnership: J. H. Oldham and Africa'. *Africa: Journal of the International African Institute*, 30:4 (1960), 356–61.

Bennett, John C. 'Breakthrough in Ecumenical Social Ethics: The Legacy of the Oxford Conference on Church, Community and State (1937)'. *Ecumenical Review*, 40:2 (1988), 132–46.

Bergunder, Michael. 'What Is Religion? The Unexplained Subject Matter of Religious Studies'. *Method and Theory in the Study of Religion*, 26 (2014), 246–86.

Besier, Erhard, Armin Boyens and Gerhard Lindemann. *Nationaler Protestantismus und ökumenische Bewegung: Kirchliches Handeln im Kalten Krieg (1945–1990)*. Berlin: Duncker & Humblot, 1999.

Bevir, Mark. 'The Logic of the History of Ideas'. *Rethinking History: The Journal of Theory and Practice*, 4:3 (2000), 295–300.

Bevir, Mark. 'Philosophy, Rhetoric, and Power: A Response to Critics'. *Rethinking History: The Journal of Theory and Practice*, 4:3 (2000), 341–50.

Blaxland-de Lange, Simon. *Owen Barfield: Romanticism Comes of Age*. Forest Row: Temple Lodge, 2006.

Bliss, Kathleen. 'The Legacy of J. H. Oldham'. *International Bulletin of Missionary Research*, 8:1 (1984), 18–23.

Bliss, Kathleen, rev. Andrew Porter. 'Oldham, Joseph Houldsworth (1874–1969)'. In *Oxford Dictionary of National Biography*. Oxford: Oxford University Press, 2004; online edn, May 2007, www.oxforddnb.com/view/article/35301.

Blissett, William. 'T. S. Eliot and Catholicity'. In Benjamin G. Lockerd, ed., *T. S. Eliot and Christian Tradition*, pp. 33–51. Madison, NJ: Fairleigh Dickinson University Press, 2014.

Bok, P. Mackenzie. 'Did the Christians Ruin Rights?'. *New Rambler*, posted 15 February 2016, http://newramblerreview.com/book-reviews/history/did-the-christians-ruin-rights.

Bowler, Peter J. *Reconciling Science and Religion: The Debate in Early-Twentieth-Century Britain*. Chicago: University of Chicago Press, 2001.

Brett, Annabel. *Liberty, Right, and Nature: Individual Rights in Later Scholastic Thought*. Cambridge: Cambridge University Press, 1997.

Brett, Annabel. 'Human Rights and the Thomist Tradition'. In Pamela Slotte and Miia Halme-Tuomisaari, eds., *Revisiting the Origins of Human Rights*, pp. 82–101. Cambridge: Cambridge University Press, 2015.

Brewer, John D. 'Sociology and Theology Reconsidered: Religious Sociology and the Sociology of Religion in Britain'. *History of the Human Sciences*, 20:2 (2007), 7–28.

Brewitt-Taylor, Sam. 'The Invention of a "Secular Society"? Christianity and the Sudden Appearance of Secularisation Discourses in the British National Media, 1961–64'. *Twentieth Century British History*, 24:3 (2013), 327–50.

Brewitt-Taylor, Sam. 'From Religion to Revolution: Theologies of Secularisation in the British Student Christian Movement, 1963–73'. *Journal of Ecclesiastical History*, 66:4 (2015), 792–811.

Brown, Callum. *The Death of Christian Britain: Understanding Secularisation 1800–2000*, 2nd edn. London: Routledge, 2009 [2001].

Brubaker, Rogers. 'Religion and Nationalism: Four Approaches'. *Nations and Nationalism*, 18 (2012), 2–20.

Bruce, Steve. 'Secularisation in the UK and the USA'. In Callum G. Brown and Michael Snape, eds., *Secularisation in the Christian World*, pp. 205–18. Farnham: Ashgate, 2010.

Bruce, Steve. *Secularization: In Defence of an Unfashionable Theory*. Oxford: Oxford University Press, 2011.

Burleigh, Michael. *Sacred Causes: The Clash of Religion and Politics, from the Great War to the War on Terror*. New York: HarperCollins, 2007.

Casanova, José. *Public Religions in the Modern World*. Chicago: University of Chicago Press, 1994.

Casanova, José. 'Secularization Revisited: A Reply to Talal Asad'. In David Scott and Charles Hirschkind, eds., *Powers of the Secular Modern: Talal Asad and His Interlocutors*, pp. 12–30. Stanford: Stanford University Press, 2006.

Catterall, Peter. 'Church Decline, Secularism and Ecumenism'. *Contemporary Record*, 5:2 (1991), 276–90.

Catterall, Peter. 'Morality and Politics: The Free Churches and the Labour Party between the Wars'. *Historical Journal*, 36:3 (1993), 667–85.

Catterall, Peter, ' "Efficiency with Freedom"? Debates about the British Constitution in the Twentieth Century', in Peter Catterall, Wolfram Kaiser and Ulrike Walton-Jordan, eds., *Reforming the Constitution: Debates in Twentieth-Century Britain*. London: Cass, 2000, pp. 1–42.

Catterall, Peter. 'The Distinctiveness of British Socialism? Religion and the Rise of Labour, *c*. 1900–39'. In Matthew Worley, ed., *The Foundations of the British Labour Party: Identities, Cultures, and Perspectives 1900–39*, pp. 131–52. Farnham: Ashgate, 2009.

Catterall, Peter. *Labour and the Free Churches, 1918–1939: Radicalism, Righteousness, and Religion*. London: Bloomsbury, 2016.

Ceadel, Martin. *Semi-Detached Idealists: The British Peace Movement and International Relations, 1845–1945*. Oxford: Oxford University Press, 2000.

Cell, J. W. *By Kenya Possessed: The Correspondence of Norman Leys and J. H. Oldham 1918–1926*. Chicago: University of Chicago Press, 1976.

Chandler, Andrew. 'Munich and Morality: The Bishops of the Church of England and Appeasement'. *Twentieth-Century British History*, 5:1 (1994), 77–99.

Chandler, Andrew. Review of John Wolffe, *God and Greater Britain: Religion and National Life in Britain and Ireland 1843–1945* (London: Routledge, 1994), *English Historical Review*, 110 (1995), 948–50.

Chandler, Andrew, ed. *Brethren in Adversity: George Bell, the Church of England and the Crisis of German Protestantism, 1933–1939*. Woodbridge: Boydell, 1997.

Chandler, Andrew. *George Bell, Bishop of Chichester: Church, State, and Resistance in the Age of Dictatorship*. Grand Rapids, MI: William B. Eerdmans, 2016.

Chapman, Alister, John Coffey and Brad S. Gregory, eds. *Seeing Things Their Way: Intellectual History and the Return of Religion*. Notre Dame: University of Notre Dame Press, 2009.

Chappel, James. 'The Catholic Origins of Totalitarianism Theory in Interwar Europe'. *Modern Intellectual History*, 8:3 (2011), 561–90.

Chappel, James. 'Beyond Tocqueville: A Plea to Stop "Taking Religion Seriously" '. *Modern Intellectual History*, 10:3 (2013), 697–708.

Cheyne, Alec C. 'The Baillie Brothers'. In David Fergusson, ed., *Christ, Church and Society: Essays on John Baillie and Donald Baillie*, pp. 3–37. Edinburgh: T. & T. Clark, 1993.

Chinitz, David. 'T. S. Eliot and the Cultural Divide'. *PMLA*, 110:2 (1995), 236–47.

Clements, Keith. *A Patriotism for Today: Dialogue with Dietrich Bonhoeffer*. Bristol: Bristol Baptist College, 1984.

Clements, Keith. 'John Baillie and "the Moot" '. In David Fergusson, ed., *Christ, Church and Society: Essays on John Baillie and Donald Baillie*, pp. 199–219. Edinburgh: T. & T. Clark, 1993.

Clements, Keith. *Faith on the Frontier: A Life of J. H. Oldham*. Edinburgh: T. & T. Clark, 1999.

Clements, Keith. ' "Friend of Africa": J. H. Oldham (1874–1969), Missions and British Colonial Policy in the 1920s'. In Frieder Ludwig and Afe Adogame, eds., *European Traditions in the Study of Religion in Africa*, pp. 175–86. Wiesbaden: Otto Harrasowitz, 2004.

Clements, Keith, ed. *The Moot Papers: Faith, Freedom and Society 1938–1944*. Edinburgh: T. & T. Clark, 2010.

Clements, Keith W. 'Oldham and Baillie: A Creative Relationship'. In Andrew. R. Morton, ed., *God's Will in a Time of Crisis: A Colloquium Celebrating the 50th Anniversary of the Baillie Commission*, pp. 45–59. Edinburgh: University of Edinburgh, 1994.

Cline, Catherine Anne. 'Ecumenism and Appeasement: The Bishops of the Church of England and the Treaty of Versailles'. *Journal of Modern History*, 61 (1989), 683–703.

Collini, Stefan. 'The European Modernist as Anglican Moralist: The Later Social Criticism of T. S. Eliot'. In Mark S. Micale and Robert L. Dietle, eds., *Enlightenment, Passion, Modernity: Historical Essays in European Thought and Culture*, pp. 207–29. Stanford: Stanford University Press, 2000.

Collini, Stefan. 'The Literary Critic and the Village Labourer: "Culture" in Twentieth-Century Britain'. *Transactions of the Royal Historical Society*, 6th series, 14 (2004), 93–116.

Collini, Stefan. *Absent Minds: Intellectuals in Britain*. Oxford: Oxford University Press, 2006.

Collini, Stefan. 'Saint or Snake'. *London Review of Books*, 8 October 2015, 29–33.

Conway, Martin. 'The Rise and Fall of Western Europe's Democratic Age, 1945–1973'. *Contemporary European History*, 13:1 (2004), 67–88.

Cooper, Frederick and Rogers Brubaker. 'Identity'. In Frederick Cooper, ed., *Colonialism in Question: Theory, Knowledge, History*, pp. 59–90. Los Angeles: University of California Press, 2005.

Coupland, Philip. 'H. G. Wells's "Liberal Fascism"'. *Journal of Contemporary History*, 35:4 (2000), 541–58.

Coupland, Philip. 'Britain, Europe and Christendom in Mid-Twentieth-Century British Christian Thought'. *Political Theology*, 6:3 (2005), 367–91.

Coupland, Philip M. *Britannia, Europa and Christendom: British Christians and European Integration*. Basingstoke: Palgrave Macmillan, 2006.

Coupland, Philip M. 'Anglican Peace Aims and the Christendom Group, 1939–1945'. In Stephen G. Parker and Tom Lawson, eds., *God and War: The Church of England and Armed Conflict in the Twentieth Century*, pp. 99–120. Abingdon: Ashgate, 2012.

Cowling, Maurice. *Religion and Public Doctrine in Modern England*, Vol. III: *Accommodations*. Cambridge: Cambridge University Press, 2001.

Crook, David. 'Universities, Teacher Training, and the Legacy of McNair, 1944–94'. *History of Education*, 24:3 (1995), 231–45.

Dale, Alzina Stone. *T. S. Eliot: The Philosopher Poet*. Wheaton, IL: Harold Shaw, 1988.

Dale, Gareth. *Karl Polanyi: The Limits of the Market*. Cambridge: Polity, 2010.

Davie, Grace. *Religion in Britain since 1945: Believing without Belonging*. Oxford: Blackwell, 1994.

DeJonge, Michael P. 'Martin Luther, Dietrich Bonhoeffer, and Political Theologies'. In *Oxford Research Encyclopedia (Religion)*, August 2016, DOI: 10.1093/acrefore/9780199340378.013.307.

Deneen, Patrick. *Democratic Faith*. Princeton: Princeton University Press, 2005.

Deneen, Patrick. *Why Liberalism Failed*. New Haven: Yale University Press, 2018.

Dietz, Bernhard. 'Christliches Abendland gegen Pluralismus und Moderne: Die Europa-Konzeption von Christopher Dawson'. *Zeithistorische Forschungen/ Studies in Contemporary History*, 9 (2012), 491–7.

Dietz, Bernhard, trans. Ian Copestake. *Neo-Tories: The Revolt of British Conservatives against Democracy and Political Modernity (1929–1939)*. London: Bloomsbury Academic, 2018.

Dorrien, Gary J. *The Making of American Liberal Theology: Idealism, Realism and Modernity, 1900–1950*. Louisville, KY: Westminster John Knox Press, 2003.

Dorrien, Gary J. *Social Ethics in the Making: Interpreting an American Tradition*. Chichester: John Wiley, 2011 [2008].

Dreher, Rod. *The Benedict Option: A Strategy for Christians in a Post-Christian Nation*. New York: Sentinel, 2017.

Dressler, Markus and Arvind-Pal S. Mandair. *Secularism and Religion-Making*. Oxford: Oxford University Press, 2011.

Duchhardt, Heinz and Małgorzata Morawiec, eds. *Die europäische Integration und die Kirchen: Akteure und Rezipienten*. Göttingen: Vandenhoeck & Ruprecht, 2010.

Edgerton, David. *Warfare State: Britain, 1920–1970*. Cambridge: Cambridge University Press, 2006.

Edwards, David L. 'Bliss, Kathleen Mary Amelia (1908–1989)', rev. In *Oxford Dictionary of National Biography*. Oxford: Oxford University Press, 2004; online edn, May 2007, www.oxforddnb.com/view/article/39995.

Edwards, Mark T. '"God's Totalitarianism": Ecumenical Protestant Discourse during the Good War, 1941–45'. *Totalitarian Movements and Political Religions*, 10 (2009): 285–302.

Edwards, Mark T. *The Right of the Protestant Left: God's Totalitarianism*. New York: Palgrave Macmillan, 2012.

Eggert, Marion and Lucian Hölscher, eds. *Religion and Secularity: Transformations and Transfers of Religious Discourses in Europe and Asia*. Leiden: Brill, 2013.

Einfalt, Michael. 'Debating Literary Autonomy: Jacques Maritain versus André Gide'. In Rajesh Heynickx and Jan De Maeyer, eds., *The Maritain Factor: Taking Religion into Interwar Modernism*, pp. 152–63. Leuven: Leuven University Press, 2010.

Elford, R. John and Ian S. Markham, eds. *The Middle Way: Theology, Politics and Economics in the Later Thought of R. H. Preston*. London: SCM, 2000.

Evans, Richard J. *The Third Reich in Power*. New York: Penguin, 2005.

Feindt, Gregor, Bernhard Gißibl, and Johannes Paulmann, eds. *Kulturelle Souveränität: Politische Deutungs- und Handlungsmacht jenseits des Staates im 20. Jahrhundert*. Göttingen: Vandenhoeck & Ruprecht, 2016.

Fergusson, David A. S. 'Theology in a Time of War: John Baillie's Political Writing'. In Andrew R. Morton, ed., *God's Will in a Time of Crisis: A Colloquium Celebrating the 50th Anniversary of the Baillie Commission*, pp. 32–44. Edinburgh: University of Edinburgh, 1994.

Fitzgerald, Timothy. *Discourse on Civility and Barbarity: A Critical History of Religion and Related Categories*. Oxford: Oxford University Press, 2007.

Fletcher, Christine M. 'An Anglican Middle-Axioms Reading of *Caritas in veritate*'. In Laurie M. Cassidy and Maureen H. O'Donnell, eds., *Religion, Economics and Culture in Conflict and Conversation*, pp. 236–54. Maryknoll, NY: Orbis, 2011.

Forrester, Duncan B. 'Some Thoughts on "Religionless Christianity"'. *Indian Journal of Theology*, 13:1 (1964), 11–19.

Forrester, Duncan B. *Beliefs, Values and Policies: Conviction Politics in a Secular Age*. Oxford: Clarendon Press, 1989.

Forrester, Duncan B. 'God's Will in a Time of Crisis: John Baillie as a Social Theologian'. In David Fergusson, ed., *Christ, Church and Society: Essays on John Baillie and Donald Baillie*, pp. 221–33. Edinburgh: T. & T. Clark, 1993.

Forstater, Mathew. 'Adolph Lowe on Freedom, Education and Socialization'. *Review of Social Economy*, 58:2 (2000), 225–39.

Fox, Richard Wightman. *Reinhold Niebuhr: A Biography*. New York: Pantheon, 1985.

Fox, Richard Wightman. 'The Niebuhr Brothers and the Liberal Protestant Heritage'. In Michael J. Lacey, ed., *Religion and Twentieth-Century American Intellectual Life*, pp. 94–115. Cambridge: Woodrow Wilson International Center for Scholars, 1989.

Freathy, Rob. 'The Triumph of Religious Education for Citizenship in English Schools, 1935–1949'. *History of Education: Journal of the History of Education Society*, 37:2 (2008), 295–316.

Fullbrook, Kate. 'Murry, John Middleton (1889–1957)'. In *Oxford Dictionary of National Biography*. Oxford: Oxford University Press, 2004; online edn, September 2012, www.oxforddnb.com/view/article/35171.

Ganiel, Gladys. 'Secularization, Ecumenism and Identity on the Island of Ireland'. In John Carter Wood, ed., *Christianity and National Identity in Twentieth-Century Europe: Conflict, Community, and the Social Order*, pp. 73–89. Göttingen: Vandenhoeck & Ruprecht, 2016.

Gentile, Emilio. 'Fascism, Totalitarianism and Political Religion: Definitions and Critical Reflections on Criticism of an Interpretation'. *Totalitarian Movements and Political Religions*, 5:3 (2004): 326–75.

Gordon, Peter E. 'Contextualism and Criticism in the History of Ideas'. In Darrin M. McMahon and Samuel Moyn, eds., *Rethinking Modern European Intellectual History*, pp. 32–55. Oxford: Oxford University Press, 2014.

Gorry, Jonathan. *Cold War Christians and the Spectre of Nuclear Deterrence, 1945–1959*. Basingstoke: Palgrave Macmillan, 2013.

Gorski, Philip S. *The Disciplinary Revolution: Calvinism and the Rise of the State in Early Modern Europe*. Chicago: University of Chicago Press, 2003.

Gorski, Philip S., David Kyuman Kim, John Torpey and Jonathan VanAntwerpen, eds. *The Post-Secular in Question: Religion in Contemporary Society*. New York: New York University Press, 2012.

Gosden, Peter. 'Putting the Act Together'. *History of Education*, 24:3 (1995), 195–207.

Graf, Friedrich Wilhelm. 'Euro-Gott im starken Plural? Einige Fragestellungen für eine europäische Religionsgeschichte des 20. Jahrhunderts'. *Journal of Modern European History*, 3 (2005), 231–56.

Green, S. J. D. *The Passing of Protestant England: Secularisation and Social Change, c. 1920–1960*. Cambridge: Cambridge University Press, 2011.

Greenberg, Udi. 'Protestants, Decolonization and European Integration, 1885–1961'. *Journal of Modern History*, 89 (2017), 314–54.

Griffin, Roger. 'The "Holy Storm": "Clerical Fascism" through the Lens of Modernism'. *Totalitarian Movements and Political Religions*, 8:2 (2007), 213–27.

Griffin, Roger. *Modernism and Fascism: The Sense of a Beginning under Mussolini and Hitler*. Basingstoke: Palgrave Macmillan, 2007.

Griffin, Roger. 'Studying Fascism in a Postfascist Age: From New Consensus to New Wave?'. *Fascism*, 1 (2012), 1–17.

Griffin, Roger. 'The Legitimizing Role of Palingenetic Myth in Ideocracies'. In Uwe Backes and Steffen Kailitz, eds., *Ideokratien im Vergleich: Legitimation – Kooptation – Repression*, pp. 279–95. Göttingen: Vandenhoeck & Ruprecht, 2014.

Grimley, Matthew. 'Civil Society and the Clerisy: Christian Elites and National Culture, c. 1930–1950'. In Jose Harris, ed., *Civil Society in British History: Ideas, Identities, Institutions*, pp. 231–47. Oxford: Oxford University Press, 2003.

Grimley, Matthew. *Citizenship, Community, and the Church of England: Liberal Anglican Theories of the State between the Wars*. Oxford: Oxford University Press, 2004.

Grimley, Matthew. 'The Religion of Englishness: Puritanism, Providentialism and "National Character", 1918–1945'. *Journal of British Studies*, 46:4 (2007), 884–906.

Grimley, Matthew and Sam Brewitt-Taylor. 'Vidler, Alexander Roper [Alec] (1899–1991)'. In *Oxford Dictionary of National Biography*. Oxford: Oxford University Press, 2004; online edn, September 2012, www.oxforddnb.com/view/article/50491.

Grossbölting, Thomas. 'Religionsgeschichte als Problemgeschichte der Gegenwart: Ein Vorschlag zu künftigen Perspektiven der Katholizismusforschung'. In Wilhelm Damberg and Karl-Joseph Hummel, eds., *Katholizismus in Deutschland: Zeitgeschichte und Gegenwart*, pp. 169–85. Paderborn: Ferdinand Schöningh, 2015.

Habermas, Jürgen. 'Faith and Knowledge'. In Jürgen Habermas, *The Future of Human Nature*, pp. 101–15. Cambridge: Polity, 2003.

Habermas, Jürgen. 'Notes on Post-Secular Society'. *New Perspectives Quarterly*, 25 (2008), 17–29.

Hannebrink, Paul. 'European Protestants between Anti-Communism and Anti-Totalitarianism: The Other Interwar *Kulturkampf*?'. *Journal of Contemporary History*, 53:3 (2018), 622–43.

Harding, Jason. '"The Just Impartiality of a Christian Philosopher": Jacques Maritain and T. S. Eliot'. In Rajesh Heynickx and Jan De Maeyer, eds., *The Maritain Factor: Taking Religion into Interwar Modernism*, pp. 181–91. Leuven: Leuven University Press, 2010.

Hardy, Dennis. *Utopian England: Community Experiments 1900–1945*. London: E. & F. N. Spon, 2000.

Harris, Alana. *Faith in the Family: A Lived Religious History of English Catholicism, 1945–82*. Manchester: Manchester University Press, 2013.

Harris, Jose. 'Enterprise and Welfare States: A Comparative Perspective'. *Transactions of the Royal Historical Society*, 40 (1990), 175–95.

Harvey, Graham, 'Defining Religion'. In John Wolffe and Gavin Moorhead, 'Religion, Security and Global Uncertainties: Report from a Global Uncertainties Leadership Fellowship', pp. 7–8. Milton Keynes: Open University, 2014, www. open.ac.uk/arts/research/religion-martyrdom-global-uncertainties/sites/www. open.ac.uk.arts.research.religion-martyrdom-global-uncertainties/files/files/ ecms/arts-rmgu-pr/web-content/blackburn-programme-may.pdf [*sic*].

Hastings, Adrian. *A History of English Christianity 1920–1990*. London: SCM, 1991.

Hastings, Adrian. 'The British Churches in the War and Post-War Reconstruction'. In Andrew R. Morton, ed., *God's Will in a Time of Crisis: A Colloquium Celebrating the 50th Anniversary of the Baillie Commission*, pp. 4–13. Edinburgh: University of Edinburgh, 1994.

Hastings, Adrian. *Oliver Tomkins: The Ecumenical Enterprise, 1908–1992*. London: SPCK, 2001.

Hauerwas, Stanley. *Dispatches from the Front: Theological Engagements with the Secular*. Durham, NC: Duke University Press, 1994.

Hawtrey, Kim. 'Anglicanism'. In Paul Oslington, ed., *The Oxford Handbook of Christianity and Economics*, pp. 177–96. Oxford: Oxford University Press, 2014.

Heater, Derek. 'The History of Citizenship Education in England'. *Curriculum Journal*, 12:1 (2001), 103–23.

Heeren, John. 'Karl Mannheim and the Intellectual Elite'. *British Journal of Sociology*, 22:1 (1971), 1–15.

Helm, Paul. *Faith with Reason*. Oxford: Clarendon Press, 2000.

Hockenos, Matthew D. 'Pastor Martin Niemöller, German Protestantism, and German National Identity, 1933–1937'. In John Carter Wood, ed., *Christianity and National Identity in Twentieth-Century Europe: Conflict, Community, and the Social Order*, pp. 113–30. Göttingen: Vandenhoeck & Ruprecht, 2016.

Holzem, Andreas. 'Die Geschichte des "geglaubten Gottes"'. In Andreas Leinhäupl-Wilke, ed., *Katholische Theologie studieren: Themenfelder und Disziplinen*, pp. 73–103. Münster: LIT, 2000.

Hoover, A. J. *God, Britain and Hitler in World War II: The View of the British Clergy, 1939–1945*. Westport, CT: Praeger, 1999.

Hughes, Michael. *Conscience and Conflict: Methodism, Peace and War in the Twentieth Century*. Peterborough: Epworth, 2008.

Hutchinson, John. *Modern Nationalism*. London: Fontana, 1994.

Huttner, Markus. *Totalitarismus und säkulare Religionen*. Bonn: Bouvier, 1999.

Itzen, Peter. *Streitbare Kirche: Die Church of England vor den Herausforderungen des Wandels 1945–1990*. Baden-Baden: Nomos, 2012.

Jackson, Eleanor M. *Red Tape and the Gospel: A Study of the Significance of the Ecumenical Missionary Struggle of William Paton 1886–1943*. Birmingham: Phlogiston, 1980.

Jacobs, Alan. *The Year of Our Lord 1943: Christian Humanism in an Age of Crisis.* Oxford: Oxford University Press, 2018.

Jacobs, Struan and Phil Mullins. 'Faith, Tradition, and Dynamic Order: Michael Polanyi's Liberal Thought from 1941 to 1951'. *History of European Ideas,* 34 (2008), 120–31.

Jha, Stefania Ruzsits. *Reconsidering Michael Polanyi's Philosophy.* Pittsburgh: University of Pittsburgh Press, 2002.

Julius, Anthony. *T. S. Eliot, Anti-Semitism and Literary Form.* Cambridge: Cambridge University Press, 1995.

Kahl, Sigrun. 'The Religious Roots of Modern Poverty Policy: Catholic, Lutheran, and Reformed Protestant Traditions Compared'. *European Journal of Sociology,* 46 (2005), 91–126.

Kaiser, Wolfram. *Christian Democracy and the Origins of European Union.* Cambridge: Cambridge University Press, 2007.

Kaplan, Sydney Janet. *Circulating Genius: John Middleton Murry, Katherine Mansfield and D. H. Lawrence.* Edinburgh: Edinburgh University Press, 2010.

Kelley, Donald R. 'Intellectual History and Cultural History: The Inside and the Outside'. *History of the Human Sciences,* 15:2 (2002), 1–19.

Kent, John. *William Temple: Church, State and Society in Britain, 1880–1950.* Cambridge: Cambridge University Press, 1992.

Kent, John. 'William Temple, the Church of England and British National Identity'. In Richard Weight and Abigail Beach, eds., *The Right to Belong: Citizenship and National Identity in Britain, 1930–1960,* pp. 19–35. London: I.B. Tauris, 1998.

Kettler, David and Volker Meja. *Karl Mannheim and the Crisis of Liberalism.* New Brunswick, NJ: Transaction, 1995.

Kettler, David, Volker Meja and Nico Stehr. *Karl Mannheim.* London: Tavistock, 1984.

Kirby, Diane. *Church, State and Propaganda. The Archbishop of York and International Relations: A Study of Cyril Foster Garbett 1942–1955.* Hull: University of Hull Press, 1999.

Kirby, Diane. 'Divinely Sanctioned: The Anglo-American Cold War Alliance and the Defence of Western Civilization and Christianity, 1945–1948'. *Journal of Contemporary History,* 35:3 (2000), 385–412.

Kirby, Diane. 'Christian Co-operation and the Ecumenical Ideal in the 1930s and 1940s'. *European History Review,* 8:1 (2001), 37–60.

Kirby, Diane, ed. *Religion and the Cold War.* Basingstoke: Palgrave, 2003.

Kojecky, Roger. *T. S. Eliot's Social Criticism.* London: Faber and Faber, 1971.

Koselleck, Reinhart, trans. Keith Tribe. *Futures Past: On the Semantics of Historical Time.* New York: Columbia University Press, 2004.

Kosmahl, Hans-Joachim. *Ethik in Oekumene und Mission.* Göttingen: Vandenhoeck & Ruprecht, 1970.

Ku, Hsiao-Yuh. 'Education for Liberal Democracy: Fred Clarke and the 1944 Education Act'. *History of Education,* 42:5 (2013), 578–97.

Ku, Hsiao-Yuh. 'Fred Clarke's Ideals of Liberal Democracy: State and Community in Education'. *British Journal of Educational Studies,* 61:4 (2013), 401–15.

Kurlberg, Jonas. 'Resisting Totalitarianism: The Moot and a New Christendom'. *Religion Compass,* 7 (2013), 517–31.

Kurlberg, Jonas. 'The Moot, the End of Civilisation and the Re-Birth of Christendom'. In Erik Tonning, Matthew Feldman and David Addyman, eds. *Modernism, Christianity and Apocalypse*, pp. 222–35. Leiden: Brill, 2015.

Kynaston, David. *A World to Build: Austerity Britain 1945–48*. London: Bloomsbury, 2007.

Lamberts, Emiel, ed. *Christian Democracy in the European Union (1945–1995)*. Leuven: Leuven University Press, 1997.

Lawson, Tom. *The Church of England and the Holocaust: Christianity, Memory and Nazism*. Woodbridge: Boydell, 2006.

Lea, Frank Alfred. *The Life of John Middleton Murry*. London: Methuen, 1959.

LeMahieu, D. L. *A Culture for Democracy: Mass Communication and the Cultivated Mind in Britain between the Wars*. Oxford: Clarendon Press, 1988.

Lepenies, Wolf. *Between Literature and Science: The Rise of Sociology*. Cambridge: Cambridge University Press, 1988.

Leustean, Lucian N. 'The Ecumenical Movement and the Schuman Plan, 1950–1954'. *Journal of Church and State*, 53:3 (2011), 442–71.

Leustean, Lucian. *The Ecumenical Movement and the Making of the European Community*. Oxford: Oxford University Press, 2014.

Linehan, Thomas. '"On the Side of Christ": Fascist Clerics in 1930s Britain'. *Totalitarian Movements and Political Religions*, 8:2 (2007), 287–301.

Loader, Colin. *The Intellectual Development of Karl Mannheim: Culture, Politics, and Planning*. Cambridge: Cambridge University Press, 1985.

Loader, Ian. 'Fall of the "Platonic Guardians": Liberalism, Criminology and Political Responses to Crime in England and Wales'. *British Journal of Criminology*, 46 (2006), 561–86.

Lockerd, Benjamin G. 'Beyond Politics: T. S. Eliot and Christopher Dawson on Religion and Culture'. In Benjamin G. Lockerd, ed., *T. S. Eliot and Christian Tradition*, pp. 217–36. Madison, NJ: Fairleigh Dickinson University Press, 2014.

Lord, Eric and Marjorie Reeves. 'Themes of the 1930s'. In Marjorie Reeves, ed., *Christian Thinking and Social Order: Conviction Politics from the 1930s to the Present Day*, pp. 3–18. London: Cassell, 1999.

Lowe, Rodney. 'The Second World War, Consensus and the Foundation of the Welfare State'. *Twentieth Century British History*, 1:2 (1990), 152–82.

Lyon, David. 'The Idea of a Christian Sociology: Some Historical Precedents and Current Concerns'. *Sociological Analysis*, 44 (1983), 227–42.

Machin, G. I. T. *Churches and Social Issues in Twentieth-Century Britain*. Oxford: Clarendon Press, 1998.

MacIntyre, Alasdair. *After Virtue: A Study in Moral Theory*. London: Bloomsbury, 2007 [1981].

Macpherson, C. B. *The Life and Times of Liberal Democracy*. Oxford: Oxford University Press, 1977.

Mandler, Peter. 'The Consciousness of Modernity? Liberalism and the English National Character, 1870–1940'. In Martin Daunton and Bernhard Reiger, eds., *Meanings of Modernity: Britain from the Late-Victorian Era to World War Two*, pp. 119–44. Oxford: Berg, 2001.

Mandler, Peter. *The English National Character: The History of an Idea from Edmund Burke to Tony Blair*. New Haven: Yale University Press, 2006.

Manow, Philip. *Religion und Sozialstaat: Die konfessionellen Grundlagen europäischer Wohlfahrtsregime*. Frankfurt: Campus, 2008.

Manz, Stefan. 'Constructing a Normative National Identity: The *Leitkultur* Debate in Germany, 2000/2001'. *Journal of Multilingual and Multicultural Development*, 25:5–6 (2004), 481–96.

Marinetto, M. 'The Historical Development of Business Philanthropy: Social Responsibility in the New Corporate Economy'. *Business History*, 41:4 (1999), 1–20.

Markham, Ian S. *Plurality and Christian Ethics*. Cambridge: Cambridge University Press, 1994.

Martin, Sarah. *Davis McCaughey: A Life*. Sydney: UNSW Press, 2012.

Marwick, Arthur. 'Middle Opinion in the Thirties: Planning, Progress and "Political Agreement".' *English Historical Review*, 79 (1964), 285–98.

Mateus, Odair Pedroso. 'José Míguez Bonino and the Struggle for Global Christian Unity in the 1970s'. In Katharina Kunter and Annegreth Schilling, eds., *Globalisierung der Kirchen: Der ökumenische Rat der Kirchen und die Entdeckung der Dritten Welt in den 1960er und 1970er Jahren*, pp. 237–54. Göttingen: Vandenhoeck & Ruprecht, 2014.

May, Samantha, Erin K. Wilson, Claudia Baumgart-Ochse and Faiz Sheikh. 'The Religious as Political and the Political as Religious: Globalisation, Post-Secularism and the Shifting Boundaries of the Sacred'. *Politics, Religion and Ideology*, 15 (2014), 331–46.

Mazower, Mark. *Dark Continent: Europe's Twentieth Century*. New York: A. A. Knopf, 1998.

McCarthy, Helen. 'Leading from the Centre: The League of Nations Union, Foreign Policy and "Political Agreement" in the 1930s'. *Contemporary British History*, 23:4 (2009), 527–42.

McCarthy, Helen. 'Whose Democracy? Histories of British Political Culture between the Wars'. *Historical Journal*, 55:1 (2012), 221–38.

McClay, Wilfred M. *The Masterless: Self and Society in America*. Chapel Hill: University of North Carolina Press, 1994.

McCleary, Joseph R. *The Historical Imagination of G. K. Chesterton: Locality, Patriotism, and Nationalism*. Abingdon: Routledge, 2009.

McCulloch, Gary. 'The Standing Conference on Studies in Education: Sixty Years On'. *British Journal of Educational Studies*, 60:4 (2012), 301–16.

McCulloch, Gary. 'Fred Clarke and the Internationalisation of Studies and Research in Education'. *Paedagogica historica*, 50:1–2 (2014), 123–37.

McCutcheon, Russell T. '"They licked the platter clean": On the Co-Dependency of the Religious and the Secular'. *Method and Theory in the Study of Religion*, 19 (2007), 173–99.

McGinn, Bernard. *Thomas Aquinas's 'Summa theologiae': A Biography*. Princeton: Princeton University Press, 2014.

McKibbin, Ross. *Classes and Cultures: England 1918–1951*. Oxford: Oxford University Press, 1998.

McLeod, Hugh. 'Introduction'. In Hugh McLeod and Werner Ustorf, eds., *The Decline of Christendom in Western Europe, 1750–2000*, pp. 1–26. Cambridge: Cambridge University Press, 2003.

McMahon, Darrin M. and Samuel Moyn, eds. *Rethinking Modern European Intellectual History*. Oxford: Oxford University Press, 2014.

McVey, Christopher. 'Backgrounds to *The Idea of a Christian Society*: Charles Maurras, Christopher Dawson and Jacques Maritain'. In Benjamin G. Lockerd, ed., *T. S. Eliot and Christian Tradition*, pp. 179–93. Madison, NJ: Fairleigh Dickinson University Press, 2014.

Mendel, Iris. 'Mannheim's Free-Floating Intelligentsia: The Role of Closeness and Distance in the Analysis of Society'. *Studies in Social and Political Thought*, 12 (2006), 30–52.

Mitchell, Frank W. *Sir Fred Clarke: Master-Teacher, 1880–1952*. London: Longmans, 1967.

Moleski, Martin X. *Personal Catholicism: The Theological Epistemologies of John Henry Newman and Michael Polanyi*. Washington, DC: Catholic University of America Press, 2000.

Morgan, D. Densil. *Barth Reception in Britain*. Edinburgh: T. & T. Clark, 2010.

Morgan, David and Mary Evans. *The Battle for Britain: Citizenship and Ideology in the Second World War*. London: Routledge, 1993.

Morgan, Dewi, ed. *They Became Anglicans: Personal Statements of Sixteen Converts to the Anglican Communion*. London: A. R. Mowbray, 1960.

Morton, Andrew R., ed. *God's Will in a Time of Crisis: A Colloquium Celebrating the 50th Anniversary of the Baillie Commission*. Edinburgh: University of Edinburgh, 1994.

Moyn, Samuel. *Christian Human Rights*. Philadelphia: University of Pennsylvania Press, 2015.

Müller, Jan-Werner. 'Die eigentlich katholische Entschärfung: Jacques Maritain und die christdemokratischen Fluchtwege aus dem Zeitalter der Extreme'. *Zeitschrift für Ideengeschichte*, 2 (2008): 40–54.

Müller, Jan-Werner. *Contesting Democracy: Political Ideas in Twentieth-Century Europe*. New Haven: Yale University Press, 2011.

Müller, Jan-Werner. 'European Intellectual History as Contemporary History'. *Journal of Contemporary History*, 46:3 (2011), 574–90.

Müller, Jan-Werner. 'Towards a New History of Christian Democracy'. *Journal of Political Ideologies*, 18:2 (2013), 243–55.

Mullins, Phil and Struan Jacobs. 'Michael Polanyi and Karl Mannheim'. *Tradition & Discovery: The Polanyi Society Periodical*, 32 (2005), 20–43.

Mullins, Phil und Struan Jacobs. 'T. S. Eliot's Idea of the Clerisy, and Its Discussion by Karl Mannheim and Michael Polanyi in the Context of J. H. Oldham's Moot'. *Journal of Classical Sociology*, 6 (2006), 147–76.

Myers, Kevin. 'National Identity, Citizenship and Education for Displacement: Spanish Refugee Children in Cambridge, 1937'. *History of Education*, 28:3 (1999), 313–25.

Nash, David. 'Reconnecting Religion with Social and Cultural History: Secularization's Failure as a Master Narrative'. *Cultural and Social History*, 1 (2004), 302–25.

Nash, David. *Christian Ideals in British Culture: Stories of Belief in the Twentieth Century*. Basingstoke: Palgrave Macmillan, 2013.

Newlands, George. 'Baillie, John (1886–1960)'. In *Oxford Dictionary of National Biography*. Oxford: Oxford University Press, 2004; online edn, September 2012, www.oxforddnb.com/view/article/40282.

Norman, E. R. *Church and Society in England, 1770–1970: A Historical Study*. Oxford: Clarendon Press, 1976.

Nurser, John. 'The "Ecumenical Movement" Churches, "Global Order", and Human Rights: 1938–1949'. *Human Rights Quarterly*, 25:4 (2003), 841–81.

Nurser, John. *For All Peoples and All Nations: Christian Churches and Human Rights*. Geneva: WCC Publications, 2005.

Nye, Mary Jo. *Michael Polanyi and His Generation: Origins of the Social Construction of Science*. Chicago: University of Chicago Press, 2011.

'Obama's Favorite Theologian? A Short Course in Reinhold Niebuhr'. 4 May 2009. www.pewforum.org/2009/05/04/obamas-favorite-theologian-a-short-course-on-reinhold-niebuhr/.

Oliver, John. *The Church and Social Order: Social Thought in the Church of England, 1918–1939*. London: A. R. Mowbray, 1968.

Olson, James Stuart, ed. *Historical Dictionary of the 1960s*. Westport, CT: Greenwood, 1999.

O'Meara, Thomas F. *Thomas Aquinas: Theologian*. Notre Dame: University of Notre Dame Press, 1997.

Ormrod, David. 'The Christian Left and the Beginnings of Christian–Marxist Dialogue, 1935–1945'. In Jim Obelkevich, Lyndal Roper, and Raphael Samuel, eds., *Disciplines of Faith: Studies in Religion, Politics and Patriarchy*, 435–50. London: Routledge and Kegan Paul, 1987.

Overy, Richard. *Why the Allies Won*. London: Pimlico, 2006 [1995].

Overy, Richard. *The Morbid Age: Britain and the Crisis of Civilisation, 1919–1939*. London: Penguin, 2010.

Overy, Richard. 'Pacifism and the Blitz, 1940–1941'. *Past and Present*, 219 (2013), 201–36.

Painter, John. *1, 2 and 3 John*. Collegeville, MN: Liturgical Press, 2002.

Palti, Elías José. 'From Ideas to Concepts to Metaphors: The German Tradition of Intellectual History and the Complex Fabric of Language'. *History and Theory*, 49 (2010): 194–211.

Parker, Stephen G. *Faith on the Home Front: Aspects of Church Life and Popular Religion in Birmingham, 1939–1945*. Bern: Peter Lang, 2005.

Parker, Stephen G. 'Reinvigorating Christian Britain: The Spiritual Issues of the War, National Identity, and the Hope of Religious Education'. In Stephen G. Parker and Tom Lawson, eds., *God and War: The Church of England and Armed Conflict in the Twentieth Century*, pp. 61–79. Aldershot: Ashgate, 2012.

Parker, Stephen G. and Tom Lawson, eds. *God and War: The Church of England and Armed Conflict in the Twentieth Century*. Aldershot: Ashgate, 2012.

Pasture, Patrick. 'Religion in Contemporary Europe: Contrasting Perceptions and Dynamics'. *Archiv für Sozialgeschichte*, 49 (2009), 319–50.

Pasture, Patrick. 'Dechristianization and the Changing Religious Landscape in Europe and North America since 1950: Comparative, Transatlantic, and Global Perspectives'. In Nancy Christie and Michael Gauvreau, eds., *The Sixties and Beyond: Dechristianization in North America and Western Europe, 1945–2000*, pp. 367–402. Toronto: University of Toronto Press, 2013.

Pasture, Patrick. *Imagining European Unity since 1000 AD*. Basingstoke: Palgrave Macmillan, 2015.

Pasture, Patrick. 'Between a Christian Fatherland and Euro-Christendom', in John Carter Wood, ed., *Christianity and National Identity in Twentieth-Century Europe: Conflict, Community, and the Social Order*, pp. 169–87. Göttingen: Vandenhoeck & Ruprecht, 2016.

Paulmann, Johannes. 'Interkultureller Transfer zwischen Deutschland und Großbritannien: Einführung in ein Forschungskonzept'. In Rudolf Muhs, Johannes Paulmann and Willibald Steinmetz, eds., *Aneignung und Abwehr: Interkultureller Transfer zwischen Deutschland und Großbritannien im 19. Jahrhundert*, pp. 21–43. Bodenheim: Philo, 1998.

Pemberton, Joanne. 'The Middle Way: The Discourse of Planning in Britain, Australia, and at the League in the Interwar Years'. *Australian Journal of Politics and History*, 52:1 (2006), 48–63.

Phillips, Paul T. *A Kingdom on Earth: Anglo-American Social Christianity, 1880–1940*. University Park: Pennsylvania State University Press, 1996.

Phillips, Paul T. *Contesting the Moral High Ground: Popular Moralists in Twentieth-Century Britain*. Montreal: McGill-Queen's University Press, 2013.

Pocock, J. G. A. 'The Reconstruction of Discourse: Towards the Historiography of Political Thought'. *MLN*, 96:5 (1981), 959–80.

Pocock, J. G. A. 'Quentin Skinner: The History of Politics and the Politics of History'. *Common Knowledge*, 10 (2004), 532–50.

Pollack, Detlef and Gergely Rosta. *Religion in der Moderne: Ein internationaler Vergleich*. Frankfurt: Campus, 2015.

Raphael, Lutz and Heinz-Elmar Tenorth, ed. *Ideen als gesellschaftliche Gestaltungskraft im Europa der Neuzeit*. Munich: De Gruyter Oldenbourg, 2006.

Reardon, Bernard G., ed. *Liberal Protestantism*. London: Adam & Charles Black, 1968.

Renaud, Terence. 'Human Rights as Radical Anthropology: Protestant Theology and Ecumenism in the Transwar Era'. *Historical Journal*, 60:2 (2017), 493–518.

Ricks, Christopher. *T. S. Eliot and Prejudice*. London: Faber and Faber, 1988.

Ritschel, Daniel. *The Politics of Planning: The Debate on Economic Planning in Britain in the 1930s*. Oxford: Clarendon Press, 1997.

Robbins, Keith. 'Britain, 1940 and "Christian Civilisation"'. In Keith Robbins, ed., *History, Religion and Identity in Modern Britain*, pp. 195–214. London: Hambledon, 1993.

Robbins, Keith. *Great Britain: Identities, Institutions, and the Idea of Britishness*. London: Longman, 1998.

Robbins, Keith. 'Avoiding the Challenge? British Churches, British Society and European Integration, 1947–1949'. In Heinz Duchhardt and Małgorzata

Morawiec, eds., *Die europäische Integration und die Kirchen: Akteure und Rezipienten*, pp. 5–20. Göttingen: Vandenhoeck & Ruprecht, 2010.

Robichaud, Paul. 'David Jones, Christopher Dawson, and the Meaning of History'. *Logos: A Journal of Catholic Thought and Culture*, 6:3 (2003), 68–85.

Robichaud, Paul. 'Eliot's Christian Sociology and the Problem of Nationalism'. In Benjamin G. Lockerd, ed., *T. S. Eliot and Christian Tradition*, pp. 207–15. Madison, NJ: Fairleigh Dickinson University Press, 2014.

Rose, Sonya O. *Which People's War? National Identity and Citizenship in Britain, 1939–1945*. Oxford: Oxford University Press, 2003.

Rosenboim, Or. 'Barbara Wootton, Friedrich Hayek and the Debate on Democratic Federalism in the 1940s'. *International History Review*, 36:5 (2014), 894–918.

Ruotsila, Markku. *The Origins of Christian Anti-Imperialism: Conservative Evangelicals and the League of Nations*. Washington, DC: Georgetown University Press, 2008.

Schloesser, Stephen. 'The Rise of a Mystic Modernism: Maritain and the Sacrificed Generation of the Twenties'. In Rajesh Heynickx and Jan De Maeyer, eds., *The Maritain Factor: Taking Religion into Interwar Modernism*, pp. 28–39. Leuven: Leuven University Press, 2010.

Scott, Christina. *A Historian and His World: A Life of Christopher Dawson, 1889–1970*. London: Sheed & Ward, 1984.

Scruton, Roger. *Our Church: A Personal History of the Church of England*. London: Atlantic, 2012.

Seidentop, Larry. *Inventing the Individual: The Origins of Western Liberalism*. London: Allen Lane, 2014.

Sell, Alan P. F. *Four Philosophical Anglicans: W. G. de Burgh, W. R. Matthews, O. C. Quick, H. A. Hodges*. Farnham: Ashgate, 2010.

Sheehan, Jonathan. 'Enlightenment, Religion, and the Enigma of Secularization: A Review Essay'. *American Historical Review*, 108:4 (2003), 1061–80.

Silver, Harold. *Higher Education and Opinion Making in Twentieth-Century England*. London: Woburn, 2003.

Simon, Brian. *Education and the Social Order, 1940–1990*. London: Lawrence and Wishart, 1991.

Simon, Joan. 'The Shaping of the Spens Report on Secondary Education 1933–38: An Inside View'. *British Journal of Educational Studies*, 25:1 (1977): 63–80 and 25:2 (1977), 170–85.

Sittser, Gerald L. *A Cautious Patriotism: The American Churches and the Second World War*. Chapel Hill: University of North Carolina Press, 1997.

Skinner, Q. R. D. 'Meaning and Understanding in the History of Ideas'. *History and Theory*, 8:1 (1969), 3–53.

Smith, Graeme. 'Christian Totalitarianism: Joseph Oldham and Oxford 1937'. *Political Theology*, 3:1 (2001), 32–46.

Smith, Graeme. *Oxford 1937: The Universal Christian Council for Life and Work Conference*. Frankfurt: Peter Lang, 2004.

Snape, Michael. *God and Uncle Sam: Religion and America's Armed Forces in World War II*. Woodridge: Boydell, 2015.

Spencer, Nick. *Freedom and Order: History, Politics and the English Bible.* London: Hodder and Stoughton, 2011.

Spurr, Barry. *'Anglo-Catholic in Religion': T. S. Eliot and Christianity.* Cambridge: Lutterworth Press, 2010.

Stamatov, Peter. 'Activist Religion, Empire, and the Emergence of Modern Long-Distance Advocacy Networks'. *American Sociological Review*, 75 (2010), 607–28.

Stapleton, Julia. 'Political Thought, Elites and the State in Modern Britain'. *Historical Journal*, 42 (1999), 251–68.

Stapleton, Julia. 'Resisting the Centre at the Extremes: "English" Liberalism in the Political Thought of Interwar Britain'. *British Journal of Politics and International Relations*, 1:3 (1999), 270–92.

Stark, Rodney. 'Secularisation, R. I. P.'. *Sociology of Religion*, 60:3 (1999), 249–73.

Steele, Tom and Richard Kenneth Taylor. 'Oldham's Moot (1938–1947), the Universities and the Adult Citizen'. *History of Education*, 39 (2010), 183–97.

Steigmann-Gall, Richard. *The Holy Reich: Nazi Conceptions of Christianity, 1919–1945.* Cambridge: Cambridge University Press, 2004.

Sterenberg, Matthew. *Mythic Thinking in Twentieth-Century Britain: Meaning for Modernity.* Basingstoke: Palgrave Macmillan, 2013.

Takayanagi, Shun'ichi. 'T. S. Eliot, the *Action française* and Neo-Scholasticism'. In Benjamin G. Lockerd, ed., *T. S. Eliot and Christian Tradition*, pp. 89–97. Madison, NJ: Fairleigh Dickinson University Press, 2014.

Taylor, Charles. *A Secular Age.* Cambridge, MA: Belknap Press of Harvard University Press, 2007.

Taylor, William. 'Education and the Moot'. In Richard Aldrich, ed., *In History and in Education: Essays Presented to Peter Gordon*, pp. 159–86. London: Woburn, 1996.

Taylor, William and Marjorie Reeves. 'Intellectuals in Debate: The Moot'. In Marjorie Reeves, ed., *Christian Thinking and Social Order: Conviction Politics from the 1930s to the Present Day*, pp. 24–48. London: Cassell, 1999.

Templeton, E. *God's February: A Life of Archie Craig.* London: CCBI, 1991.

Thompson, Michael G. *For God and Globe: Christian Internationalism in the United States between the Great War and the Cold War.* Ithaca, NY: Cornell University Press, 2015.

Tibi, Bassam. *Europa ohne Identität? Die Krise der multikulturellen Gesellschaft.* Munich: Bertelsmann, 1998.

Tyldesley, Mike. 'Max Plowman's Pacifism'. *Peace & Change*, 27 (2002), 20–36.

Valderrama, Paula. '"Planning for Freedom": Hayekian and Polanyian Policies in Latin America'. *International Journal of Political Economy*, 41:4 (2012–13), 88–105.

Van Eijnatten, Joris, Ed Jonker, Willemijn Ruberg and Joes Segal. 'Shaping the Discourse on Modernity'. *International Journal for History, Culture and Modernity*, 1 (2013), 3–20.

Vanheste, Jeroen. *Guardians of the Humanist Legacy: The Classicism of T. S. Eliot's Criterion Network and Its Relevance to Our Postmodern World.* Leiden: Brill, 2007.

Veldman, Meredith. *Fantasy, the Bomb, and the Greening of Britain: Romantic Protest, 1945–1980.* Cambridge: Cambridge University Press, 1994.

Veevers, Nick and Pete Allison. *Kurt Hahn: Inspirational Visionary, Outdoor and Experiential Educator*. Rotterdam: Sense, 2011.

Villis, Tom. *British Catholics and Fascism: Religious Identity and Political Extremism between the Wars*. Basingstoke: Palgrave Macmillan, 2013.

Vischer, Lukas. 'The Ecumenical Movement and the Roman Catholic Church'. In Harold C. Fey, ed., *A History of the Ecumenical Movement*, Vol. II: *1948–1968*, pp. 311–52. Geneva: WCC Publications, 2004.

Wallis, Roy and Steve Bruce. 'Secularization: The Orthodox Model'. In Steve Bruce, ed., *Religion and Modernization: Sociologists and Historians Debate the Secularization Thesis*, pp. 8–30. Oxford: Clarendon Press, 1992.

Walsh, Michael J. 'Ecumenism in War-Time Britain: The Sword of the Spirit and Religion and Life, 1940–45'. *Heythrop Journal*, 23 (1982), 243–58, 377–94.

Warren, Heather A. *Theologians of a New World Order: Reinhold Niebuhr and the Christian Realists, 1920–1948*. Oxford: Oxford University Press, 1997.

Weight, Richard. *Patriots: National Identity in Britain, 1940–2000*. London: Macmillan, 2002.

Weir, Todd. 'The Christian Front against Godlessness: Anti-Secularism and the Demise of the Weimar Republic 1928 to 1933'. *Past and Present*, 229:1 (2015), 201–38.

Welby, Justin. *Dethroning Mammon: Making Money Serve Grace*. London: Bloomsbury, 2017.

Whatmore, Richard. 'Intellectual History and the History of Political Thought'. In Richard Whatmore and Brian Young, eds., *Palgrave Advances in Intellectual History*, pp. 109–29. Basingstoke: Palgrave Macmillan, 2006.

Whatmore, Richard. *What Is Intellectual History?* Cambridge: Polity, 2016.

Wilkinson, Alan. *Dissent or Conform? War, Peace and the English Churches 1900–1945*. London: SCM, 1986.

Wilkinson, Alan. *Christian Socialism: Scott Holland to Tony Blair*. London: SCM, 1998.

Wilkinson, Alan. *The Church of England and the First World War*. Cambridge: Lutterworth Press, 2014 [1996].

Williams, Rowan. *Faith in the Public Square*. London: Bloomsbury, 2012.

Williams, S. C. *Religious Belief and Popular Culture in Southwark c. 1880–1939*. Oxford: Oxford University Press, 1999.

Williamson, Philip. 'Christian Conservatives and the Totalitarian Challenge, 1933–1940'. *English Historical Review*, 115: 462 (2000), 607–42.

Wilson, James Matthew. 'An "Organ for a Frenchified Doctrine": Jacques Maritain and *The Criterion*'s Neo-Thomism'. In Benjamin G. Lockerd, ed., *T. S. Eliot and Christian Tradition*, pp. 99–116. Madison, NJ: Fairleigh Dickinson University Press, 2014.

Wolffe, John. *God and Greater Britain: Religion and National Life in Britain and Ireland 1843–1943*. London: Routledge, 1994.

Wollenberg, Bruce. *Christian Social Thought in Great Britain between the Wars*. Lanham, MD: University Press of America, 1997.

Wolterstorff, Nicholas. *Justice: Rights and Wrongs*. Princeton: Princeton University Press, 2008.

Wood, John Carter. 'Zwischen Mammon und Marx: Christliche Kapitalismuskritik in Großbritannien 1930–1939'. In Robert König, ed., *Religion und Kapitalismus*, pp. 147–76. Kaltenleutgeben: Ferstl & Perz, 2014.

Wood, John Carter. '"Blessed Is the Nation"? Christianity and National Identity in Twentieth-Century Europe'. In John Carter Wood, ed., *Christianity and National Identity in Twentieth-Century Europe: Conflict, Community, and the Social Order*, pp. 11–31. Göttingen: Vandenhoeck & Ruprecht, 2016.

Wood, John Carter, ed. *Christianity and National Identity in Twentieth-Century Europe: Conflict, Community, and the Social Order*. Göttingen: Vandenhoeck & Ruprecht, 2016.

Wood, John Carter. '"A Fundamental Re-Orientation of Outlook": Religiöse Intellektuelle und das Ziel einer "christlichen Gesellschaft" in Großbritannien, 1937–1949'. In Gregor Feindt, Bernhard Gißibl and Johannes Paulmann, eds., *Kulturelle Souveränität: Politische Deutungs- und Handlungsmacht jenseits des Staates im 20. Jahrhundert*, pp. 165–94. Göttingen: Vandenhoeck & Ruprecht, 2016.

Wood, John Carter. '"The rock of human sanity stands in the sea where it always stood": Britishness, Christianity, and the Experience of (Near) Defeat, 1937–1941'. In John Carter Wood, ed., *Christianity and National Identity in Twentieth-Century Europe: Conflict, Community, and the Social Order*, pp. 131–48. Göttingen: Vandenhoek & Ruprecht, 2016.

Wood, John Carter. 'When Personalism Met Planning: Jacques Maritain and a British Christian Intellectual Circle, 1937–1949'. In Rajesh Heynickx und Stéphane Symons, eds., *So What's New about Scholasticism? How Neo-Thomism Helped Shape the Twentieth Century*, pp. 77–108. Berlin: Walter de Gruyter, 2018.

Zeilstra, Jurjen A. *European Unity in Ecumenical Thinking 1937–1948*. Zoetermeer: Boekencentrum, 1995.